Basic Financial Accounting

Robert Bowman
ACIS InstM CertEd
Lecturer in the School of Economics
and Accounting Leicester Polytechnic

Edward Arnold

© Robert Bowman 1983

First published 1983
by Edward Arnold (Publishers) Ltd
41 Bedford Square London WC1B 3DQ

Edward Arnold (Australia) Pty Ltd
80 Waverley Road
Caulfield East 3145
PO Box 234
Melbourne

British Library Cataloguing in Publication Data

Bowman, Robert
   Basic financial accounting.
   1. Accounting
   I. Title
   657'.48   HF5635

   ISBN 0-7131-0729-4

To Mum and Dad

All rights reserved. No part of this publication may be reproduced, stored in a retrieval system, or transmitted in any form or by any means, electronic, mechanical, photocopying, recording or otherwise, without the prior permission of Edward Arnold (Publishers) Ltd.

Text set in 10/11pt Times Compugraphic by Colset Private Limited Singapore
Printed and bound in Great Britain by Richard Clay (The Chaucer Press) Ltd, Bungay, Suffolk.

Contents

Schedule of questions	vi
Author's note	vii
Acknowledgements	viii

Section I
Final accounts — 1

Unit			
	1	Introduction to financial accounting	1
	2	The accounts of sole traders	4
	3	Presentation of final accounts I	5
	4	The layout of accounts I	8
	5	The trading account	9
	6	The profit and loss account	13
	7	The balance sheet	15
		Questions (and selected answer guides)	21

Section II
Recording individual entries — 27

Unit			
	1	Arriving at final accounts	27
	2	Double entry principles	29
	3	Sales and purchases – double entry	35
	4	Expenses – double entry	39
	5	Returns of purchases and sales – double entry	40
	6	Carriage inwards and outwards and discount allowed and received	43
	7	Balancing off ledger accounts	45
	8	The trial balance	47
	9	Presentation of final accounts II	55
		Questions (and selected answer guides)	58

Section III
Adjustments to final accounts — 69

Unit			
	1	The nature of adjustments	69
	2	Expense – prepayments and accruals	75
	3	Subsidiary income – delayed and advanced receipt	79
	4	Provisions for depreciation in final accounts	81
	5	Bad debts and provisions for doubtful debts in final accounts	89
	6	Double entry for provisions	94
	7	A method for dealing with adjustments	105
	8	Examination notes on final accounting questions	106
		Questions (and selected answer guides)	108

Section IV
Collection of data　　　　　　　　　　　　　　　　　　　　**117**

Unit			
	1	A diagrammatic presentation of the accounting system	117
	2	Accounts documentation	119
	3	The collection and processing of accounting information I – day books and returns daybooks	122
	4	The cash book	125
	5	The petty cash book	132
	6	Stock	134
	7	Drawings	137
	8	Classification of accounts	140
	9	The collection and processing of accounting information II – journal entries	147
	10	Goodwill and other reducible assets	160
	11	Accounting for Value Added Tax	162
		Questions (and selected answer guides)	166

Section V
The extension of final accounts presentations　　　　　　**174**

Unit			
	1	Limited company accounts	174
	2	Partnership accounts	188
	3	Non-profit or club accounts	195
	4	Manufacturing accounts	203
		Questions (and selected answer guides)	211

Section VI
Account controls　　　　　　　　　　　　　　　　　　　　**227**

Unit			
	1	Control accounts	227
	2	Bank reconciliation	237
	3	Incomplete records	246
		Questions (and selected answer guides)	252

Section VII
Additional information and statements from final accounts　**263**

Unit			
	1	Accounting ratios (including mark-up and margin)	263
	2	Funds flow statements (including SSAP 10)	278
	3	Cash budgeting	289
		Questions (and selected answer guides)	294

Section VIII
Regulatory matters   **313**

Unit 1 Statute   313
    2 Accounting concepts, conventions and standards   315
    3 Auditing and auditors   318

Conclusion   321

Appendices
1. Accounting for price level changes   322
2. Accounts documents and flow of documents   339
3. Business final accounts – first six years trading for a fashion shop   348
4. Professional questions and answers – foundation level   367

Glossary   419
Index   437

Schedule of questions

Section I
Equations of assets and liabilities	21
The trading account	22
The profit and loss account	24
The trading and profit and loss account	24
The balance sheet	25

Section II
The accounting transaction equation	58
Debits and credits in columns	58
The trial balance	60
Final accounts from trial balance	62
Ledger accounts and the trial balance	64
Correction of layout	67

Section III
Adjustments to final accounts	108
Accruals and prepayments in ledger accounts	112
Depreciation in ledger accounts	114
Bad debts in ledger accounts	117

Section IV
Ledger records to final accounts	166
The cash book	167
Day books	170
The journal and adjustments to final accounts	171

Section V
Company accounts	211
Partnership accounts	216
Income and expenditure accounts	220
Manufacturing accounts	223

Section VI
Control accounts	252
Control accounts in the accounting system	254
Bank reconciliation statements	256
Incomplete records	259

Section VII
Accounting ratios	294
Accounting ratios and final accounts	297
Funds flow statements	302
Cash budgeting	307

Author's note

The aim has been to devise a straightforward text that is serviceable at several different academic levels. The higher the level the greater the input from other sources, namely, lecturers and more advanced text books. The rationale behind this is that all students tackling accounting for the first time need to have a knowledge of double-entry book-keeping. For example, the BEC General or National student at a College of Further Education, should find this acceptable as a basic text for learning financial accounting, so too would the ordinary and advanced level GCE student. Whereas the BEC Higher, Professional Foundation, and Degree student, should regard it as a primer or introduction, depending on the level of accounting input within his or her course.

The text is divided into sections and units, each section classifies a number of units as an integrated part of the book. An overview is used at the start of each unit, not only to summarise the contents, but also provide the more experienced student with a knowledge of what can confidently be omitted.

Explanation based on a diagrammatic presentation supported by appropriate text has been used wherever possible to provide a straightforward understanding of the mechanics of double entry. Examples are provided at the conclusion of sections, with an answer book available to teachers direct from the Publishers.

A glossary is provided to explain technical terms where necessary which is both supplementary and complimentary, but additional to those provided in the text. There are four appendices to reinforce and extend knowledge of the subject. Their subject matter ranges from some aspects of accounting for price level changes to containing professional (Foundation Level) examination questions.

It is possible to gain a fair appreciation of the principles of double-entry by just reading the Overviews and studying the diagrams. Where this method is used (say in support of comprehensive lectures) it could be followed by selective reading of the notes and the attempted working of examples.

Acknowledgements

I would like to extend my sincere thanks to everyone who has helped me, from my parents and friends to colleagues mainly at Leicester Polytechnic and Hull College of Further Education. Particular thanks should be given to David Berridge (Hull College of Higher Education) Keith Auty, Dennis Hampson and John Marsden from Hull. Malcolm Roper, Alan Hill, Roy Thody, Anne Dilks, David Anderson, Keith Brown, Lynne Coates, Geoffery Poultney and Barry Weeks from Leicester and Steve Marshall from Lowestoft. Many thanks are also due to the examining authorities for permitting me to use their questions, in particular the Association of Certified Accountants and the Institute of Cost and Management Accountants for the questions in Appendix 4.

Special thanks to my mother, Norah Bowman, and Grace Norris for typing a technically difficult manuscript and Mike Rigby and Margaret Owens from Edward Arnold for their encouragement and support throughout the writing and editing stages of the book. Finally thanks to my past students for all their unknowing but helpful assistance. In spite of all this help the ideas and decisions in the end were my own, for which I accept full responsibility.

Robert Bowman
Leicester
September 1983

Section I
Final accounts

Unit 1   Introduction to financial accounting
Unit 2   Accounts of sole traders
Unit 3   Presentation of final accounts I
Unit 4   Layout of accounts
Unit 5   The trading account
Unit 6   The profit and loss account
Unit 7   The balance sheet

Unit 1
Introduction to financial accounting

Overview

1 Accounting has, as a body of knowledge, responded to the changes required of it according to the demands of business.

2 An important feature has been, and is, concerned with stewardship.

3 Business accounts are generally prepared for a given period of time, a point related to the need to assess stewardship.

4 Conditions in which businesses operate have changed and accounting has changed to meet those needs.

5 The modern profession has adapted and today consists of three branches. These are:
a) financial accounting,
b) management accounting, and
c) responsibility for auditing.

6 The organization of professional institutes is discussed to draw a distinction between both management and financial aspects within the business and external to it.

Accounting has developed since the Renaissance according to the requirements of business. The theory is today an amalgamation of the different practices that have emerged over the period to show the results of organized businesses and commercial activities trading for profit. The development to some extent explains the accountant's problem in providing absolute answers to matters of principle since these frequently involve a conflict of interest.

Students sometimes confuse the necessity for arithmetical accuracy and consistency with the expression of differing opinion and interpretations. To illustrate this, the comparatively recent introduction of financial accounting standards in the United Kingdom has been an attempt to minimise differences of opinion and interpretation.

However, traditionally the accountant has been concerned with what is known as stewardship. As understood by accountants, stewardship generally requires the recording of transactions that assist in the protection of business property by those involved in running it, on behalf of those who own it. These may or may not be the same persons.

Although many years ago businesses were a good deal smaller than those of today many, like todays, would not have the attention of their owners all the time. This could increase the incidence of bad accounting practice and even fraud. Owners may have, for instance, numerous business interests and would appoint trusted individuals to oversee one or more business ventures, leaving these individuals to supervise and record the financial transactions. Good financial accounting assists the process of stewardship and has the preparation of final accounts as its end product. But to achieve this a business should maintain a sufficiently accurate record of its transactions to enable the process to be completed at the close of a trading period — usually one year in length.

The very nature of modern business activities leads to an expectation of continuance. Businesses take time to grow and achieve a status in the market sufficient to operate efficiently; their owners expect them to continue if not indefinitely, at least over the forseeable future. Dealings and prospects do not (normally) come to an abrupt halt at the close of a trading period but for the purpose of preparing financial information, accountants in the main have to check assertions about continuance. For example, can the business pay its debts as they become due? To provide year-end information, adjustments to figures have to be made to produce a periodic review. It is this adjustment process that largely creates the problems and difficulties of reporting financial information.

The mystique of accounting knowledge can be removed by an appreciation of commercial activity and work on accounting principles. Such a knowledge requires an understanding of the mechanics behind the production of year-end and financial accounts.

Essentially then owners have long required protection of their business property and the means of recording changes in it as a result of trading activities. Although arrangements in the past were a good deal less complex than today and modern accountants would be less than satisfied with what was provided, records did generally give owners sufficient information for their trading activities.

Conditions for the conduct of business have changed and even the smallest business cannot isolate itself from the trends. Changes such as:

1 size (increases) through merger, take-over and general economic conditions,
2 patterns of ownership ie the change to limited liability companies,

3 social conditions eg a better educated and relatively wealthy population,
4 goods produced eg more complex consumer durables,
5 styles of management eg an understanding of the psychology of employees' behaviour.

All of which have had effects on the type of business activities undertaken and the accounting requirements needed.

Without elaborating further, the modern profession has responded to these changes. However there are three main headings which though not entirely distinct, serve as a suitable division of the profession to be used at this stage. These are:

1 financial accountants, in the firm,
2 management accountants, in the firm,
3 auditors (professional practice) outside the firm whose role is governed by statute so far as corporate enterprise is concerned.

Financial accounting leads to the creation of records and auditing the evaluation of those records against source documents, surrounding information and circumstance. Quite apart from the split in the financial aspects of accounting, namely (as stated above):

1 in company accountants (internal employees);
2 auditors (external practitioners),

there is a more fundamental division between financial, and cost and management accountants. Financial accounting (and auditing) is largely concerned with recording past information. In earlier years this was probably the only reliable method and today is practised since it can be verified by historic fact. However, modern developments (and this is where cost and management accountants have the upperhand) have required management to request information about:

a) present conditions, and
b) future prospects.

Therefore a separate branch has developed concentrating on, primarily, costs (present conditions) and latterly, management information (future prospects).

Auditors act as independent assessors of financial accounting, but also more recently management information – that cannot be entirely divorced from financial considerations and may assist in providing an overall guide to financial aspects of that firm.

Emphasis of the divisions within the accounting profession adds a dimension to, and puts into perspective, the study of financial accounting given that the process of learning accounting begins with financial aspects. This book will concentrate on that activity.

Unit 2
The accounts of sole traders

Overview

1 The sole trader is usually identified as the small one-man business.
2 Although he or she may employ people, responsibility rests with him or her as the owner.
3 Practical accounting examples usually begin with sole traders.
4 The sole trader must comply with the minimum accounting and legal requirements.

Many businesses continue to operate as sole traders. Usually they are small and under the control of the one owner, proprietor or manager. Examples of such businesses are easily found in the service sector eg small newsagents, cafes, hairdressers and greengrocers. It is not so much the type of business that is important but the fact that the responsibility rests with one person, namely the owner. The owner may of course employ people (and usually does) for he or she cannot always be expected to do all the work.

From the accounting point of view this is the simplest type of business since responsibility rests with one person and there are no other owners, partners or shareholders to consider. It is for this reason more than any other that the accountancy student usually begins a course by dealing with the accounts of sole traders.

The sole trader, trading as an individual without limited liability, is in a less onerous position so far as financial reporting is concerned than are other organizations. Unless money is owed to a bank, through a bank loan or overdraft, he or she has only himself or herself to satisfy so far as information requirements are concerned. This has obvious advantages because if the business is small enough the proprietor will usually have a good understanding of its financial state, keeping only the minimum records. However, it would be unwise to take such an attitude too far because minimal accounts are necessary if only to satisfy the requirements of tax authorities, particularly the Inland Revenue.

The legal requirements are less for sole traders than other business organizations, but if the proprietor makes an error of judgement, sufficient to prejudice the claims of creditors and goes out of business, it is he or she who is responsible and mainly suffers alone. Without the privilege of limited liability, sole traders are personally liable for the full debts of their business to the extent of their own personal savings. Since limited liability and corporate status go hand in hand, except in the obscure case of limited partnerships, the loss of this privilege would be quite serious but for the fewer legal and accounting reporting requirements that tend to make a sole trader's status more attractive.

Unit 3
Presentation of final accounts I

Overview

1 A business has to report periodically to interested parties eg owners lenders, trade creditors and the Inland Revenue on the state of its financial affairs.
2 Three separate parts are to be considered when presenting final accounts:
   a) the trading account,
   b) the profit and loss account, and
   c) the Balance Sheet.
3 The following formulae are considered as a preliminary explanation and developed to a limited extent:
   a) Trading account: gross profit = sales − purchases (ignoring stock),
   b) Profit and loss account: net profit = gross profit − expenses,
   c) Balance sheet: assets = liabilities.
4 The balance sheet is further sub-divided into:
   Long term liabilities (capital),
   Short term liabilities (current liabilities),
   Long term assets (fixed assets),
   Short term assets (current assets).
5 Net profit − the return to owners (a liability) is added to owner's capital.
6 Careful thought should be given to the presentation of information.

A business has to report periodically on the state of its financial affairs. This is clearly important to the owners of the business, is largely (and has been traditionally) for their benefit, but other persons and authorities will be interested, namely financiers with an interest, trade creditors, and the Inland Revenue.

The preparation of final accounts has traditionally served this purpose and is the most common form of financial reporting although other methods of financial reporting will also be considered.

Final accounts consist of three interrelated stages of preparation as follows:

1 the trading account,
2 the profit and loss account, and
3 the balance sheet.

Before moving on to explain these a proviso might be advantageous at this stage. It has to be presumed that all the stages of recording information are in order. Although it may appear strange to commence an examination of the subject at a point close to the final stages, it has been the writer's experience that some preliminary knowledge of where one is going is an important part of the building process. This fact is quite simple to appreciate since most readers will no doubt have had at least sight of final accounts of some organization, even if it is a local club or voluntary association.

A reference is often made to accounts balancing or not, and although the process of preparing final accounts has to be carried out accurately, a non-balancing account can in practice, more often than not, result from errors in the system that have not been eliminated earlier. This point will be discussed at some length later (see pp 49–51, 153–9).

In all cases, it has to be pointed out, the effect of taxation on the allocation of profit in preparing final accounts is ignored. The techniques of the three stages will be dealt with in the following sections, but some definitions may be useful at this stage:

The trading account

This is designed to find the gross profit, that is the difference between sales (or outputs of the business) and purchases (or inputs contributing to sales) including certain adjustments made for stocks of goods to satisfy accountants and, as we shall learn, these have important consequences for the calculation of gross profit. For the time being however, stock is ignored.

ie *Gross profit = sales − purchases*

eg Sales: £48,754
    Purchases: £21,236
    Gross profit = £48,754 − £21,236 (ignoring stock)
                 = £27,518

The profit and loss account

This account takes the gross profit and converts it to the net profit by deducting expenses (accountants adjust these for accuracy, according to when they occur – this will be dealt with in due course). This means that the gross profit as calculated is reduced by expenses. Examples of expenses are rent, rates, wages, salaries and electricity. If the expenses are too great for the business then a net profit cannot be expected and a net loss will be shown.

ie *Net profit = gross profit − expenses*

eg Gross profit: £27,518
    Expenses: £14,489
    Net profit = £27,518 − 14,489
               = £13,029

A distinction can now conveniently be made between certain terminology used in connection with the trading and profit and loss accounts.

Expenditure and expenses Expenditure is the description applied to a specific type of cost, paid through cash or bank funds, this amount does not necessarily represent the full amount accountants will accept as the claims against the business in any one period, some of which will remain unpaid at the time of preparing accounts or to be paid in advance. Expense is the full liability accepted by accountants under its appropriate expense heading.

ie *Expenditure*   ± *Adjustment*   = *Expense*

eg Light & heat   + unpaid   = full light and heat
    Expenses paid   light & heat expenses   expense for the period
    540   + 40   = 580

Receipts and revenue Receipts (like expenditures) are the bank or cash amounts, in this case received by the business as income. Again this income may not be the full amount due to a business in a given period and will be recognized as such by accountants. Revenue will be the adjusted receipts by amounts due but unpaid (to be added) and not due but paid (to be deducted).

ie   Receipt   ± Adjustment   = Revenue

eg   Rent income received   + rent income due but unpaid   = full rent revenue for the period
    625   + 125   = 750

The balance sheet

This is arguably the most important stage in the preparation of final accounts. Just as the gross profit was used in the profit and loss account, so the net profit (or net loss) is used or carried down to the balance sheet, and used in a different manner to adjust the capital balance of the proprietor up (or down).

The balance sheet is a statement prepared for a point in time and collects together relevant information – balances from different sources, records and displays them in a traditional way acceptable to accountants.

Items that are included are capital – funds belonging to the owners that are a long-term liability and other short-term liabilities eg trade creditors, plus those items that are supported by the liabilities (on the opposite side) known as assets. Assets can also be divided into long term eg buildings and motor vehicles and short term eg cash, bank and trade debtor balances.

ie   *Total assets = fixed assets + current assets*

eg   Fixed assets: £150,600
    Current assets: £ 45,834
    Total assets   = £150,600 + 45,384
        = £195,984

ie   *Total liabilities = capital + current liabilities*

eg   Capital: £163,720
    Current liabilities: £ 32,264
    Total liabilities   = £163,720 + £32,264
        = £195,984

Net profit This is the surplus from trading for the year, earned by the business for its owners (a net loss is a deficit). The calculation that occurred in the profit and loss account is taken to the balance sheet and adjusts the owner's long term retained funds, except for withdrawals. A sole proprietor and partner are usually entitled to withdraw part of this surplus to meet their living expenses; such a withdrawal will result in complimentary changes in the balance sheet.

ie   *Total assets = total liabilities + net profit (for current revenue period)*

eg   Total liabilities: £182,955
    Net profit: £ 13,029
    Total assets   = £182,955 + £13,029
        = £195,984

All of these matters will be discussed further since collectively they form a major part of financial accounting.

In all three stages of final accounts there are different methods of presentation that are acceptable to accountants, some traditional, others of comparatively recent introduction. Method of presentation is to some degree a matter of opinion, but recent innovations are favoured. Examples of different methods (new and old) will be illustrated in the text.

A further point to mention at this stage is that accounts, especially final accounts, are concerned with presentation of information to users and care should be taken not only with respect to the accuracy of the information but also the way it is presented − this includes matters of clarity and neatness. (For an illustration of final accounts, if necessary or out of curiosity, refer to final accounts II pages 55−7.)

Unit 4
The layout of accounts I

Overview

1 Accounting statements can be presented in a variety of formats.
2 Accounting records in the main are restricted to two types:
   a) the ledger, and
   b) the journal.
3 Each has a different purpose and will be employed in the explanation of accounting systems.
4 The modern, vertical or whole page presentation of final accounts is discussed.

The trading account along with the profit and loss account and balance sheet is part of the final statement.

Accounting statements can be presented in a variety of formats according to the requirements of information implicit in each. However, traditionally, accounting records take two major forms. These are:

1 the ledger, and
2 the journal.

These names often cause students needless difficulties since the purpose of each is only to present and retain information in the best possible way. Visually these two types can be illustrated as follows:

The ledger:

Account name

The journal:

Description of entry		

Part of the text will involve the use of these.

So far as final accounts are concerned, there has been a tendency to move away from the ledger presentation to a whole page or vertical format. This modern approach started with the balance sheet, which as has been said, is purely a listing of closing balances. Such a rearrangement has many advantages that extend to the trading account and profit and loss account. However it is suggested that some care should be taken when adopting this method in the two latter cases, since reference is made to, say debit or credit one or other account when transferring amounts from the ledgers, and clearly the corresponding entry is less obvious when the debit and credit two-sided account has been rearranged. To be fair, such a problem only exists in the early stages when learning the process of double entry but is nevertheless crucial at this point. Therefore, in the following units the modern method is illustrated and explained as subsidiary to the conventional method, but will be increasingly used in later stages of the text.

Unit 5
The trading account

Overview

1 The trading account is presented in the traditional ledger format and again in the modern 'whole page' format.

2 The initial formula, Gross profit = sales − purchases, is amended to include figures for opening stock and closing stock.

3 The term 'Cost of goods sold' is explained, namely as:
Cost of goods sold = opening stock + purchases − closing stock.

4 The trading account enables a further relationship to be visualized:
Sales = Cost of goods sold *plus* gross profit.

5 The trading account presents the gross profit calculation.

The trading account and, for that matter, the profit and loss account have been traditionally produced in a ledger format. However, a completed 'whole page' version will be illustrated beneath the full layout.

It has already been stated that the trading account is primarily concerned with sales and purchases to show the gross profit. The explanation progresses through the following diagrammatic presentations to develop the trading account from its simplest to its more familiar layout.

The conventional presentation is purchases on the left, sales on the right. Since sales should in all cases be greater than purchases — gross profit (the difference) is shown on the left.	Purchases (ignoring adjustments for stock) Gross profit	x	Sales	x

The equality of the entries — the account balances with the inclusion of total figures. Note the formula: gross profit = sales − purchases.	Purchases (ignoring adjustments for stock) Gross profit	x x x	Sales	x x

It is a fundamental principle of ledger accounts that they balance, and in this case the balance is then utilized in the profit and loss.

These are some of the adjustments required by accountants, namely opening stock and closing stock.	Opening stock Add Purchases Less Closing stock Gross profit	x x x x x	Sales	x x

Adjustments for stock

A business is usually regarded as continuing ie, it carries on from one year to the next. Accountants recognize this and call it the 'going concern' basis, used as a fundamental principle on which to prepare accounts. Therefore, if we choose to prepare accounts for a given period, a business that continues from an earlier period and proceeds to a later period will almost certainly have a balance of stock of goods for sale.

Two interim points should be recognized at this stage:

a) status and
b) calculation

Status When the business is not regarded as a going concern it is likely to be either just starting up or, in the majority of cases, just finishing. Both aspects contain legal and accounting complications which will be discussed later, but a feature so far as stock is concerned is that there may not be a significant opening or closing stock figure.

Calculation The calculation of stock figures will be dealt with in a subsequent section.

To continue beyond the two interim points, a small newsagent and tobacconist who is trading can be expected to have a supply of goods for sale eg cigarettes, tobacco, magazines and confectionery (but not newspapers) that are of value, but remain unsold at the close of an accounting period. Newspapers will not be of much value once they are out of date.

Often you will notice a sign in a shop window reading 'closed for stock taking'. Although the business is continuing to trade and only stops temporarily, perhaps for a day, it means that the work of stock taking, done at the close of the financial period, cannot be successfully carried out while actively participating in normal trading activities.

The following layout represents a common trading account as used by accountants to determine the gross profit after making adjustments for stock.

1. A sub-total is shown for the addition of purchases and opening stock. A similar sub-total is the cost of goods sold figure, and this is considered more important.
2. The importance of cost of goods sold or cost of sales is highlighted in the second, alternative (modern) presentation. The purpose is the same; it is just that the layout has been rearranged.

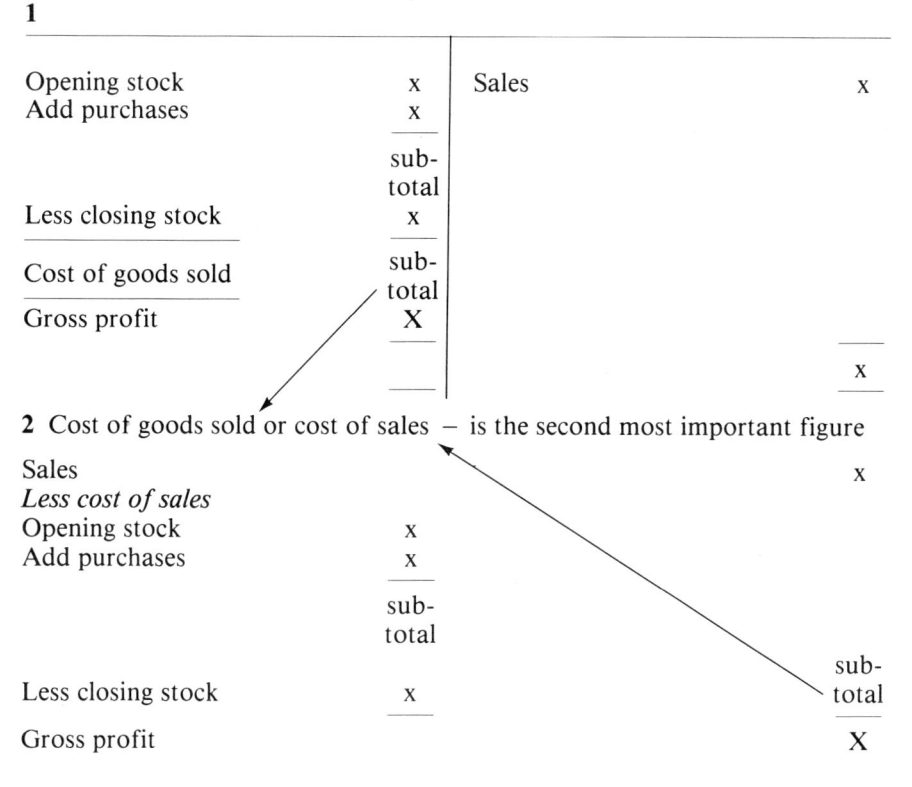

1

Opening stock	x	Sales	x
Add purchases	x		
	sub-total		
Less closing stock	x		
Cost of goods sold	sub-total		
Gross profit	X		
			x

2 Cost of goods sold or cost of sales — is the second most important figure

Sales			x
Less cost of sales			
Opening stock	x		
Add purchases	x		
	sub-total		
Less closing stock	x		sub-total
Gross profit			X

The addition of opening stock and purchases to give a sub-total could be described as goods available for sale; it is merely convention that it is not. Perhaps a description would unnecessarily clutter up the account. However, it is from this sub-total that closing stock is *deducted*, that is the goods available for sale that have not been sold at the close of the accounting period, thus providing the cost of goods sold. Therefore we can re write our initial equation as:
Sales = cost of goods sold + gross profit.

A point of interest that will be useful later on is that in the ledger variant of the trading account, closing stock is occasionally shown on the opposite side of the account beneath sales, but it is not shown as a deduction on that side. The reason for this is that some entries can be shown differently on opposite sides.

To re-emphasize an earlier point, the trading account correctly prepared produces a record of the gross profit of the business.

Example
The 'traditional' method

Opening stock	4,637	Sales	39,925
Add purchases	28,488		
	33,125		
Less closing stock	5,250		
Cost of goods sold	27,875		
Gross profit	12,050		
	£39,925		£39,925

The 'modern' method

Sales		39,925
Less cost of sales		
Opening stock	4,637	
Add purchases	28,488	
	33,125	
Less closing stock	5,250	27,875
Gross profit		£12,050

The gross profit will be used in the profit and loss account described in the next unit.

Unit 6
The profit and loss account

Overview

1 The profit and loss account is presented in the traditional ledger format and again in the modern 'whole page' format.
2 The gross profit from the trading account is applied to the profit and loss account.
3 The profit and loss account is often a continuation of the trading account – the heading for both being that of the trading and profit and loss account.
4 The two accounts are for the whole of the accounting period. The term 'for year ended' is used as part of the heading for these accounts (a close alternative is 'year ending').
5 The expenses ie costs are listed and totalled on the left-hand side of the profit and loss account.
6 The abbrieviations for and the terminology of 'carried down' (c/d) and 'brought down' (b/d) are introduced in the ledger account version as a preliminary step to use in subsequent ledger accounts.
7 The profit and loss account presents the net profit (loss).

The profit and loss account takes the gross profit from the trading account and subjects the trading profit to the recognition of expenditure. The balance remaining is the net profit that may be supplemented by any non-trading revenue.

In the ledger format the gross profit is said to be brought down from the trading account and in the trading account itself it is said to be carried down. This is a familiar procedure that is adopted with ledger accounts.

The familiar layout of a trading account with the gross profit carried down (abbreviated c/d) and the adjoining profit and loss account with the gross profit brought down (abbreviated b/d).

The 'ledger' layout

Gross profit c/d	x			
			Gross profit b/d	x
	x			
	x			
	x			
	x			
	x			
Net profit c/d	X			

In the new layout the sales less the cost of sales give the gross profit – there is no need for the abbreviations c/d and b/d. The expenses are sub-totalled and inset. The final figure provides the net profit.

The 'modern' layout
Sales   x

Gross profit   x
Less expenses   x
                                                                                         X

                                                    x
                                                    x
                                                    x
                                                    x
                                                    x   x
Net profit   X

It is common practice to treat the profit and loss account as a continuation of the trading account. The heading for both would be: trading and profit and loss account for year ending 31st December 19-1 at the top of the trading account. Note 'The year ending' as opposed to 'as at' in the balance sheet. The balance sheet is a compilation of ending balances whereas the profit and loss account contains an accumulation of the progressive costs for the whole year.

Expenses These are the 'costs' contained in the profit and loss account on the left-hand side of the ledger version alternative presentations total them as in the modern format. Consider the following expenditures (totalling £9,160):

The 'ledger' format
Wages	4,210	Gross profit b/d	12,050
Salaries	3,100		
Rent	980		
Rates	240		
Light	100		
Heat	250		
Repairs to vehicles	88		
Repairs to property	192		
Net profit c/d	2,890		
	£12,050		£12,050

The 'modern' format

Gross profit		£12,050
Less expenses		
Wages	4,210	
Salaries	3,100	
Rent	980	
Rates	240	
Light	100	
Heat	250	
Repairs to vehicles	88	
Repairs to property	192	9,160
Net profit		£2,890

A listing of expenditure is totalled and set against the gross profit leaving a net profit £2,890. It is the net profit that in the case of sole traders account is carried directly to the balance sheet.

Unit 7
The balance sheet

Overview

1 The balance sheet is first shown in ledger format.
  assets = liabilities

2 Assets are classified into fixed (long term) and current (short term).

3 Liabilities are classified into capital (long term) and current (short term).

4 A distinction is drawn between long term and short term according to accountants' rules ie the long term period is usually greater than a year.

5 An explanation is given of all terms appearing in the balance sheet.

6 An example is given of both the ledger and vertical presentation.

7 In the ledger presentation, total liabilities are compared with total assets:
  Fixed assets + current assets = capital + current liabilities.

8 In the whole page presentation, there is a rearrangement of sub totals:
  Fixed assets + net current assets = financed by

The balance sheet is the last and probably the most important part in the preparation of final accounts. It is, as has been said, a statement of assets and liabilites and is first illustrated in a ledger format.

This layout has been traditional in the United Kingdom for many decades.

Liabilities	Assets

However, a reversed ledger format is also acceptable.

This layout is accepted as the traditional layout in the United States.

Assets	Liabilities

The point I want to make about this at the outset, without causing confusion, is that the balance sheet is to some degree independent of other accounting entries even though it is often shown as a ledger account. What is important is that both parts balance.

ie Assets = Liabilities

The balancing is like that of any other ledger account so far as totalling is concerned except there is no balancing figure that is not usually known already. We have already seen that assets and liabilities can be subdivided as follows:

Assets into: fixed assets
current assets

Liabilities into: capital
current liabilities

The presentation and sub-classification so far would be:

The major sub-divisions are used in outline.	Capital	Fixed assets
The balance sheet is a total of these.	Current liabilities	Current assets

Listed below are the types of balances that would be shown:

Capital of owners	Land and buildings
Add Net profit	Plant and machinery
Less Drawings	Fixtures and fittings
Long term loans	Motor vehicles
Creditors	Stock (closing)
Accruals	Debtors
Bank overdraft	Pre payments
	Bank balance
	Cash

Both assets and liabilities can be long term or short term. Accountants have sometimes found difficulty drawing the distinction for the purpose of making a general rule. Many factors affect the classification not least the particular circumstances of the business. Therefore as an arbitrary rule most accountants accept the distinction as:

whether they will remain for longer or less than a year.

A current item will then be prescribed as having a 'life' of less than a year and a fixed, long-term or capital item as more than a year.

There are exceptions to this yearly rule. For instance, net profit (and drawings) only relate to a particular year but since they affect owners' capital in the long run, they are seen as a yearly or periodic adjustment of this figure. Problems such as decisions about classifications of this nature do cause difficulty. Students are inclined to think that everything about accounts is absolute when this is really not the case.

A brief explanation will now be given for those items many of which will be recognized by name and some understood in an accounting context, others not previously encountered will require explanation. The composition and treatment of these balances listed form a large section of accounting theory and will be returned to, many under separate headings (a reference to the Contents, Index and Glossary would be useful at this stage). However, for the moment, the following explanations are sufficient.

Capital of owners – are funds belonging to the proprietor, in the case of a sole trader, and other owners in different types of business. These are the long term funds of the business belonging to the owners.

Net profit – is the trading or revenue surplus after meeting expenditure that is added to the long term funds of the proprietor. Part of the long term funds of the owners may already be made up of earlier years profits, similarly added.

Drawings – are funds taken out of the business by the proprietor. As net profit (funds obtained by trading) is added to the funds belonging to the owner, so drawings are funds taken out for private use (deducted from net profit or capital).

Long-term loans – not only the proprietor but other parties may lend funds to the business, over a period of time, that would vary according to the terms of contract for the loan. It is important to distinguish between bank loans and overdrafts.

Creditors – the total balance of money owed by the business to its suppliers of goods and service, often referred to as trade creditors.

Accruals – these are similar to creditors in that they represent a total of amounts owing, but for reasons not so much related to trade as to the complexities of preparing accounts for a given period.

Bank overdraft – this is the balance of money owed to a bank, and the opposite of an asset balance where the business keeps some of its money in the bank. Note that an overdraft is not regarded as a loan, because it is considered unlikely to remain for longer than a year, were this not the case the bank would probably wish to consider it on a more formal basis ie a loan.

Land and buildings – this is property that is owned by the business or in the process of being purchased, ie used for some business purpose to assist in the trading activities, to earn a profit for the business.

Plant and machinery – this is similar to land and buildings. These are assets used for the purpose of manufacturing a saleable commodity. Such assets have to be owned, or be in the process of being owned, to be so recognized.

Fixtures and fittings – these are assets used for trading usually found in retail businesses, for example shelving systems.

Motor vehicles – all businesses require some form of transport – delivery vans or sales representatives' cars – and these like other fixed assets, are used to earn a profit.

Each of the above has a life usually longer than a year. What is important is that they are used for the purpose of earning revenue and not actively traded in. From time to time such assets will be traded in and accounting aspects relating to this procedure will be dealt with under depreciation.

For example a used car business would not show a valuation for motor vehicles in the fixed asset section, but in the current asset section under closing stock, since in this case they are traded in

Stock – this is the closing valuation of goods on hand for resale. These are usually complete but there are cases where unfinished goods and raw materials have to be shown.

Debtors (the opposite of creditors) – this is the total balance of money owed to the business by its customers for sales made that have not been paid. Often referred to as trade debtors.

Pre payments – similar to debtors in that they represent value to be gained from sums paid out in advance, but for reasons not so much related to trade, as to the complexities of preparing accounts for a given period.

Bank balance – this is the amount held by a business in one or more bank accounts. Information about the balance is easily obtainable from bank records, eg statements. Such current account funds together with cash are the most liquid funds. It is unlikely there will be both a positive balance and an overdraft in theoretical examples.

Cash – the total balance of money held by the business for various uses. Where there are many accounts eg at different locations, then it is important that all amounts are included.

Owners' capital		42,000	*Fixed assets*		
			Land and buildings		25,000
Add: Net profit	2,890		Fixtures & fittings		3,500
			Motor vehicle		7,800
Less: Drawings	2,250	640			36,300
		42,640			
Loan (repayable in 5 years)		4,000	*Current assets*		
			Stock	8,250	
			Debtors	2,390	
			Prepayments	280	
Current liabilities			Bank balance	1,210	
			Cash	475	12,605
Creditors	2,070				
Accruals	195	2,265			
		£48,905			£48,905

Note Transfer of: a) Net profit from profit and loss, and
            b) Closing stock from trading account.

A point about presentation is that a balance sheet can be shown in other ways. An alternative method is the vertical balance sheet that is increasingly becoming accepted as the method of presentation. It is simply a rearrangement of the ledger format. First refer to the diagram below and then to the above statement rewritten in vertical form. An important point to note is that there is more than one type of 'modern' presentation. In this respect, as in others in accounting, both the user and compiler should be flexible in considering which is best, given the circumstances of each case.

Owners' capital　　　*Fixed assets*　　　　*Fixed assets*

Current liabilities　　*Current assets*　　　*Net current assets*
　　　　　　　　　　　　　　　　　　　　Current assets

　　　　　　　　　　　　　　　　　　　　Less current liabilities

　　　　　　　　　　　　　　　　　　　　Financed by

Balance Sheet as at 31 December 19-1
Fixed assets
Land and buildings   25,000
Fixtures and fittings   3,500
Motor vehicles   7,800
                                                             36,300
Net current assets
Current assets
Stock   8,250
Debtors   2,390
Prepayments   280
Bank balance   1,210
Cash   475   12,605

Less current liabilities
Creditors   2,070
Accruals   195   (2,265)   10,340
                                                            £46,640

Financed by
Owners capital   42,000
Add: Net profit   2,890
Less: Drawings   2,250   640
Bank loan   4,000
                                                            £46,640

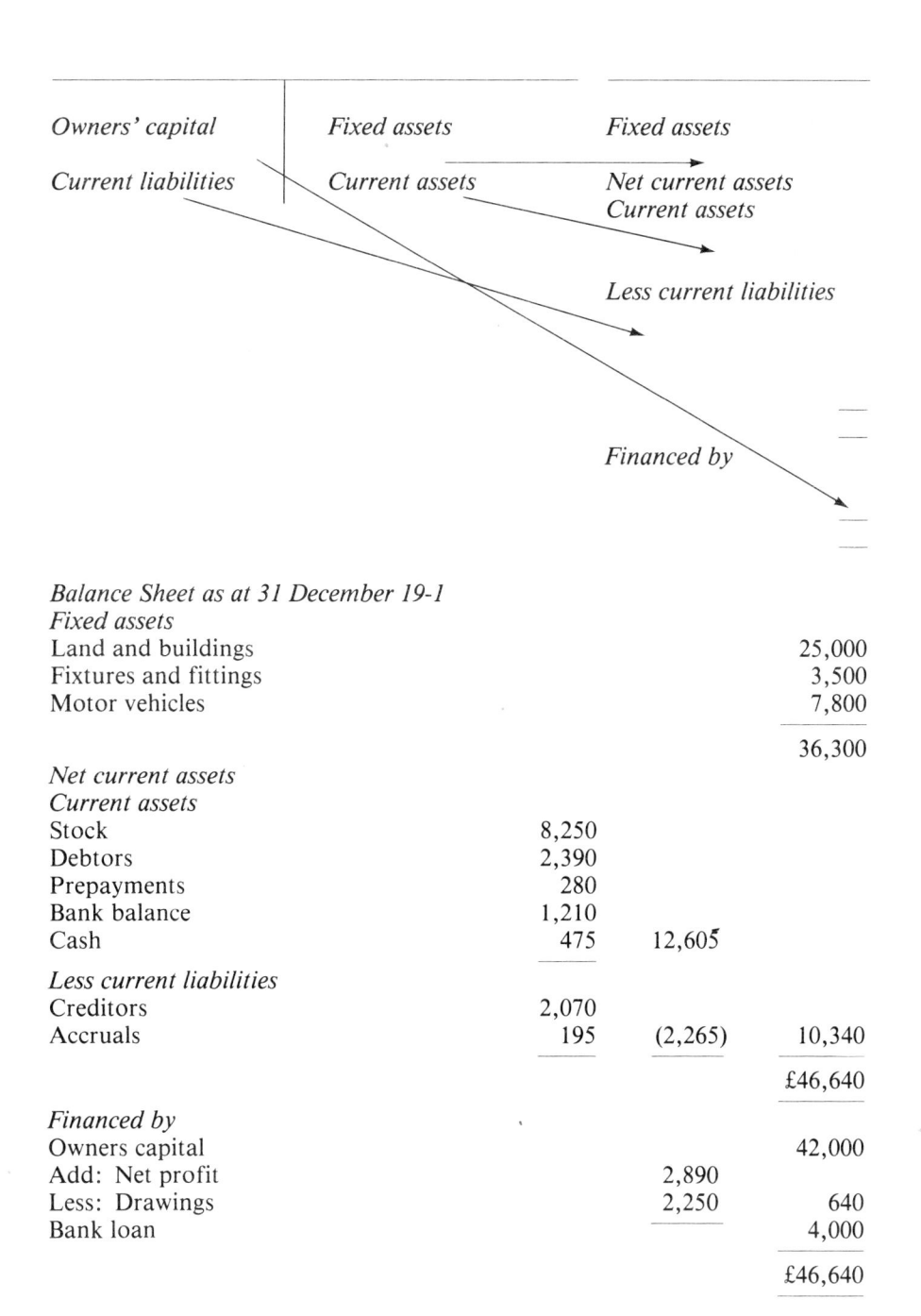

Note 1 The total balancing figure may be different, but check the sub-totals of each section.
2 Figures in brackets are minus and therefore deducted.
3 The vertical balance sheet takes the whole width of a page.
4 Current liabilities are deducted from current assets (that should be greater) to give net current assets.
Net current assets = working capital
Working capital = current assets − current liabilities
5 Current liabilities are still regarded as the opposite of current assets; but they are not shown in the conventional ledger format as opposites to the right and left of a dividing line down the centre.
6 In the vertical format it is the top half that balances with the bottom half.

ie Fixed assets + net current assets
            (current assets − current liabilities)
        = Financed By
          (Long term capital)

Questions

Equations of assets and liabilities

1 Complete the gaps in the following tables:

	Assets	Liabilities	Capital
1a	22,900	–	13,480
b	108,756	63,984	–
c	–	109,519	54,321
d	35,330	21,568	–
e	29,817	–	14,440
2a	1,039,856	987,318	–
b	62,436	–	24,829
c	97,810	60,010	–
d	578,450	393,630	–
e	–	214,891	178,612
3a	913,240	754,221	–
b	58,338	–	26,212
c	37,814	21,515	–
d	–	72,506	36,663
e	15,205	7,888	–
4a	–	489,288	134,930
b	24,344	–	6,790
c	–	54,330	20,015
d	29,555	19,843	–
e	107,081	–	34,438
5a	333,996	257,188	–
b	1,512,778	–	485,111
c	10,721,000	8,342,850	–
d	–	29,818	14,640
e	–	33,773	20,130

2 Complete the gaps in the following tables:

	Fixed assets	Current assets	Capital	Long term loan	Current liabilities
1a	90,960	28,730	–	10,000	14,895
b	–	45,221	33,730	15,000	42,836
c	128,000	36,960	106,110	–	35,850
d	504,322	64,110	350,560	125,000	–
e	255,350	–	216,588	30,000	88,942
2a	–	7,210	19,500	2,000	6,980
b	308,630	–	208,020	75,000	54,226
c	1,566,288	215,843	–	375,500	205,110
d	898,440	–	454,230	250,000	100,320
e	312,880	156,534	286,014	–	98,400
3a	–	65,575	250,960	100,000	54,325
b	–	89,170	329,600	52,500	50,240
c	725,800	102,619	27,612	225,000	75,727
d	545,100	60,480	350,650	155,500	–
e	53,571	–	25,964	25,250	5,842

21

4a	684,910	90,060	527,330	–	82,140	
b	54,981	25,242	38,516	25,000	–	
c	233,382	–	187,980	60,250	50,765	
d	–	80,090	797,440	100,000	60,110	
e	1,090,223	200,540	–	485,750	198,623	
5a	200,338	63,800	180,800	–	59,500	
b	60,555	–	57,725	10,500	12,802	
c	–	45,034	42,180	5,650	39,220	
d	332,112	76,923	192,185	–	71,100	
e	121,646	11,086	61,191	62,000	–	

Answer guide: 3c £527,692; 4c £65,613

The trading account

3 How would the following items be classified by accountants in the Trading Account?

1a Goods sold to customers
 b Goods held at the start of the year
 c Goods sold to customers for cash
 d Goods held at the close of the year that remain unsold
 e Goods bought from suppliers that have not been paid for
 f Goods sold to customers who have yet to pay
 g Goods purchased from suppliers for cash
 h Goods in the store at the end of the year.
 i Goods bought by business proprietor for his own use
 j Goods in the store at the start of the year.

2a Goods bought for business use during the year stored in the proprietors own home
 b Goods sold to customers on credit
 c Purchases bought for business from a legitimate trader
 d Goods sold to proprietors friend who has yet to pay
 e Goods bought for the proprietors home
 f Machinery bought for use in business
 g Unsold goods in store on premises other than the main location at the end of a trading year
 h Goods sold at close of trading period, but not delivered
 i Exchange of goods with another trader
 j Goods bought during a trading period, but not delivered.

4 The following lists of entries should be arranged as a Trading Account and the cost of sales and gross profit calculated.

1	Opening stock	3,000	2 Opening stock	49,800	
	Purchases	15,000	Purchases	536,333	
	Sales	30,000	Closing stock	51,608	
	Closing stock	4,000	Sales	1,271,444	
3	Opening stock	5,400	4 Sales	92,310	
	Purchases	45,600	Closing stock	11,827	
	Closing stock	7,200	Opening stock	9,935	
	Sales	76,330	Purchases	54,180	

5 Sales   236,952
   Purchases   113,640
   Opening stock   –
   Closing stock   24,330
   Can you think why the opening stock should be nil?

Answer guide: 1 GP = £16,000.

5 The following lists of entries contain some missing information but this can be calculated, using the Trading Account format, figures may have to be rounded up or down to use whole numbers.

1			2		
Sales		125,960	Opening stock		51,010
Purchases		?	Closing stock		?
Gross profit – 25% of sales			Sales		350,575
Closing stock		6,730	Purchases		260,885
Opening stock		5,520	Gross profit – 20% of sales		

3			4		
Sales		483,993	Opening stock		82,160
Purchases		316,218	Closing stock		96,348
Opening stock		?	Sales		?
Closing stock		33,893	Purchases		724,336
Gross profit – 33⅓% of sales			Gross profit – 50% of purchases		

5 Opening stock   12,989
   Closing stock   21,656
   Purchases   86,414
   Sales   ?
   Gross profit – 40% of purchases

Answer guide: 3 GP £161,331

6 Prepare trading accounts from the following information:

1	£	2	£
Opening stock	15,500	Opening stock	8,900
Closing stock	17,300	Closing stock	?
Purchases	?	Purchases	44,250
Sales	200,000	Sales	55,000
Gross profit – 25% of sales		Gross profit – 20% of sales	

3	£	4	£
Opening stock	13,700	Opening stock	?
Closing stock	15,880	Closing stock	29,370
Purchases	76,182	Purchases	166,200
Sales	?	Sales	200,000
Gross profit – 33⅓% of purchases		Gross profit – 25% of cost of sales	

5   £
   Opening stock   18,970
   Closing stock   26,440
   Purchases   136,915
   Sales   ?
   Gross profit 20% of purchases

23

The profit and loss account

7 How would the following items be classified by accountant in the Profit and Loss Account?

1a Bills for electricity
 b Payment of rent
 c Payment of rates
 d Bills for gas
 e Repairs to motor vehicles
 f Building of an extension to property
 g Payment of wages
 h Purchase of motor vehicles
 i Rent paid in advance
 j Payment of salaries

2a Salaries paid in arrears
 b Distribution and warehouse costs
 c Wages paid in arrears
 d Purchase of property
 e Receipt of income from rent
 f Rates paid in advance
 g Rent owing
 h Repairs to property
 i Rent paid in advance
 j Gross profit

8 The following lists of entries apply to the Profit and Loss Account, and should be arranged in the required manner.

1			2		
	Gross profit	5,000		Gross profit	47,280
	Rent	1,000		Rent	2,100
	Rates	250		Rates	600
	Wages	2,500		Delivery costs	5,250
	Net profit	1,250		Electricity	1,760
				Gas	2,390
				Wages	15,840
				Salaries	9,230
				Net Profit	10,110

3			4		
	Gross profit	189,620		Gross profit	55,186
	Rent income	2,512		Rent and rates	6,254
	Rent and rates	42,980		Electricity	1,233
	Heating and lighting	18,244		Wages	13,438
	Carriage outwards	1,027		Salaries	5,879
	Wages and salaries	75,740		Motor van repairs	783
	Vehicle maintenance	2,150		Net profit	?
	Building repairs	1,860			
	Net profit	50,131			

5 Gross profit   100,036
   Rent income   7,288
   Rates   10,116
   Rent   15,630
   Salaries   20,222
   Wages   40,178
   Electricity   1,821
   Repairs to machines   973
   Net profit   ?

The trading and profit and loss account

9 Prepare a Trading and Profit and Loss Account from the following lists of entries, the two accounts can be combined, first calculating the gross profit then utilizing it to calculate the net profit. Only one combined heading is necessary.

1	Opening stock	5,600	2	Purchases	42,643
	Closing stock	6,300		Sales	100,925
	Purchases	25,850		Salaries	10,819
	Sales	56,720		Wages	21,442
	Staff wages	10,900		Electricity	1,960
	Insurance	256		Gas	570
	Light & heat	843		Rents & rates	4,830
	General expenses	2,970		Opening stock	21,118
				Closing stock	25,333
3	Purchases	336,824	4	Salaries & wages	31,220
	Sales	680,560		Repairs to buildings	1,582
	Opening stock	76,930		Electricity & gas	2,320
	Closing stock	104,310		Rent	4,690
	Building maintenance & repairs	15,550		Rates	1,313
	Motor van expenses	2,446		Vehicle repairs	1,116
	Light & heat	6,754		Vehicle running cots	1,584
	Rent & rates	20,480		Purchases	104,717
	Wages & salaries	151,718		Sales	186,424
				Opening stock	33,927
				Closing stock	46,820
5	Opening stock	19,240			
	Closing stock	33,883			
	Purchases	207,660			
	Sales	301,540			
	Wages	50,110			
	Salaries of staff	22,920			
	Vehicle maintenance & repairs	1,142			
	Rent & rates	6,340			
	Light & heat	2,119			
	Building repairs	833			
	Vehicle running costs	2,691			

Answer guide: 1 Gross profit £31,570; Net profit £16,601

The balance sheet

10 How would the following items be classified by accountants in the Balance Sheet?

1a Lathes
 b Delivery vans
 c Fork lift trucks
 d Money owed to business
 e Cash retained for business use
 f Money held at the bank
 g Capital of the proprietor
 h Drawings made by the proprietor
 i Net profit
 j Money owed by the business

2a Freehold land and buildings
 b Articulated lorries
 c Drilling machines
 d Fixed conveying equipment
 e Proprietors own private car, not used by business
 f Milling machines
 g Sales of goods made during year.
 h Purchases of goods made during year
 i Proprietors private house being purchased through a building society mortgage
 j Stock of goods unsold at the close of the year.

11 The following lists of entries apply to the Balance Sheet, they should be arranged in the appropriate format.

1 Owner's capital	15,600	2 Owner's capital	5,000
Net profit	7,220	Net profit	3,200
Trade creditors	11,490	Drawings	1,840
Motor van	4,850	Trade creditor	50
Stock	10,210	Motor van	2,300
Trade debtors	17,100	Stock	2,580
Bank	2,150	Bank	1,530

3 Owner's capital	50,000	4 Owner's capital	45,300
Net profit	25,000	Net profit	20,168
Drawings	10,000	Drawings	4,550
Machinery	20,000	Trade creditors	22,672
Creditors	10,000	Fixtures and fittings	10,200
Stock	27,500	Motor vans	17,660
Debtors	17,800	Stock	34,980
Bank	9,200	Trade debtors	12,340
Cash	500	Bank	8,410

5 Owners capital	96,200
Net profit	?
Drawings	10,850
Creditors	32,710
Debtors	14,400
Land and buildings	100,000
Fixture and fittings	20,000
Motor vehicles	10,000
Stock	24,860
Bank	4,320

Answer guide: 4 Balances (ledger method) £83,590

Section II
Recording individual entries

Unit 1   Arriving at final accounts
Unit 2   Double entry principles
Unit 3   Sales and purchases – double entry
Unit 4   Expenses – double entry
Unit 5   Returns of purchases and sales – double entry
Unit 6   Carriage inwards and outwards, discount allowed and received
Unit 7   Balancing off ledger accounts
Unit 8   The trial balance
Unit 9   Presentation of final accounts II

Unit 1
Arriving at final accounts

Overview

The stages are:

1 Prime entry,

2 Ledger accounts,

3 Balancing off,

4 Preparation of a trial balance and

5 Preparation of final accounts.

Five distinct stages can be illustrated in the accounting cycle, following on one from another and leading up to final accounts. These are briefly illustrated:

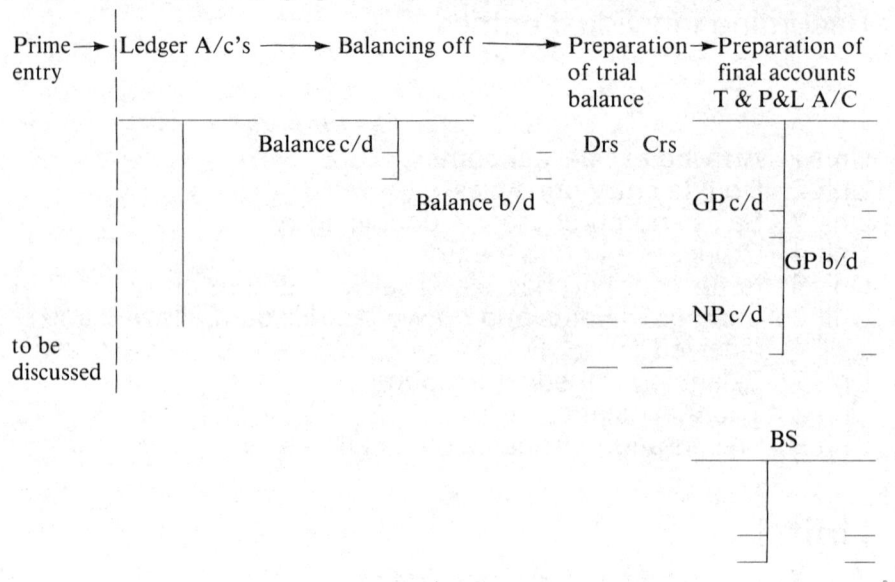

```
Prime ──► Ledger A/c's ──────► Balancing off ──────► Preparation ──► Preparation of
entry                                                of trial         final accounts
                                                     balance          T & P&L A/C

                         Balance c/d                 Drs   Crs

                                        Balance b/d                  GP c/d

                                                                             GP b/d

                                                           ──  ──   NP c/d

to be
discussed                                                                         BS
```

1 Prime entry   Transactions are collected together in a listing arrangement. Broadly there are two types of list — daybook for sales and purchases; and journal for items of special importance.

2 Ledger accounts   The actual double entry is carried out in the form of a 'T' account.

3 Balancing off   Where a balance for a period is extracted from each ledger account, it is to be used in final accounts.

4 Preparation of a trial balance   An intermediate step checking that balances extracted as debits and credits are equal when totalled. If figures do not balance at this stage it is unlikely they will balance later (in the final accounts) and therefore steps should be taken to discover discrepancies. Many accountancy questions provide a Trial balance as a starting point.

5 Preparation of final accounts: The three stages (i) trading account,
                                           (ii) profit and loss, and
                                           (iii) balance sheet.

Unit 2
Double entry principles

Overview

1 Entries require classification in a ledger format.

2 Entries are made twice for each transaction — considered as both an asset and a liability.

3 Transactions shown as debits and credits follow the format:

		Debit	Credit
Increase to an asset	(+)	X	
Increase to a liability	(+)		X
Decrease to an asset	(−)		X
Decrease to a liability	(−)	X	

providing the four permutations.

4 An example is given outlining the major points of double entry. Some points are presented before full discussion.

The principles stated here are the essence of book-keeping. Problems are often encountered because double entry is introduced at an early stage and compounded by use of the terms debit and credit in a manner which presumes instant understanding.

The decision to make entries includes other features namely, that entries are simultaneously:

1 classified according to the type of asset or liability,
2 presented in a ledger format,
3 shown as either a debit or a credit, and
4 considered in two ways — double entry proper.
(Points 3 and 4 will be considered below.)

Double entry — each entry is included in the books in two ways, once as a debit and once as a credit, to ensure that the accounts, taken as a whole balance, from which final accounts are prepared according to the principles outlined earlier.

There are essentially four permutations of entry. These are:

a) increasing or adding to an asset,
b) increasing or adding to a liability,
c) decreasing or deducting from an asset, and
d) decreasing or deducting from a liability
    depending on (i) how accountants classify the entry in the first place, and
                    (ii) its effect on that classification.

The following diagrams illustrate the four permutations of entry in a ledger format.

29

```
    An Asset
  ─────────────          Increasing an asset
       │
    +  │
       │
```

```
    A Liability
  ─────────────          Increasing a liability
       │
       │  +
       │
```

```
    An Asset
  ─────────────          Decreasing an asset
       │
       │  −
       │
```

```
    A Liability
  ─────────────          Decreasing a liability
       │
    −  │
       │
```

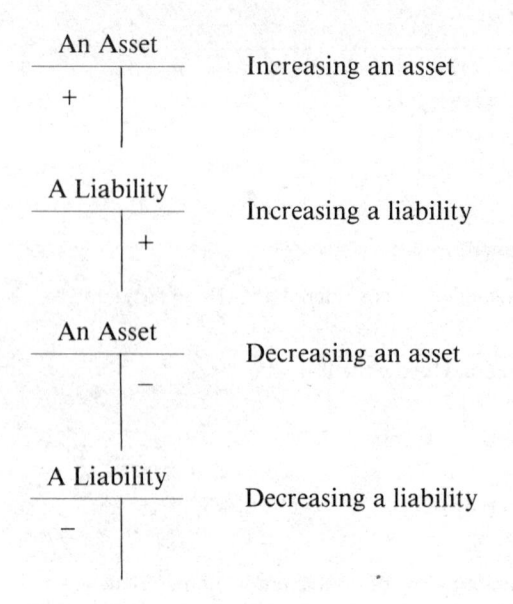

Depending on whether the entry is on the left or right, it is a debit or credit respectively.

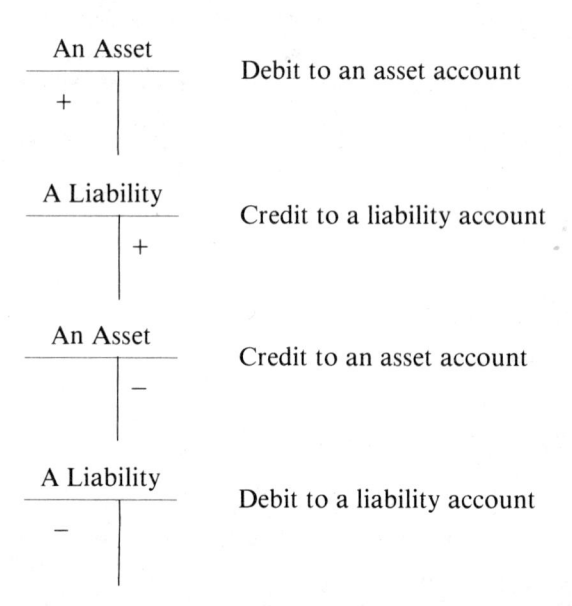

```
    An Asset
  ─────────────          Debit to an asset account
       │
    +  │
       │
```

```
    A Liability
  ─────────────          Credit to a liability account
       │
       │  +
       │
```

```
    An Asset
  ─────────────          Credit to an asset account
       │
       │  −
       │
```

```
    A Liability
  ─────────────          Debit to a liability account
       │
    −  │
       │
```

Therefore an asset account can have both a debit entry (on the left) and a credit entry (on the right), so too can a liability account, but the respective entries represent different aspects of accounting classification.

Essentially, every debit entry must have a corresponding credit entry and vice versa. The description of the appropriate account is part of the classification process.

The basic principles of double entry can be represented diagrammatically as follows:

Debit (Dr)   Credit (Cr)

```
     Debit ⬎                    |                    ⬋ Credit
                                 |
                                 |
   Dr           Cr    Dr                Cr
  ─────────────────  ──────────────────────
     Debit ⬋          |                    ⬊ Credit
                      |
```

So far as classification is concerned, one or other part of the transaction is likely to be more recognizable. Take that part first and consider it from the point of view of the following questions:

1 how can it be classified, and
2 is it a debit or credit?

Having made one or other decision will invariably help in making the other.

Illustration

Look at transaction 3 the purchase of a motor vehicle for £2,900 in the following tabulation.

Questions	Answer
1 Will it belong to the business?	Yes
2 Is it an asset?	Yes
3 What type of asset is it?	Motor van
4 Is it a debit?	Yes

Therefore **debit** Motor Van Account – adding to the assets. The corresponding entry must, therefore, be a credit.

```
Dr           Motor van           Cr
             ─────────────────────
             2,900 |
```

Questions	*Answer*
1 Does the asset have to be paid for?	Yes
2 Is payment by cash or cheque?	Cheque (through bank)

Therefore **credit** Bank Account – reducing the assets (money at the bank).

```
Dr             Bank              Cr
             ─────────────────────
                   | 2,900
```

A debit entry is made (in different accounts) for both short-term assets – expenses, and long-term assets – fixed assets used in the business.

Two points remain:

1 descriptions have to be added, and
2 dates have to be inserted.

The descriptions, adjacent to the amounts, have to be added, each description referring to the heading of the account in which the corresponding entry is made.

31

```
Dr              Motor van              Cr
                Bank 2,900 |


Dr                Bank                 Cr
                           | Motor van 2,900
```

Then the relevant date for the transaction has also to be added this time adjacent to the description.

```
Dr              Motor van              Cr
        Oct 3 Bank 2,900 |


Dr                Bank                 Cr
                           | Oct 3 Motor van 2,900
```

The dates and descriptions serve as a reference point; other reference features will become apparent later in the text.
Here is a tabulated, worked example:

Transaction		Effect		Action
1 Oct 1 Started wholesale business putting £20,000 into business bank account.	1	Increases assets of bank.	(a)	Debit bank account.
	2	Increases capital of proprietor.	(b)	Credit capital account.
2 Oct 2 Pays a year's rent in advance £1,000 through bank.	1	Increases expenses − rent.	(c)	Debit expense account − rent.
	2	Decreases assets bank.	(d)	Credit bank account.
3 Oct 3 Bought a van second-hand paying £2,900 through bank.	1	Increases asset motor van.	(e)	Debit motor van account.
	2	Decreases asset bank.	(f)	Credit bank account.
4 Oct 5 Bought goods for resale £1,490 from S Jones on credit.	1	Increases asset purchases.	(g)	Debit purchases account.
	2	Increase liability to S Jones.	(h)	Credit S Jones' account.
5 Oct 6 Transfers £200 from bank to cash.	1	Increases asset cash.	(i)	Debit cash account.
	2	Decreases asset bank.	(j)	Credit bank account.

6	Oct 9	Paid for casual labour £50 by cash.	1	Increases expenses – wages.	(k)	Debit expense account – wages.
			2	Decreases asset cash.	(l)	Credit cash account.
7	Oct 10	Sold goods to J Williams for £632 on credit.	1	Increases (creates) asset debtors.	(m)	Debit J Williams' account.
			2	Increases sales.	(n)	Credit sales account.
8	Oct 11	Paid S Jones by cheque for goods purchased on credit.	1	Decreases liability to S Jones.	(o)	Debit S Jones' account.
			2	Decreases asset bank.	(p)	Credit bank account.
9	Oct 12	Bought goods for resale £820 from P Smith on credit.	1	Increases asset purchases.	(q)	Debit purchases account.
			2	Increases (creates) liability to P Smith.	(r)	Credit P Smith's account.
10	Oct 14	Received cheque from J Williams in payment for goods sold on credit.	1	Increases asset bank.	(s)	Debit bank.
			2	Decreases liability of J Williams.	(t)	Credit J Williams' account.

```
                        Capital
                        |  19-1
                        |  Oct 1  Bank         (b)   20,000

                        Bank
19-1                    |  19-1
Oct 1   Capital   (a) 20,000 | Oct 2  Rent           (d)    1,000
Oct 14  J Williams (s)   632 | Oct 3  Motor Van      (f)    2,900
                             | Oct 6  Cash           (j)      200
                             | Oct 11 S Jones        (p)    1,490

                        Rent
19-1                    |
Oct 2   Bank       (c)  1,000 |

                      Motor Van
19-1                    |
Oct 3   Bank       (e)  2,900 |
```

33

Purchases

19-1			
Oct 5 S Jones	(g)	1,490	
Oct 12 P Smith	(q)	820	

Note Debits of goods for resale go to Purchases not stock.

S Jones

19-1				19-1		
Oct 11 Bank	(o)	1,490		Oct 5 Purchases	(h)	1,490

Cash

19-1				19-1		
Oct 6 Bank	(i)	200		Oct 9 Wages	(l)	50

Wages

19-1			
Oct 9 Cash	(k)	50	

P Smith

			19-1		
			Oct 12 Purchases	(r)	820

J Williams

19-1				19-1		
Oct 10 Sales	(m)	632		Oct 14 Bank	(t)	632

Sales

			19-1		
			Oct 10 J Williams	(n)	632

Note Sales result in entirely opposite entries to Purchases, compare entries (n) and (m) with (g) and (h)

Unit 3
Sales and purchases − double entry

Overview

1 A diagrammatic outline is reproduced.

2 Sales and purchases are recorded:
Purchases − debit purchases account.
Sales − credit sales account.

3 Corresponding entries are made to one of:
a) Personal ledgers − purchases and sales on credit,
b) Bank or
c) Cash.

4 Entries in 3 are shown as corresponding to:
a) Purchases − credit relevant account.
b) Sales − debit relevant account.

Given that transactions for purchases and sales are expressed in monetary terms, the purchase and sale of goods by a business ultimately affect either cash or bank, depending on the method of payment. The point is, that for cases where there is other than an immediate cash settlement, there may well be some delay ie

a) goods bought, but not paid for, or
b) goods sold, but not paid for,

depending on the direction of the flow of goods − in or out of the business. Such transactions still have to be shown in the double-entry system, and the presentation of information involving credit (delay) is as important as that for immediate payment.

Transactions are recognized, in accounting, as purchases and sales, as soon as they are invoiced, and the two-way character of the effect on assets and liabilities can be illustrated diagrammatically, showing, in both cases the effect of a cash or *credit* (delayed) impact on the business accounting system.

Purchases and sales

If goods are available for resale, this will ultimately affect cash at bank depending on the medium of transaction, assuming it is expressed in monetary terms.

An intermediate stage may be a credit transaction, in other words, a purchase or sale not immediately affecting monetary terms.

Such items have to be shown in double-entry system to show outstanding amounts, ie goods bought but not paid for
               goods sold but not paid for.
These transactions are still recognised as sales and purchases.

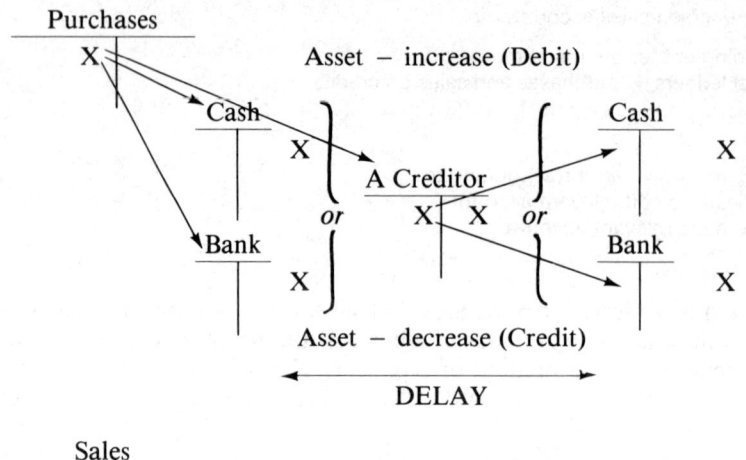

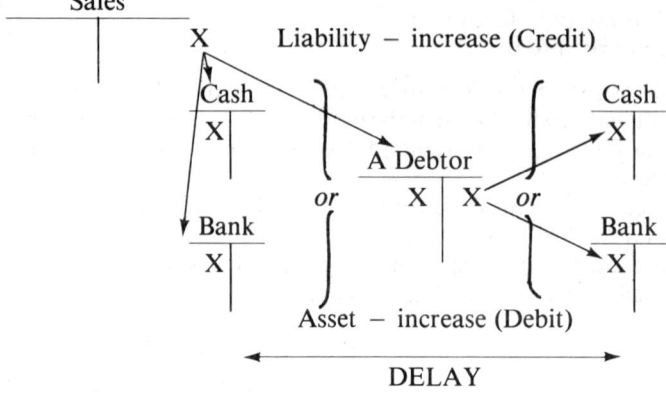

Main entries

Sales and purchases are the two major classifications of trade transactions a business undertakes. They take different physical forms depending on the type of business. Considerable care has to be taken in practice to ensure that these are accurately recorded. The collection of this information by the use of daybooks is examined on pages 122–5.

However, assuming these items are recorded directly through the ledger as debits and credits, the following transactions are carried out:
Purchases – debit the Purchase Account with every item purchased.
Sales – credit the Sales Account with every item sold.

It will be apparent that these entries are only part of the double entry process and require corresponding entries. A glance at a purchase and sales account will illustrate the position to date.

Illustration

Purchases

19-1		19-1	
June 2 B James	1950		
June 3 K Muxloe	280		
June 5 J Rogers	620		
June 6 B Hill	402		
June 6 Cash	90		
June 7 Bank	115		

Purchases are recorded as debits.

Sales

19-1		19-1	
		June 1 F Brownhill	180
		June 1 K Brand	53
		June 2 P Myers	250
		June 2 K Brand	844
		June 4 Bank	210
		June 6 Cash	136

Sales are recorded as credits.

Corresponding entries

The double entry for sales and purchases will occur as follows:

1 Transactions on credit in the personal ledger of debtors (for sales), and creditors (for purchases).
2 Bank account – where payments or receipts are made through the bank.
3 Cash account – where payments or receipts are made via cash.

For entries in the personal ledgers (as in 1 above), credit transactions will be recorded in the Purchases Ledger and Sales Ledger for creditors and debtors respectively, under the account names of the various parties to whom they apply.

Purchases

B James
19-1	
June 2 Purchases	1950

K Muxloe
19-1	
June 3 Purchases	280

J Rogers
19-1	
June 5 Purchases	620

and so on.

Note The corresponding entry is recorded as a credit

Sales

F Brownhill
19-1	
June 1 Sales	180

K Brand
19-1	
June 1 Sales	53
June 2 Sales	844

and so on.

Note The corresponding entry is recorded as a debit.
There are two sales recorded against K Brand and this is a common enough feature where there is more than one transaction. Other entries for bank and cash will also be made as follows:

Bank
19-1		19-1	
June 1 Balance b/d	560	June 7 Purchases	115
June 4 Sales	210		

Cash
19-1		19-1	
June 1 Balance b/d	80	June 6 Purchases	90
June 6 Sales	136		

Note Both the Bank and Cash accounts have money brought forward from an earlier period — shown as Balances b/d.

An important point to remember is that accounts record transactions in monetary amounts, the point mentioned at the start of this Unit. Therefore we do not necessarily know the quantity of goods involved. When comparing sales and purchases, it is likely that a given monetary amount will represent fewer actual sales than purchases, broadly speaking, sales cost more ie they contain added profit.

Unit 4
Expenses — double entry

Overview

1 Expense records have to be maintained in books of account prior to inclusion in final accounts.
2 Expenses are shown in the double entry system as debits.
3 Types of expenses include rent, rates, lighting and heating, wages and salaries.

The presentation of expenses has been illustrated in the final accounts, but it is important to appreciate how accountants can extract these figures from the books of account with a reasonable degree of confidence in their accuracy (assuming that the accounting system is efficiently controlled).

To do this expenses have to be entered into the double entry system and classified as **debits** under appropriate headings:
eg   rent and rates
      light and heat
      wages and salaries
   . . . to name but a few.

Why debits? While it is reasonably easy (given practice) to appreciate that assets are recorded as debits, it may not be so easy with expenses. When buying a fixed asset, say a machine, use is obtained of that machine for loss of an agreed amount of cash or money in the bank.

Assets
one asset   — cash or bank balance
is exchanged for . . .
another asset — a machine.

So too with expenses
one asset — cash or bank balance
is consumed in exchange for . . .
a service — a value has been obtained by the business.

Note That as well as the cash or bank balance being reduced a liability to reduce these (in the future) can also be incurred as an alternative.

Double entry

Incurring an expense leads to the following entries (for the moment ignoring timing, and assuming a bill has been received):
Take the following ledger example.

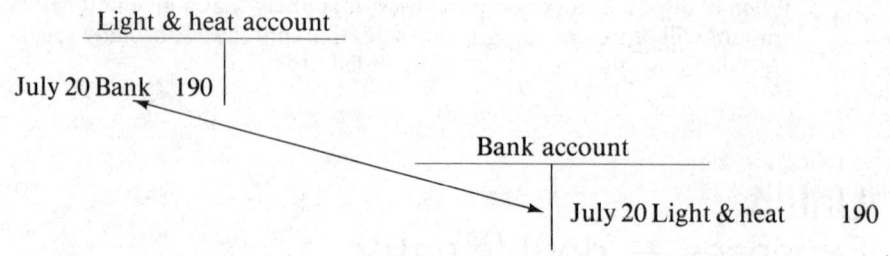

```
           Light & heat account
           ─────────────────────
July 20 Bank    190 |
                    |
                            Bank account
                            ─────────────────────
                                         | July 20 Light & heat    190
```

ie **debit** light and heat — value has been obtained in the form of light and heat that is expected to assist towards the provision of a saleable product or service.

   credit bank — reduction of the asset (total money in the bank) to pay for a service consumed.

Similar aspects apply to other expenses, arranged on the debit side and classified according to type. Here are some accounts:

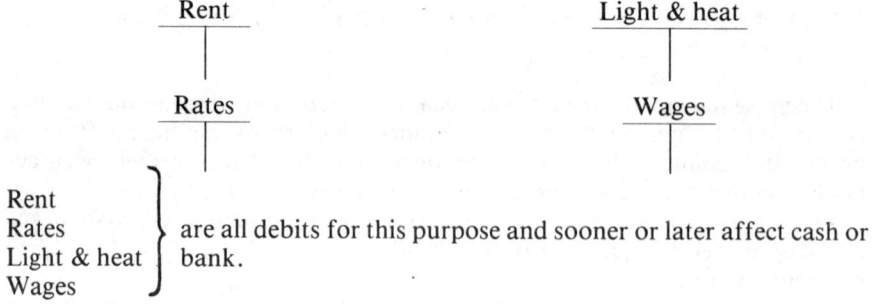

```
        Rent                     Light & heat
        ────                     ────────────
         |                            |
        Rates                      Wages
        ─────                      ─────
         |                            |
```

Rent
Rates } are all debits for this purpose and sooner or later affect cash or
Light & heat } bank.
Wages

In the majority of cases (where there are no adjustments) expense accounts will contain only debits prior to balancing off.

Unit 5
Returns of purchases and sales — double entry

Overview

1 Just as purchases and sales are collected together in their respective accounts so too are returns of these.

2 Returns of sales = returns inward (sales returns) as the account is so titled.

3 Returns of purchases = returns outward (purchase returns) also used to describe an account.

40

4 Opposite entries for the return of sales and purchases compared to the original entries will have to be made.
5 Entries opposite to those originals in the personal accounts also have to be made.
6 The return transaction is illustrated in the context of:
   a) the trial balance, and
   b) the trading account,
   as to their effect on these presentations.

As has been demonstrated, purchases and sales have been collected together as follows:
Purchases — a **debit**

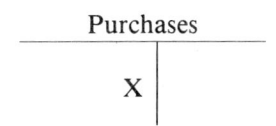

```
        Purchases
    _____
           |
        X  |
           |
```

Sales — a **credit**

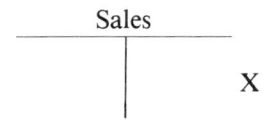

```
                    Sales
                _____
                       |
                       |  X
                       |
```

The respective entries for transactions on credit will occur in the personal account of the debtor or creditor.

Often goods have to be returned by the customer because they may be faulty, are the wrong type, or have been incorrectly delivered. There may be other reasons but certain goods, ie goods on sale or return, will be excluded from this discussion.

It will be clear that the return of goods represents the adjustment of a recorded sale or purchase, and amendments will have to be made to the original accounting entries. But only under the rules applicable to double entry.

Entries are as follows:
a) (i) Transactions for cash require adjustment to cash received or paid.
   (ii) Transactions on credit require adjustments to the respective entry in personal accounts.
b) Both types require adjustment to the sales and purchases account, but by use of returns accounts.

The returns account entries and the personal account entries will be opposite to those originally made for sales and purchases on credit.

```
  Returns outward
 _____
       |
       |  X
       |
```
or Purchase returns

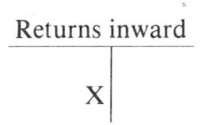

```
                Returns inward
               _____
                      |
                   X  |
                      |
```
or Sales returns.

41

Compare the positioning of the entry in the Returns account to the original Sales or Purchases entry — they are opposites.

Example
From the previous section on Sales and Purchases:
1 B James, from whom purchases had been made, had delivered £50 of faulty goods that were returned.

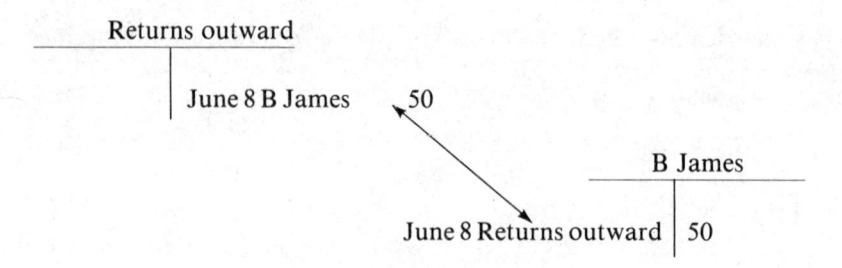

```
             Returns outward
        ─────────────────────────
             │ June 8 B James   50

                                        B James
                                  ─────────────────────────
                                  June 8 Returns outward │ 50
```

Thus the principle of double entry is conformed to:
Returns outward (purchase returns)   =   credit
B James (reducing amount owed)   =   debit
2 F Brownhill had found incorrect goods delivered and had returned the whole consignment.

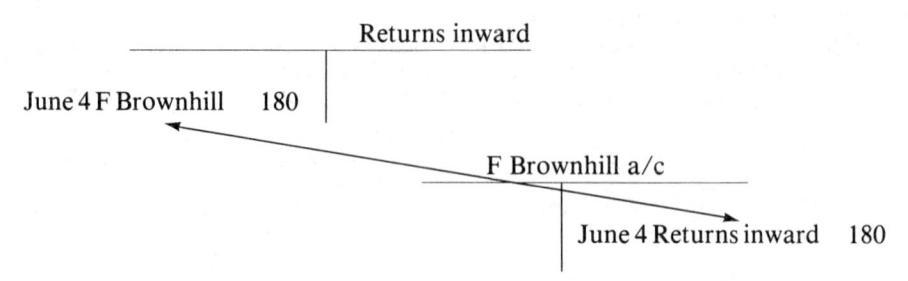

```
                         Returns inward
        ──────────────────────────────────────
        June 4 F Brownhill   180 │

                              F Brownhill a/c
                         ──────────────────────────────
                                  │ June 4 Returns inward   180
```

Thus the principle of double entry is conformed to:
Returns inward (sales returns)   =   debit
F Brownhill (reducing amount owed)   =   credit

The return of goods is subordinate to and necessarily smaller in amount than the original, otherwise the business would be less than successful! Returns will be shown in the trial balance and final accounts — the Trading Account — as balances extracted from the ledger accounts.

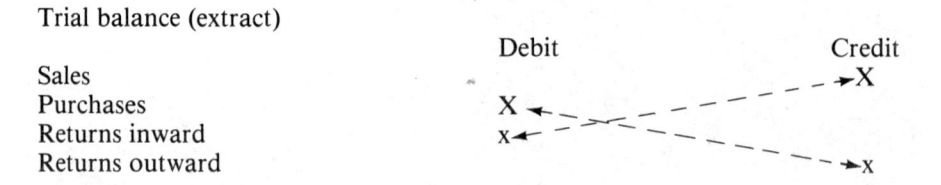

Trial balance (extract)

	Debit	Credit
Sales		X
Purchases	X	
Returns inward	X	
Returns outward		X

Note A full examination of the Trial Balance is not intended at this stage.

Trading account (extract)

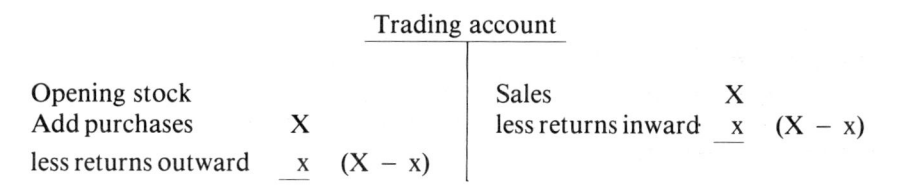

		Trading account		
Opening stock		Sales X		
Add purchases X		less returns inward x	(X − x)
less returns outward x	(X − x)			

The algebraic notation is really superfluous. The point of the exercise is to derive a net sales and a net purchases figure ie net of returns.

Unit 6
Carriage inwards and outwards and discount allowed and received

Overview

1 Carriage inwards and carriage outwards are presented how they would appear both in final accounts and the supporting ledgers:
Carriage inwards   = debit in Trading Account,
Carriage outwards = debit Profit & Loss Account,
both are debits in the ledgers.

2 Discount allowed and received are similarly contrasted and represented
Discount allowed = debit in Profit & Loss Account
Discount received = credit in Profit & Loss Account
and each is collected in the ledgers as a debit and credit respectively.

Carriage inwards and outwards

These expenses on purchases coming into the business and sales going out of the business are dealt with in different ways in the accounting procedure and reflect the fundamental difference between such expenses.

Carriage inwards   = an additional cost of purchases that is concerned with delivery to the business.
Carriage outwards = an additional cost of sales that is concerned with delivery to the customer.

It has to be said that the process is somewhat anachronistic under modern trading conditions, nevertheless it is one that still prevails in accounting questions.

Accounting treatment − final accounts

Carriage inwards is added to Purchases in the Trading Account.

Trading Account

Opening stock		X	Sales	X
Add Purchases	X		Less Returns inwards	X X
plus carriage inwards	X			
Less Returns outwards	X	X		

Note the distinction between carriage inwards and returns outwards and inwards. The descriptions may be deceptively similar, but the differences arise both in the nature of the transaction and the accounting treatment. Carriage outwards is added to the expense section of the Profit & Loss Account, since it is much the same as a normal delivery expense.

Profit & Loss Account

		Gross profit b/d	X
Lighting & heating	X		
Carriage outwards	X		
Rent & rates	X		

There is no particular order for presenting these expenses in the profit and loss account.

Accounting treatment — ledger accounts

Both carriage inwards and carriage outwards are expenses and therefore debits, and both appear as such in the ledger accounts.

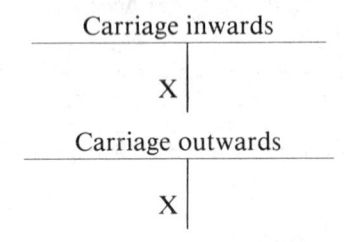

Carriage inwards

X |

Carriage outwards

X |

Discount allowed and received

Discount is frequently granted and taken in the case of both sales and purchases, reducing the amounts receivable and payable.

Accounting treatment — final accounts

Both items appear in the Profit & Loss Account, one as a debit, the other as a credit.

Rent & rates	X	Gross profit b/d	X
Discount allowed	X	Discount received	X

Accounting treatment — ledger accounts
The collection of discounts is a matter for further treatment but discounts allowed are collected as debits and discounts received are collected as credits.

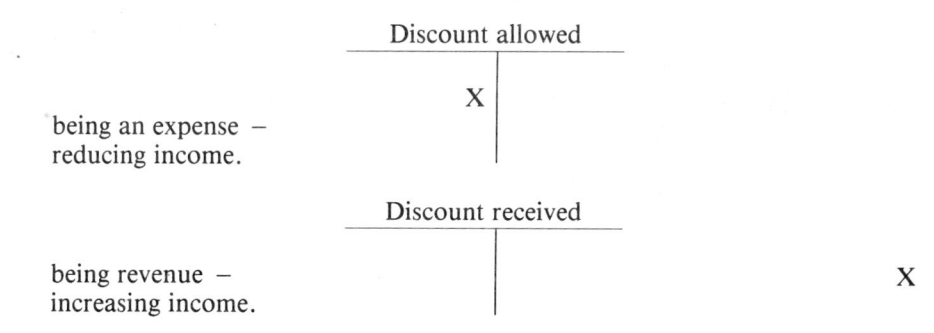

	Discount allowed	
being an expense – reducing income.	X	

	Discount received	
being revenue – increasing income.		X

Unit 7
Balancing off ledger accounts

Overview

1 Each ledger account has to be balanced off.
2 The resulting balance is produced with other balances in the preparation of final statements.
3 The procedure for balancing off is given and illustrated by diagrams.
4 Aggregate debtor and creditor balances derived from individual personal accounts are taken to the trial balance.

Once entries are made in ledger accounts, each account has to be balanced off to arrive at a statement of account for a given period. The purpose is to extract a figure that can be used to compile the final accounts. Balance figures represented in aggregate as debits and credits are checked in a trial balance.

Rules for balancing off

1 Add up both sides.
2 Consider which side is the smaller.
3 Make up the difference between the larger and smaller item as a balance.
4 Now both sides of the account equal the larger figure.
5 Give 'balance' the description Balance c/d.
6 Add end of month date so that entry becomes say June 30 Balance c/d.
7 Bring balance down beneath totals and across to the other side of the account.
8 Call this second balance Balance b/d.
9 Add opening (usually month) date.
10 Balance b/d is the opening figure for the new period of transactions.

Balancing off is only a matter of addition and subtraction. However, some accounts notably cash and bank, will be arithmetically more difficult than others, for example expenses, where there are usually only debits, where no adjustments are shown.

45

Diagrams for Balancing off:
total (larger figure) = 100
total (smaller figure) = 80. Then balance is 20
diagrams are numbered 1 to 3

1

```
                    ⎫ 80
                    ⎭
                      20
                     ___
         100         100
```

2

```
              │ June 30 Balance c/d   20
              │                      ___
    100       │                      100
```

3

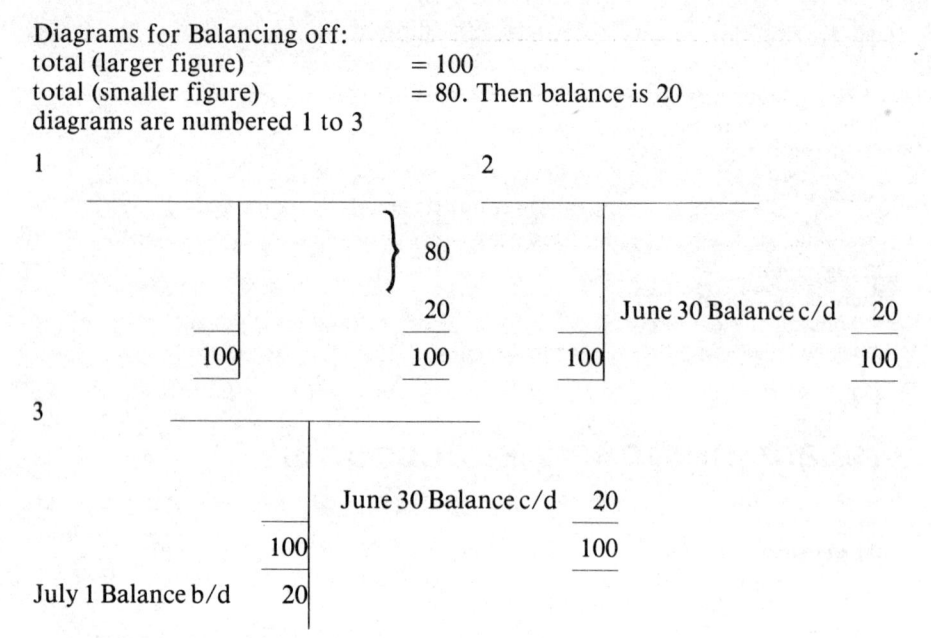

```
              │ June 30 Balance c/d   20
              │                      ___
    100       │                      100
July 1 Balance b/d   20
```

Credit purchases
The aggregate of personal account balances for amounts owing on purchases
= Creditors (closing balance).

Credit sales
The aggregate of personal account balances for amounts owed on sales
= Debtors (closing balance).

Each of these two closing balances is represented in the trial balance
. . . the former as a credit
. . . the latter as a debit.

Unit 8
The trial balance

Overview

1 The trial balance is a listing of closing balances taken from the ledger accounts.
2 It is produced in 'journal' format.
3 It consists of the arrangement of items as debits or credits according to the closing balance from which they are derived.
4 The balance used is the 'Balance b/d'.
5 In many respects the Trial Balance is the pivot between the collection of data and presentation of final accounts.
6 Two aspects have to be covered:
   a) preparing a trial balance, and
   b) using a trial balance.

The trial balance is a listing of closing balances, as shown in the previous Unit, before using the figures to prepare final accounts. There is a given procedure to be followed, namely a listing of items as debits and credits. If the totals balance then there is a reasonable degree of certainty that entries are correct, subject to the fact that certain errors may not be revealed. Two major aspects will now be covered

1 preparing a trial balance, and
2 using a trial balance.

Preparing a trial balance

1 List balances taken from individual ledger accounts.
2 Arrange these balances in two columns according to whether they are debit or credit balances.
3 Ensure that total debits equal total credits ie the trial balance checks the arithmetic accuracy of accounting entries.

Illustration
Assume the following is a list of balances taken from conventional ledger accounts.

Freehold land and buildings	65,000
Motor vehicles	12,250
Purchases	133,320
Sales	208,900(*)
Capital	130,000(*)
Opening stock	23,130
Cash	6,840
Bank	25,620
Rent	2,010
Commission paid	530

Wages and salaries	58,580
Insurance	1,250
Debtors	23,060
Creditors	18,950(*)
General expenses	4,590
Advertising	1,220

Distinguishing debit balances from credit balances requires examination of the Balance b/d figure within the ledger account; its positioning will suggest one or the other.
(* Asterisk denotes a credit)
a debit balance = balance b/d on the left-hand side

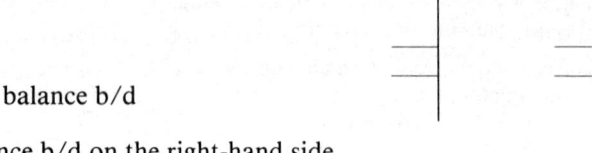

balance b/d

a credit balance = balance b/d on the right-hand side

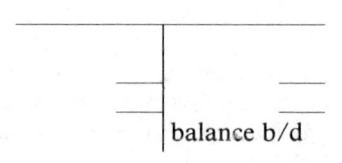

balance b/d

Usually the majority of entries will be debits (those that are credits have been marked with an asterisk). There are three credit entries. A two column trial balance can now be prepared, listing items as debits or credits.

	Debits	Credits
Freehold land and buildings	65,000	
Motor vehicles	12,250	
Purchases	133,320	
Sales		208,450
Capital		130,000
Opening stock	23,130	
Cash	6,840	
Bank	25,620	
Rent	2,010	
Commission paid	530	
Wages & salaries	58,580	
Insurance	1,250	
Debtors	23,060	
Creditors		18,950
General expenses	4,590	
Advertising	1,220	
	357,400	357,400

The trial balance works!

Using a trial balance

There is no sectionalization of entries to the trial balance as there is for final accounts since it is only broadly a check list and entries are usually made as they are read from the ledgers. For instance, examination questions make no attempt to collate entries into any specific order. Therefore when using a trial balance to prepare final accounts it is worthwhile devising a method of marking off items as they are used eg ticking them.

A further point of interest would be the rearrangement of a trial balance into a sectionalized format. The illustration below uses the previous trial balance.

Illustration

		Debits	Credits	
Trading Account	Purchases	133,320		To calculate the gross profit.
	Sales		208,450	
	Opening stock	23,130		
Profit & Loss Account	Rent	2,010		To calculate the net profit.
	Commission paid	530		
	Wages & salaries	58,580		
	Insurance	1,250		
	General expenses	4,590		
	Advertising	1,220		
Balance sheet	Freehold land & buildings	65,000		to use remaining figures to check overall balance *including* Net profit and Closing stock.
	Motor vehicles	12,250		
	Cash	6,840		
	Bank	25,620		
	Debtors	23,060		
	Creditors		18,950	
		£357,400	£357,400	

Notes

1. Certain items to be included in the final accounts are not shown in the trial balance. These are either:
    a) calculated in preparing final accounts eg gross profit and net profit, cost of goods sold,
    or
    b) recorded differently and derived from a different source eg closing stock.
2. Treat the 'journalized' format at this stage as accounting entries (debits and credits) presented in two columns to the right of a description.

Errors in a trial balance

Errors in accounts that prevent a trial balance from balancing generally relate to one of two aspects:
a) incorrect addition,
   or
b) incorrect double entry.

In practice every effort should be made to eliminate these errors but in examinations it may not be possible and a Suspense Account can be used, as a repository for the non-balancing amount.

Trial balance (extract)
Supposing a suspense account was required for the above trial balance:

Debtors	23,060	
Creditors		18,950
General expenses	4,590	
Advertising	1,220	
	357,140	357,400

The trial balance does not balance.
Therefore a suspense account could be used, allowing the trial balance to balance, as follows:

Debtors	23,060	
Creditors		18,950
General expenses	4,590	
Advertising	1,220	
Suspense account	260	
	357,400	357,400

Suspense account

19-2
Dec 31 Difference per trial balance 260

The same principle would apply for a *credit* adjustment.

An example now follows, opening up and maintaining ledger accounts, balanced off, with results extended to a trial balance.

Example
Newton started a small business in August, from the following information, write up the accounts, balance them off and extract a trial balance.

August   1 Introduced £10,000 in capital
          2 Of the £10,000, £8,000 was used to open a Bank account
          3 Bought goods for resale, on credit from T Moloney £560, D Burton £325 and K Smith £283
          4 Paid rent on premises £1,640, by cheque
          5 Purchased a delivery van £3,980 paying by cheque
          7 Made sales on credit to B Cheney £431 and P Denver £822
          9 Made sales for cash amounting to £148
        10 Purchased fixtures on credit from Fixtures Ltd £1,218
        12 Goods returned by B Cheney £56

13 Made cash sales of £267
14 Goods returned to D Burton £32
15 Purchased goods for resale paying cash £242
16 Transferred £1,000 cash into Bank
20 Received a loan from R Jacques £2,000, by cheque
21 Received payment from P Denver £822 by cheque
23 Paid T Moloney, D Burton and K Smith by cheque
24 Bought stationery on credit from Suppliers Ltd £33.
25 Paid salary to assistant £399 by cheque
28 Sold goods on credit to T Briars £434, B Gregory £86 and, P Lowe £149
31 Purchased goods for resale, on credit, from S Parker £264 and, G Childs £97.

Cash

Aug	1	Capital	10,000	Aug	2 Bank	8,000
	9	Sales	148		15 Purchases	242
	13	Sales	267		16 Bank	1,000
					31 Balance c/d	1,173
			10,415			10,415
Sept	1	Balance b/d	1,173			

Bank

Aug	2	Cash	8,000	Aug	4 Rent	1,640
	16	Cash	1,000		5 Delivery van	3,980
	20	Loan	2,000		23 T Moloney	560
	21	P Denver	822		D Burton	293
					K Smith	283
					25 Salary	399
					31 Balance c/d	4,667
			11,822			11,822
Sept	1	Balance b/d	4,741			

Sales

Aug	31	Balance c/d	2,337	Aug	7 B Cheney	431
					9 P Denver	822
					9 Cash	148
					10 Cash	267
					28 T Briars	434
					B Gregory	86
					P Lowe	149
			2,337			2,337
				Sept	1 Balance b/d	2,337

Capital

Aug	31	Balance c/d	10,000	Aug	1 Cash	10,000
				Sept	1 Balance b/d	10,000

Loan

Aug	31	Balance c/d	2,000	Aug	20 Bank	2,000
				Sept	1 Balance b/d	2,000

Delivery Van

Aug	5	Bank	3,980	Aug	31 Balance c/d	3,980
Sept	1	Balance b/d	3,980			

Fixtures

Aug	10	Fixtures Ltd.	1,218	Aug	31 Balance c/d	1,218
Sept	1	Balance b/d	1,218			

Rent

Aug	4	Bank	1,640	Aug	31 Balance c/d	1,640
Sept	1	Balance b/d	1,640			

Stationery

Aug	24	Suppliers Ltd.	33	Aug	31 Balance c/d	33
Sept	1	Balance b/d	33			

Salary

Aug	25	Bank	399	Aug	31 Balance c/d	399
Sept	1	Balance b/d	399			

Purchases

Aug	3	T Moloney	560	Aug	31	Balance c/d		1,771
		D Burton	325					
		K Smith	283					
	15	Cash	242					
	31	S Parker	264					
		G Childs	97					
			1,771					1,771
Sept	1	Balance b/d	1,771					

G Childs

Aug	31	Balance c/d	97	Aug	31	Purchases		97
				Sept	1	Balance b/d		97

Fixtures Limited

Aug	31	Balance c/d	1,218	Aug	10	Fixtures		1,218
				Sept	1	Balance b/d		1,218

Suppliers Limited

Aug	31	Balance c/d	33	Aug	24	Stationery		33
				Sept	1	Balance b/d		33

B Cheney

Aug	7	Sales	431	Aug	12	Returns		56
					31	Balance c/d		375
			431					431
Sept	1	Balance b/d	375					

T Moloney

			560	Aug	3	Purchases		560

D Burton

Aug	23	Bank	32	Aug	3	Purchases		325
			293					
			325					325
				Sept	1	Balance b/d		293

K Smith

Aug	23	Bank	283	Aug	3	Purchases		283

S Parker

Aug	14	Returns	264	Aug	31	Purchases		264
	31	Balance c/d		Sept	1	Balance b/d		264

53

P Denver
Aug	7	Sales	822	Aug	21	Bank	822

B Gregory
Aug	28	Sales	86	Aug	31	Balance c/d	86
Sept	1	Balance b/d	86				

P Lowe
Aug	28	Sales	149	Aug	31	Balance c/d	149
Sept	1	Balance b/d	149				

T Briars
Aug	28	Sales	434	Aug	31	Balance c/d	434
Sept	1	Balance b/d	434				

Returns Inward
Aug	12	B Cheney	56	Aug	31	Balance c/d	56
Sept	1	Balance b/d	56				

Returns Outward
Aug	31	Balance c/d	32	Aug	14	D Burton	32
			32	Sept	1	Balance b/d	32

Trial Balance

	Dr	Cr
Cash	1,173	
Bank	4,667	
Sales		2,337
Purchases	1,771	
Capital		10,000
Loan		2,000
Delivery van	3,980	
Fixtures	1,218	
Rent	1,640	
Stationery	33	
Salary	399	
Creditors (264 + 97 + 1,218 + 33)		1,612
Debtors (375 + 86 + 149 + 434)	1,044	
Returns inward	56	
Returns outward		32
	15,981	15,981

Unit 9
Presentation of final accounts II

Overview

1 The trading and profit and loss account is prepared (calculating the gross and net profits respectively).
2 Using the net profit the balance sheet is prepared.
3 The remaining information in the trial balance, together with the net profit and closing stock, is used to compile the balance sheet.
4 Both traditional and vertical balance sheets are illustrated.
5 The trial balance from the previous Unit is used as the starting point.

Using the information supplied in the trial balance in the previous Unit, with the supplementary figure closing stock £28,550, the final accounts can be prepared using the fictitious person A Jones.

A Jones

Trading and Profit and Loss Account for year ended 31 December 19-2

	Opening stock	23,130	Sales	208,450
	Add Purchases	133,320		
		156,450		
1	Less closing stock	28,550		
2	Cost of goods sold	127,900		
3	Gross profit c/d	80,550		
		208,450		208,450
	Wages & salaries	58,580	Gross profit b/d	80,550
	Commission	530		
	Insurance	1,250		
	General expenses	4,590		
	Advertising	1,220		
	Rent	2,010		
4	Net profit c/d	12,370		
		80,550		80,550

Note
1 The closing stock has been introduced,
2 the cost of goods sold calculated,
3 the gross profit calculated, and
4 the net profit calculated.

At this stage a reference to the original trial balance would be useful before going on to prepare the balance sheet.

The used figures have been ticked

	Debits	Credits
Freehold land and building	65,000	
Motor vehicles	12,250	
Purchases	133,320 ✓	
Sales		208,450 ✓
Capital		130,000
Opening stock	23,130 ✓	
Cash	6,840	
Bank	25,620	
Rent	2,010 ✓	
Commission paid	530 ✓	
Wages & salaries	58,580 ✓	
Insurance	1,250 ✓	
Debtors	23,060	
Creditors		18,950
General expenses	4,590 ✓	
Advertising	1,220 ✓	
	357,400	357,400

Closing stock £28,550.

Those figures that remain unticked will now be entered in the balance sheet.

A Jones

Balance Sheet as at 31 December 19-2

Capital			*Fixed assets*		
Opening balance	130,000		Freehold land & buildings	65,000	
Add Net profit	12,370		Motor vehicles	12,250	
	142,370				77,250
Current liabilities			*Current assets*		
Creditors		18,950	Closing stock	28,550	
			Debtors	23,060	
			Bank	25,620	
			Cash	6,840	84,070
		£161,320			£161,320

... illustrates the traditional presentation

A Jones Trading & Profit & Loss Account for year ended 31 December 19-2

Sales		208,450
Less cost of sales		
Opening stock	23,130	
Add Purchases	133,320	
	156,450	
Less closing stock	28,550	127,900
		£ 80,550
Less expenses		
Wages & salaries	58,580	
Commission paid	530	
Insurance	1,250	
General expenses	4,590	
Advertising	1,220	
Rent	2,010	68,180
Net profit		£ 12,370

A Jones Balance Sheet as at 31 December 19-2

Fixed assets			
Freehold land & buildings			65,000
Motor vehicles			12,250
			77,250
Net current assets			
Current assets			
Closing stock	28,550		
Debtors	23,060		
Bank	25,620		
Cash	6,840	84,070	
Less current liabilities			
Creditors	18,950	(18,950)	65,120
			£142,370
Financed by			
Opening capital			130,000
Add net profit			12,370
			£142,370

. . . illustrates the vertical position.

Note
1 Net profit (calculated) in the profit and loss of £12,370 and Closing stock (given) of £28,550 are introduced.
2 Net profit is shown in the balance sheet and the profit and loss because it is the surplus of current period revenue over current period expenses that permits additional funding of assets, and is an additional liability of the business to its owners so long as it remains in the business and is not withdrawn in the form of drawings, dividends or taxation.
3 Closing stock is the valuation of purchases which remain unsold at the close of an accounting period. They have either been:
   a) paid for and represent a reduction of the cash or bank figure
   or
   b) recognized as a liability to be paid for in the following period.
In both cases they should be represented by a short term asset (closing balance) shown in the Balance Sheet.

Questions

The accounting transaction equation

1 Complete the columns to show the effect of the following transactions:

                                                            Assets   Liabilities   Capital

1a J introduced capital £5,000, by opening a business bank account
b Rented premises for a year £1,500 paid by cheque
c Received loan from J Owens £2,000 paid into bank
d Bought machinery on credit from N Revel, costing £3,000
e Bought goods for resale accepting credit terms offered by P Smart, total amounted to £1,250
f Sold goods for cash £50
g Bought more goods from P Smart on same terms £600
h Made sales on Credit to B Saint £450
i Proprietor made drawings to extent of £100 cash from bank account
j Proprietor decided to keep cash on business premises up to £250 and withdraws funds from bank for this purpose

2a P commences trading with £1,000 cash
b Pays rent for small shop – £500 for a year
c Receives a loan of £2,000 from his uncle, who suggests he opens a bank account
d Buys fixtures for shop at a cost of £350 from U-Fix on credit
e Purchases goods for resale from S Silly £1,850 who gives credit
f Makes a sale for cash of £200
g Proprietor introduces additional capital £800, paying it into the bank
h Buys a second-hand delivery van for £1,020 paying by cheque
i Goods returned to Silly because they are damaged, amounting to £150
j Proprietor takes £30 cash to meet his living expenses

    Answer guide: 1d Assets: Machinery + £3,000; Liabilities: N Revel + £3,000.

Debits and credits in columns

2 Complete the columns to show the effect of the following transactions:

                                                              Debited   Credited

1a Bought goods paying cash immediately
 b Bought goods from J Bennett on credit
 c Sold goods on credit to A Downs
 d Paid J Bennett by cheque for goods bought
 e Sold goods for cash, money received immediately
 f A Downs settled his account by paying cash
 g Goods sold to V Peers on credit
 h Purchased goods for resale from D Coleman on credit
 i Bought more goods from J Bennett on credit
 j Sold more goods to A Downs on credit

2a Purchased machinery on credit from R Paterson for use in business
 b Paid rent by cheque
 c D Bond made a loan paying by cheque
 d Purchased a delivery van on credit from F Towers for use in business
 e Bought goods from T Smith on credit
 f Bought goods for resale paying cash
 g Sold goods for cash
 h Sold goods on credit to S Palmer
 i S Palmer settled his account paying by cheque
 j Paid T Smith by cheque for goods bought

Answer guide: 1d Debit J Bennett; Credit Bank

3 Complete the columns to show the effect of the following transactions:

                                                                Debit   Credit

1a Proprietor started business introducing cash
 b Brought premises paying cash
 c Bought goods for resale paying cash
 d Bought goods for resale from P Peters on credit payable in a week
 e Sold goods for cash
 f Sold goods on credit to B Brown payable in two weeks
 g Sold more goods for cash
 h Purchased goods for cash
 i Paid P Peters for goods in cash
 j Received payment from B Brown by cash

2a Proprietor started business paying money into bank
 b Paid rent on premises by cheque
 c Purchased motor van paying by cheque
 d Proprietor decided to keep some cash on business premises
 e Made purchases on credit from I Brown
 f Made sales for cash
 g Sales made on credit to K Maloney
 h Further purchases made for cash
 i K Maloney paid for sales by cheque
 j Paid I Brown for purchases by cheque

3a Proprietor started business paying capital into bank ($\frac{3}{4}$) and cash ($\frac{1}{4}$)
 b Rented premises paying by cheque
 c Purchased delivery van paying by cheque
 d Bought goods for resale on credit from P Smith

59

e Bought goods for resale paying cash
f Sold goods for cash
g Paid P Smith by cash
h Bought materials for repairs from D Hind on credit
i Sold goods on credit to F Grimes
j Paid D Hind by cheque

The trial balance

4 Compile a trial balance from the following lists of entries:

1			2		
	Sales	136,890		Land & buildings	186,835
	Purchases	63,123		Fixtures & fittings	22,912
	Returns inward	680		Motor vehicles	14,516
	Returns outward	336		Rent	70,550
	Land & buildings	90,840		Rates	10,811
	Plant & machinery	26,720		Carriage inwards	2,336
	Debtors	18,119		Carriage outwards	24,531
	Creditors	20,510		Debtors	25,902
	Delivery expenses	8,176		Creditors	30,306
	Rent & rates	10,322		Sales	545,822
	Wages	20,189		Purchases	336,118
	Salaries	8,560		Capital	218,383
	Capital	88,993			

3			4		
	Rent	30,021		Purchases	1,236,943
	Light & heat	12,927		Sales	2,185,132
	Land & buildings	325,320		Returns inward	5,863
	Plant & machinery	108,740		Returns outward	7,310
	Motor vehicles	46,655		Debtors	74,222
	Capital	252,864		Creditors	88,335
	Purchases	286,780		Land & buildings	890,780
	Sales	547,826		Machinery	225,775
	Returns outwards	1,122		Fixtures	50,815
	Returns inwards	1,556		Rent & rates	101,770
	Debtors	25,632		Wages & salaries	329,639
	Creditors	35,819		Repairs	45,724
				Electricity	23,079
				Gas	13,612
				Capital	?

5		
	Land & buildings	329,774
	Plant	101,220
	Fixtures	54,960
	Motor vehicles	29,440
	Capital	?
	Creditors	84,766
	Debtors	53,299
	Sales	432,180
	Purchases	256,420
	Returns inwards	4,480
	Returns outwards	7,312
	General expenses	46,309
	Repairs to buildings	13,113
	Motor vehicle expenses	8,542
	Rent & rates	53,256

Light & heat	28,741
Wages	58,902
Salaries	46,630

Answer guide: 3 Trial Balance balances £837,631.

5 An inexperienced book-keeper has drawn up the following trial balances, these need correcting and you are asked to do so.

1

	Dr	Cr
Capital		36,609
Bank Overdraft	3,056	
Debtors	23,160	
Creditors		31,420
Sales		201,333
Purchases	120,115	
Drawings	19,430	
Returns inwards	466	
Returns outwards		575
Stock		58,176
Provision for depreciation of fixtures	527	
Office furniture	7,455	
Premises	44,500	
	£218,709	£328,113

2

	Dr	Cr
Buildings	60,600	
Capital		82,439
Creditors	34,320	
Debtors		28,190
Sales		150,510
Purchases	98,780	
Opening stock		14,330
Provision for depreciation of machinery		2,155
Machinery	35,840	
Drawings		11,990
Returns inwards	1,416	
Returns outwards		982
Bank balance	19,260	
	£250,216	£290,596

Final accounts from trial balance

6 From the trial balance of R Alderson you are to prepare final accounts for the year ending 31 December 19-4.

	Dr	Cr
Capital		183,214
Purchases	46,130	
Sales		99,388
Purchase returns		256
Sales returns	742	
Discount allowed	818	
Discount received		631
Wages	20,630	
Salaries	10,118	
Rent	2,455	
Rates	1,760	
Delivery expenses	3,414	
Trade debtors	20,523	
Bank balance	5,083	
Trade creditors		35,110
Stock	7,846	
Land & buildings	110,100	
Plant and machinery	54,300	
Motor vehicles	34,680	
	£318,599	£318,599

Closing stock £10,332

7 From the following trial balance of A Bone you are to prepare final accounts for year ending 31 March 19-1.

	Dr	Cr
Land and buildings	1,036,280	
Fixtures and fittings	133,891	
Motor vehicles	335,712	
Capital		1,503,382
Drawings	63,288	
Debtors	100,026	
Creditors		150,433
Cash in hand	15,134	
Bank balance	30,218	
Wages and salaries	214,110	
Administrative expenses	23,996	
Vehicle expenses	17,444	
Building repairs	3,081	
Light and heat	20,729	
Sales		836,211
Purchases	424,199	
Opening stock	50,021	
Sales returns	4,234	
Purchase returns		3,187
Discount allowed	56,753	
Discount received		35,903
	£2,529,116	£2,529,116

Closing stock £68,814

8 From the trial balance of D Fernside you are asked to prepare a Trading, Profit and Loss Account and Balance Sheet for the year ending 31 May 19-5.

	Dr	Cr
Purchases	98,080	
Sales		185,630
Returns inwards	3,121	
Returns outwards		2,343
Stock at 1 June 19-4	25,554	
Plant and machinery	52,900	
Fixtures and fittings	14,240	
Motor vehicles	25,790	
Discount received		10,924
Discount allowed	19,636	
Wages and salaries	38,440	
Rent and rates	14,600	
Administrative expenses	3,080	
Carriage inwards	496	
Carriage outwards	869	
Motor vehicle expenses	8,330	
Capital		105,217
Debtors and creditors	15,216	36,112
Drawings	9,300	
Bank balance	10,020	
Cash in hand	544	
	£340,226	£340,226

Stock at 31 May 19-5   £33,611

9 From the trial balance of L Hirst you are asked to prepare an Income Statement and Position Statement for the year ended 30 November 19-9.

	Dr	Cr
Purchase and sales	60,180	115,495
Returns inward	5,113	
Returns outward		2,734
Capital		69,178
Drawings	10,265	
Debtors	15,046	
Creditors		31,229
Opening stock	19,622	
Delivery costs	3,550	
Vehicle maintenance & repairs	2,117	
Building repairs	1,010	
Wages and salaries	25,978	
Rents and rates	9,210	
Light and heat	4,330	
Bank overdraft		10,711
Machinery	55,770	
Fixtures	3,360	
Motor vehicles	12,180	
Cash balance	1,616	
	£229,347	£229,347

Closing stock   £25,788

10 From the trial balance of G Lincoln you are asked to prepare a Trading, Profit and Loss Account and Balance Sheet for the year ending 30 September 19-7.

	Dr	Cr
Capital		169,992
Drawings	25,150	
Land and buildings	88,500	
Plant and machinery	23,630	
Fixtures and fittings	12,140	
Motor vehicles	8,810	
Purchases and sales	75,050	156,336
Returns inwards and outward	8,984	3,367
Carriage inwards	342	
Carriage outwards	821	
Administrative expenses	32,011	
Trade debtors and creditors	36,160	51,386
Stock at 1 October 19-6	25,142	
Discount received and allowed	10,130	5,680
Bank balance	14,441	
Cash in hand	1,228	
Wages and salaries	24,222	
	£386,761	£386,761

Stock at 30 September 19-7   £29,175

Answer guide:
GP = £79,360
NP = £17,856
Balance sheet totals = £214,084
(ledger method)

Ledger accounts and trial balance

11 Pearson used £10,000 of his own funds to put into a business he was just starting, employing one assistant. During June, Pearson made the following transactions, all of which are for cash.

June 1 Introduced £10,000
     3 Purchased goods for £3,000
     4 Paid rent of shop £150
     6 Sold goods for £1,860
     7 Paid for newspaper advertisement £40
     8 Sold more goods for £830
    15 Paid insurance amounting to £75
    18 Sold more goods for £1,400
    25 Paid wages to assistant amounting to £250
    30 Sold remaining goods for £120

You are required to enter the above transactions in the books of Pearson, and to prepare a Trial Balance as at 30th June 19-8.

Answer guide: Bank £10,695; Trial Balance balances £14,210

12 Andrews made the following credit transactions:

Sept 1 Purchase of goods from F   £250
     2 Sold goods to P   £70
     6 Sold goods to X   £180
    10 Purchased goods from B   £760
    13 Sold goods to D   £485
    14 Purchased goods from R   £390

	17	Sold more goods to P £230
	20	Sold more goods to P £55
	25	Sold more goods to X £295
	30	Purchased more goods from B £1,020
Oct	8	Paid F £250 for goods purchased on 1 Sept
	9	Received £70 from P for goods sold on 2 Sept
	12	Received £180 from X for goods sold on 6 Sept
	16	Paid B £760 for goods purchased on 10 Sept
	18	Received £200 from D for goods sold on 13 Sept
	19	Paid R £250 for goods purchased on 14 Sept
	21	Received £230 from P for goods sold on 17 Sept
	23	Received £50 from P in full settlement, for good sold on 20 Sept
	27	Received £295 from X for goods sold on 25 Sept
	29	Paid B £1,020 for goods purchased on 30 Sept

Consider what is the likely outcome for amounts owed by P & D, and to R? Can you think of any reason why the shortfall for P will be different? If not these points will be dealt with later in the text.

13 Lark took £7,750 of his own money to use in a business he was about to open.

The following cash transactions are for the month of February:

February	1	Introduced £7,750
	2	Purchased goods for £2,950
	5	Bought a sales vehicle £3,680
	6	Paid for insurance of sales vehicle £183
	12	Made a sale of £1,030
	15	Made further sales of £230 & £165
	19	Placed advertisement in trade magazine £45
	23	Paid for repairs & service to vehicle £230
	24	Purchased more goods for resale £556
	28	Bought a typewriter for £95
	29	Stock of goods is valued at cost, £3,544

You are required to enter the above transactions in the books of Lark, and prepare a Trial Balance as at 29 February 19-2

Can you think why the closing stock of goods is not included in the trial balance?

14 Clements started a business on 1 January and proceded to trade, conducting the following initial transactions. You are required to write up the accounts, balance them off and extract a trial balance.

January	1	Capital introduced £15,000 to open up a business bank account
	2	Withdrew £1,000 to hold as business cash
	3	Paid rent on business premises £2,320 by cheque
	5	Bought goods on credit from P Smithers £1,460
	6	Purchased fixtures and fittings paying by cheque £2,810
	7	Made cash sales amounting to £187
	10	Purchased a delivery van paying by cheque £3,650
	11	Paid P Smithers by cheque for goods purchased on credit
	12	Sold goods on credit to G Jackson £1,985
	14	Made cash sales amounting to £336
	16	Bought more fixtures on credit from S Timothy £4,670
	18	Made cash sale of £87
	19	Sold goods on credit to K Rankin £321
	20	Received payment from G Jackson by cheque
	22	K Rankin returned faulty goods to the value of £47

23 Purchased goods for re-sale on credit from L Plummer £1,087
25 Made cash sale £246
26 Returned goods to L Plummer, because they were not the correct type £75
27 Paid S Timothy for fixtures, by cheque
31 Sold goods to J Bright on credit £2,153

Answer guide: Bank £1,075; Sales £5,315; Trial Balance totals £21,402.

15 Enter the following transactions in the books of Pollard for the month of July, balance off the accounts and compile a trial balance.

July 1 Started a business with £2,000 in cash
2 Received a loan of £5,000 from P Hind which was used to open a bank account
4 Bought stocks of goods for sale £540, from J Lang on credit
5 Paid rent on trading premises £910 by cheque
6 Bought more goods for resale at a cost of £440 paying by cash
7 Purchased stationery £53, and a typewriter £109 for use in the business paying by cheque
8 Paid for advertisement in newspaper in cash £37
9 Sold goods for cash £174
10 Sold goods to value of £343 on credit to S Mears
11 Returned goods valued at £49 to J Lang
14 S Mears returned goods to value of £29

16 H Marvin has previously been earning her living as a pop musician, but has now decided to retire and set up a hi-fi and record business.

Jan 1 Started business with £8,000 deposited in the bank
2 Paid month's rent on premises £200
   Bought shop fittings £1,800 and motor van £3,000 paying for each immediately
3 Bought £400 goods for resale on credit from VMH Records Ltd
5 Cash sales £160
6 Paid motor expenses £10
8 Bought £150 goods for resale on credit from Punk Records Ltd
10 Sold goods on credit to Dave's Disco £270
11 Cash sales £85
   Bought £200 goods for resale on credit from Motown Moaners Incorporated
12 Credit sales: 'Krazy Kats Nite Spot' £90; 'Tramps' £160; 'Plastic Goblet' £150
14 Bought £350 goods on credit from VMH Records
15 Returned goods to Motown Moaners £50
16 Krazy Kats Nite Spot paid amount owing to Marvin
18 Dave's Disco returned goods value £20
19 Paid amount owing to Motown Moaners
20 Credit sales: Dave's Disco £140; Plastic Goblet £36
21 Paid office expenses £75
22 Paid £400 to VMH Records
23 Cash sales £178
   Plastic Goblet paid amount owing to Marvin
   Paid motor expenses £54
25 Bought £450 goods on credit from Punk Records
26 Paid £300 for additional shop fittings
27 Sold goods on credit to Krazy Kats Nite Spot £174
28 Returned £28 goods to Punk Records
29 Cash sales £91
30 Dave's Disco paid £250

At the end of the month's trading, the stock was calculated at £500.

Required

Enter the above transactions in appropriate accounts, then prepare a set of final accounts, showing the profit or loss made during the period, and a Balance Sheet at the end of the month.

Correction of layout

17 A Mann produced the following as a Trading and Profit and Loss a/c for the year ended 31 December and Balance Sheet as at that date.

Trading and Profit and Loss Account

	£	£		£	£
Opening stock		1,200	Purchases	575	
Sales	950		Less Returns in	25	550
Less returns out	35				
		915			
		2,115	Gross loss		320
Less closing stock		1,250			
		865			
Stationery		5			
		870			870
Gross loss b/d		320	Discounts allowed		15
Fixtures & fittings		250			
Discount received		20			
Wages		200	Net loss		780
Cleaning		5			
		795			795

Balance Sheet

	£	£		£	£
Capital	3,225		Creditors		710
Less loss	708	2,445	Motor vehicles	500	
			Less motor expenses	25	475
Debtors		1,300	Furniture		45
			Stock		1,250
			Bank		770
			Rates		25
		3,745			3,275

Required

Redraft the accounts and Balance Sheet.

18 J Boot produced the following as an Income Statement for the year ended 31 December and a Position Statement as at that date.

67

Income statement

Purchases		2,350	Sales		4,920
Less opening stock	1,350		Add closing stock	1,440	
less returns in	65	1,285	less returns out	90	1,350
		1,065			6,270
Discount allowed		65	Discount received		45
		1,130			6,315
Gross profit		5,185			
		6,315			6,315
Motor vehicles		3,314	Gross profit		5,185
Motor expenses		120			
Wages and salaries		1,735			
Net profit		16			
		5,185			5,185

Position statement

Capital		6,132	Light and heat		80
Add net profit		16	Creditors		2,119
		6,148	Rent and rates		1,440
			Fixtures and fittings		950
Debtors	2,821		Furniture		526
Bank overdraft	1,510	4,331			
		10,479			5,115

Required
A redraft of the above statements in the correct form.

Section III
Adjustments to final accounts

Unit 1 The nature of adjustments
Unit 2 Expense – prepayments and accruals
Unit 3 Subsidiary income – delayed and advanced receipt
Unit 4 Provisions for depreciation in final accounts
Unit 5 Bad debts and provisions for doubtful debts in final accounts
Unit 6 Double entry for provisions
Unit 7 A method for dealing with adjustments
Unit 8 Examination notes on final accounting questions

Unit 1
The nature of adjustments

Overview

1 A brief introduction is made retracing the process of accounting to the presentation stage.
2 Certain information contained in the trial balance will need to be adjusted, often because events occurring at the year end remain unrecorded in the books.
3 Reference is made to closing stock that has already been presented as an adjustable balance.
4 Adjustments are dealt with only so far as they affect final accounts.
5 Two examples of adjusted final accounts questions are given, the former, an earlier question is worked out in its current format.

This section presents many of the routine adjustments that have to be made when preparing final accounts. The principles behind the adjustments are explained under each of the following unit headings.

Up to this point the key aspects of accounting have been the collection, recording, extraction and presentation of information as follows:

collection → recording → extraction → presentation
(prime entry) (ledgers) (trial balance) (final accounts)

However, certain information is either
a) not recorded in its entirety, or
b) requires amending for one reason or another − usually relating to events close to the year end.
. . . it is for this reason adjustments are made.

One such adjustment of primary importance that has already been encountered is that of closing stock.

Unit 9 Section II shows the positioning of closing stock after the balancing of the trial balance. A presentation, similar to closing stock, applies as an introduction to all adjustments as they are presented in final accounting questions − see example of a final accounts questions based on the Trial Balance of:

Example I R Alderson, a sole trader − the question is from Section 2.
Example II Cluriber Ltd a company − used as an example in Section 5.
Remember that in the trial balance the list of debits equals the list of credits.
Debits = Credits

and this duality of entry made so meticulously has to be maintained when making adjustments.

Final accounts, like a trial balance, are concerned with the presentation of information relevant to a specific accounting period. It should be remembered that for the majority of cases, double entry transactions involve money or liquid transfers. It is only at the final accounts stage where profit (or loss) is considered in financial accounting that adjustments are made to affect the presentation of the current position.

Adjustments to final accounts

These have to be considered as increases or decreases to either expenses or income in the profit and loss account, supported by corresponding entries in the balance sheet. Adjustments are made so far as these have not been recorded as cash transactions.

Most adjustments affect expenses, amendments to these are dealt with as follows:

	Profit & loss	Balance sheet
Expenses − increases to:	add to expenses	add to current liabilities
	(a debit)	(a credit)
decreases from:	deduct from expenses	add to current assets
	(a credit)	(a debit)

Adjustments to receipts can be dealt with in a similar manner:

	Profit & loss	Balance sheet
Receipts − increases to:	add to income	add to current assets
	(a credit)	(a debit)

| | decreases from: | deduct from income (a debit) | add to current liabilities (a credit) |

A reference to the amended example of the accounts of R Alderson, (that follows) would be useful, that incidentally only adjusts expenses.

Illustration
Wages owed at the end of the trading period are 305, this means that these should be treated as follows:

an increase is an expense in the profit and loss account
ie a debit (20,630 + 305)
an increase in a current liability (an accrual)
in the balance sheet
ie a credit (305)
thus the adjustment is:
debit: profit and loss account
credit: balance sheet.

The terms accrual (referred to) and prepayment are used as follows:
accrual — subsidiary creditor in the current liabilities
    section of a balance sheet and a debit in the profit and loss account.
prepayment — subsidiary debtor in the current assets
    section of a balance sheet and a credit in the profit and loss account.

Example I
From the trial balance and adjustments for R Alderson you are to prepare final accounts for the year ending 31 December 19-4

	Dr	Cr
Capital		183,214
Purchases	46,130	
Sales		99,388
Purchase returns		256
Sales returns	742	
Discount allowed	818	
Discount received		631
Wages	20,630	
Salaries	10,118	
Rent	2,455	
Rates	1,760	
Delivery expenses	3,414	
Trade debtors	20,523	
Bank balance	5,083	
Trade creditors		35,110
Stock	7,846	
Land and buildings	110,100	
Plant and machinery	54,300	
Motor vehicles	34,680	
	£318,599	£318,599

Adjustments
1 Closing stock is valued at £10,332
2 Rates paid in advance amount to £536
3 Rent paid in advance amounts to £122
4 Wages owing are calculated at £305
5 Delivery expenses outstanding amount to £18

Original answer and amendments.

R Alderson
Trading and Profit and Loss Account for year ended 31 December 19-4

Opening stock		7,846	Sales		99,388
Add purchases	46,130		Less returns		742
Less returns	256	45,874			
					98,646
		53,720			
Less closing stock		10,332			
Cost of sales		43,388			
Gross profit c/d		55,258			
		£98,646			£98,646
Discount allowed		818	Gross profit b/d		55,258
Wages			Discount received		631
(20,630 + 305)	20,935	20,630			
Salaries		10,118			55,889
Rent (2,455 − 122)	2,333	2,455			
Rates (1,760 − 536)	1,224	1,760			
Delivery expenses					
(3,414 + 18)	3,432	3,414			
Net profit c/d	17,029	16,694			
		£55,889			£55,889

R Alderson
Balance sheet as at 31 December 19-4

Owner's Capital			*Fixed Assets*		
Opening balance		183,214	Land and Buildings		110,100
Add net profit	17,029	16,694	Plant and machinery		54,300
	200,243	199,908	Motor vehicles		34,680
					199,080
Current Liabilities			*Current Assets*		
Trade creditors		35,110	Stock		10,332
Accruals (305 + 18)		323	Trade debtors		20,523
			Prepayments (536 + 122)	658	
			Bank balance		5,083
		£235,018			£235,018
	£235,676			£235,676	

Note:
1 To think about the adjustments for accruals and prepayments in this way will be useful later when considering the effect of errors.
2 The ledger accounts (to be presented later pp 75−9) show examples of the treatment of expenses.

Rates				Wages			
Bank	1,760	Profit & Loss	1,224	Bank	20,630	Profit & Loss	20,935
		Balance c/d	536	Balance c/d	305		
	1,760		1,760		20,935		20,935
Balance b/d	536					Balance b/d	305

Rewritten amended answer.

R Alderson
Trading and Profit and Loss Account for year ended 31 December 19-4

Opening stock		7,846	Sales		99,388
Add purchases	46,130		Less returns		742
Less returns	256	45,874			98,646
		53,720			
Less closing stock		10,332			
Cost of sales		43,388			
Gross profit c/d		55,258			
		£98,646			£98,646
Discount allowed		818	Gross profit b/d		55,258
Wages (20,630 + 305)		20,935			631
Salaries		10,118			55,889
Rent (2,455 − 122)		2,333			
Rates (1,760 − 536)		1,224			
Delivery expenses (3,414 + 18)		3,432			
Net profit c/d		17,029			
		£55,889			£55,889

R Alderson
Balance Sheet as at 31 December 19-4

Owner's capital		*Fixed assets*	
Opening balance	183,214	Land and buildings	110,100
Add Net profit	17,029	Plant and machinery	54,300
	200,243	Motor vehicles	34,680
			199,080
Current liabilities		*Current assets*	
Trade creditors	35,110	Stock	10,332
Accruals (305 + 18)	323	Trade debtors	20,523
		Prepayments (536 + 122)	658
		Bank balance	5,083
	£235,676		£235,676

Example II
The following trial balance was extracted from the books of Cluriber Ltd a trading concern, as at 31 December 19-4.

	Dr	Cr
Share capital		100,000
Share premium		25,000
8% debentures		10,000
Freehold land and buildings	105,000	
Motor vehicle at cost	40,000	
Provision for depreciation on motor vehicles as at 1 January 19-4.		15,000
Purchases and sales	120,000	158,000
Stock in trade at 1 January 19-4.	15,000	
Rent and rates	4,500	
Rent received		900
Salaries and wages	12,000	
General expenses	3,500	
Debenture interest to 30 June 19-4.	400	
Bad debts	500	
Advertising	3,000	
Debtors and creditors	13,000	12,500
Profit & loss account as at 1 January 19-4.		3,500
Interim dividend on ordinary shares at 30 June 19-4.	5,000	
Discount allowed	800	
Discount received		1,300
Balance at bank	3,500	
	£326,200	£326,200

You are given the following additional information:

(i) Stock in trade at 31 December 19-4 £20,000
(ii) Three months rates have not been paid at 31 December 19-4 £1,000
(iii) Depreciation is charged on motor vehicles at the rate of 20% per annum on cost.
(iv) The directors propose to pay a final dividend on ordinary shares of 6%.
(v) The share capital consists of 100,000 ordinary shares of £1 each fully paid up.
(vi) One quarter year's rent is still to be received at 31 December 19-4 £300.

Prepare an Income Statement for 19-4 and a Balance Sheet as at 31 December 19-4.
THIS QUESTION WILL BE DEALT WITH UNDER COMPANY ACCOUNTS – its presentation here is purely for an appreciation of the adjustment notes to the main trial balance, as they affect organizations other than sole traders.

Unit 2
Expense – prepayments and accruals

Overview

1 Each adjustment for a prepayment or accrual presented in the note section outside the trial balance must contain an additional debit and credit entry in the final accounts.
2 One adjustment will be in the income statement (profit & loss account) and the other in the position statement (balance sheet).
3 A prepayment is a time-based payment that depletes cash/bank in the current year but is not expected to yield its full value until a later period.
4 An accrual (opposite to a prepayment) is a payment that has yet to be made at the close of an accounting period for which a benefit has already been received.
5 Illustrations of prepayments and accruals are provided.

The payment of certain expenses (and receipt of subsidiary income) does not coincide with the accounting period, since the business trades and continues to trade independently from the preparation of final accounts. The adjustments are termed pre-payments and accruals. Both affect the profit & loss account and balance sheet in some specific way according to whether:

1 they are an expense (or income), and
2 they are paid before time or owing.

Prepayments

These are also referred to as prepaid or paid in advance and apply to such items as: rent, rates, insurance, telephone rental etc. Cash or bank funds have been paid, that is value given by the business, but no service has, as yet been received.
  In other words an unused amount is shown in final accounts as:

a) a deduction from the relevant expense in the profit & loss accounts, and
b) a current asset in the balance sheet.

It is understood to be used in the following year.

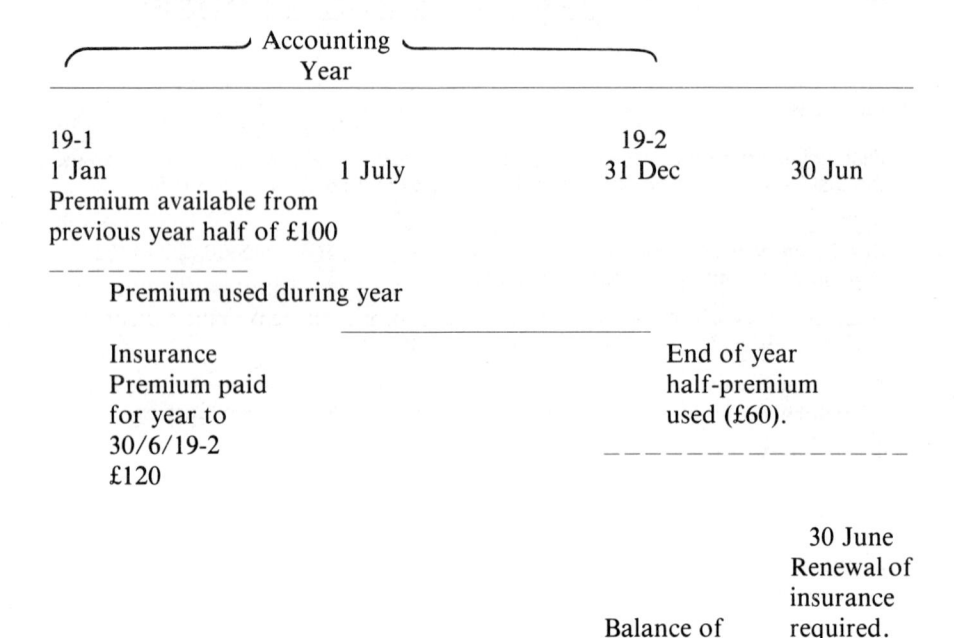

Illustration
Insurance prepaid

```
                    ┌──────── Accounting ────────┐
                                Year
```

19-1		19-2	
1 Jan	1 July	31 Dec	30 Jun
Premium available from previous year half of £100			

- - - - - - - - - -

　　Premium used during year

　　　Insurance　　　　　　　　　　　　　　　End of year
　　　Premium paid　　　　　　　　　　　　　half-premium
　　　for year to　　　　　　　　　　　　　　used (£60).
　　　30/6/19-2
　　　£120

- - - - - - - - - - - - - - -

　　　　　　　　　　　　　　　　　　　　　　　　　30 June
　　　　　　　　　　　　　　　　　　　　　　　　　Renewal of
　　　　　　　　　　　　　　　　　　　　　　　　　insurance
　　　　　　　　　　　　　　　　Balance of　　　 required.
Note　　　　　　　　　　　　　　premium unused
Insurance premium　　　　　　　　(£60)
paid 1 July 19-0　£100
paid 1 July 19-1　£120
ie annual increase　£20
Expense of insurance for accounting year end 31/12/19-1
($\frac{1}{2} \times$ £100)　+　($\frac{1}{2} \times$ £120)
= 　£50　　　+　　　£60
= 　£110

But:　£100 will have been paid in Year 19-0 and only £50 used by business.
　　　£120 will have been paid in Year 19-1 and only £60 used by business.
Therefore: Accounts Year Ended 31/12/19-1 will show

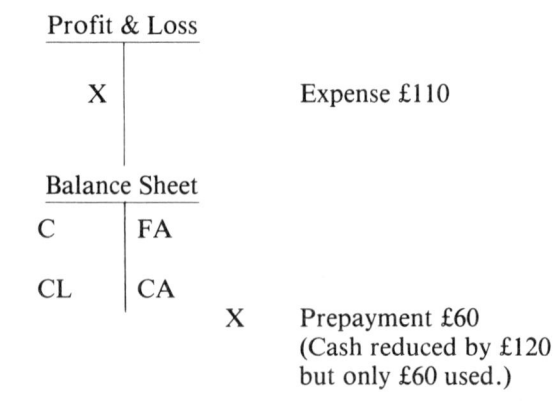

　　　Profit & Loss
　　　　　　│
　　　X　　│　　　　Expense £110
　　　　　　│
　　　　　　│
　　　Balance Sheet
　　　　　　│
　　　C　　│　FA
　　　　　　│
　　　CL　 │　CA
　　　　　　│　　　X　　Prepayment £60
　　　　　　　　　　　　　(Cash reduced by £120
　　　　　　　　　　　　　but only £60 used.)

Accruals

These are also referred to as amount accrued, expense owing, amount outstanding and apply to such items as general expenses, wages, salaries etc. Cash or bank funds have not been paid but value had been received by the business. In other words an amount used has to be shown in the final accounts as:

a) an addition to the relevant expense in the Profit & Loss account, and
b) a current liability in the Balance Sheet.
It is understood to be paid for in the following year.

Illustration
Weekly wages outstanding

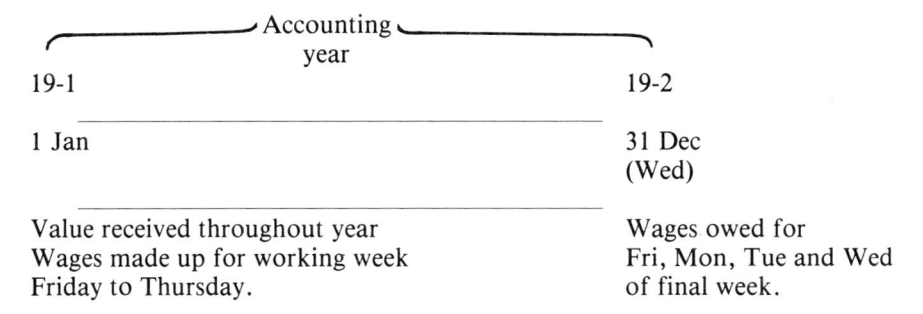

```
                    ⌒ Accounting ⌒
                        year
19-1                                            19-2

1 Jan                                           31 Dec
                                                (Wed)

Value received throughout year          Wages owed for
Wages made up for working week          Fri, Mon, Tue and Wed
Friday to Thursday.                     of final week.
```

Wages paid during the year £28,460 to date, but with £332 outstanding. Business will have received £28,792 of work from its weekly paid work force at close of trading on Wednesday 31 December 19-2, but will only have paid out of cash £28,460

Therefore: Accounts year ended 31/12/19-2 will show

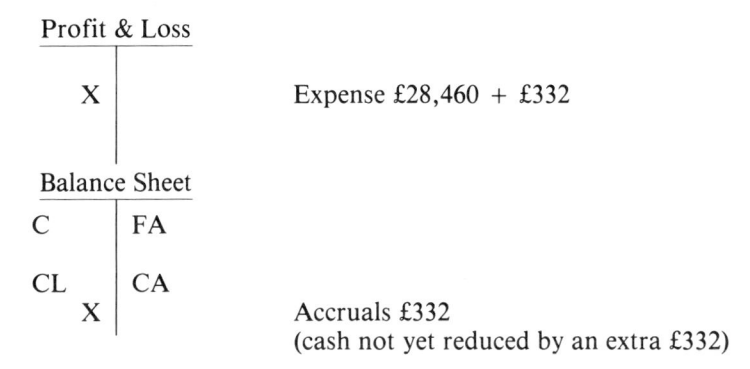

```
    Profit & Loss

        X               Expense £28,460 + £332


    Balance Sheet
  C   |  FA

  CL  |  CA
   X  |                 Accruals £332
                        (cash not yet reduced by an extra £332)
```

Value Purchased, transferred to Profit & Loss and Retained
Value purchased = money spent
Value transferred to profit & loss account = amount used up
Value retained = balance carried down = amount left over
for the purpose of the following illustration

Illustration
Complete the missing figures.

Account	Value purchased	Transferred to profit & loss account	Balance carried down	
Insurance	240	180	60	Dr
Machinery leased	9,000		750	Dr
Heating & lighting	300	280	?	
Advertising	150	150	?	
Carriage	85	?	25	Cr
Salaries	?	4,500	300	Cr

The type of entry will affect the nature of the closing balance. Once the difference is found the nature of the balance will be more easily ascertainable.
You can decide on the nature of the entry by looking carefully at the balances carried down from above.

Machinery leased	9,750	– is an expense for the year
Heating & lighting	20Cr	– is unused
Advertising	Nil	– all value is used
Carriage	60	– is an expense for the year
Salaries	4,800	– is the value purchased during the year.

Look at the double entry for insurance:

Insurance

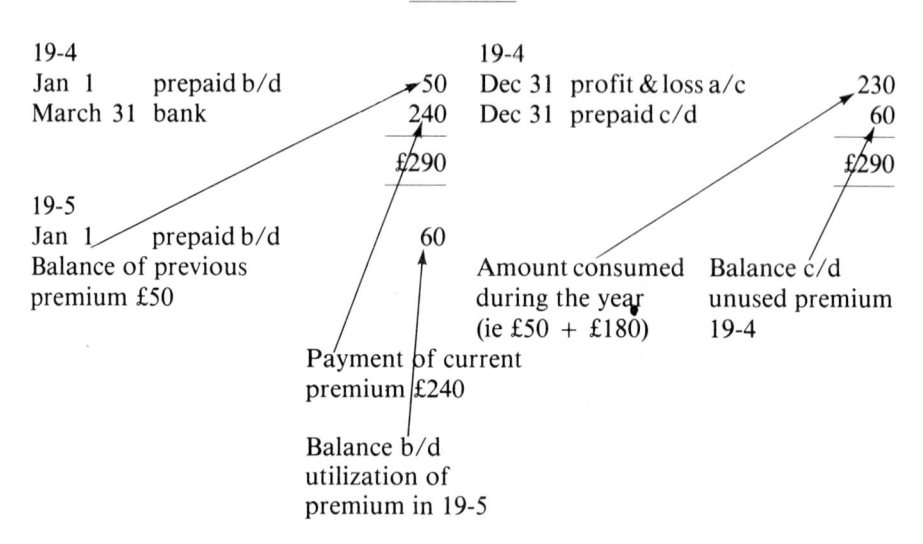

```
19-4                              19-4
Jan 1    prepaid b/d      50     Dec 31  profit & loss a/c   230
March 31 bank            240     Dec 31  prepaid c/d          60
                        ————                                 ————
                        £290                                 £290

19-5
Jan 1    prepaid b/d      60
Balance of previous              Amount consumed    Balance c/d
premium £50                      during the year    unused premium
                                 (ie £50 + £180)    19-4

                  Payment of current
                  premium £240

                  Balance b/d
                  utilization of
                  premium in 19-5
```

The insurance premium is paid annually.

Question	Answer
What insurance premium was paid in 19-3? (one quarter is the pre-payment)	£200

Illustration

The following applies for machinery. A new five year leasing agreement for machinery provides for payment to be made quarterly in advance, the first payment occurring on February 1 in 19-7 at £3,000 per quarter.

For the point of this discussion assume leasing to be the long-term rental of production plant and machinery, an alternative to straightforward purchasing.

Machinery leasing a/c

19-7				19-7			
Feb 1	Bank		3,000	Dec 31	Profit & Loss A/c		11,000
May 1	Bank		3,000	Dec 31	Prepaid c/d		1,000
Aug 1	Bank		3,000				
Nov 1	Bank		3,000				
			£12,000				£12,000

19-8
Jan 1 Prepaid b/d   1,000

With the exception of payments to employees (and related payments) most adjustments in practice relate to payments in advance.

Final accounts summary

Prepayments: 1 deducted from amounts for expenses in the profit & loss account, and
2 added to current assets in the balance sheet.

Accruals: 1 added to amounts for expense in the profit & loss account, and
2 added to current liabilities in the balance sheet.

Unit 3
Subsidiary income — delayed receipt and advance receipt

Overview

1 Income as well as expense items often have to be adjusted in a similar manner.
2 Such income includes rent and commissions, usually subsidiary to trade income and much smaller.
3 Again a similar process of adjustment applies as that for prepayments and accrual of expenses.
4 An illustration is provided.

Subsidiary income usually refers to non-trade income or income not directly related to sales. A trading activity is mainly confined to buying and selling goods. The Inland Revenue amongst others will be particularly interested in this distinction for applying the rules for taxation appropriate to different sources of income. Other activities might include:

1 letting off surplus premises – providing rent income, or
2 engaging specialized selling – providing commission income.

Adjustment

Apart from the fact that the income itself is derived from a different source it might, like accruals and prepayments – that were related to expenses, require adjustment.

Similar principles apply as those for prepayments and accruals; the income brought into the income statement has to be adjusted for that due during the relevant accounting period. Any note outside but related to an item of income contained in the trial balance will require a double-entry adjustment, ie an entry in the income statement (profit & loss) and balance sheet depending on whether it is:

1 value owed to the business – payments due to the business, or
2 value owed by the business – payment in advance for which the business has to give value.

Delayed receipt

This is an amount not received but due and will be shown in the final account as:

a) an addition to the relevant income in the profit & loss account, and
b) a current asset in the balance sheet ie to be received as cash in the following year.

Advanced receipt

This is an amount paid to the business in advance and shown in the final accounts as:

a) a deduction from the relevant income in the profit & loss account, and
b) a current liability in the balance sheet, ie to give value in the following year.

Illustration
Rent received in advance

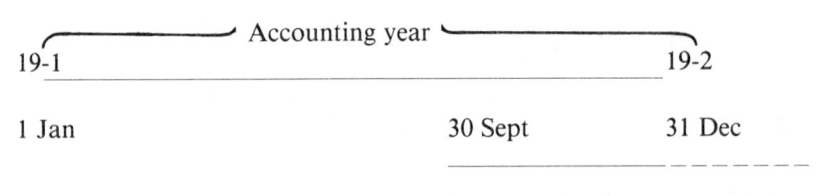

```
                  Accounting year
19-1                                                     19-2
_____

1 Jan                        30 Sept           31 Dec
                                      _____

                             Rent received quarterly 3 months
                             in advance – paid £100 30 December.
                             For 1/1/19-2 to 31/3/19-2.
```

Therefore: Accounts year ended 31/12/19-1 will show

Profit & Loss

        X Income for year £400
           (£500 less £100 paid in advance).
           ie cash received £500.

Balance Sheet

  C   FA

  CL   CA   Accrual £100
    X   (value to be given.)

Final accounts summary

Delayed receipt: 1 increases amount for income in the profit & loss account and
                          2 is added to current assets in the balance sheet.

Advance receipt: 1 deducted from amount for income in the profit & loss account and
                          2 is added to current liabilities in the balance sheet.

Unit 4
Provision for depreciation in final accounts

Overview

1 Assets depreciated (losing value) over a period of time is a recognizable feature of ownership, but the accountant attempts to regulate this for business fixed assets.

2 The traditional method for recording assets has been to start with historic cost as a point of reference that can be verified.

3 The problem is just how much depreciation to take and what method to use. Generally this is solved on the basis of past experience.

4 An adjustment reflecting a decline in historic cost has been conventionally recorded in the final accounts, and this is usually done through an adjustment to the trial balance figures.

5 The appropriate entries required in profit & loss account and balance sheet are illustrated, providing the distinction between amounts recorded as an expense and amounts shown as a cumulative deduction.

6 The adjustments for depreciation can at best only be regarded as estimates.

7 Adjustments are usually expressed as percentages of the capital cost taken as an expense in each trading period.

8 In considering methods of depreciation, accountants are concerned with retaining a balance between retention and distribution of profits.
9 Two practical methods are:
   a) straight-line and
   b) reducing balance.
10 Variations in estimates for depreciation can arise for reasons outside the control of the business. These variations although briefly noted here are considered in a later part of the book, in particular the effect of inflation (see Appendix I accounting for price level changes).

Most of us are familiar with the notion of assets losing value during the course of the life expectancy of each. Some more quickly than others eg the motor car. For an initial period after the vehicle is first put to use it depreciates (loses value) quite quickly, and then more slowly over the remainder of its life until it is virtually worthless.

To proceed further with the analogy of the motor car is useful, since most car owners roughly know the value of their vehicle, so too in business, must the business person have some idea of the value of assets.

Provision

The terminology is common to accountants and follows the dictionary definition. The accountant's assessment of loss in value causes an adjustment to be made in the accounts. The accountant aims to produce figures that accurately show the worth of fixed assets, given certain assumptions about the way value falls. To do this the traditional method has been one based on historic cost.

Historic cost

You would probably agree that there is some difficulty in obtaining the value of a second-hand asset. Take the following situation: A used car salesman is putting a value on your car because you are considering a part-exchange deal:

Salesman: I would offer you £750.
Yourself: I want at least £850 (rather taken back).
Salesman: Well, the paint work needs some attention and there is rust round the wheel arches. . .
Yourself: Yes but I only had it MOT tested last week, and the brakes relined.
Salesman: Well, £775 is my final offer.

Now the accountant faces the same problem but with a large number of different fixed assets that a business may own. The accountant has to devise a general method that is applicable to all. Starting from the purchase, as a known point of reference, the price of an asset can be ascertained by looking at the original documents of purchase. What was paid for the asset is known as the historic cost.

Depreciation

The general aim is to adjust the monetary worth of long-term assets reflecting (the usual) loss through use, eg a machine purchased a year ago is worth less than what it cost originally. But by how much, and by what method this is decided is a problem. The solution will generally be based on the experience within a business. (These aspects will be considered in more detail later.)

Inflation

The problems of declining money values do not affect the principle of depreciation but the sufficiency of the amount. The intention of a provision for depreciation has been to maintain the operating capability of a business and thereby its ability to replace assets.

Since we are primarily concerned at this stage with double entry and the presentation of information, let us assume that the problems of amount and method have been solved and look at the mechanics of adjustment for depreciation.

Adjustment for depreciation

This is often referred to as a provision. Technically the term represents the accountant's assessment of the loss in value of an asset that requires an adjustment to be made in the accounts. The usage of the term follows the accepted dictionary definition, (see pp 94–100 for the instruction for adjustment).

Final accounts

The adjustment for a provision for depreciation occurs in the final accounts – the balance sheet and profit and loss account.

The balance sheet

Deduct the amount of depreciation from the cost of the asset, (to reduce a debit the Balance Sheet is credited). Look at this standard extracted presentation of depreciation in a balance sheet.

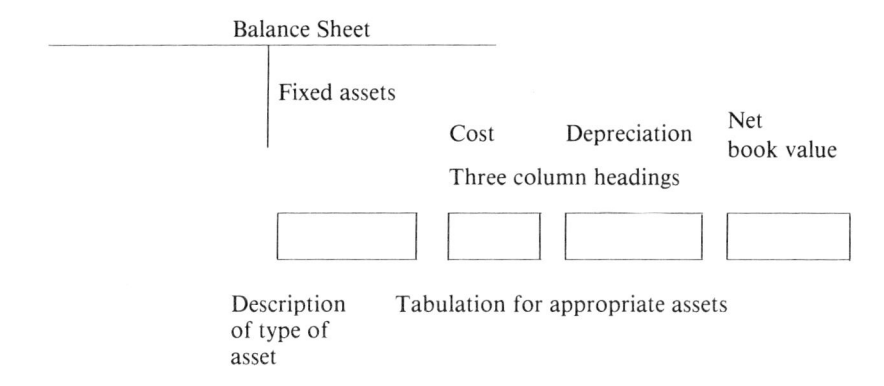

Balance Sheet

Fixed assets

Cost   Depreciation   Net book value

Three column headings

Description of type of asset   Tabulation for appropriate assets

Cost: Historic cost
Depreciation: depreciation to date
Net Book Value: Cost less the depreciation to date ie the *debit* net of the *credit*

The profit & loss account

A provision for depreciation is treated as a reduction of profit for the year in which it arises. (To reduce profit the profit & loss account is debited). Look at this standard extracted presentation of depreciation in a profit and loss account.

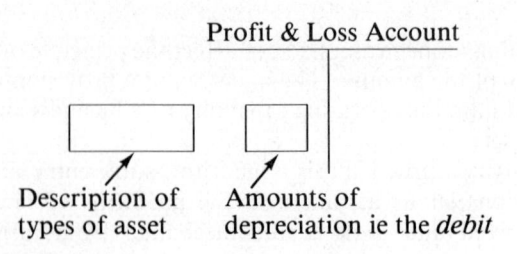

Profit & Loss Account

Description of types of asset ／ Amounts of depreciation ie the *debit*

Depreciation over time and type of asset

Assume start of business.

Year 1 P&L A/C	Year 2 P&L A/C	Year 3 P&L A/C	Year 4 P&L A/C
Dep'n yr 1	Dep'n yr 2	Dep'n yr 3	Dep'n yr 4
B S	B S	B S	B S
FA COST less dep'n yr 1	FA Cost less dep'n yr 1 + 2	FA Cost less dep'n yr 1, 2, + 3	FA Cost less dep'n yr 1, 2, 3 + 4

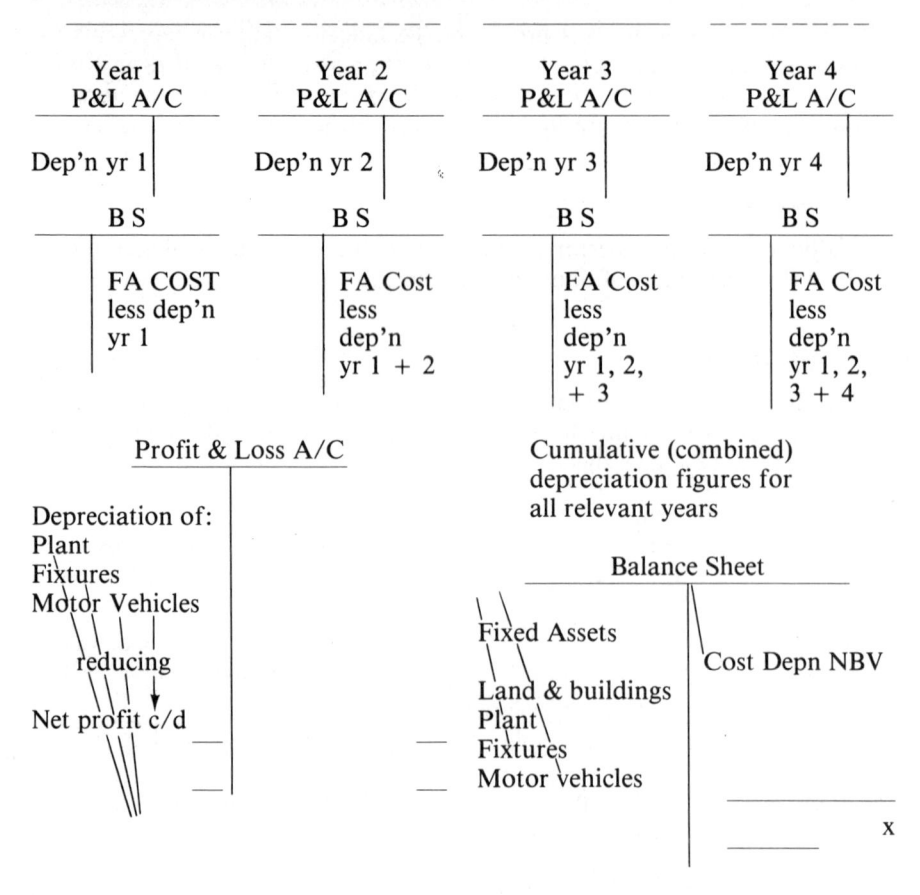

Profit & Loss A/C

Depreciation of:
Plant
Fixtures
Motor Vehicles

reducing

Net profit c/d

Yearly depreciation figures shown for each type of asset.

Cumulative (combined) depreciation figures for all relevant years

Balance Sheet

Fixed Assets   Cost Depn NBV
Land & buildings
Plant
Fixtures
Motor vehicles
                                    x

The aggregate figures for each type of asset are collected together.

Note
1 The total net book value (NBV) figure is the important summary figure marked with a 'x' to be introduced into a balance sheet.
2 In many examples land and buildings are not depreciated yearly, are recorded at cost (subject to adjustment) and therefore an amount of depreciation does not appear in the profit & loss. However, current practice does treat land and buildings separately, and requires buildings to be depreciated, if only by smaller percentage amounts than are required for other assets.

Calculation of depreciation

The calculation is related to the estimated useful life of an asset spread over a number of years. Clearly the life of an asset will depend on its type and the use to which it is put, but any conclusions can only be estimates and fairly rough and ready at that! In practice the estimate is based on the number of accounting periods (usually years) during which the asset will decline in value from cost to a negligible amount. The proportion for one period is then related to the estimate for life and expressed as a percentage reduction to be applied as a charge to profit and loss (debit) for each period of use.
Look at the following examples:

Buildings	– having an extended life span	– say $2\frac{1}{2}$% per year
Plant & machinery	– having a life of 10 years	– 10% per year
Fixture & fittings	– having a life of 5 years	– 20% per year
Motor vehicles	– having a life of 4 years	– 25% per year

Estimates of life expectancy that form the basis of the percentage reduction are a problem and can depend on so many economic, commercial and political circumstances. However, these factors can usefully be put aside for the purpose of explaining the double entry treatment. Because whatever life expectancy decision is arrived at the method will be largely unaffected.

Method of depreciation

Much discussion has traditionally centred around the method of depreciation. This has taken place not only amongst professional accountants but other specialists, chief amongst them economists who might argue the advantages of writing off the whole cost in the year of acquisition. The prime argument centres on a realistic method that is uncomplicated.

The problem for accountants is not one of the theoretical advantages but of practice providing that:

1 sufficient funds are retained to provide for eventual replacement,
2 enough profit is available for distribution to make the business attractive to investors, and
3 the method is consistent taking one year with another.

Two methods to be considered are:

1 Straight-line and
2 reducing balance.
Neither of these affect the principles for double entry.

Straight line

This is the most popular method among accountants because of its:
1 simplicity, and
2 consistency
   a) from year to year, and
   b) between different assets.

Annual
depreciation
£'s

Years

It is also the method to be most commonly applied in examination questions.

Illustration
A machine costing £10,000 has an estimated useful life of five years. Calculate the depreciation.
depreciation — percentage is 20% per year of £10,000
ie   £2,000 per year

Profit & Loss = debit of £2,000 a year for 5 years.
Balance Sheet = a net book value of:
   end of year 1 (10,000 − 2,000) = £8,000
              2 (10,000 − 4,000) = £6,000

              5 (10,000 − 10,000) = nil.

Reducing balance

Instead of applying a fixed percentage to the cost, the figure to which it is applies is the reduced balance.

Annual
depreciation
£'s

Years

The result is that the amounts of depreciation taken in later years is less, since a constant percentage is applied to a diminishing figure. This method is consistent but lacks simplicity, since a formula has to be applied to deduce a percentage figure that will reduce the value of an asset from cost or appropriate valuation to a negligible amount eg scrap value over a given period. To apply the formula a scrap value has to be taken, however small, otherwise a zero would be introduced.

The formula is

$r = 1 - \sqrt[n]{\dfrac{s}{c}}$ where n = number of years
s = end value
c = cost
r = rate of depreciation to be calculated.

Illustration
A machine costing £32,768 has an estimated life of 5 years and an end of life value of £32.
depreciation — (three stages)
(i) Calculating the percentage:

$$r = 1 - \sqrt[n]{\dfrac{s}{c}}$$
$$= 1 - \sqrt[5]{\dfrac{32}{32,768}}$$
$$= 1 - \dfrac{2}{8}$$
$$= 1 - 0.25 = 75\%$$

Note
1 The percentage figure may look excessively high, but remember the calculation is on a diminished value after each successive application.
2 The example is contrived and this probably reflects its difficulty in use.

ie $\sqrt[5]{\dfrac{128}{32,768}} = \sqrt[5]{\dfrac{2 \times 2 \times 2 \times 2 \times 2}{8 \times 8 \times 8 \times 8 \times 8}}$

(ii) Applying the percentage:

Year 0	Cost	32,768
Year 1	Less depreciation (75%)	24,576
	Valuation	8,192
Year 2	Less depreciation (75%)	6,144
	Valuation	2,048
Year 3	Less depreciation (75%)	1,536
	Valuation	512
Year 4	Less depreciation (75%)	384
	Valuation	128
Year 5	Less depreciation (75%)	96
	Valuation	32

(iii) The adjustment
Profit & Loss – debits of:
Year 1	Year 2	Year 3	Year 4	Year 5
24,576	6,144	1,536	384	96

Balance Sheet – net book value of:
Year 1	Year 2	Year 3	Year 4	Year 5
8,192	2,048	512	128	32

Variations in estimates

Changes in:

a) trading conditions, and
b) monetary value

can affect the validity of estimates.
A machine thought to have many useful years of life can suddenly become obsolete and have to be replaced, through technological advance, making the machine worthless, ie estimates for depreciation will have to be increased.
A building increases in monetary value largely through inflation even so depreciation should be taken though there are two opposite trends reflecting:

a) the time span of use, and
b) the current cost of replacement,

ie some revision of the cost will have to be agreed and accounted for. (A reference to Appendix I: Accounting for price level changes, would be useful at this or a later stage.)

Depreciation in final accounts

Illustration
Extract of a trial balance

	Dr	Cr
Land at valuation	40,000	
Buildings at valuation	68,000	
Buildings depreciation to date		18,460
Plant & machinery at cost	75,000	
Plant & machinery depreciation to date		15,000
Fixtures & fittings at cost	36,000	
Fixtures & fittings depreciation to date		12,000
Motor vehicles at cost	40,000	
Motor vehicles depreciation to date		20,000

Note
   The net value for each type of asset is the *debit* figure less the *credit* figure eg Plant & machinery £75,000 – £15,000 = £60,000
Extract of notes for adjustment
The directors' policy for depreciation is the straight-line method applied to the assets as follows:

Plant & machinery	20%	Buildings	4%
Fixture and fittings	33⅓%	Land	nil
Motor vehicles	25%		

You are required to show the entries in the profit & loss account & balance sheet.

```
                          Profit and Loss Account
Provision for depreciation:
Buildings 4% on valuation        2,720
Plant & machinery 20% on cost   15,000
Fixture & fittings 33⅓% on cost 12,000
Motor vehicles 25% on cost      10,000
```

```
                    Balance Sheet

        Fixed assets
                              Cost or
                              valuation    Dep'n     NBV
        Land                    40,000       –      40,000
        Buildings               68,000    21,180    46,820
        Plant & machinery       75,000    30,000    45,000
        Fixtures & fittings     36,000    24,000    12,000
        Motor vehicles.         40,000    30,000    10,000
                               -------   -------   -------
                               259,000   105,180   153,820
```

Note

1 Depreciation figures shown in the Balance Sheet are up to date at the time of presentation whereas they are unlikely to be in the Trial Balance.
2 Total cost or valuation less total depreciation should equal the net book value.

Final accounts summary

Depreciation as an expense	: Should be shown in the profit & loss account as a debit for each class of depreciable asset in the year in which it arises.
Depreciation as it reduces the value of assets	: Should be shown in the balance sheet as a credit, a cumulative figure for all years, leaving the net book value as the figure to be utilized.

Unit 5
Bad debts and provisions for doubtful debts in final accounts

Overview

1 The distinction is made between bad debts and provisions for doubtful (or bad) debts.
   a) a bad debt is revenue lost, and
   b) a provision is an estimate against future possible loss.
2 The contribution made by credit control towards the reduction in bad debts is noted.

89

3 Bad debts are illustrated as an expense to profit & loss.

4 The adjustments required for provisions are illustrated as they affect both the profit & loss and balance sheet.

There are two distinct classifications for bad debts in final accounts. These are:
a) bad debts (proper) and
b) provision for doubtful debts (or bad debts).

Each type will be dealt with separately since they are largely distinct, require different treatment, and have different commercial origins. The term provision is used in the second case, and it will be realized the same terminology is applied here as with a provision for depreciation. The accounting treatment is similar for provisions ie for both depreciation and doubtful debts.

Bad debts

These consist of funds lost through trading and are generally unlikely to be recovered. Treated as an expense to profit & loss, they are extracted from the main body of the trial balance. Strictly then, they are not an adjustment but it is convenient to treat provisions for doubtful debts and bad debts under one main heading. Given that bad debts are funds lost, there ought to be some remedial action a business can take. These precautions are matters of common commercial knowledge and are the concern of good credit control.

Credit control requires:

1 maintenance of records in sufficient detail to monitor debts,
2 appointment of a person(s) whose responsibility is credit control,
3 investigation of new customers — to test their credit rating,
4 early transactions to be completed for cash only,
5 setting individual credit limits in line with a policy of overall credit control,
6 introduction of a discount (allowed) policy to encourage prompt payment, and
7 a policy to decide when bad debts should be recognized as such.

Accounting treatment for bad debts

In final accounts the method is to debit profit and loss because they are an expense. This should not be regarded as a substitute to action for recovery and can be recognized at least partially as a failure to recover.

Other entries will have to be made in the ledger accounts to maintain an on-going record of bad debts when they are considered to arise, ie adjustment to the personal account of debtors. Remember that in this case funds have effectively been lost through loss of revenue following a sale.

Illustration
Trial balance extract

	Dr	Cr
Wages	29,242	
Rent and rates	3,680	
Light and heat	2,190	
Bad debts	670	

Profit and loss account extract

	Profit & Loss Account
Wages	29,242
Rent and rates	3,680
Light & heat	2,190
Bad debts	670

Note A debt remains unpaid and a deficiency has arisen for either part of or the whole amount leaving an imbalance in a debtor's account were it allowed to remain.

```
                                        Sales
                                          |
                                          |   X

         A debtor
           |
         X |
```

By treating it as an expense in the period a bad debt arises prevents its being allowed to remain.

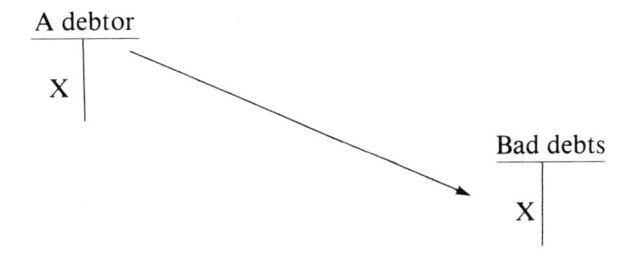

```
         A debtor
           |
         X |  ───────────────┐
                             ↓
                          Bad debts
                             |
                           X |
```

Provision for doubtful debts

This is also referred to as a provision for bad debts in some text books and examination questions, introducing an element of uncertainty because of the projection into the future. A provision for doubtful or bad debts is an estimate of the possibility of bad debts arising in a future accounting period.

This provision has arisen through the accountant's need to record as accurately as possible periodic events in an end period statement, bearing in mind that some credit sales (debtors balances) will remain unpaid at the close of an accounting period and may not ever be paid. The adjustment required will be shown as a note to the trial balance and will (like all the notes) affect both the profit and loss account and the balance sheet. A figure for a provision for doubtful debts will appear in the main body of the trial balance. It is how the adjustment affects this figure that is important.

Illustration
Trial balance extract

	Dr	Cr
Wages	29,242	
Rent and rates	3,680	
Light and heat	2,190	
Bad debts	670	
Provision for doubtful debts		1,500

(The directors' have decided that the provision for doubtful debts shall be increased to £2,250.)

Final accounts

The entries in final accounts will occur in:

a) the profit & loss, and
b) the balance sheet.

Profit & Loss Account

Wages	29,242
Rent and rates	3,680
Light and heat	2,190
Bad debts	670
Increased provision for doubtful debts	750

Balance Sheet

Debtors
less provision for doubtful debts 2,250

The profit and loss account

There is an important subsidiary point here, the adjustment to a provision for bad debts can either be:

a) up — the trial balance figure can be increased, or
b) down — the trial balance figure can be reduced.

Therefore the adjustment figure shown in the profit & loss account will be either the increase or the decrease that will be reflected in whether the entry is a debit or a credit.

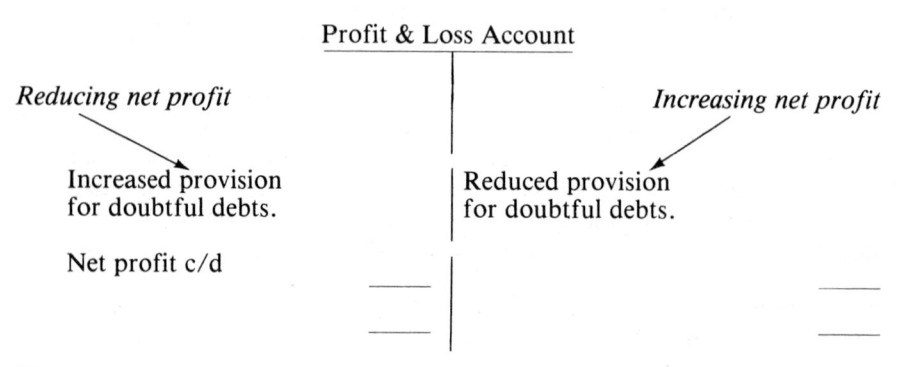

Profit & Loss Account

Reducing net profit → Increased provision for doubtful debts.

Net profit c/d

Increasing net profit → Reduced provision for doubtful debts.

The actual decision about bad debts is the responsibility of management; it is a matter for business judgement based on experience. The book-keeping relates only to the state of the records. It is the convention for a provision for doubtful debts (the adjusted figure) to be carried forward from one year to another and adjusted in the profit & loss account as illustrated above. An increase in a provision will *reduce* the profit available for distribution to the owners. A decrease in a provision will *increase* the profit available for distribution to the owners.

Question : In a period of increasing difficulties for businesses would directors (in a company) be inclined to increase or decrease a provision for bad debts?

Answer : In my opinion they would think very carefully about the related aspects (not least the effect on profits) but would probably decide to increase.

The balance sheet

As was stated earlier an adjustment for a doubtful (bad) debts provision will also affect the balance sheet. The *new adjusted figure* (suitably increased or decreased) will be taken to the Balance Sheet, but in the following, more unusual way, as a deduction from the current asset debtors. Think about it, a reduction of an asset is a credit and any provision (no matter whether it is adjusted up or down) is in itself a reduction of debtors. Thus a credit can be used as a reduction of an asset.

Remember closing stock – a credit was treated as a deduction from debits in the trading account.

Balance Sheet extract

Balance Sheet

Current assets			
Stock			8,798
Debtors	19,224		
less provision for doubtful debts	2,250	16,974	

Summary

1 Bad debts are debited to profit & loss as an expense.
2 a) The provision for doubtful debts is adjusted in the profit & loss (the difference from the amount stated in the trial balance) as either:
   (i) an increase – debited, or
   (ii) a decrease – credited.
   b) The provision for doubtful debts is deducted from the Current Asset figure for debtors – this is the new adjusted figure, often given in the Notes to a question.

Unit 6
Double entry for provisions

Overview

1 The underlying ledger accounts that support the entries in final accounts are discussed for:
   a) depreciation, and
   b) doubtful debts.
2 Depreciation provisions:
   a) The method used employs three accounts:
      (i) Cost of asset account,
      (ii) Provision for depreciation account, and
      (iii) Disposal account.
   b) Transfers to final accounts are included, and
   c) an example is provided with diagrammatic and notation explanations.
3 Doubtful debts provision (including bad debts)
   a) The method used employs two accounts:
      (i) Provision for doubtful debts account, and
      (ii) bad debts account.
   b) Transfer to final accounts are included.
   c) An example is provided with diagrammatic and notational explanations.

Provisions as they have hitherto been explained and shown in final accounts do not present a sufficiently detailed record to meet book-keeping requirements. For the purpose of final accounts, provisions are shown to have an effect on profit and the valuation of assets at the year end.

To support final account records for depreciation and doubtful and bad debts, entries in the books should comprise:

1 yearly divisions,
2 balances transferred to year end statements,
3 other periodic adjustments,
4 conventional presentation in ledger (or alternative 'two-way') format.

In particular, taking depreciation and bad debts separately:

depreciation requires a record of the:

1 acquisition price that is maintained as cost,
2 accumulated provisions for depreciation, and
3 adjustment at disposal.

bad debts require a record of the:

1 acknowledged bad debts, and
2 accumulated provision for doubtful (bad) debts.

There are different methods adopted within the ledger for accounting for provisions, but demonstration of one method in each case should be sufficient to illustrate the principles involved.

Depreciation provisions

Three ledger accounts are used showing separate aspects of the accounting record, these show the:

a) Cost of the asset − as brought into the ledger at purchase (debit) and removed from at disposal (credit).
   Shown as a debit balance at the start of a year.
b) Provision for depreciation of the asset − as a yearly accumulation of amounts transferred to profit & loss (credit) and removed from at disposal (debit).
   Shown as a credit balance at the start of a year.
The two accounts are opposites and taken together provide a net figure.
c) Disposal − each disposal requires a merging adjustment of figures from Cost and Provision accounts, plus the introduction of any cash proceeds from the sale
   The balance is taken as either a debit or credit to profit and loss ie an adjustment beyond the annual amount.

Cost

Debit entries are for:
(i) purchase − cash or bank, or
(ii) balance b/d.

| Year 1 | Year 1 |
| Year 2 | Year 2 |

Credit entries are for:
(i) disposals − the sale or removal, or
(ii) balance c/d

Provision for depreciation

Credit entries are for:
(i) yearly transfers to profit & loss, or
(ii) balance b/d

| Year 1 | Year 1 |
| Year 2 | Year 2 |

Debit entries are for:
(i) disposals (amount of depreciation taken over the years), or
(ii) balance c/d

Disposal

Debit entries are for:
(i) disposal value at cost, or
(ii) transfer to profit & loss (alternative to (iii) below)

| Cost | Proceeds of sales |
| | Provision for depreciation (accumulated) |

Credit entries are for:
(i) disposal proceeds,
(ii) the provision for depreciation, or
(iii) transfer to profit & loss (alternative to (ii) Debit − above).

Profit & Loss ⇄ on disposal

Note Separate records will be kept for assets:
a) of different classes eg motor vehicles and machinery, and
b) where different percentages for depreciation have been used.

Transfers to profit & loss

There are two types of transfer:
a) the standard periodic provision, and
b) the adjustment at disposal.

The standard periodic adjustment has been dealt with but the adjustment at disposal has not. The adjustment at disposal requires comparison of the written down value (cost less accumulated depreciation) against the disposal proceeds, and unless the amounts exactly coincide an adjustment taking either:
a) more depreciation, or
b) less depreciation,
will be required.

More depreciation requires an additional expense and is therefore a debit to profit & loss – ie a shortfall against market value over the years of ownership. Less depreciation provides a release of earlier provisions and is therefore a credit to profit & loss (giving extra income) – ie a surplus against market value over the years of ownership.

A look at a profit & loss extract will demonstrate the position.

A provision for depreciation remains for the year unless (and this is unlikely) all assets are disposed of at once. It is possible to have both too much and too little depreciation in one year, when (for instance) more than one asset is disposed of.

Profit & Loss

Provision for depreciation. plus Previous under provision for depreciation.	OR	Previous over provision for depreciation.
(too little earlier depreciation)		*(too much earlier depreciation).*

Thus an adjustment to depreciation in the year of sale of an asset usually affects the net profit (either increasing or decreasing it).

End of year or part-year provisions

This does not affect either:
a) the principle of the provision, or
b) its adjustment,
but does often affect the amount especially when assets are unlikely to be sold exactly at the year end.

Illustration

A machine is sold on 31 August 19-7, therefore it can be depreciated:
a) for eight months, incurring part-year depreciation,
b) regarded as not owned at the start of the year and therefore incurring no depreciation, or
c) regarded as owned at the close of the year and therefore incurring a full year of depreciation.

The amount would depend entirely on the policy of the business, but what is important is that the policy should be consistently applied from year to year. Any examination question would provide full instructions on what to do.

Method of depreciation

The method:
a) reducing balance, or
b) straight-line
has already been discussed and does not affect:
(i) the method of account in the ledgers, or
(ii) the adjustment in the profit & loss,
but does affect the overall amount.

Reason for the adjustment
It is unlikely the estimate for depreciation and the assumptions made at commencement of ownership will turn out to be correct . . .
ie net book value at sale = market price
             (exactly equals)
If it did then accountants could be relied on as clairvoyants, and may be more profitably employed in business in that role!

Remember, the attempt at making an estimate of the life of an asset, can be no more precise than this, and adjustments will nearly always have to be made. For some examples, for instance, those more complicated types using the reducing balance method and or part years; a schedule of the arithmetic may be usefully prepared, outside the double-entry accounts, but supporting the entries.
It is now useful to look at the following worked question:

Example
Jones asks you to calculate and summarize his machinery and depreciation for machinery positions for the years 19-1, 19-2, 19-3 and 19-4 given the following information:

19-1 Balance brought down on machinery and provision for depreciation of machinery are £4,000 and £400 respectively.

He purchases two machines, one by cheque on June 30 for £300, and one for cash − £500 on October 1.

19-2 He purchases a further machine costing £400, paid by cheque on March 31.

19-4 Jones sells one of the machines brought forward from 19-0 for £100 cash on September 30 that originally cost £500 and was valued in the books at £50.

Depreciation should be calculated at 20% on cost per annum.
You are required to:

1 Prepare a machinery account, a provision for depreciation account and a disposals account for the relevant years.
2 Show the profit and loss account and balance sheet extracts for the relevant years.
   Ignore part years of depreciation − thus any part year has been regarded as a full year.

The Ledger Entries

Machinery a/c

19-1				19-1			
Jan 1	Balance b/d	4,000		Dec 31	Balance c/d (1)	4,800	
Jun 30	Bank	300					
Oct 1	Cash	500					
		£4,800				£4,800	
19-2				19-2			
Jan 1	Balance b/d (4)	4,800		Dec 31	Balance c/d	5,200	
Mar 31	Bank	400					
		£5,200				£5,200	
19-3				19-3			
Jan 1	Balance b/d	5,200		Dec 31	Balance c/d	5,200	
		£5,200				£5,200	
19-4				19-4			
Jan 1	Balance b/d	5,200		Sept 30	Disposal (6)	500	
				Dec 31	Balance c/d	4,700	
		£5,200				£5,200	
19-5							
Jan 1	Balance b/d	4,700					

Depreciation a/c

				19-1			
				Jan 1	Balance b/d	400	
Dec 31	Balance c/d (2)	1,360		Dec 31	P & L (3)	960	
		£1,360				£1,360	
				19-2			
				Jan 1	Balance b/d	1,360	
Dec 31	Balance c/d	2,400		Dec 31	P & L	1,040 (5)	
		£2,400				£2,400	
				19-3			
				Jan 1	Balance b/d	2,400	
Dec 31	Balance c/d	3,440		Dec 31	P & L	1,040	
		£3,440				£3,440	
				19-4			
Sept 30	Disposal	450 (7)		Jan 1	Balance b/d	3,440	
Dec 31	Balance c/d	3,930		Dec 31	P & L	940	
		£4,380				£4,380	
				19-5			
				Jan 1	Balance b/d	3,930	

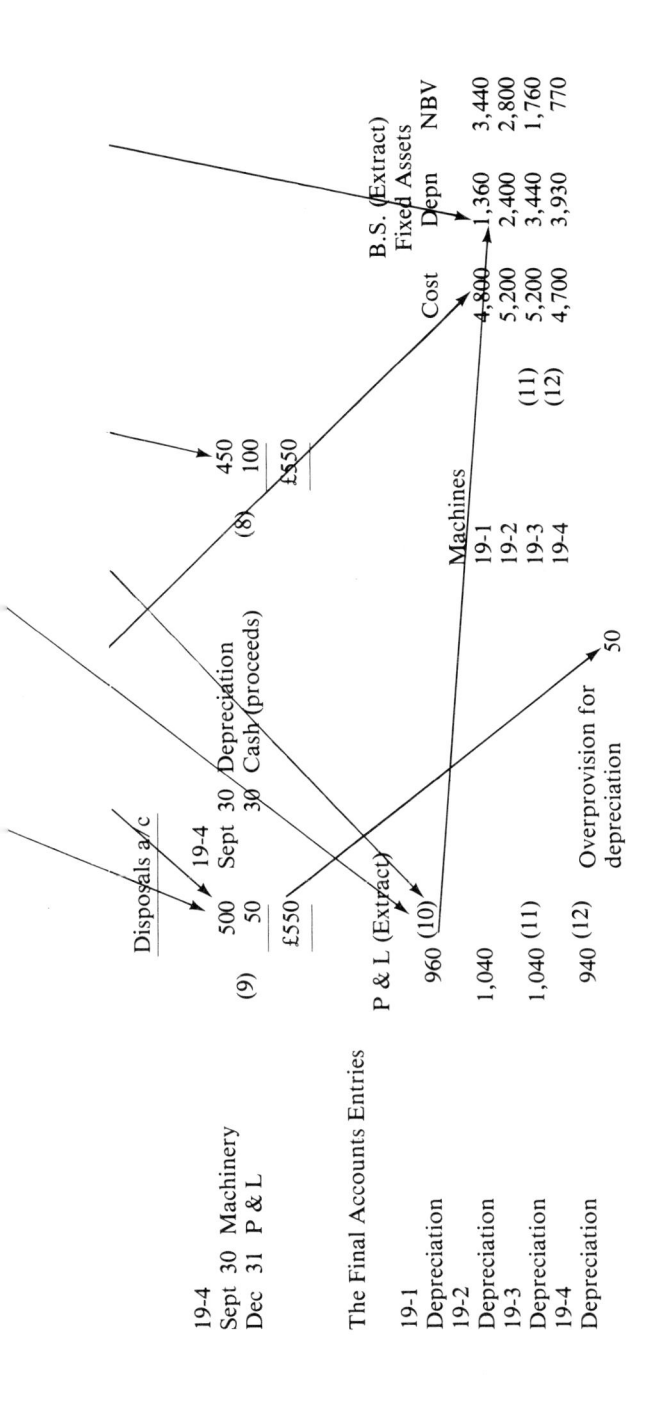

	Disposals a/c		
19-4		19-4	
Sept 30 Machinery	500	Sept 30 Depreciation	450
Dec 31 P & L	50	30 Cash (proceeds)	100
	£550		£550
(9)		(8)	

The Final Accounts Entries

P & L (Extract)

19-1 Depreciation	960 (10)
19-2 Depreciation	1,040
19-3 Depreciation	1,040 (11)
19-4 Depreciation	940 (12)
	Overprovision for depreciation	50

B.S. (Extract)
Fixed Assets
Machines

	Cost	Depn	NBV
19-1	4,800	1,360	3,440
19-2	5,200	2,400	2,800
19-3	5,200 (11)	3,440	1,760
19-4	4,700 (12)	3,930	770

Note Yearly accounting entries
1. Balance c/d in Year 1 becomes balance b/d in Year 2. Read the debit balance as the cost.
2. Balance c/d in Year 1 becomes balance b/d in Year 2. Read the credit balance as the cumulative amount of depreciation to date (£960 + £400).
3. The depreciation for the year is transferred to the profit & loss account for the year as an expense.
4. The cumulative balance for cost of the asset (machinery in this case) becomes the cost figure in the balance sheet.
5. The cumulative balance for depreciation becomes the depreciation figure in the balance sheet.

Entries to account for a disposal
6. The cost value of the asset is taken out of the asset account (once sold it is no longer an asset) and transferred to a specific disposal account:
Credit: machinery a/c
Debit: disposal a/c
7. The accumulated depreciation for the asset disposal is taken out of the depreciation account and transferred to the same specific disposal account (as in 6):
Debit: depreciation a/c
Credit: disposal a/c
8. The agreed cash proceeds will be introduced to the disposal account and be a debit to either cash or bank (initially increasing cash/bank):
Debit: cash a/c or bank a/c
Credit: disposal a/c
9. To balance the disposal account will provide the amount to be transferred to the profit & loss account and indicate whether it is to be regarded as an *over or under provision* ie a debit or credit to profit & loss in this case:
Debit: disposal a/c
Credit: profit & loss.

Therefore, an over provision for depreciation is needed. Our policy suggested the asset was worth only £50 (£500 − £450) but we were fortunate enough to sell it for £100.

10. Thus it is the yearly depreciation figure that contributes to the overall cumulative figure for depreciation.

11 & 12 The diminished figures for cost and depreciation between year three and year four arise because part of the assets have been disposed of and the cumulative balances diminished.

Calculations
Year 1: 4,800 × 20% = £ 960
     2: 5,200 × 20% = £1,040
     3: 5,200 × 20% = £1,040
     4: 4,700 × 20% = £ 940

Comment
A provisions policy for depreciation is designed to prevent excessive distribution (by reducing the profit) in order to leave funds in the business. These funds could, if desired, be released to fund the purchase of new assets, provided an appropriate amount of cash was available.

Doubtful debts provisions (Bad debts page 104)

In this case it is only a provision account that requires on-going adjustments, to show:
a) the full provision that is taken to the balance sheet, and
b) the adjustment that is taken to profit & loss.

Balance Sheet

The final provision is shown in the balance sheet as a credit ie a reduction of debtors.

Current Assets

Debtors   X
less provision for
doubtful
debts   X   X

Profit & Loss

The adjustment either up or down is:
debit = increase
credit = decrease

Increased provision for doubtful debts	Reduced provision for doubtful debts
increase the amount provided	*reduce* the amount provided

Effect on profit

| *reduces* profit | *increases* profit |

The Provision Account

Credit entry will be the opening or existing balance — balance b/d
Debit entry will be the closing newly adjusted balance — balance c/d

Year 1	Year 1
Year 2	Year 2

The Provision Account

The profit & loss adjustment:
INCREASE a provision
Credit provision a/c
Debit profit & loss a/c

REDUCE a provision
Debit provision a/c
Credit profit & loss a/c

Year 2	Year 2 Balance b/d
PROFIT LOSS ADJUSTMENT	
Balance c/d	

Ledger entries:

Provision for Doubtful Debts A/c				Bad Debts A/c			
19-0		19-0		19-0		19-0	
Dec 31 Balance c/d	449	Dec 31 Profit & Loss	449	Dec 31 Sundry Debtors	460	Dec 31 Profit & Loss	460
			(2)				(1)
19-1		19-1		19-1		19-1	
Dec 31 Balance c/d	(5)522	Jan 1 Balance b/d	449	Dec 31 Sundry Debtors	510	Dec 31 Profit & Loss	510
	(4)	Dec 31 Profit & Loss	(3) 73				
	522		522	19-2		19-2	
19-2		19-2		Dec 31 Sundry Debtors	330	Dec 31 Profit & Loss	330
Dec 31 Balance c/d	698	Jan 1 Balance b/d	522				
		Dec 31 Profit & Loss	176	19-3		19-3	
	698		698	Dec 31 Sundry Debtors	690	Dec 31 Profit & Loss	690
19-3		19-3					
Dec 31 Profit & Loss	62	Jan 1 Balance b/d	698				
Dec 31 Balance c/d	636						
	698		698				
19-4		19-4					
		Jan 1 Balance b/d	636				

Note The differences between these two accounts. One shows the provision and its adjustment, the other merely a record of an expense.

102

The Final Accounts entries

Profit & Loss (extract)

19-0			
Bad debts	460		
Provision for doubtful debts	449		
19-1			
Bad debts	510		
Provision for doubtful debts	73		
19-2			
Bad debts	330		
Provision for doubtful debts	176		
19-3			
Bad debts	690	19-3 Provision for doubtful debts	62

Balance Sheet (extract)

19-0		
Debtors	8,980	
less provision for doubtful debts	449	8,531
19-1		
Debtors	10,440	
less provision for doubtful debts	522	9,981
19-2		
Debtors	13,960	
less provision for doubtful debts	698	13,262
19-3		
Debtors	12,720	
less provision for doubtful debts	636	12,084

Notes
Yearly accounting entries:

1 Profit & loss amount in the bad debts account is transferred to the profit & loss.
2 & 3 Profit & loss amounts in the provisions account is transferred to the profit & loss in 2 the whole amount since it represents the creation of a *new* provision in 3 the additional amount that represents the *increase* in the provision.
4 & 5 Provision account balances carried down from year 0 to year 1 in the provision account, but also to the balance sheet (for respective years) to form the total provision by which the debtors are adjusted.

Bad debts

Although not a provision, bad debts are shown in the ledger accounts.

		Bad Debts Account	
Credit entry will be a transfer to profit & loss.	Year 1	Year 1	
Debit entry will be a reference to sales ledger as sundry debtors. Look for bad debts in Unit on Control Accounts. (pp 227–36)	Year 2	Year 2	

	Bad Debts	
There is no balance to carry to the following period.	Sales Ledger Control X	Profit & Loss X

	Profit & Loss
Bad debts have been incurred and are a straight expense to profit & loss.	Bad debts X

It is now useful to look at the following worked question, but first remember the distinction between bad debts and provisions for doubtful (bad) debts, because the question is designed to illustrate this too.

Example
The directors of X limited decide to introduce a new bad debts policy at the close of 19-0, on the basis of creating a provision for debtors of 5% on closing year debtors. Records are required showing the accounting entries in ledgers and final accounts, to effect the policy according to the following information.

Required provision for bad debts (5% of debtors)	Bad debts	Balance of debtors
19-0	460	8,980
19-1	510	10,440
19-2	330	13,960
19-3	690	12,720

Calculation of provision:
19-0   449   (8,980 × 5%)
19-1   522   (10,440 × 5%)
19-2   698   (13,960 × 5%)
19-3   636   (12,720 × 5%)
It is assumed that debtor balances do not include the amounts for bad debts.

Comment
The exercise comprises of funds being taken out (or added to) the trading funds of a business to prevent excessive distribution where debts may not have actually been paid by customers.

Unit 7
A method for dealing with adjustments

Overview

1 Final accounts questions usually require a method for dealing with adjustments.
2 An acceptable method for dealing with adjustments usually increases the speed and accuracy for obtaining the final answer.
3 An adaptation of the journal layout is used for this purpose.

Adjustment notes are a familiar part of most final accounts examination questions. The student who can reduce the complexities of such adjustments to straightforward debits and credits is often at an advantage over others who cannot.

Just as it is important to plan out answers in advance when writing essay-type examination questions, so too is it important to consider the effect of the adjustments before preparing final accounts. A simple method is to use the journal format as the basis for considering the effect of such adjustments, remembering that each must have a double entry.

The journal format

	Dr	Cr
Description		

Instead of the traditional format this can be amended to:

1 Use the debit and credit columns for instructions about entries — namely which account is to be debited and which credited. An abbreviated notation for the names of final accounts can be used.
2 Enter the amount in a third column adjacent to but inset from the debit.
3 Add a description to merely list the adjustment.

Illustration
From the question on company accounts at the start of the section on page 74 (which is completed in Section 5 Unit 1 on Company Accounts page 174):

		Dr	Cr
1 Closing stock	£ 20,000	BS	T a/c
2 Rent (rent & rates)	£ 1,000	P & L a/c	BS
3 Depreciation — motor vehicles	£ 8,000	P & L a/c	BS
6 Rent (receivable)	£ 300	BS	P & L a/c

Notes 4 & 5 relate specifically to companies, but will be included for purpose of illustration — principles discussed in the later unit and section.

| 4 Final dividend (proposed) | £ 6,000 | P & L (Appropriation) | BS |
| 5 Paid up shares | £100,000 | — | — |

105

The notation is:
BS = Balance sheet
T a/c = Trading account
P & L a/c = Profit & loss account
P & L (Appropriation) = Profit & loss appropriation account.

It is recommended that this or a similar method be used for adjustments when preparing final accounts.

Unit 8
Examination notes on final accounts questions

Overview

1 To test the student's understanding of accounting theory some complications may be introduced into final accounts.
2 These do not detract from the basic process of preparing final accounts.
3 What is required is a full appreciation of the trial balance.
4 Examples are given; the student could think of others.

In order to test the competence of students to adjust information for use in final accounts, examiners may introduce complications into the presentation in the trial balance. The point to remember is that marks are awarded for correct answers and small errors are not going to be sufficient to prevent a pass. A student who has practised examination questions will know that the prime aspects of final accounts remain irrespective of what 'tricks' are introduced.

A few tricks are detailed here for educational reasons to ask you to think about their implications. Obviously these are not exhaustive but will provide sufficient insight for the resourceful student. Most of these items are minor deviations from the information we have so far encountered in the trial balance. The debit and credit entry has to be recognized by the student.

	Dr	Cr
Debtor and creditors – one balance relates to outstanding sales and the other to outstanding purchases.	Debtor	Creditor
Discounts – there are two types of discount allowed and received, these are not distinguished	Discount allowed	Discount received

Purchases & sales
− the most fundamental debit & credit distinction, but little indication is given of which is which.

	Purchases	Sales

Returns
− outward and inward, one affects the sales the other purchases.

	Returns inward	Returns outward

Carriage (both in this case are debits)
− inwards and outwards, one increases the cost of purchases the other is just a delivery expense. Note carriage inwards is added to purchases in the trading account.

inwards
T a/c
outwards
P&L a/c

Questions

Adjustments to final accounts

1 From the following trial balance of A Bone you are to prepare final accounts for year ending 31 March 19-1

	Dr	Cr
Land and buildings	1,036,280	
Fixtures and fittings	133,891	
Motor vehicles	335,712	
Capital		1,503,382
Drawings	63,288	
Debtors	100,026	
Creditors		150,433
Cash in hand	15,134	
Bank balance	30,218	
Wages & salaries	214,110	
Administrative expenses	23,996	
Vehicle expenses	17,444	
Building repairs	3,081	
Light and heat	20,729	
Sales		836,211
Purchases	424,199	
Opening stock	50,021	
Sales returns	4,234	
Purchase returns		3,187
Discount allowed	56,753	
Discount received		35,903
	£2,529,116	£2,529,116

Notes
1 Closing stock £68,814
2 Wages outstanding amounted to £2,711
3 Electricity owed for period £389
4 Administration expenses included £574 for rates that had been paid in advance
5 Vehicle expenses owed amounted to £84

Answer guide: GP = £429,758; NP = £126,938; Balance Sheet totals £1,720,649 (ledger method).

2 From the trial balance of D Fernside you are asked to prepare a Trading, Profit and Loss Account and Balance Sheet for the year ending 31 May 19-5

	Dr	Cr
Purchases	98,080	
Sales		185,630
Returns inwards	3,121	
Returns outwards		2,343
Stock at 1 June 19-4	25,554	
Plant and machinery	52,900	
Fixtures and fittings	14,240	
Motor vehicles	25,790	
Discount received		10,924
Discount allowed	19,636	
Wages and salaries	38,440	

Rent and rates	14,600	
Administrative expenses	3,080	
Carriage inwards	496	
Carriage outwards	869	
Motor vehicle expenses	8,330	
Capital		105,217
Debtors and creditors	15,216	36,112
Drawings	9,300	
Bank balance	10,020	
Cash in hand	554	
	£340,226	£340,226

Notes
1. Carriage outwards accrued was £36
2. Stock at 31 May 19-5 £33,611
3. Rates prepaid were £631 and rent owing was £974
4. Motor vehicle expenses outstanding were £347
5. Wages owed amounted to £723
6. Administrative expenses included a stock of office supplies value at £191

Note Stock is a type of prepayment

3 From the trial balance of L Hirst you are asked to prepare an Income Statement and Position Statement for the year ended 30 November 19-9.

	Dr	Cr
Purchases & sales	60,180	115,495
Returns inward	5,113	
Returns outward		2,734
Capital		69,178
Drawings	10,265	
Debtors	15,046	
Creditors		31,229
Opening stock	19,622	
Delivery costs	3,550	
Vehicle maintenance & expenses	2,117	
Building repairs	1,010	
Wages & salaries	25,978	
Rent & rates	9,210	
Light & heat	4,330	
Bank overdraft		10,711
Machinery	55,770	
Fixtures	3,360	
Motor vehicles	12,180	
Cash balance	1,616	
	£229,347	£229,347

Notes
1. Electricity prepaid due to error in bill £96
2. Building repair costs outstanding £1,045
3. Gas outstanding £153
4. Closing stock £25,788
5. Vehicle maintenance unpaid £522
6. Delivery costs paid in advance £108

Answer guide: GP = £59,102; NP = £11,391; Balance Sheet totals = £70,304 (vertical method).

4 From the trial balance of G Lincoln you are asked to prepare a Trading, Profit and Loss Account and Balance Sheet for the year ending 30 September 19-7.

	Dr	Cr
Capital		169,992
Drawings	25,150	
Land and buildings	88,500	
Plant and machinery	23,630	
Fixtures and fittings	12,140	
Motor vehicles	8,810	
Purchases and sales	75,050	156,336
Returns inward and outward	8,984	3,367
Carriage inwards	342	
Carriage outwards	821	
Administrative expenses	32,011	
Trade debtors and creditors	36,160	51,386
Stock at 1 October 19-6	25,142	
Discount received and allowed	10,130	5,680
Bank balance	14,441	
Cash in hand	1,228	
Wages and salaries	24,222	
	£386,761	£386,761

Notes
1. Stock at 30 September 19-7 £29,175
2. Carriage inwards prepaid amounted to £28
3. Administrative expenses contained amounts paid in advance for rent £3,066 and rates £1,199
4. Wages outstanding amounted to £521
5. Carriage outward outstanding was £256

5 The following trial balance was extracted from the books of L Pirrie on 31 December 19-4.

	Dr	Cr
Capital account		9,000
Drawings account	700	
Purchases	5,221	
Sales		14,984
Returns outwards		424
Returns inwards	182	
Stock January 1st 19-4	1,146	
Salaries	628	
Manufacturing wages	3,856	
Leasehold factory	2,500	
Rent, rates and insurance	694	
Carriage inwards	231	
Carriage outwards	324	
Office expenses	952	
Plant and machinery	2,400	
Bad debts provision January 1st 19-4		324
Factory fuel	795	
Discounts received		118
Discounts allowed	100	
Sundry debtors	4,021	
Sundry creditors		1,698
Cash at bank	1,240	

Cash in hand	221	
Office furniture	350	
Travellers salaries and commission	987	
	£26,548	£26,548

You are required to prepare Trading and Profit and Loss Accounts and Balance Sheet after taking the following adjustments into consideration.
1 Depreciation to be written off: leasehold factory 5%; plant and machinery 10%, office furniture 5%
2 Provision for bad debts to be made up to £400
3 Value of stock at 31 December 19-4 was £1,429
4 Wages amounting to £57 had accrued due but had not been paid on closing the books
5 Unexpired insurance premiums amounting to £68 are to be carried forward to next year

6 A Flowers is in business as a florist and landscape gardener. The following trial balance is extracted from his books at 30 September 19-3.

	Dr £	Cr £
Capital account		12,500
Freehold nursery and gardens	6,198	
Leasehold warehouse and office	5,547	
Loose tools	700	
Workmen's wages	2,586	
Rent and rates	870	
Purchases	9,642	
Sales		17,894
Charges for constructing customers' gardens		1,963
Stock 1 October 19-2	3,861	
Returns outwards		94
Returns inwards	39	
Carriage inwards	127	
Carriage outwards	98	
Insurance	118	
Office salaries	697	
Discounts received		137
Discounts allowed	100	
Motor lorries	1,900	
Office furniture	320	
Lease on mortgage at 10% per annum		2,000
Interest account	100	
Bank charges	36	
Sundry debtors	3,742	
Sundry creditors		2,520
Heating and lighting	107	
Advertising	975	
Bank overdraft		462
Cash in hand	107	
Provision for bad debts 1 October 19-2		300
	£37,870	£37,870

Prepare trading, profit and loss accounts for year ended 30 September 19-3 and a balance sheet as at that date after taking the following adjustments into consideration:

1 Office salaries £32 had accrued due on 30 September 19-3.
2 Insurance £12 had been paid in advance.
3 Interest for half year to 30 September 19-3 on loan and mortgage had accrued due.
4 Provide Depreciation: motor lorries 15%: loose tools 25%:
                     office furniture 5%: leasehold premises £547.
5 Provision for bad debts to be increased to £400.
6 Stock on hand at 30 September 19-3 was valued at £4,062.

7 B Clewless a retailer of limited accounting and business knowledge has prepared a Trial Balance at the year end — 31 December, 19-5 as follows:

	Dr		Cr
Purchases	36,300	Sales	45,800
Opening stock	6,500	Returns inwards	300
Closing stock	7,000	Returns outwards	200
Wages and salaries	6,000	Light and heat	600
Bank charges	200	Discounts allowed	900
Rent payable	390	Discounts received	610
Rent receivable	260	Capital — 1.1.19-5.	18,480
Rates	560	Drawings	3,080
Insurance	840	Debtors	4,800
Bad debts written off	800	Cash	80
Trade creditors	4,000	Provision for	
Bank overdraft	2,000	depreciation	
Motor vehicles — at cost	6,000	Motor vehicle	
Premises — at cost	7,000	1.1.19-5.	3,000
	£77,850		£77,850

Notes:
1 Depreciation on motor vehicles to be provided at 25% on cost
2 Rates prepaid £160
3 Insurance prepaid £240
4 Light and heat owing £400

Required:
a) Amended trial balance at 31 December, 19-5
b) Trading and profit and loss accounts for the year ended 31 December 19-5
c) Balance sheet as at 31 December, 19-5

Accruals and prepayments in ledger accounts

8 Adjustments — expenditure and income.

1	*Account*	*Amount paid*	*Transfer to P & L*	*Balance c/d*
	a) Wages	4,650	4,800	—
	b) Telephone	233	—	67 Cr
	c) Heating	3,230	—	208 Dr
	d) Rent	—	5,550	650 Cr
	e) Expenses	1,776	1,540	—
2	*Account*	*Amount paid*	*Transfer to P & L*	*Balance c/d*
	a) Insurance	540	—	36 Dr
	b) Advertising	1,219	—	285 Cr
	c) Lighting	—	780	25 Dr
	d) Rates	2,334	4,620	—
	e) Wages	108	214	—
3	*Account*	*Amount paid*	*Transfer to P & L*	*Balance c/d*
	a) Rent	2,587	3,000	—
	b) Interest	506	580	—
	c) Fees	—	126	36 Dr
	d) Commission	1,210	—	58 Cr
	e) Discount	1,998	1,998	—

4	Account	Amount paid	Transfer to P & L	Balance c/d
a)	Interest	334	–	88 Dr
b)	Commission	774		91 Dr
c)	Discount	587	587	–
d)	Fees	1,514	1,404	–
e)	Rent	1,206	1,376	–

5	Account	Amount paid	Transfer to P & L	Balance c/d
a)	Wages	3,500	3,650	–
b)	Telephone	422	–	112 Dr
c)	Heating & lighting	1,050	–	Nil
d)	Rent & rates	–	780	115 Dr
e)	Expenses	130	–	130 Cr

9 Complete the missing figures and state what they represent.

1   *Rent Account*

19-4				19-4			
March	31	Bank	30	Dec	31	Profit & loss a/c	120
July	1	Bank	30				
Oct	3	Bank	30				
Dec	31	Balance c/d					
			120				120
				19-5			
				Jan	1	Balance b/d	

2   *Electricity Account*

19-1				19-1			
Jan	4	Cash	45	Jan	1	Balance b/d	45
March	28	Cash	45	Dec	31	Profit & loss a/c	
June	30	Cash	45				
Sept	29	Cash	45				
Dec	31	Cash	45				

3   *Gas Account*

19-7				19-7			
March	31	Bank	200	Jan	1	Balance b/d	50
June	30	Bank	200	Dec	31	Profit & loss a/c	400
Sept	30	Bank	200			Balance c/d	
			600				600

19-8			
Jan	1	Balance b/d	

4   *Fees Earned*

19-3				19-3			
Jan	1	Balance b/d	4,000	Jan	4	Bank	3,600
Dec	31	Profit & loss		June	14	Bank	20,530
				Sept	23	Bank	
				Dec	31	Balance c/d	5,400
			48,410				

19-4			
Jan	1	Balance b/d	5,400

5   Rent Received

19-5				19-5			
Jan	1	Balance b/d		Feb	18	Bank	6,112
Dec	31	Profit & loss	20,787	May	3	Cash	813
				July	11	Bank	3,412
				Sept	14	Cash	955
				Nov	23	Bank	4,830
				Dec	31	Balance c/d	

19-6
Jan   1   Balance b/d   8,324

10 The final accounts of A Parfitt are made up to 30 September every year.

Parfitt let buildings to D Ganny and P Dean. D Ganny paid Parfitt £180 on 30 June 19-8, amounting to rent for the month of July. But Dean at the same date owed Parfitt £130 for the rent for June 19-8.

The year 19-9 saw the payment by Ganny of £1,800 ten months rent and from Dean £1,820 fourteen months rent to 31 July 19-9. The rent due from Ganny for June 19-9 was not paid until July 19-9.

Show the rent receivable account in the ledger of A Parfitt for the year to 30 June 19-9. No personal accounts for Ganny or Dean are required.
Note
The buildings were first let as follows:
(i) to Dean from 1st June 19-8.
(ii) to Ganny from 1st July 19-8.

11 T Briars has a rental agreement that permits sub-letting, but requires him to pay £4,800 per annum.

He sub-lets parts to Hennesey and Noble at a rental of £2,700 and £2,100 per annum respectively. On 1 January 19-6 Briars had paid his rent up to date, but Hennesey's rent was four months in arrears and Noble had paid his rent up to 30 April 19-6.

During the year: Briars paid his rent at the end of each quarter, and did in fact pay £2,400 on 1 October. Briars received the following sums from Hennesey 12 January £750, 2 February £150, 3 April £900, 25 August £900 and 30 November £1,800. Briars also received from Noble £700 on 30 April. All receipts and payments were made through the bank.

You are required to show accounts for rent payable and receivable in Briar's ledgers for year ending 31 December 19-6. There is no need to keep personal accounts for Hennesey and Noble for the purposes of this exercise.

12 Harris let premises to Hogan and Hodges on a quarterly basis. Harris himself paid rent of £1,450 quarterly. Annual payments by Hogan and Hodges amounted to £5,300 and £4,600 respectively. Financial years run from July to June.

On September 30 Harris paid £1,450 by cash, on December 31 the same amount by cheque. On March 31 Harris paid cash £900. On July 1 Hogan owed a quarters rent, but by June 30 Hodges had already paid his rent. During the year payments were made by Hogan on October 1 and March 8 of £2,650 in cash on each occasion. Hodges paid £1,150 also by cash, on January 4.

You are asked to show rent accounts – receivable and payable, in the books of Harris for year ending June 30 19-5. Personal accounts are not required.

Answer guide: 10 Opening balances: Debit £130; Credit £180.

Depreciation in ledger accounts

13 A company starts in business on 1 January 19-1. The following assets were purchased:-
1 January 19-1, 2 cars for £5,000 each, paying cash
1 July   19-2, 5 cars for £6,000 each, paying by cheque.
Depreciation is calculated on a straight line basis at 20% pa, for complete years irrespective of when purchased during any one year.

Write up for the Cars a/c and the Provision for Depreciation a/c for the years ended 31 December 19-1 and 19-2.

14 A company starts in business on 1 January 19-1
   The following assets were purchased:
   1 January   19-1, 1 machine costing £8,000, paying in cash
   1 July   19-2, 2 machines costing £5,000 each, paying by cheque
   30 October 19-2   1 machine costing £6,000, paying by cheque
   1 April   19-3   1 machine costing £4,000, paying cash.
   Depreciation is calculated on a reducing balance basis at 10% pa, for complete years irrespective of when purchased during any one year.
   Show a) the Machinery a/c, and
         b) the Provision for Depreciation a/c
   for years ending 31 December 19-1, 19-2 and 19-3 and Balance Sheet and Profit and Loss extracts for periods.

15 A company's financial year ends on 31 December. Two large vans were purchased for £13,000 on 1 January 19-1 and three vans for £20,000 on 1 October 19-2, payment was by cheque in both cases.
   The original two vans are sold for £3,850 on 30 June 19-3.
   Depreciation is calculated on a straight line basis at 20% pa, and should be calculated on a monthly basis, reflecting a more accurate assessment than otherwise.
   Show the following: a) Vans a/c,
                       b) Provision for Depreciation a/c, and
                       c) Disposal a/c
   for the years ending 31 December 19-1, 19-2, 19-3, and a Balance sheet and Profit and Loss a/c extracts for periods.

16 A company starts in business on 1 January 19-1. The following purchases and sales of machinery take place, all transactions are through the bank account.
   1.1.19-1   2 machines purchased for £16,000
   1.10.19-1   1 machine purchased for £8,000
   1.7.19-3   1 machine purchased for £15,000
   1.10.19-4   2 machines sold for £12,500
               (originally cost £16,000 on 1.1.19-1)
   Depreciation is calculated on a reducing balance basis at 10% pa, taking account of purchases and disposals on a monthly basis.
   Show a) Machinery a/c
         b) Provision for Depreciation a/c
         c) Disposals a/c
   for the years ended 31st December, 19-1, 19-2, 19-3, 19-4 and a Balance Sheet and Profit and Loss extracts for periods.

   Answer guide: 2 Total depreciation machine £2,168 (year 3)
                 Total depreciation £5,608 (year 3)

17 R Ltd bought four vehicles at £4,000 each on 1 January, 19-3.
   On 7.7.19-5 he sold one of these vehicles for £1,850, replacing it on the same day with a new vehicle costing £3,800.
     You are required to write up the following accounts (where relevant) for the year ended 31 December 19-3, 19-4, 19-5 and 19-6:
   a) Motor vehicles a/c
   b) Disposal of motor vehicles a/c
   c) Provision for depreciation a/c
   assuming R Ltd depreciates his vehicles
     (i) at 25% straight line per annum
     (ii) at 30% reducing balance per annum
   Note
   R. Ltd provide a full year's depreciation in the year of acquisition and none in the year of disposal.

   Answer guide: Motor vehicle a/c – closing balance £15,800; Depreciation a/c – closing balance £13,900; Disposal a/c – Profit & Loss £150.

18 Pusher commenced business on 1 January 19-9 with two lorries A and B. A cost £10,000 and B cost £16,000. On 3 March 19-0 A was written off in an accident and Pusher received £7,500 from the Insurance Company. This vehicle was replaced on 10 March 19-0 by C which cost £20,000.

A fully year's depreciation is charged in the year of acquisition and no depreciation is charged in the year of disposal.

a) You are required to show the appropriate extracts from Pusher's balance sheet and profit and loss accounts for the years to 31/12/-9, 31/12/-0 and 31/12/-1 assuming that:
   (i) the vehicles are depreciated at 20% on the straight line method and
   (ii) the vehicles are depreciated at 25% on the reducing balance method.
b) Comment briefly on the pros and cons of using the straight line and reducing balance methods of depreciation.

Association of Certified Accountants

Answer guide: Motor vehicle a/c − closing balance £3,600; Depreciation a/c: Straight line − closing balance £1,760; Reducing balance − closing balance − £1,800; Disposal a/c: Profit & Loss balance: Straight line − £50; Reducing balance-nil.

Bad debts in ledger accounts

19 From the following information prepare a bad debts account and provision account and show the entries as they would appear in final accounts.

Year to 31 December	Debtors end of year − after bad debts written off	Bad debts written-off during year	Debts estimated to be non-collectable
1 19-6	26,000	734	540
19-7	27,500	812	780
19-8	28,950	928	890
19-9	31,300	545	1,020
19-0	32,650	692	1,050

Consider that the business to which the above set of figures apply, started trading in 19-6.

2 19-3	10,560	874	
19-4	11,220	1,131	5% debtors after
19-5	13,480	924	deducting bad debts
19-6	15,720	722	written off
19-7	16,660	1,203	

The closing provision for doubtful debts in 19-2 was £330

3 Year to 31 March

19-0	53,610	1,812	1,640
19-1	74,880	2,021	2,350
19-2	65,390	2,565	1,900
19-3	78,104	2,370	2,580
19-4	73,220	2,740	2,150
19-5	68,530	3,005	3,420

The opening provision for bad debts in year ended 31 March 19-0 was £1,490

4 Year to 30 June	Debtors end of year − before bad debts written off		Debts estimated to be non-collectable (rounded to nearest £)
19-3	31,340	1,270	5% of debtors after
19-4	36,730	3,310	deducting bad debts
19-5	40,150	1,430	written off
19-6	43,450	2,060	
19-7	46,780	1,840	

The opening provision for bad debts in year ended 30 June 19-3 was £1,156

Answer guide: 1 Year 7 Bad debts £812; Provision £780.

Section IV
Collection of data

Unit 1　A diagrammatic presentation of the accounting system
Unit 2　Accounts documentation
Unit 3　Collection and processing of accounting information I
　　　　　– daybooks and returns
Unit 4　The cash book
Unit 5　The petty cash book
Unit 6　Stock
Unit 7　Drawings
Unit 8　Classification of Accounts
Unit 9　Collection and Processing of Accounting Information II
　　　　　– journal entries
Unit 10　Goodwill and other reducible assets
Unit 11　Accounting for Value Added Tax

Unit 1
A diagrammatic presentation of the accounting system

Overview

Double entry
1 The diagram illustrates primarily purchases and sales systems.

2 Systems are shown through the documentation and books of account to the trial balance.

3 The system includes treatment of assets and expenses.

4 Capital is introduced to enable the trial balance to balance.

5 Accounts procedures are shown in Appendix 2
　Sales on credit
　Purchases on credit
　Payments

6 Accounts documents are shown in Appendix 2
　Order
　Delivery note
　Invoice
　Goods received note (internal to acknowledge receipt)
　Statement.

A DIAGRAMMATIC PRESENTATION OF THE DOUBLE ENTRY SYSTEM

– four sections: **i** Purchases (including expenses); **ii** Capital; **iii** Sales and **iv** Trial Balance

i PURCHASES

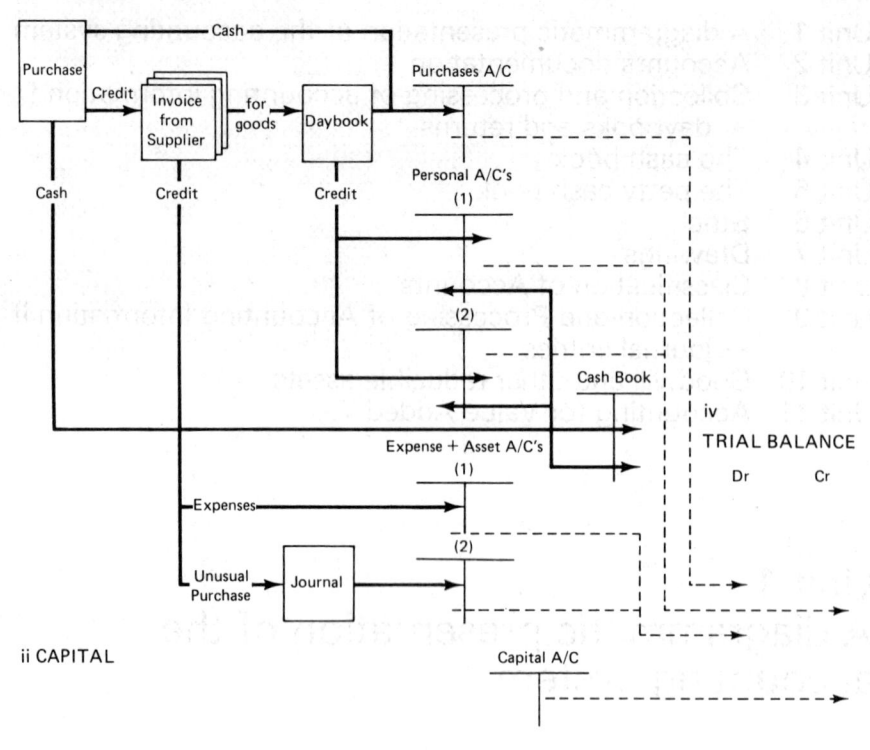

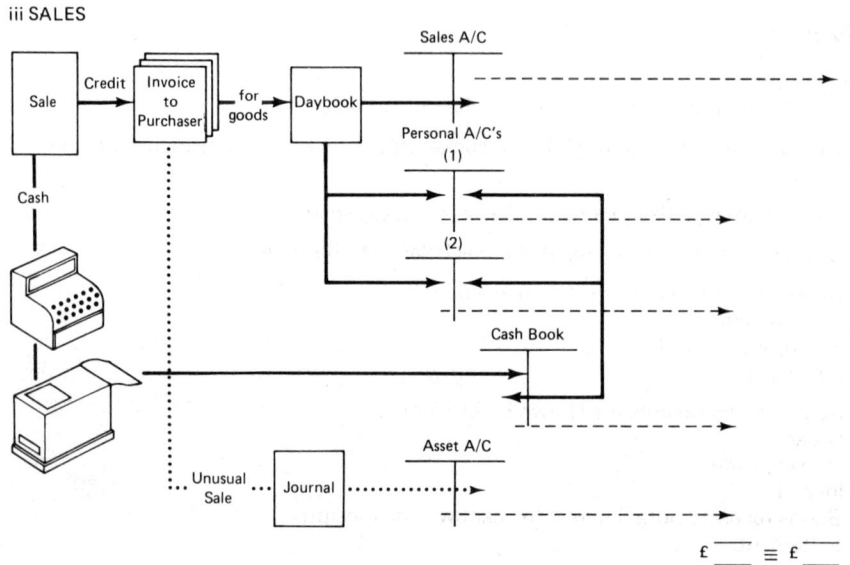

ii CAPITAL

iii SALES

iv TRIAL BALANCE

Unit 2
Accounts documentation

Overview

1 Different procedures and requirements of businesses over the years have produced different systems and descriptions for documents eg Daybooks described in Unit 3, pages 122–5.

2 Arithmetic (or procedural) accuracy is always required. This is not to be confused with alternative principles for treatment of an entry.

3 Original documents used in accounting for trade transactions are:
   a) Purchases
      (i) Order
      (ii) Delivery note
      (iii) Goods received note – goods in note
      (iv) Invoice
      (v) Statement
   b) Sales
      (i) Order
      (ii) Delivery note
      (iii) Goods received note – goods in note
      (iv) Invoice
      (v) Statement

   It will be noticed that the documents are the same but the source and direction of flow will not be.

4 Other activities and their records are as follows:
   a) Purchases not for re-sale eg fixed assets, and
   b) Expenses – distinguished as to whether evidence for occurrence is created internally or externally.

5 An illustration of procedures and documentation will be shown in Appendix 2.

Accountancy as a body of knowledge is an amalgamation of experience drawn from practice over the years as was mentioned in the introduction. It is a legacy of this joining from experience that causes different ideas on what is 'right' and different names for documentation and records to remain. This point is echoed in this section and elsewhere in the book.

The idea that there is no absolute answer to many accounting problems may appear strange to students, especially when in another breath, the accountant shows such concern for making the books balance. Is such arithmetic accuracy (for that is what it is) compatible with certain vague ideas about the valuation of assets and the like? Some progress has already been made to prove that these two positions are not incompatible and are extremely necessary, and by the end of the text, I hope you will see some sense in it. Starting a discussion of accounting principles with one of the end products may seem curious. It is suggested that in a building process (such as accountancy is), an understanding of the intermediate principles involved can be more easily achieved once the final picture is known. Going right back to the collection of data – the other end of the spectrum – it is hoped will now be easier, and will provide the student with some immediate answers to problems, as they arise, that might not otherwise have been possible.

Original documents used in accounting

Illustrations of systems and documents are provided in Appendix 2. The major transactions consist of:

1 purchases (for resale),
2 sales,
3 other purchases (not for resale),
4 expenses.

In many cases these transactions are conducted for credit that involves delivery and some agreement to pay at a later stage.

1 Purchases (for re-sale)

The process of purchasing goods for resale begins with an agreement by authorized persons in a business – with a sole proprietor it is usually the owner.

The next step is to place an order on an official order form. (Even when placed by telephone in the smallest business, it is usual for a verbal order to be followed by a written acknowledgement.) The supplier will usually process this order and confirm it stating the delivery date.

The next important stage from the accounting point of view is the delivery or receipt of an invoice. Usually delivery is made first and has as evidence a delivery note, followed by an invoice sent through the post. This flow of documentation may not always be the case, for instance the goods may be delayed and the invoice arrive first. Whatever the case the invoice, delivery note and order should at some point be matched up, certainly before payment is made.

Accountants recognize invoicing as the fundamental acceptance of a liability and the invoice as written evidence of this.

Summary

```
                          Goods
                            ↓
Order to supplier ——→ Delivery note received ——→ Invoice received
```

2 Sales

On this occasion the origination of the order occurs outside the business at the customer's premises.

In this case the positions are reversed and the customer will raise the order and the business the delivery note and invoice. The documents are essentially the same and serve a similar but opposite purpose considering the relationship between parties.

Summary

```
                       Goods
                         ↓
Order to customer  →  Delivery note sent  →  Invoice sent
```

Differences in presentation between documents sent to and from respective sources will almost certainly be apparent except where, coincidentally, both businesses are using the same standardized system.

3 Other purchases (not for resale)

In order to operate successfully a business not only has to purchase items with which to trade but also assets that enable it to trade. These transactions usually occur less frequently and are usually held for a long period of time – long term assets, eg buildings and plant and machinery.

Fundamentally, the double entry procedure to purchase is the same. What is different is that they are not usually a routine transaction, require careful planning before making a decision, and then proper authorization from top management or a committee of managers.

4 Expenses

Expenses occur in many different forms and original evidence will vary according to the type of expense. For instance expenses that are incurred through suppliers eg gas, electricity and fuel oil will occur regularly and be invoiced, as a statement of use. Other expenses, also from outside suppliers may arise less frequently, eg paint for redecorating premises. These items will again be invoiced. However, other expenses will originate internally and require an entirely different record and method of collection eg wages. These aspects of recording and managing are more properly dealt with by the cost accountant, but it has to be remembered that the system will have to be sufficiently reliable to provide a record of say wages actually incurred, so that they can be used as an expense in the profit and loss account. Such records for wages may be based on a clocking-in system.

Note
Statements are used by suppliers for the purpose of providing customers with a periodic record (usually monthly) of credit sales made that represent purchases of the receiving organization. Set against the record of items contracted for, there will be the amount of funds paid by customers for these goods, plus any refunds or reductions, thus providing a current total of the amount outstanding or owed.

Goods received notes (goods in notes) are raised internally by the purchaser to inform all departments interested in the receipt of particular goods. Some systems dispense with this; much would depend on the individual organization and its requirements.

Unit 3
The collection and processing of accounting information I – daybooks and returns daybooks

Overview

1 Daybooks are the first stage for entering credit sales and purchases information in accounting books.
2 Daybooks are lists of entries.
3 There are four uses:
 a) Purchases,
 b) Sales,
 c) Returns outward, and
 d) Returns inward.
4 Returns apply to both sales (returns inward) and purchases (returns outward).
5 Examples of daybooks are given.

The use of daybooks is the first stage for entering accounting information on sales and purchases in to the main books of account. Such recording has to be carried out in a logical and organized manner according to the needs and requirements of a business. Daybooks are used for listing purchases and sales that are made on credit, ie sales and purchases made for cash (immediate payments) are not included.

There are four daybooks that are used in most businesses. These are:

1 Purchases daybook
2 Sales daybook
3 Purchases returns daybook
4 Sales returns daybook.

First of all just consider purchase and sales daybooks, although you can no doubt think of occasions when purchases and sales have to be returned for one reason or another eg faulty goods.

Sometimes instead of daybook, the name 'journal' is given, ie Purchases journal. (I would like to see the use of the description 'journal' restricted to a method of recording more complex information which will be discussed in a further unit, (pp 147–59). However, while we are considering descriptions let me also mention sales returns and purchases returns daybooks are often referred to differently as returns inward and returns outward daybooks, respectively.)

ie *Sales returns daybook* ≡ *returns inward daybook.*

Purchase returns daybook ≡ *returns outward daybook.*

The terms inward and outward reflect the movement of goods relative to the business. Returns that come inwards have to be related to sales because sales themselves form the outflow of goods. Returns that go outwards, by the same token, have to be related to purchases because purchases form the inflow of goods. Therefore returns of purchases are purchases sent back to suppliers and returns of sales are sales returned from customers. The trading account (as shown in the trial balance unit) will indicate the place of returns in final accounts.

Opening stock		X	Sales	X	
Add purchases	X		Less returns inward	X	X
less returns outward	X	X			

Thus after deducting returns, the accountant is referring to net sales and net purchases respectively.

The daybook, as has been stated, is a method of listing recent purchases and sales transactions. Presumably they were called daybooks because they were closed daily. This procedure is currently followed but not necessarily daily. The balances once totalled can be periodically transferred to other accounts. The time period depends on the frequency of transactions, the type of business and its requirements.

The layout of a daybook in its simplest form is as follows:

| Date | Description | Reference columns | Amount |

The 'reference columns' can be ignored for the purpose of instruction if the student accepts them as necessary in practice when entries are much more numerous and cross-referencing is vital. Examples of the four types of daybook will now be given.

Sales daybook

Date		Description	Amount £
May	2	J Atkins	55
	2	D Fennel	210
	2	F Jones	89
	3	S Wood	36
	4	B Flowers	572
	4	M Linnel	363
	10	Transferred to general ledger	1,325

Purchases daybook

Date		Description	Amount £
May	1	E Saint	28
	1	J Johns	96
	2	A Palmer	229
	2	R Peach	438
	4	T Bower	53
	4	W Anderson	171
	10	Transferred to general ledger	1,015

Returns inward daybook

Date		Description	Amount £
May	16	S Wood	10
	17	P Dunn	48
	20	Transferred to general ledger	58

Returns outward daybook

Date		Description	Amount £
May	15	A Palmer	67
	17	T Butt	86
	20	Transferred to general ledger	153

The general ledger would contain the Sales, Purchases, Returns inward and Returns outward accounts as follows:

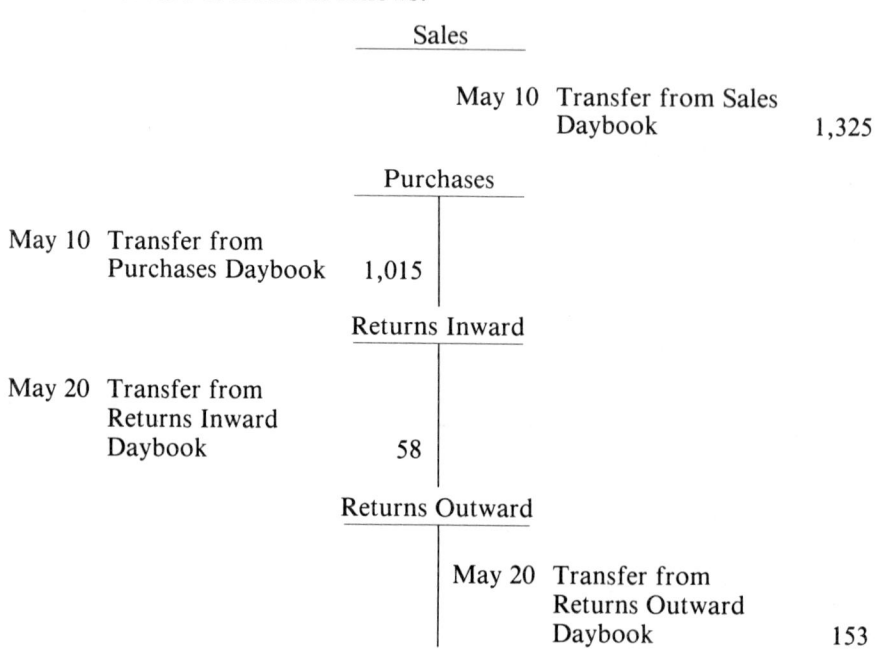

Sales

May 10 Transfer from Sales Daybook   1,325

Purchases

May 10 Transfer from Purchases Daybook   1,015

Returns Inward

May 20 Transfer from Returns Inward Daybook   58

Returns Outward

May 20 Transfer from Returns Outward Daybook   153

The purchases ledger would contain the accounts of the various creditors

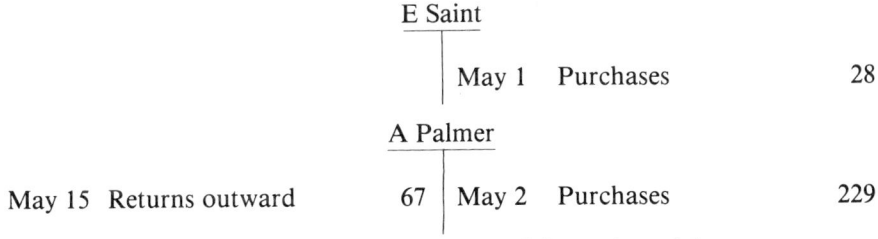

E Saint

	May 1 Purchases	28

A Palmer

| May 15   Returns outward | 67 | May 2   Purchases | 229 |

The sales ledger would contain the accounts of the various debtors.

J Atkins

| May 2   Sales | 55 | | |

S Wood

| May 3   Sales | 36 | May 16   Returns Inward | 10 |

. . . and so on.

Note Further points on the classification of accounts can be found in Unit 8 of this section.

Unit 4
The cash book

Overview

1 The cash book, so termed, is an amalgamation of the cash account and bank account retaining the ledger format, hence the description two column cash book.

2 Discount accounts are inset to cash and bank on both the debit and credit sides of the ledger layout:
Debit   =   discount allowed
Credit =   discount received
– hence the description three column cash book.

3 The discount columns do not form part of the double entry system and are purely a convenient means of collecting discounts together.

4 There is no balancing off of the discount sections.

5 The double entry for discounts is contained in either a separate discount allowed account, or discount received account depending on the nature of the transaction.

6 Each individual discount will be dealt with in the respective personal accounts of debtors and creditors.

7 An extension of the cash book is discussed and illustrated that classifies entries not only into receipts and payments, but also sub-headings for various types of receipt and payment.

The cash book forms an important part in a system of accounts. There are two types, the first contains the cash account and the bank account.

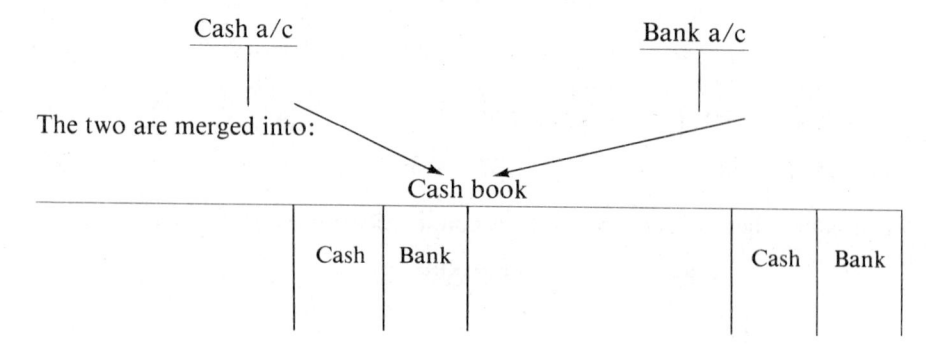

```
         Cash a/c                          Bank a/c
            |                                 |
            |                                 |
The two are merged into:
                          Cash book
```

	Cash	Bank		Cash	Bank

This contains both the cash column and a bank column maintaining the principle of double entry. The second contains the cash account and the bank account but is a development of the former containing the columns for discount.

Cash book

Disc	Cash	Bank		Disc	Cash	Bank

Hence the terms two and three column cash book.

I think it is only necessary to concentrate on the three column version because the same principles that have been applied to both cash account and bank account apply to it and the two column form. The addition of discount is important not only as a development in this context but also because it is:

a) a convenient means of introducing discount into the double entry system, and
b) discount can be noted here on individual transactions and collated into period totals but is not balanced off and is integrated into the double-entry system later (see pp 145–7).

In this manner discount is recorded two ways, on both the goods and services the business buys and the goods and service it sells. In the first case discount (received) is being offered to it to make its purchases cheaper; in the second case discount (allowed) is being granted to its customers, as a cost to the business, in order to make its sales cheaper. Double entry occurs in the personal account of a debtor/creditor and in aggregate transferred to the general ledger (see pp 00) or nominal ledger.

Discount is often given:
1 as part of the terms of trade for a particular product,
2 to assist in prompt payment of accounts eg $2\frac{1}{2}$% for settlement within a month. Sometimes a scale of discounts arises based on the time in which payment is made eg 5% for settlement within two weeks and $2\frac{1}{2}$% for settlement within two to four weeks. Discount shown in the cash book is very largely that related to times of settlement.

The following is an example of a completed three column cash book given the instructions below:

May 1 Brown commences his business and introduces £5,000 capital. The same day he opens a bank account to put the money into.
    2 Brown transfers £1,000 out of the Bank a/c into the Cash a/c.
    3 He agrees to rent business premises for five years and pays one-year's rent £1,250 in advance by cheque.
    4 He buys a second-hand van for £1,600, paying by cheque.
    5 Brown received a loan of £2,000 from E Hebbutt paid into the bank by cheque.
    6 Brown paid for purchases of £600 being granted a 5% discount because he paid cash.
    7 He received payment for sales to the value of £120 from J Hindes who paid by cheque, and he gave no discount.
    8 He received for sales payment from B Goodwin £480; P Sears £40; T Harmer £160; each received a $2\frac{1}{2}$% discount, each paid by cheque.
    8 Brown purchases display fittings off Shelves Ltd for £1,050. He claimed a 10% discount and paid by cheque.
  10 Brown paid for motor expenses and repairs £45 by cash, without getting any discount.
  14 He received further payment for sales from J Hasluck £50; S Mears £100 who paid by cash and were granted 5% discount.

After two weeks' trading Brown's cash book was as follows:

Cash book

Date	Description	Disc	Cash	Bank	Date	Description	Disc	Cash	Bank
May 1	Capital			5,000	May 2	Cash ₵			1,000
2	Bank ₵		1,000		3	Rent			1,250
5	E Hebbutt (loan)			2,000	4	Motor Van			1,600
7	J Hindes			120	6	Purchases	30	570	
8	B Goodwin	12		468	8	Shelves Ltd	105		945
8	P Sears	1		39	10	Motor Van repairs		45	
8	T Harmer	4		156	15	Balance c/d		542	2,988
14	J Hasluck	3	57						
14	S Mears	5	100						
		25	1,157	7,783			135	1,157	7,783
15	Balance b/d		542	2,988					

Discount allowed 25

May 15 Total per cash book

Discount received

May 15 Total per cash book   135

127

Note

1 The collection of discounts allowed and received occurs in the Cash Book from individual entries.

2 The double entry for each occurs in the respective personal accounts.

3 The aggregate discount in the ledgers (discount allowed and discount received accounts) occurs on the same side as in the cash book.

4 The discount accounts are contained in the general ledger.

5 Discount in the cash book is given (usually as a percentage) on gross invoice cost.

6 The difference between discount and gross amount (the net amount) is recorded in either the bank or cash column according to the instructions, on either side of the cash book.

7 The symbol '$\mathcal{C}$' shows the contra entry. This is used where the double entry occurs within the cash book and usually comprises transfers between:
either a) bank and cash, or
      b) cash and bank.

A further worked example may now be useful to illustrate all aspects of the cash book. The following cash book entries are to be made for Jones a trader continuing in business for the month of August.

Aug 1 Opening balances cash at bank and cash in hand £1,590 and £230 respectively.

     5 Sales made to customers in July, payments received by cheque. D Simms £180. T Little £440, D Palmer £70, each deducted 10% discount.

     8 Cash received for sales made to P Small £150, S Marshall £280, A Nixon £330 allowing 10% discount.

   10 Cash paid into bank £500.

   14 Jones paid for servicing and repairs to office machinery by cash £40.

   15 Payment made for purchases of goods for resale invoiced in July: J Hill £900, B Pears £660, 5% discount agreed – payment made by cheque.

   17 Purchased goods for resale off A Truman £50 paid for by cash, no discount granted.

   20 Received payment for sales made earlier in the month from the following debtors F Howell £90, P Francis £170, J Soar £390, S Brown £210, P Smetham £80, all of whom paid by cheque and were allowed 10% discount.

   21 Paid motor expenses by cash £19.

   22 Received payment for sales made in previous month by cheque allowing 5% discount from B Sales £240, G James £920, F Smiles £450,

V Davis £300. Cash sales to various customers were also made during the day, allowing 10% discount, totalling £1,020.

23 Jones decided to buy a new van which was needed, paying by cash £1,000 and cheque £800.

24 Purchases of goods were paid for by cheque from L Lever £220, J McCauley £480, O Glynn £320, J Hill £30, all of whom granted discount of 5% except J Hill.

27 Payments for goods were made by cheque to J Soames £190, L Lever £400, A Gartham £390, F Boothby £90, J Seymour £30, a discount of 10% was taken.

28 A transfer from the bank account to the cash account of £150 was made.

29 Payment for sales was received by cheque from V Davis £200, J Jackson £630, P Small £150, A Divet £230, a 10% discount was deducted by all customers.

29 Payment for purchases was made by Jones out of the bank to J McCauley £860, T Palmer £420, a 5% discount was taken. L Dexter was also paid £55 by cash and no discount was received.

30 Jones purchased a second hand machine for £1,200 from Recondition Ltd paying by cheque.

31 The following debtors settled their accounts by cash and were granted a 5% discount, B Pears £180, F Thornton £280, J McCauley £360 and S Grimes £120.

Cash book

Date	Description	Disc	Cash	Bank	Date	Description	Disc	Cash	Bank
Aug 1	Balance b/d		230	1,590	Aug 10	Bank ₵		500	
2	D Simms	18		162	14	Repairs to office machinery		40	
5	T Little	44		396					
	D Palmer	7		63					
8	P Small	15	135		15	J Hill	45		855
	S Marshall	28	252			B Pears	33		627
	A Nixon	33	297		17	A Truman		50	
10	Cash ₵			500	21	Motor expenses		19	
20	F Howell	9		81					
	P Francis	17		153	23	Van		1,000	800
	J Soar	39		351	24	L Lever	11		209
	S Brown	21		189		J McCauley	24		456
	P Smetham	8		72		O Glynn	16		304
22	B Sales	12		228		J Hill			30
	G James	46		874	27	J Soames	19		171
	F Smiles	23		436		L Lever	40		360
	V Davis	15		285		A Gartham	39		351
	Sales	102	918			F Boothby	9		81
28	Bank ₵		150			J Seymour	3		27
29	V Davis	20		180	28	Cash ₵			150
	J Jackson	63		567	29	J McCauley	43		817
	P Small	15		135		T Palmer	21		399
	A Divet	23		207		L Dexter		55	
31	B Pears	9	171		30	Machinery			1,200
	F Thornton	14	266		31	Balance c/d		1,211	
	J McCauley	18	342						
	S Grimes	6	114						
	Balance c/d			368					
		605	2,875	6,837			303	2,875	6,837
Sept 1	Balance b/d		1,211		Sept 1	Balance b/d			368

Discount Allowed

Aug 31 Total per cash book   605

Discount Received

Aug 31 Total per cash book   303

Treatment of individual discounts

In order that an accurate record of account balances can be maintained, a record of individual discounts must also be kept, and is posted to the appropriate personal account of the party concerned. Using the above example this can be clearly illustrated for sales and purchases.

Sales

Take the account of P Small who made two purchases (let us assume) during the month of August, paying one week after purchase. The transactions were as follows:

1 August £150 of goods, payment 8 August − 10% discount.
22 August £150 of goods, payment 29 August − 10% discount.

P Small

Aug	1	Sales	150	Aug 8	Cash	135
	22	Sales	150		Discount allowed	15
				29	Bank	135
					Discount allowed	15
			300			300

Sales and payments were made in this case within the month, so there is no balance to carry forward.

Purchases

Take the account of J McCauley who, for sake of argument, allows the business two weeks' credit. The transactions disclosed in the Cash Book (where payment had been made) were as follows:
 10 August £480 of goods, payment 24 August 5% discount
 15 August £860 of goods, payment 29 August 5% discount
but McCauley has also sold us goods on 30 August for £550 subject to the same terms.

J McCauley

Aug 24	Bank	456	Aug 10	Purchases	480
	Discount received	24	15	Purchases	860
29	Bank	817	31	Purchases	550
	Discount received	43			
31	Balance c/d	550			
		1,890			1,890
			Sept 1	Balance b/d	550

Thus there is an amount outstanding on the 31 August that is owed to J McCauley for purchases on credit of £550. Further aspects of accounting concerning the use of the cash book will be dealt with under appropriate headings.

Extension of the cash book

The cash book can be extended and used as the basis of an accounting system by classifying different receipts and payments under various sub-headings, as well as entering them according to whether they affect cash or bank. Taking the standard columns for cash and bank (and discount where appropriate) it is merely a matter of inserting additional columns. This usually occurs through the purchase of a lengthened, specially designed cash book with multiple columns, headed when used. A design with fifteen or more columns for receipts and payments is common, see illustration below:

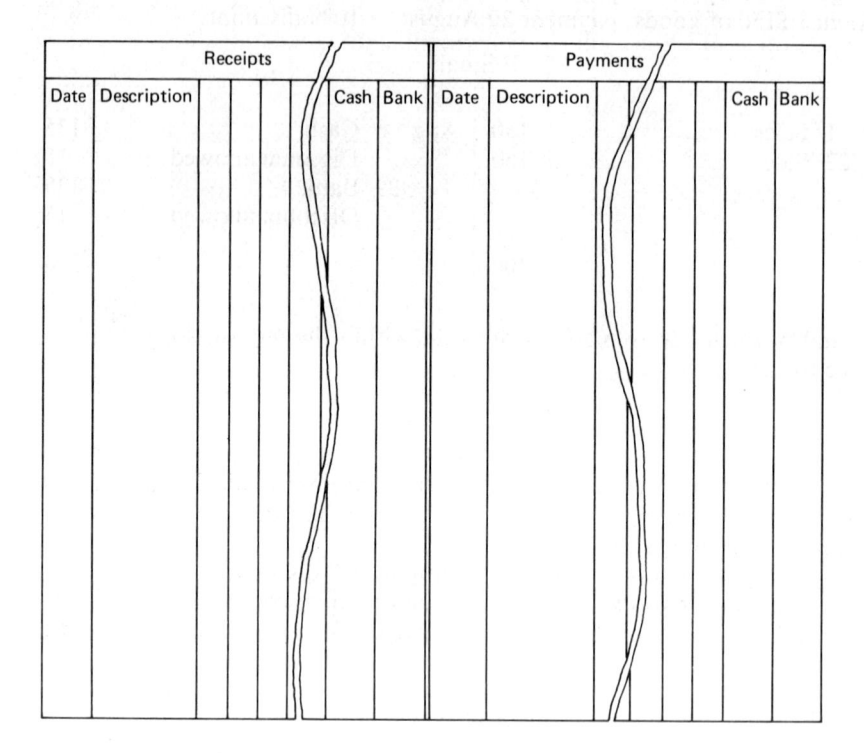

Receipts						Payments					
Date	Description				Cash	Bank	Date	Description			Cash	Bank

Unit 5
The petty cash book

Overview

1 The petty cash book is designed to facilitate the payment of numerous small expenses.
2 The imprest system is used to replenish the fund.
3 At the end of the period the classified minor expenses are transferred to the ledgers.

In most firms, a petty cash book is required to assist in the payment of a variety of small regular expenses. It has a distinctive ruling and is used for the classification of expenses under major headings. Examples of classification are:

postage, travelling, stationery.

Such amounts in total (at the close of an accounting period) will be transferred to a relevant expense heading in the double entry ledger accounts.

Imprest system

A sufficient sum is determined to meet the needs of petty cash expenditure. This forms the initial float and is topped up periodically by the amount of expenditure.

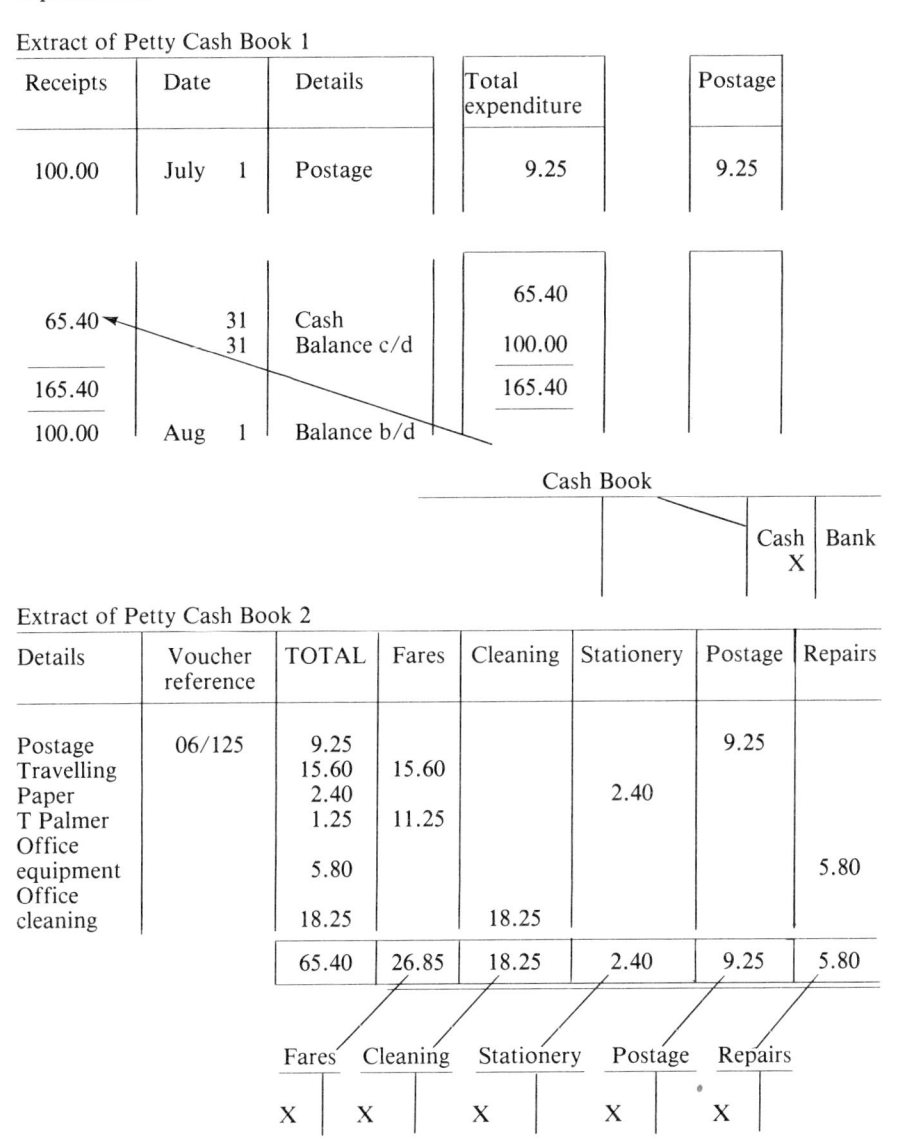

Extract of Petty Cash Book 1

Receipts	Date	Details	Total expenditure	Postage
100.00	July 1	Postage	9.25	9.25
			65.40	
65.40	31	Cash		
	31	Balance c/d	100.00	
165.40			165.40	
100.00	Aug 1	Balance b/d		

Cash Book

	Cash	Bank
	X	

Extract of Petty Cash Book 2

Details	Voucher reference	TOTAL	Fares	Cleaning	Stationery	Postage	Repairs
Postage	06/125	9.25				9.25	
Travelling		15.60	15.60				
Paper		2.40			2.40		
T Palmer		1.25	11.25				
Office equipment		5.80					5.80
Office cleaning		18.25		18.25			
		65.40	26.85	18.25	2.40	9.25	5.80

Fares	Cleaning	Stationery	Postage	Repairs
X	X	X	X	X

Note It is usual for all expenditure to be supported by a voucher and, wherever possible, a receipt.

133

Unit 6
Stock

Overview

1 Consideration has to be given to the positioning of opening and closing stock.
2 A stocktake is used to count closing stock.
3 A valuation has to be made of closing stock.
4 The relevance of stock in final accounts is examined in its constituent parts, namely:
   a) trading account and
   b) balance sheet.
5 Stock is examined in the context of ledger accounts.

The presentation of stock in final accounts is an important aspect in the representation of balances. The two types of stock are: Opening stock Closing stock . . . that occur at different points in the same accounting period, although the closing stock of one period, clearly becomes the opening stock of a consecutive period.

The close of a financial year

At the close of any accounting period it is important to obtain a valuation of goods, remaining unsold, that will be available for sale in the following accounting period. Just because accounts are prepared for a given period, does not prevent a business continuing from one period to the next, with as little disruption as possible. In fact it is important to keep the disruption to a minimum.

Stocktake

The process for arriving at a valuation of goods unsold at the close of a period is known as stocktake. This simply involves a physical count of the goods, under the various types and categories and the assignment of a value to each.

Valuation

What value to take has been the subject of much discussion. Traditionally in most cases it has been cost via various methods of input, but this aspect of accounting requires discussion of methods and bases that are omitted from this book. Further reference should be made to cost and management, and other textbooks.
It is the physical count that is important at this stage.

Illustration

					Sheet No.1	
James Wiley & Son		Stock Sheet				
				Date: 31 March 19-6		
Quantity	Description	Code	Price		£	p
12 doz	Water-tight jars	J006	£15.00 per doz		180.	00
108	Assembly cases	C013	£10 each		1080.	00
20 doz	Knock-down cases	C104	£55.00 per doz		1100.	00
85 stones	Packaging material	P205	£ 0.50 per stone		42.	50
750 yds	PVC sheeting	P209	£ 0.95 per yard		712.	50
30 gross	Brackets	B062	£ 4.30 per gross		129.	00
			. . . and so on			
			Total stock	£		

Final accounts

The trading account

The goods available for sale during the year will comprise:

Opening stock — goods at the start of the year
Plus
Purchases — goods bought during the year.

It is assumed at this stage that the business is purely retail, buying goods/purchases in a completed state, without conducting any conversion or manufacturing activity, thus making the treatment of stock easier.

The record in the trading account with which you are now familiar is:

Opening stock	
Add purchases	————
Less closing stock	————

The input of goods into the business, assuming it to be retail, is always through purchases. The distinction between opening stock and purchases is that opening stock is the balance of purchases remaining unsold at the start of an accounting period, brought forward from earlier periods.

Therefore the opening stock of one period must equal the closing stock of the earlier period. The record of double entry for stock, unlike other items, occurs in the final accounts.

```
        Trading Account 2              Trading Account 3
    |    Opening stock            |    Opening stock            |
    |    Add purchases            |    Add purchases            |
    |                             |                             |
    |    Less closing stock       |    Less closing stock       |
             Credit      the same stock      Debit
             Stock           figure          Stock
```

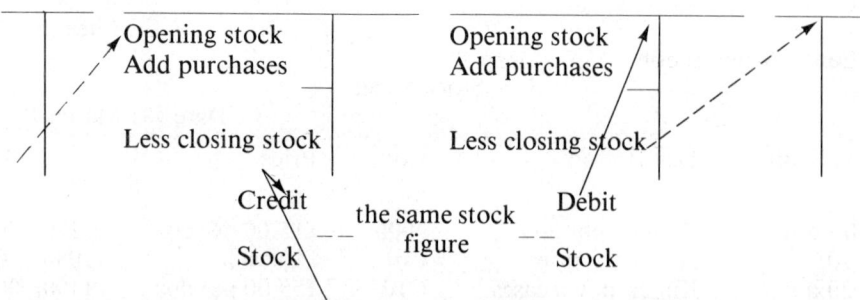

Within the current accounting year once a credit to the trading account has been made a debit has to be raised in the balance sheet.

The balance sheet

```
                    Balance Sheet
                    
                    Fixed Assets
                    
                    Current Assets
                    Stock
```

Closing stock is a current asset and is likely to be partially consumed or changed during the following accounting year. It is because closing stock is an asset (balance sheet debit) and represents value given by the business that it is important, contributing to the surplus assets.

Note Surplus assets ⅛ profit and is available for distribution to the owners. This is why accountants take such care over the valuation of closing stock and attempt to ensure, so far as possible, it is valued correctly.

The ledgers

Opening stock for the period under consideration (the previous period closing stock) is held in the ledger during the period, and usually represented in the trial balance. The double entry occurs in the trading account.

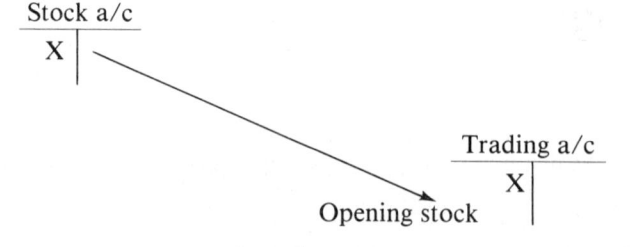

```
         Stock a/c
         X |
                                    Trading a/c
                                    X |
                         Opening stock
```

Closing stock is presented in Ledger accounts in one of two ways; either (i) or (ii) in the Trading Account below (both are regarded as *credit* entries).

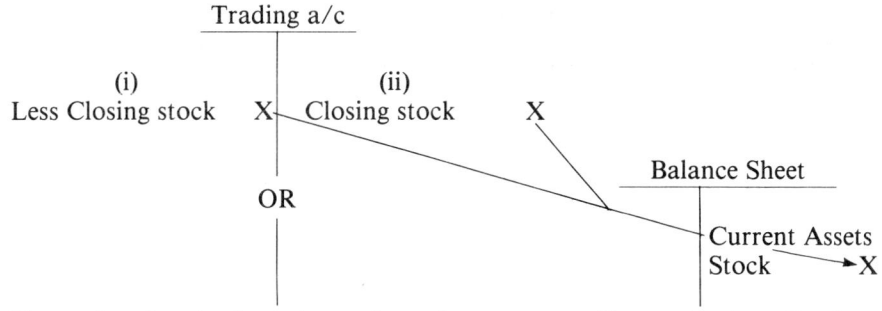

```
                Trading a/c
        (i)            │    (ii)
 Less Closing stock  X─┴─Closing stock    X
                       │                              Balance Sheet
                       │                              ─────────────
                       OR                             │Current Assets
                       │                              │Stock      ►X
```

Thus value already given via purchases is counteracted by a reduction of cash or bank, or an agreement to reduce these during an existing or future accounting period

ie the asset stock will be exchanged for the asset cash or bank.

```
        Purchase a/c
       ──────────────
         X │
           │                          Cash/Bank
           │                         ──────────
           │                                  │ X
```

When a payment is outstanding for a purchase (a debit) this will be supported by a credit in a personal account that will ultimately result in a cash/bank settlement.

```
        Purchase a/c
       ──────────────
         X │
           │                          A Creditor
           │                         ──────────
           │                                  │ X
```

Closing stock is an important residual balance that is not usually shown in the main body of the trial balance, but as a note beneath the trial balance.

Unit 7
Drawings

Overview

1 Drawings reduce owner's funds (proprietors and partners) retained in the business.

2 It is owner's capital or net profit that is reduced both of which are credit balances.

3 The double entry for drawings will occur in the ledger accounts.

4 The trial balance will show cash drawings as a debit having reduced another debit balance − cash or bank.

5 Adjustments for drawings may affect other entries namely:
   a) Purchases — when goods are removed for private consumption, or
   b) Expenses — when assets are used for private purposes.

Drawings are the funds certain owners take out of business during the course of a trading year. Drawings are made by sole proprietors and partners in order that they can pay living expenses in the period before profits are declared. The amount (that is not always regulated) may be in addition to or instead of a salary to the proprietor(s). Drawings are regarded as a direct reduction of profit in the balance sheet of sole traders — the Net profit is calculated in the profit and loss account and is added directly to capital in the balance sheet — assuming there are no drawings (see example on p 57).

The final accounts

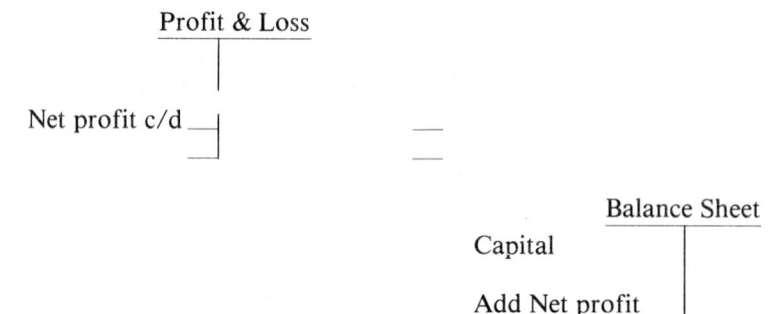

```
            Profit & Loss
           _____
                 |
Net profit c/d __|
                _|
```

```
                                    Balance Sheet
                                    _____
                          Capital         |
                          Add Net profit  |
```

Where there are drawings the following balance sheet presentation would occur (from earlier examples).

```
                         A Jones
                  Balance Sheet as at _____
Capital
                             130,000
Add Net profit    12,370
Less: Drawings     6,200      6,170
                  _____
                            136,170
```

The net overall surplus is reduced by drawings.

The double entry

This being the case, you may ask, what about the double entry?

```
              Drawings Account
              _____
                     |
                  X  |
                  X  |
```

138

The drawings made by the proprietor(s) will affect bank or cash ie the medium of payment.
The double entry will be

$$\text{Debit} - \text{drawings}$$
$$\text{Credit} - \text{bank/cash}$$

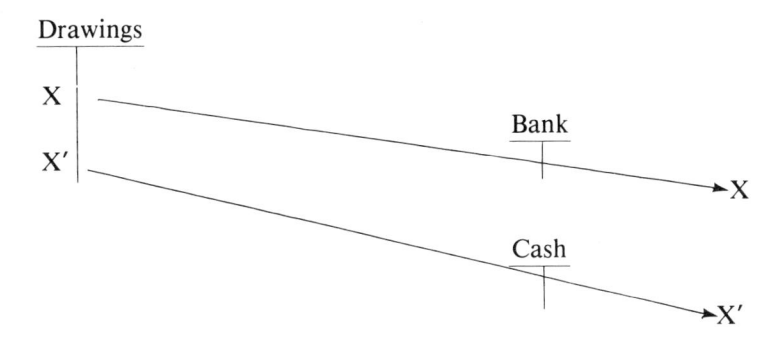

```
Drawings
   |
 X |————————————
   |              \         Bank
 X'|———————————————\————————|————————————→ X
                    \       |
                     \      Cash
                      \—————|————————————→ X'
```

It will be apparent that a debit to drawings is the opposite to capital (a credit balance) and so reduces it.

The trial balance

Of course such entries will also affect and be included in the trial balance. Funds paid or taken out will affect bank/cash for whatever purpose they may be used so there will be a reduced cash and/or bank balance. Such a deficiency will require a debit entry under drawings.

		Debit	Credit
Bank	(25,620 – 6,170)	19,450	
Drawings		6,170	

Drawings in a form other than cash taken by proprietors

Drawings can take forms other than cash for instance:

a) removing goods for personal consumption, or
b) usage of business assets for private purposes.

Goods for personal consumption

Goods have been purchased and put through the business books. Had they not been removed from the business, these goods would have been available for sale, or alternatively the business was merely used as a convenient medium for purchase eg the availability of credit. Since cash has been (or will be) depleted by such action, further entries are required to adjust the asset position for the true value of goods remaining.
The double entry will be

Debit – drawings (as usual)
Credit – purchases

```
        Drawings
          X  ←──────────────┐
                            │
                       Purchases
                            ├──────── X
```

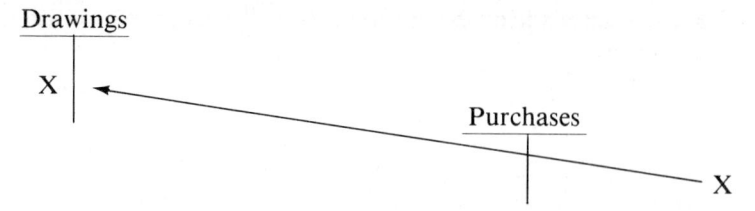

Valuation of the drawing is on the same basis as its initial recording (usually cost). Obviously, potential profit is also lost but this is the proprietor's affair. Adjustments in final accounts for such drawings are made as a deduction from purchases — showing the correct amount of goods available for sale.

Use of business assets for private means

It is also popular to use business assets for private purposes that again amounts to another form of drawings eg use of vehicles.

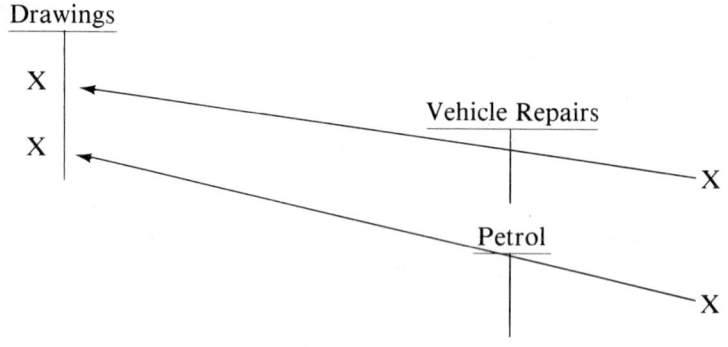

```
        Drawings
          X  ←──────────────┐
                            │
          X  ←──────┐   Vehicle Repairs
                   │        ├──────── X
                   │
                   └────  Petrol
                            ├──────── X
```

The business bears the cost of running these assets so it is only fair that if some private benefit is obtained the business does not bear all the running costs, although in the case of sole proprietors and partnerships it is not essential from the business point of view. In the majority of cases the Inland Revenue sees to it that adjustments are made, although amended accounts are prepared for this purpose. Adjustments may have to be made for these matters prior to preparing final accounts.

Unit 8
Classification of accounts

Overview

1 Ledger accounts have to be subdivided.
2 There are divisions into:
   a) type, and
   b) alphabetic.

3 A division into type refers to the:
   a) Sales ledger,
   b) Purchase ledger,
   c) Nominal ledger,
   d) Private ledger, and
   e) Cash book.
   } all part of the general ledger

4 A brief mention is made of related aspects, namely allocation and control.

The term ledger entry has been used to refer to the 'T' shaped layout, but the term also refers to the bound book that contains these accounts.

The bound ledger has itself been replaced by a variety of loose-leaf systems and, more recently, mechanical and electronic systems. But in all cases a system of division is usually required especially as a business grows.

Division into type

Rather than have numerous ledger accounts mixed together, a method of classification has grown up that divides the 'books' into the following:

Sales ledger (or debtors ledger)
containing the accounts relating to sales on credit – debtors personal accounts.

Purchases ledger (or creditors ledger)
containing the accounts relating to purchases on credit – creditors personal accounts.

Nominal ledger (or general ledger – including private ledger)
containing the general accounts and expense accounts but excluding the cash book. The sales and purchase accounts are contained in this ledger.

Cash book (three-column containing discounts)
produced in a 'ledger' format but containing the bank and cash accounts. It is worthwhile to note how important it is that the cash book should be separate because of the volume of entries contained – most transactions ultimately affect cash or bank.

The cash book can also be regarded as a book of prime entry ie for receipts and payments.

Private ledger (as part of the general ledger)
usually separated from the general ledger providing restricted access to the private accounts. It is confined to those accounts that relate to ownership eg proprietors capital, drawings and fixed assets.

Alphabetic sub-division
As the business grows it will be necessary to further sub-divide the main ledgers, sales, purchases and nominal into alphabetical ordered sections, say A to D; E to H; I to P; and Q to Z.

Allocation of work and control
The division of ledgers also assists in the allocation of clerical duties amongst different members of staff, and the control of those duties.

The points are straight forward and can be best illustrated by examples.

Example
On 1 March 19-0 Fleetwood & Brown had the following balances in their ledger accounts

Creditors		*Debtors*	
Jackson	236	Holmes	50
Peters	58	Cooper	71
Smith	427	Farlie	33
Ladd	404	Crocker	161
Wigglesworth	133		

The opening balances for cash & bank were: cash £2,020 & bank £130 overdrawn. During the month of March the following purchases and sales were made, all transactions are for credit unless stated otherwise.

Sales				*Purchases*		
March 3	Holmes	55	(cash)	March 2	Jackson	65
10	Farlie	170		13	Ladd	103
15	Burroughs	30		21	Peters	110
23	Frost	138			Stead	128
25	Holmes	78		23	Wigglesworth	38
	Gordon	56		28	Rudd	212 (cash)

The following returns were made during the month:

Inwards			*Outwards*		
March 12	Farlie	35	March 10	Jackson	20
20	Burroughs	10	29	Wigglesworth	15
28	Gordon	17	31	Rudd	8

During the month the following receipts & payments were made

Payments				*Receipts*			
March 2	Smith	300		March 3	Holmes	50	(discount £5)
15	Ladd	507	(discount £51)	16	Farlie	168	
17	Jackson	236	(discount £24)	22	Burroughs	20	(discount £2)
27	Stead	65		26	Cooper	71	
31	Rudd	8		28	Rudd	212	
				29	Frost	138	

On 20th March Fleetwood and Brown decided to purchase a reconditioned drilling machine for £1,500 and were granted a trade-in allowance on their old machine of £120. The net settlement was made by cheque. On 31 March it was decided to write off Crocker's debt as irrecoverable. All trade transactions were settled by cash.

You are required to write up the daybooks and ledger accounts and complete appropriate control accounts for the month of March.

Note Control accounts are merely a small aspect of the system and will be discussed later (pp 227–36).

Sales Daybook				*Purchases Daybook*			
March 10	Farlie		170	March 2	Jackson		65
	15	Burroughs	30		13	Ladd	103
	23	Frost	138		21	Peters	110
	25	Holmes	78			Stead	128
		Gordon	56		23	Wigglesworth	38
	31	Transferred to Ledger	472		31	Transferred to Ledger	444

Returns Inward Daybook				*Returns Outward Daybook*			
March 16	Farlie		35	March 10	Jackson		20
	20	Burroughs	10		29	Wigglesworth	15
	28	Gordon	17		31	Transferred to Ledger	35
	31	Transferred to Ledger	62				

Purchases Ledger

Jackson
March 10	Returns	20	March 1	Balance b/d	236		
17	Cash	212	2	Purchases	65		
	Disc. rec'd	24					
31	Balance c/d	45					
		301			301		
			April 1	Balance b/d	45		

Peters
March 31	Balance c/d	168	March 1	Balance b/d	58
			21	Purchases	110
		168			168
			April 1	Balance b/d	168

Smith
March 2	Cash	300	March 1	Balance b/d	427
31	Balance c/d	127			
		427			427
			April 1	Balance b/d	127

Ladd
March 15	Cash	456	March 1	Balance b/d	404
	Disc. rec'd	51	13	Purchases	103
		507			507

Sales Ledger

Holmes
March 1	Balance b/d	50	March 3	Cash	45
25	Sales	78		Disc. alld	5
			31	Balance c/d	78
		128			128
April 1	Balance b/d	78			

Cooper
March 1	Balance b/d	71	March 26	Cash	71

Farlie
March 1	Balance b/d	33	March 12	Returns	35
10	Sales	170	16	Cash	168
		203			203

Crocker
March 1	Balance b/d	161	March 31	Bad Debts	161

Wigglesworth

March 29	Returns	15	March 1	Balance b/d	133
31	Balance c/d	156	March 23	Purchases	38
		171			171
			April 1	Balance b/d	156

Stead

March 27	Cash	65	March 21	Purchases	128
31	Balance c/d	63			
		128			128
			April 1	Balance b/d	63

Burroughs

			March 15	Sales	30
March 20	Returns	10			
22	Cash	18			
	Disc. alld	2			
		30			30

Frost

			March 23	Sales	138
March 29	Cash	138			

Gordon

			March 23	Sales	56
March 28	Returns	17			
	Balance c/d	39			
		56			56
			April 1	Balance b/d	39

General Ledger

Sales

March 31	Transfer SD	472
	Cash	212

Purchases

March 31 Transfer P.D. 444

Returns Inward

March 31 Transfer RID 62

Returns Outward

	March 31	Transfer ROD 35

Discount Allowed

March	3 Holmes	5
	22 Burroughs	2

Discount Received

	March 15 Ladd	51
	17 Jackson	24

Bad Debts

March 31 Crocker	161

Machinery

March 20 Bank	1,500

Sales Ledger Control

March	1 Balance b/d	315	March 31	Cash	440
	31 Sales	472		Disc. alld	7
				Bad Debts	161
				Returns	62
				Balance c/d	117
		787			787

Purchases Ledger Control

March 31	Cash	1,033	March	1 Balance b/d	1,258
	Disc. rec'd	75		31 Purchases	444
	Returns	35			
	Balance c/d	559			
		1,702			1,702

Cash & Bank A/c's

Cash

March	1 Balance b/d	2,020	March	2 Smith	300
	3 Holmes	45		15 Ladd	456
	16 Farlie	168		17 Jackson	212
	22 Burroughs	18		27 Stead	65
	26 Cooper	71		31 Rudd	8
	28 Rudd	212		Balance c/d	1,631
	29 Frost	138			
		2,672			2,672
April 1	Balance b/d	1,631			

Bank

March 31	Balance c/d	1,510	March	1 Balance b/d	130
				20 Machine	1,380
		1,510			1,510
			April 1	Balance b/d	1,510

Note The Sales ledger control and Purchases ledger control are only included here as a matter of completeness. The importance and computation of these is discussed in Section 6 Unit 1, pages 227–36.

Unit 9
The collection and processing of accounting information II — journal entries

Overview

1 The journal has two different connections with other accounting operations:
   a) as with the ledger its description applies to a book and a layout,
   b) as with daybooks it is a book of prime entry.
2 Its uses are for:
   a) unusual transactions,
   b) infrequent transactions,
   c) a means of correcting errors, and
   d) a reference point for setting up an accounting system.
3 A method for determining capital is introduced through the journalization of valued assets.
4 Journalized opening entries are transferred to ledgers to begin the double entry system of accounting.

Mention has already been made of the journal layout in connection with the trial balance. Just as the ledger can be a method of layout and a book of account, so too can the journal.

The journal layout

This two columns debit and credit to the right of the page, plus other details (to be presented below).

Date	Description	Reference	Debit	Credit
	_____		X	
	_____			X
	_____			
	_____			

The journal book

This is a book of prime entry, it is *not* part of the double entry system (as one the ledgers) but is ancillary too and an important check on aspects of double entry.

Daybooks, for initially recording sales, purchases, sales returns and purchase returns are also books of prime entry. Remember daybooks are sometimes themselves (I think) misleading if referred to as journals.

The journal is:
1 a diary of
   a) unusual transactions, and
   b) infrequent transactions;

147

2 a means of correcting errors in accounts once they are discovered; and
3 a reference point for introduction into a double entry system.
    eg   purchase and sale of assets.
            set-offs of purchases against sales to same trader.
– expressed in terms of a debit and credit entry. It is merely a separate informative listing and is especially useful to auditors.

The journal shows:
1 the date,
2 account names and amounts of debit and credit,
3 an explanation, and
4 a reference to the ledger – with a full system (in practice).

Illustration
the books of Metalworker.
The purchase
On March 1 a milling machine is purchased from Unitary Tools for £35,000 on one month's credit.
The journal entry will be:

	Dr	Cr
March 1 Machinery	35,000	
Unitary Tools		35,000
Purchase of a milling machine on credit – a capital purchase.		

Note purely for convention:
1 the debit entry is made first,
2 the credit entry is inset below the debit,
3 the explanation is written within the description section, and
4 the complete entry is ruled off prior to making a fresh entry.
As a reminder, the ledger entry as part of the double entry system would be.

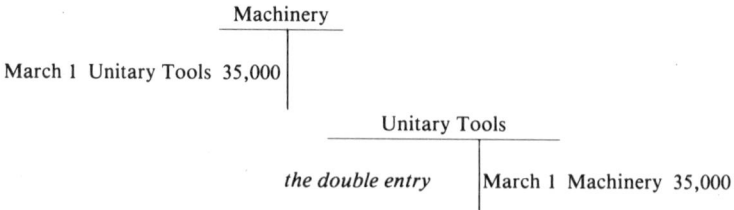

                       Machinery
March 1 Unitary Tools 35,000 |

                       Unitary Tools
             the double entry | March 1 Machinery 35,000

The payment
On March 30 Metalworker pays Unitary Tools through the bank.
The journal entry would be:

	Dr	Cr
March 30 Unitary Tools	35,000	
Bank		35,000
Payment for milling machine purchased March 1 – a capital purchase.		

– again the ledger entry would be

```
              Unitary Tools
                     |
March 30 Bank 35,000 | March 1 Machinery 35,000
```

the double entry

```
       Bank
        |
        | March 30 Unitary Tools 35,000
        |
```

Examples

The following entries will be made in the journal of Metalworker:

May 1 A delivery van is purchased from Cox Garages Ltd for £3,800.

May 3 A credit sale of goods to J Green for £640 was recorded as £460.

May 4 A credit purchase from I Smith for £870 was incorrectly posted to J Smythe's account.

May 10 An old grinding machine is sold for scrap to Breakers Ltd who paid £120 cash.

May 13 R Peters a debtor has business taken over by A Jones who accepts debt of £230.

		Dr	Cr
May 1	Motor van	3,800	
	Cox Garages Ltd.		3,800
	Purchase of a delivery van on credit – a capital purchase.		
May 3	J Green	180	
	Sales		180
	Sale of goods on credit was incorrectly recorded as £460 instead of £640		
May 4	J Smythe	870	
	I Smith		870
	Purchase of goods on credit was incorrectly posted to J Smythe instead of I Smith.		
May 10	Cash	120	
	Machine disposals		120
	Grinding machine is sold for scrap to Breakers Ltd – a capital sale		
May 13	A Jones	230	
	R Peters		230
	A Jones takes over business of R Peters and accepts debt.		

Errors corrected in the journal

As has been seen the journal is a place for explaining unusual entries that affect accounts, this also extends to the correction of errors once detected. These errors can be of several types:
1 omission,
2 recognition (commission),
3 classification (principle),
4 elimination (compensating),
5 transcription (original entry),
6 reversal,
and incidentally will not affect the balancing of the trial balance.
These errors are now explained:

1 Omission – entries that should have been recorded are missing from the books.
2 Recognition – an entry that should have been made to a specific personal account is put to another, creating errors on two outstanding account balances. Such an entry could be a debit of £330 entered in P Smith's account instead of D Smith's.
3 Classification – an item is entered in the wrong class of account eg the purchase of machinery is put to a machinery repairs account.
4 Elimination – certain errors can cancel each other out eg an addition of an extra £1,000 in the sales account can be compensated by £1,000 in the purchases account.
5 Transcription – where the incorrect reading of a figure, say from an invoice, is followed by correct double entry, eg a credit purchase of £72 is entered in both the purchase account and the personal account of the creditor as £27.
6 Reversal – correct amounts are taken but shown on the wrong side of, say, an expense account and the cash or bank account or a contra entry in the cash book itself.

Setting up a system
One use of the journal is for – determining and recording the current state of business, and a reference point for setting up accounts.

Suppose a trader has been in business for some months and had not established a complete double entry system.
Initially this may be through:

a) ignorance,
b) mistakes, or
c) a conscious decision that it is unnecessary.

At some point it may seem opportune to do so and a journalized listing would serve as a sufficient initial record. Most of the assets can be valued by various means including bringing in experts. The most usual method however is cost except where assets have been accumulated through trade and cannot be so valued. Here are some examples:
Land and buildings – cost or current valuation, the latter by a recognized expert.
Motor vehicles, machinery and fixtures – traditionally by cost less amounts for usage, or occasionally current valuation.

Stock of goods – by a stocktake, using records of cost, or an alternative.
Debtors – by some record, if not double entry, and also by circularization (writing to confirm with customers).
Bank balance – through bank statement (updated) or direct advice from bank.
Cash – total of cash balances on hand.

Some liabilities can also be determined by inspection:
Creditors (like debtors) – by some record, if not double entry creditors statements, but also by circularization.
Loans (by outside parties) – by agreement.

The missing figure is capital belonging to the owners, remember the earlier equation:

assets = liabilities (all liabilities)
from this
assets = liabilities + owner's capital
therefore
owner's capital = assets – liabilities

Setting this out in a journalized format requires listing
assets as debits
and liabilities as credits.

Illustration
P Burke has been in business for over a year and what started as a part-time venture, has now become a full-time occupation. In the meantime she has been to evening classes and learned some book-keeping. On October 1 she calculates her assets and liabilities as follows:
Land and buildings £25,000; Motor-vehicle £3,600; Stock £4,500; Debtors – J Drew £650, T Plumber £920, G Greenhill £80, Bank £570, Cash £136.
Creditors – M Stark £330, C Manthorpe £1,050
Her capital will be balancing figure.

	Dr	Cr
Land and buildings	25,000	
Motor vehicle	3,600	
Stock	4,500	
Debtors: J Drew	650	
T Plumber	920	
G Greenhill	80	
Bank	570	
Cash	136	
Creditors: M Stark		330
C Manthorpe		1,050
Capital of owner		34,076
The assets and liabilities are entered to open the books		
	£35,456	£35,456

P Burke's capital is £34,076

Note
No attempt has been made to prepare a revenue statement and her profit would be reflected in the growth of capital. Emphasizing that the journal is only a diary of transactions even though they are to open the books, the entries must now be made in the Ledger accounts as follows:

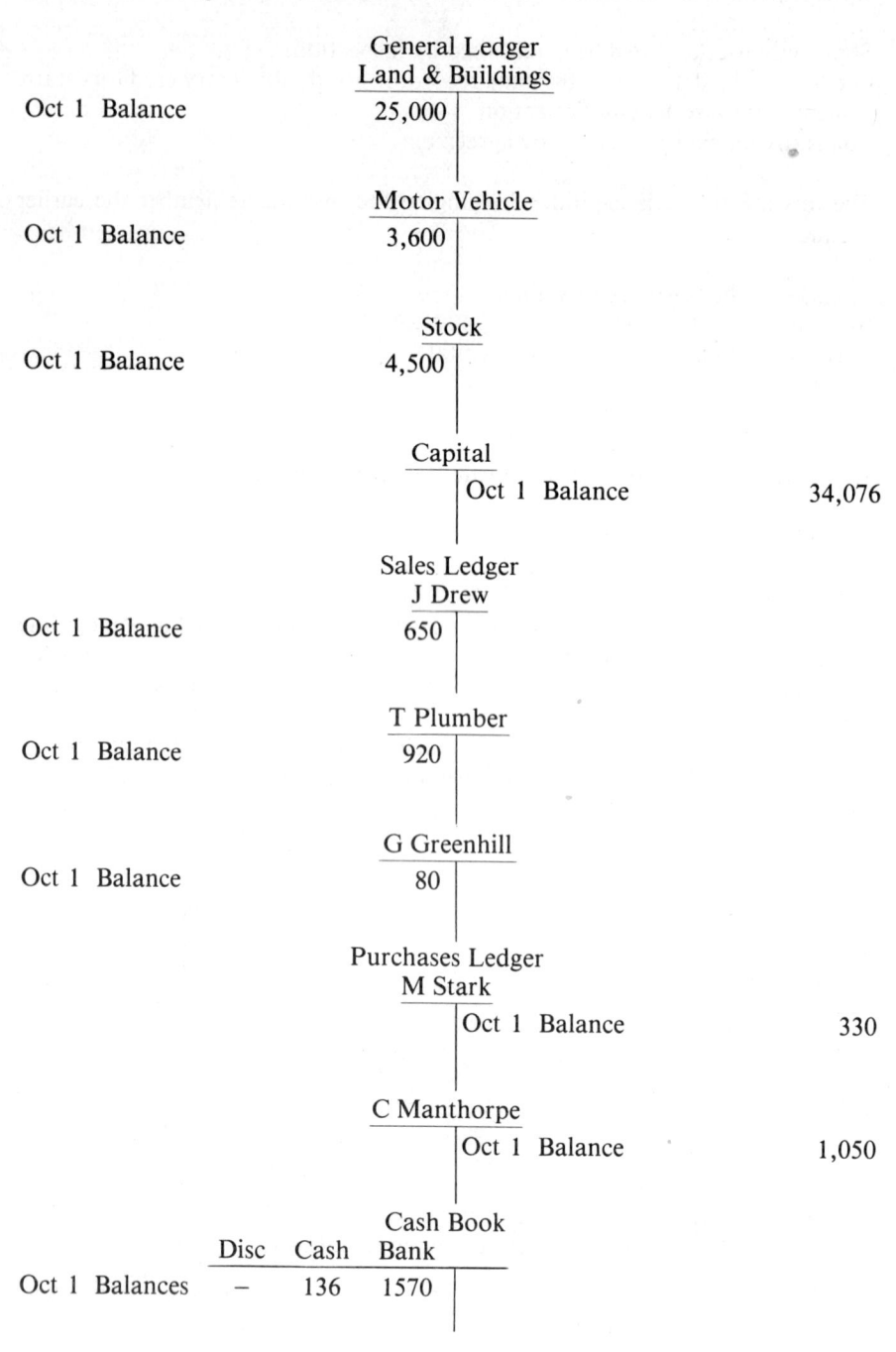

General Ledger
Land & Buildings

Oct 1 Balance   25,000

Motor Vehicle

Oct 1 Balance   3,600

Stock

Oct 1 Balance   4,500

Capital

| | | Oct 1 Balance | 34,076 |

Sales Ledger
J Drew

Oct 1 Balance   650

T Plumber

Oct 1 Balance   920

G Greenhill

Oct 1 Balance   80

Purchases Ledger
M Stark

| | | Oct 1 Balance | 330 |

C Manthorpe

| | | Oct 1 Balance | 1,050 |

Cash Book

	Disc	Cash	Bank
Oct 1 Balances	—	136	1570

152

Adjustments for errors — suspense

The theory of accounting adjustments can be taken further. The crux of the matter rests in its application as a test of double-entry knowledge and the accounting system. It will be apparent that adjustments are of two types, these are those that:
a) affect the balance of the trial balance, and
b) do *not* affect the balance of the trial balance.

Adjustments affecting the balance of the trial balance are those where the double entry is incomplete in some respect, remember that every transaction requires two entries, and it follows that one or other has not been made or made incorrectly.

The procedure is to transfer the aggregate difference (since there will probably be multiple errors) to an intermediate account — the Suspense Account, as either a debit or credit opening balance, and then attempt to reduce the composite figure by making corrections for individual errors as they are found. Transfers out of the Suspense Account to make the correction will be accompanied by Journal entries to support them. In most examination questions the information supplied is sufficient to exhaust the suspense balance, but this is not necessarily the case.

Adjustments not affecting the balance of the trial balance have been listed 1 to 6 above, and are those where the incorrect figure has had double entry applied to it and will retain the balance, but despite this equilibrium is still incorrect, and will lead (without discovery) to incorrect figures being taken to final accounts. Correction of these errors will require journal evidence to support them, but will not require use of a suspense account.

The procedure for adjusting entries that affect the trial balance can now be illustrated.

Trial Balance

	Dr	Cr
Suspense account	X	

Suspense Account

Balance per trial balance	X	Entries to clear balance to original accounts via supporting journal entries.

and vice versa for a credit balance in the Journal.

The Balance Sheet too (for examination purposes) can have a suspense account balance.

153

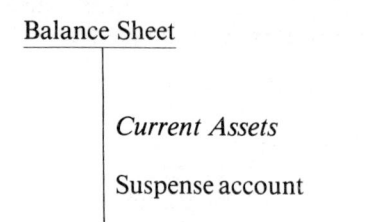

Balance Sheet

	Current Assets	
	Suspense account	X

Note
That the debit balance is shown as an asset-in the Current Assets section.

Adjusted profit statements

Some examination questions ask for the preparation of an adjusted profit statement, where adjustments that affect profit have to be singled out from others, and recorded as either:
a) additions to profit, or
b) deductions from profit,
as in the Illustration.

Statement of Adjusted Net Profit

Net profit per accounts			X
Add	X		
	X		
	X	X	
			X
Less	X		
	X		
	X	X	
			X

Visually, the presentation is rather like bank reconciliation and other special purpose statements.

Adjustment to balance sheet

Invariably adjustments elsewhere will require adjustments in the Balance Sheet, especially to remove any suspense account balance. These should be carried out in the course of presentation, and may well commence with the transfer of an adjusted profit.

Questions

Because examination and other questions adopt one or more features of the above notes, three examples are included to cover the various aspects.

In attempting some questions, assistance may be required from lecturers, remember that they are sometimes an awkward test of double-entry principles.

Example I
A young book-keeper has presented the following Trial Balance for period ended 31 March 19-2:

	Dr	Cr
Bank overdraft		7,280
General expenses	9,270	
Salaries	16,210	
Drawings	17,400	
Creditors		20,170
Debtors	13,710	
Purchases	54,790	
Returns inwards	1,150	
Rent and rates	4,740	
Sales		85,620
Discount allowed	4,330	
Discount received		1,760
Stock	12,750	
Provision for doubtful debts		1,040
Provision for depreciation of machinery		1,120
Machinery	111,660	
Capital		142,950
	£246,010	£259,940

You are required to draw up an 'amended' trial balance, debiting or crediting any residual error to a suspense account.

Further investigation leads to the origin of the various errors.

(i) Goods bought from P Smithers amounting to £170 had been posted to his account as £710.
(ii) Machinery which had cost £5,150 had been debited to the general expense account.
(iii) An invoice from Sellers Ltd for £4,650, had been omitted from the Purchase account, but credited to Sellers Ltd account.
(iv) Sales on credit to D O'Brien Ltd for £5,450 had been posted to the Sales account, but not to the debtors' ledger.
(v) The balance on the capital account had been incorrectly brought forward in the ledger, and should have been £140,250.
(vi) An amount of £1,430 received from N Pearce, a debtor, in settlement of his account had been treated as a cash sale.
(vii) Discount allowed had been undertotalled by £590.

Now that these errors have been revealed it is possible to enter the corrections in the journal and the suspense account, this you are required to do.

Corrected trial balance

	Dr	Cr
Bank overdraft		7,280
General expenses	9,270	
Salaries	16,210	
Drawings	17,400	
Creditors		20,170
Debtors	13,710	
Purchases	54,790	

Returns inwards	1,150	
Rent and rates	4,740	
Sales		85,620
Discount allowed	4,330	
Discount received		1,760
Stock	12,750	
Provision for doubtful debts		1,040
Provision for depreciation of machinery		1,120
Machinery	111,660	
Capital		142,950
Suspense account	13,930	
	£259,940	£259,940

Suspense Account

Balance from Trial Balance	13,930	P Smithers	540
		Purchases	4,650
		D O'Brien Ltd	5,450
		Capital	2,700
		Discount allowed	590
	13,930		13,930

Journal

	Dr	Cr
(i) March 31 P Smithers	540	
Suspense a/c		540
Excessive posting to P Smithers		
(ii) March 31 Machinery a/c	5,150	
General expense a/c		5,150
Machinery incorrectly posted in expenses account		
(iii) March 31 Purchases a/c	4,650	
Suspense a/c		4,650
Understatement of purchases in purchases account		
(iv) March 31 D O'Brien Ltd	5,450	
Suspense a/c		5,450
Understatement of debtor in debtors ledger		
(v) March 31 Capital a/c	2,700	
Suspense a/c		2,700
Overstatement of capital in capital account		
(vi) March 31 Sales a/c	1,430	
N Pearce		1,430
A debtor settlement incorrectly treated as a cash sale		

(vii) March 31 Discount allowed   590
      Suspense a/c   590
      Discount allowed incorrectly totalled

Example II
C Fairweather has been in business for many years as a barometer manufacturer. The following is a list of balances taken out after preparing his trading and profit and loss account.

Trial Balance Year ended 30 September 19-7

	Dr	Cr
Capital		80,000
Bank	5,000	
Drawings	2,000	
Stock	30,000	
Debtors	23,000	
Creditors		40,000
Equipment	80,000	
Net profit		20,000
	£140,000	£140,000

After these have been prepared the following errors were discovered:
1 Stock was undervalued by £2,000,
2 Purchases on credit of £3,000 have been completely missed out from the books,
3 £5,000 in the wages account related to the installation of new equipment,
4 Depreciation of 10% on equipment had not been taken,
5 Sales returns of £400 had not been entered in either the customers account or the returns inward account,
6 £2,000 worth of goods had been withdrawn by the proprietor from the business for his own use, no entry had been made for this in the books.
Prepare a statement of the true profit made and a corrected balance sheet as at 30 September 19-7.

C Fairweather Statement of Revised Net Profit year ended 30 September 19-7

Original Net profit		20,000
Add: Drawings	2,000	
Wages and capital	5,000	
Stock – previous undervaluation	2,000	9,000
		29,000
Less: Depreciation (10% × 85,000)	8,500	
Returns inwards	400	
Purchases on credit	3,000	11,900
Revised Net profit		£17,100

C Fairweather Balance Sheet as at 30 September 19-7

Equipment (80,000 + 5,000)	85,000
less depreciation	8,500
	76,500

Net current assets
Current assets

Stock (30,000 + 2,000)	32,000		
Debtors (23,000 − 400)	22,600		
Bank	5,000	59,600	

Less current liabilities

Creditors (40,000 + 3,000)	43,000	(43,000)	16,600
			£93,100

Financed By

Capital			80,000
Add net profit	17,100		
Less: drawings (2,000 + 2,000)	4,000		13,100
			£93,100

Example III
The balance sheet of G Chimes at 31 August, 19-6 was as follows:

G Chimes − Capital Account		Fixed Assets	Cost	Depn.	WDV
Balance − 1.9.19-5	10,000	Fixtures & fittings	3,000	2,000	1,000
Add − Net profit for year	5,500	Plant & machinery	4,000	2,500	1,500
		Motor vehicles	6,000	3,000	3,000
	15,500		13,000	7,500	5,500
Less − Drawings	4,400				
	11,100				

Current Liabilities			Current Assets			
Trade creditors	7,000		Stock		7,500	
Wages	200		Debtors	4,200		
		7,200	Less provision	250	3,950	
			Bank		1,350	12,800
		18,300				18,300

G Chimes has asked you to examine the accounts, and you have discovered the following items:

1 Motor repairs of £300 have been incorrectly charged to motor vehicles (depreciation on motor vehicles − 25% pa on cost).
2 A credit purchase of £100 has been omitted from the books. These goods remain unsold, and were also omitted from stock.
3 The provision for bad debts should be reduced to £200.
4 General expenses of £50 was unpaid at the year end and has been omitted from the books.
5 Bank charges − £40 has been omitted.
6 G Chimes withdrew £500 goods for his own use. No entry has been made for this.
7 Rent and rates amounting to £20 has been charged to general expenses.

Required: a) Journal entries to correct the above items where necessary;
b) A corrected balance sheet at 31 August, 19-6.

G Chimes — Journal

		Dr	Cr
1 Aug 31	Motor repairs	300	
	Motor Vehicles		300
	Incorrect recording of motor repairs to capital not revenue account		
Aug 31	Motor Vehicle Depreciation	75	
	Profit & Loss		75
	Charge of motor vehicle repairs to under vehicles account (debit) resulting in overcharging depreciation		
2 Aug 31	Purchases	100	
	Creditor		100
	A credit purchase omitted from books		
Aug 31	Stock	100	
	Profit & Loss		100
	Omission of closing stock from records		
3 Aug 31	Provision for bad debts	50	
	Profit & Loss		50
	Reduction in provision for bad debts from 250 to 200		
4 Aug 31	General expenses	50	
	Creditors		50
	General expenses unpaid that remain outstanding		
5 Aug 31	Bank Charges	40	
	Bank		40
	Bank charges omitted from the accounts		
6 Aug 31	Drawings	500	
	Purchases		500
	Proprietors drawings not recorded		
7 Aug 31	Rent & rates	20	
	General expenses		20
	Rent & rates incorrectly charged to general expenses account		

Balance Sheet (amended)

Balance		10,000	*Fixed Assets*	Cost	Depn'	NBV
Add Net profit			Fixtures & fittings	3,000	2,000	1,000
(5,500 − 300 + 75 + 50 −			P & M	4,000	2,500	1,500
50 − 40 + 500)		5,735	M V	5,700	2,925	2,775
		15,735		12,700	7,425	5,275
Less Drawings		4,900				
		10,835				
Current Liabilities			*Current Assets*			
Trade creditors (+ 100 + 50)			Stock (+ 100)		7,600	
	7,150		Debtors	4,200		
Wages	200	7,350	Less provision			
			(− 50)	200	4,000	
			Bank (− 40)		1,310	12,910
		£18,185				£18,185

159

Unit 10
Goodwill and other reducible assets

Overview

1 Such assets to be considered are
   a) Leases,
   b) Goodwill,
   c) Patents,
   d) Trade marks, and
   e) Copyright
      b) to e) are regarded as intangible assets.

2 A type of depreciation provision arises to write off the cost of the assets over an estimate of useful life or relevant worth to the business eg fifteen years in the case of a patent.

3 The writing off occurs against
   a) revenue for a particular year, and
   b) the recorded cost, less accumulated reduction.

4 The accounts used are (familiarly) the
   a) profit and loss, and
   b) balance sheet.

General

Assets other than fixed suffer a reduction in their value (usually cost) to the business over their expected life period. Such assets are:

a) leases,
b) goodwill,
c) patents,
d) trade marks, and
e) copyright.

Some are regarded as intangible ie not real, including goodwill, patents, trade marks and copyright. Different types have different names applied to the process of reduction eg leases are said to be amortized (not depreciated). They arise through different operations and probably only patents, trade marks and copyright have any intrinsic similarity.

Leases

There are different types of leases; most people are familiar with a lease in respect to property that is let. In this case the leasing (deed) provides a right of use for a given period, in exchange for some consideration, but does not confer any rights of ownership. There are other rather more complex types of leasing arrangements (that are quite a popular means of finance to business). However, these are more akin to a special method of raising finance and are sometimes referred to as 'off balance sheet finance'. This latter type are not dealt with because they are more complex than the former and are subject to accounting difficulties that have not been fully resolved by the profession.

Accounting entries on the balance sheet are recorded below the fixed asset part, as follows:

Lease(s) at cost	X	
less amortization to date	X	X

The profit and loss account records that part which is written off against profit in an accounting period, as follows:

Amortization of lease   X

Goodwill

As noted earlier this arises in accounts through the purchase of one business by another when a price is paid which is in excess of the total value of assets in the acquired business. The buyer, either sole trader, partnership or company, has paid cash or given value to the extent of the agreed sale price, that is, in excess of the assets gained. Therefore the deficiency of non-cash assets remains, when compared to the amount of cash or other consideration given up in the buyer's account, until written off against future profits.

Current accounting practice requires goodwill to be written off as soon as possible. Only goodwill can be written off by a method that is less than consistent, taking one year with another. Goodwill is regarded as an intangible asset, unlike other assets, eg plant and machinery that are tangible and very real.

The place for intangible assets on the balance sheet, so far as they are not written off is immediately beneath the tangible assets (ie after leases where they are recorded) as follows:

Goodwill at cost	X	
less amount written off (cumulative)	X	X

The profit and loss account records that part (if any) which is written off against profit, as follows:

Goodwill written off during year   X

Patents

These grant a statutory monopoly to exploit an invention over a period of years, usually fifteen. Patent rights can only be granted to an individual and are assigned to a corporate undertaking. They are recorded at the cost of the effort and resources employed in experimentation etc or the cost of acquisition where this is the case, in the balance sheet as *assets*. The amounts written off periodically are recorded as *debits* in the profit and loss.

Trade marks and copyright

These provide a monopolistic licence to use, and are written off in a manner similar to patents, but usually over a less restrictive time scale that could be longer or shorter than that for patents depending on the estimated 'productive' life of the trade mark or copyright.

Unit 11
Accounting for Value Added Tax

Overview

1 VAT is levied on goods and services by recognized traders and collected by Customs and Excise Department.

2 The types of business are as follows:
   a) Exempted,
   b) Zero rated,
   c) Partly exempt, and
   d) Taxable.

3 The taxable business is examined as for:
   a) Sales − outputs
   b) Purchases − inputs

4 Attention is drawn to cases where firms cannot recover VAT.

5 Principles are outlined in cases where VAT applies to items other than revenue purchases and sales.

6 A brief statement is made about recording VAT as debtor or creditor balances in the balance sheet.

Value Added Tax (VAT) is a tax levied on the supply of goods and services by businesses that are taxable. Some goods and services are not liable, some have attracted rates other than basic which is currently 15%. The Government department responsible for VAT is Customs and Excise.

Types of business

Exempted businesses

Such firms do not have to add VAT on to the price at which they sell goods and services. Nor will they get a refund on the amount that has been paid for goods and services eg insurance companies, banks, firms with small turnover (the latter is optional).

Zero rated businesses

These do not add VAT to the final selling price of their products or service, but do obtain a refund of all VAT paid by them − distinguishing them from exempt firms.

Partly exempt businesses

These find themselves selling goods some of which are: exempt, standard rated or zero rated − they thus have to separate turnover accordingly.

Taxable businesses

The collection of tax is by taxable firms, although the burden falls on the final consumer so far as payment is concerned.

Accounting for VAT

This depends on the type of firm and goods. There are three major classifications with subdivisions on the first case, listed as follows:

1 Businesses which can recover VAT
a) Taxable businesses
   (i) Sales and VAT
   (ii) Purchases and VAT
b) Zero rated businesses
2 Businesses which cannot recover VAT paid
3 VAT on items other than sales and purchases

Businesses which can recover VAT – taxable and zero rated

a) Taxable businesses

(i) *Sales and VAT – outputs*
A taxable business will have to add VAT to the value of sales after any trade discount has been deducted, but VAT is calculated on the net amount after any cash discount for speedy payments (even if cash discount is lost).

Sales day book – will normally have an extra column for VAT

Date	Description of customer	Invoice no	Folio no	VAT	Net amount

Transfer to general ledger   GL__ __ GL__ __

Sales ledger – will be debited with the whole amount for the goods to debtors personal accounts

A Debtor
| X

General ledger – the total sales amount will be credited to sales account (net amount) and VAT account.

```
        Sales
          |
          |    x
          |

         VAT
          |
          |    x
          |
```

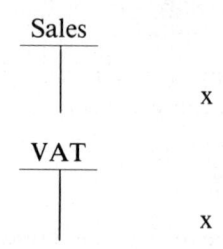

(ii) *Purchases and VAT-inputs*
A taxable business will be able to claim VAT on its purchases. This can be offset against the amount collected on sales which will normally be the greater — reducing the net payment to Customs and Excise. Where the purchases (and amounts paid) are greater than sales (amounts received), VAT can be reclaimed. Purchases day book — like the sales book will have an extra column for VAT

Date	Description of customer	Goods document no – internal	Folio no	VAT	Net amount

Transfer to general ledger   GL__   __   GL__   __

Purchases ledger — personal accounts of creditors will be credited with the full amount of goods.

```
        A Creditor
          |
          |    X
          |
```

General ledger — the total purchases will be debited to purchase account (net amount) and VAT account.

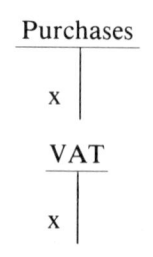

```
        Purchases
          |
     x    |
          |

          VAT
          |
     x    |
          |
```

Value Added Tax   Page 46

19-5			19-5		
June 30	Purchase day book		June 30	Sales day book	
	VAT content PB22	221		VAT content SB25	266
31	Balance c/d	45			
		266			266
			July 1	Balance b/d	45

Note
Trading Account: (i) debited with net purchases
(ii) credited with net sales
Balance sheet: amount outstanding will appear as a creditor in the Balance Sheet as at 30 June 19-5 ie VAT is owed to the Customs and Excise, and vice versa where there is a debtor balance.

b) Zero-rated businesses

These need only keep records of VAT paid on purchases and the amounts outstanding at close of period will appear as a debtor in the Balance Sheet until settled by Customs and Excise.

Businesses which can recover VAT — taxable and zero-rated
Businesses which cannot recover VAT paid
There is no VAT tax account. The VAT paid is included in cost of goods and no VAT is added to sales.

VAT on items other than sales and purchases
VAT is payable, not just on purchases for resale, but expense items and fixed assets.

Sellers (providers) books	— show an addition for VAT
Buyers books	— depend on whether VAT is reclaimable
(i) VAT reclaimable	— item should be shown *net*
	— in fixed asset account (and balance sheet) or as expense in expense account (profit and loss).
(ii) VAT not reclaimable	— item of expenditure should include VAT
	— in fixed asset account (and balance sheet) or expense account.

VAT owed — by or to firm — will be included with debtors or creditors as the case may be — there is no need to show as a separate amount in the Balance Sheet.

Settlement is made quarterly, different businesses settle at different times, so that there are funds coming into Government revenue monthly.

There are many more complex rules dealing with specific circumstances and cases, and reference when meeting these in practice will have to be made to Customs and Excise publications.

Questions

Ledger records to final accounts

1 Rankin in the course of business conducted the following credit transactions.

Aug 2 Sold goods to U for £150
      6 Bought goods from V for £350
      9 Sold goods to W for £230
     12 Bought goods from X for £540
     13 Sold goods to Y for £140
     21 Sold goods to Z for £160

Aug 4 Received £135 from U in payment
     11 Paid V £315 in payment
     16 Received £207 from W in payment
     19 Paid £486 to X in payment
     24 Received £126 from Y in payment
     29 Received £144 from Z in payment

You are required to:
1 Record the transactions as above.
2 Assume all payments were by cash and Rankin had a cash balance of £300 at the start of August show how much the closing cash balance was.
3 Show what the total discount figures were, and how these were shown in respective accounts.

2 P Lamb, a retailer went into business on 1 April and during the first month of trading made the following transactions:

April 1 Introduced £6,000 cash into the business
      3 Purchased goods for £3,200
      8 Paid one months rent £80
      9 Sold goods to value of £950
     10 Sold goods to value of £1,000
     11 Bought goods for £400
     12 Paid advertising amounting to £50
     16 Sold goods to value of £2,000
     20 Paid insurance £85
     25 Paid wages to one assistant £160
     29 Paid wages to second assistant £100
     30 Sold remaining goods for £800

You are required to record the above transactions, extract a trial balance and prepare a trading, profit and loss account for the month of April and a balance sheet as at 30 April.

3 P Williams, who opens a mobile grocery business, on 1 September conducts the following transactions during the opening month.

September 1 Introduced £12,500 cash into the business from his private funds and opened up a business bank account
            2 Purchased a large van for £7,800 paying by cheque
            3 Transferred £150 to a cash account for business use
            4 Bought supplies from R Rogers on credit £6,518
            5 Made cash sales of £1,022, the cash was then banked
            8 Returned goods to R Rogers as damaged £155
            9 Rented storage space in a warehouse, paying £2,050 by cheque
          11 Made cash sales of £1,583 the cash was then banked
          15 Made drawings from bank of £630 for own use

18 Made cash sales of £886, the cash was then banked
23 Paid R Rogers £2,000 for supplies by cheque, the balance remaining outstanding
27 Made cash sales for £1,363 the cash was then banked

Closing stock of goods is valued at £3,122 on September 30

From the above information you are asked to show the transactions in appropriate ledger accounts, extract a trial balance and prepare a trading, profit and loss account for the month of September and a balance sheet as at 30 September.

Would you consider it appropriate for any other expenses to be included?

Would you consider the trading position of P Williams to be satisfactory?

Answer guide: Cash £150; Trial Balance balance £21,872; GP £1,613; Balance Sheet balances £15,796. (ledger method)

4 R Sellers, a market trader went into business on 1 February, during the first month of trading made the following transactions:

February 1 Introduced £20,000 cash into business from his private funds and opened up a business bank account
3 Purchased goods for £2,720 paying by cheque
4 Paid rent for warehouse space £650 by cheque
6 Bought a goods van £3,850 paying by cheque
7 Withdrew £200 from bank for business use as a cash float
10 Made sales £3,520 giving credit to J Spike a retailer to the extent of £2,010 the balance was for cash
14 Purchased goods on credit costing £4,160 from H Milligan
16 Made sales £2,190 for cash
17 Transferred £3,000 from cash to bank account
19 Paid wages of £186 to assistant by cash
20 Made drawings from bank for his own personal use £855
24 Paid goods van expenses £236 by cheque
25 Bought superior stall fittings from Markets Limited for £1,045 on credit
28 Made sales of £1,500 for cash
29 Purchased goods for resale £920 paying cash

Closing stock of goods is valued at £5,617 on February 29.

From the above information you are asked to show the transactions in appropriate ledger accounts, extract a trial balance and prepare a trading, profit and loss account for month of February and a balance sheet as at 29 February.

The cash book

5 Meadows, a small trader, opened up a business and decided to keep a full double-entry system, based on a three column cash book. Meadows records the following list of transactions and asks you to enter them, then balance off the accounts and show the relevant discount accounts.

November 1 Meadows introduces Capital of £10,000, opening a bank account for the whole amount, but for £200 that he keeps as business cash
2 Goods were purchased on credit from J Jackson to the value of £1,400
3 Cash sales were made for £360
4 Goods were sold on credit to B Hughes £830
5 Meadows paid rent for premises £2,190 by cheque
6 A goods van was purchased for £4,636 and payment was made by cheque
7 B Hughes paid account outstanding £830 by cheque and took a cash discount of 10%
9 J Jackson was paid in full and offered a 15% cash discount as part of his terms for cash settlement
11 Cash sales were made for £172

12 Purchases were made on credit from F Poole £546, T Ferry £329, N Emerson £177 and P Lake £245
14 Sales were made on credit to D John £598, S Richard £729, R Robinson £441 and P Mann £211
15 Cash sales were made for £292
16 Storage racks were purchased paying £1,319 by cheque
17 The garage account was settled by cheque with Botchit Garage for petrol, since the agreed maximum of £100 had been attained
18 Meadows paid wages to part-time assistant £163 by cash
19 Stationery was purchased for £195 paying cash
20 D John and R Robinson, settled their accounts paying by cheque, no discount was granted
21 Paid F Poole by cheque, no discount received
25 Paid for repairs to warehouse by cash £350
26 Paid T Ferry, N Emerson and P Lake by cheque, no discount received
27 Cash sales were made for £343
28 S Richard settled his account by cheque, no discount allowed
   Purchased goods for resale on credit from D Dickenson £1,209, F Major £1,310 and P O'Neil £568
29 Sold goods on credit to J Moore £2,082
30 Transferred £1,000 cash to bank

Answer guide: Closing balances: Cash £156, Bank £1,486, Discount allowed £83, Discount received £210.

6 A three column cash book needs to be written up for the following transactions to incorporate them in part of a double-entry book-keeping system. The listing presented is for the month of July. The cash book should be balanced off at the end of the month and discount totals transferred to the general ledger accounts. It may be necessary to round off discount to the nearest pound sterling.

July 1 Balances brought forward: Cash £1,016, Bank £2,043 (overdraft)
2 Received payment from the following customers, cash discount allowed was 5%. R Wright £75 T Verne £497 P Taylor £712 H Cartwright £1,008. D White £84 B Lyons £2,010. Payments were all by cheque
3 Paid rent by cheque £295
5 Received payment from the following customers, cash discount allowed was 5%. S Augustus £155 B Allbones £512 T Bate £349 K Dent £460 A Greenside £121. All payments were received by cheque
7 Paid electricity bill from previous quarter by cheque £914
8 Paid suppliers for goods and received a $2\frac{1}{2}$% cash discount P McGivern £1,310 T Norrie £2,118 R Richardson £767 F Rowley £324 G Shayler £144 L Smith £152. Payments were made by cheque
10 Paid gas bill from previous quarter by cheque £1,115
15 Paid suppliers for goods and received a 5% cash discount J Sparks £233 D Taylor £441 S Burton £526. T Fryer £98. All payments were received by cheque
16 Made cash sales of £157
17 Received payment from the following customers, cash discount allowed was 10% S Aitken £1,017 B Atkinson £227 K Bocock £648 A Burrows £789 T Chatterton £1,134 A Dennis £2,026 and T Girling £3,105. All payments were received by cheque
19 Made cash sales of £627
21 Paid motor vehicle expenses £1,440 by cash
23 Transferred funds from Bank to Cash £500
26 Paid suppliers for goods and received a $7\frac{1}{2}$% cash discount F Horsman £123 M Melzack £466 D Mullet £633 C Peard £222 and S Robinson £1,081. Payments were made by cheque
29 Paid for building repairs by cheque £1,566
30 Received payment for goods from P Shanks formerly regarded as a bad debt, no discount allowed. £2,088 received by cheque

7 Selby, a small trader is continuing in business and has the following opening balances; cash £129; bank £1,011.

From the information given below for the month of September, you are required to complete the cash book, balance off and transfer the discount balances to general ledger accounts. Discount calculations should be taken to the nearest pound sterling.

September 1 Received payment from J Patrick £608; V Bourne £115; K Slater £991; respective discounts allowed were £46; £9 and £74
2 Cash sales were made of £721
3 R Warner paid his account of £854 and was allowed £47 discount
5 Paid rent by cheque £225
6 Paid the following suppliers and in each case received the respective discount: D McIntosh £548, £36; K Grimes £1,222, £84; A Kennedy £72, £6. Payments were made by cheque
10 Received payments from the following customers and in each case allowed the respective discount: D Taylor £516, £24; P Gifford £1,092, £142; L Thorn £1,520, £126; J Selby £1,980, £185. Payments were by cheque
11 Cash sales were made of £352
12 Paid motor expenses by cash £58. Purchased some specialised goods for resale paying by cash £143
18 Received payments from the following customers and in each case allowed the respective discount: S Vine £586, £28; G Whitfield £1,212, £63; J Thomas £672, £35; B Stone £814, £42
22 Paid the following suppliers and in each case received the respective discount: P Sharpe £73, £7; D McMaster £132, £7; A Smithson £295, £30
28 Paid wages by cash £326
29 Transferred £150 from bank to cash

8 Write up the following entries in three column cash book format, balance off at the end of the month and show discount accounts as they would be in the general ledger.

January 1 Balances brought forward: Cash £546, Bank £7,834
4 Loan was received from Newtown Bank of £50,000
5 Purchased new machinery for £25,500 and was given a trade in allowance of £450 on the old machinery. The payment was made by cheque but the allowance was received in cash
8 Paid the following accounts by cheque, in each case deducting a 10% cash discount. B Green £1,110; K Lyon £540; P Sears £920
12 Paid the following accounts by cash T Granger £54; S Rankin £88; R Fuller £29, no cash discounts were received in each case
15 Made cash sales of £1,452 and allowed no discount
18 Transferred £1,250 from the cash to bank account
20 Paid gas bill to NEGB for quarter ending in December £921 by cheque
21 Received payment from P Scargill £870; T Moss £1,340; L Evans £1,820 and J Jenkins £2,230, allowing a 10% cash discount in each case
Payments were made by cheque
24 Made sales, to the value of £488, immediate payment made by cheque and no cash discount allowed
25 Received payments from L Billington £920; D Martin £1,500; P Morris £1,660 by cheque, each took a 5% cash discount
28 Purchased a typewriter for use in business, paying by cheque £295
29 Transferred funds from bank to cash to pay wages £1,500
30 Paid wages to employees in cash, totalling £1,079
31 Settled outstanding garage bill for petrol, oil and servicing £336 with Garages Limited

Daybooks

9 You are asked to make entries for credit sales, and credit purchases and returns inwards and outwards relating to those transactions in a day book listing for the purpose of writing up ledgers.

April   1 Credit sales: P Gallimore £8,010, K Johnson £546, R Milne £3,227
          2 Credit purchases: G Tait £1,038, S Pearce £2,177
          5 Credit sales: K Johnson £181
              Credit purchases: N Barnes £816, D Goodman £1,355
          6 Goods returned to us: R Milne £1,088
          7 Credit purchases: G Tait £2,021. N Barnes £630
          8 Credit sales: S Pollock £823. L Ness £1,615, R Milne £854
              Goods returned by us: S Pearce £346
       10 Credit sales: K Johnson £2,949
       11 Credit purchases: C Langley £119, S Pearce £884
       13 Goods returned by us: G Tait £153
             Goods returned to us: L Ness £514
       14 Credit sales: S Pollock £774
       15 Credit purchases: N Barnes £1,789, D Goodman £552
       16 Goods returned by us: N Barnes £627
       17 Goods returned to us: K Johnson £162
       18 Credit Sales: P Gallimore £2,668, S Pollock £92
       21 Credit purchases: T Ward £685, O Waldron £422
       23 Credit sales: K Johnson £133, L Ness £5,054, R Milne £992
       25 Credit purchases: T Ward £1,812
             Goods returned to us: S Pollock £135
       28 Credit purchases: S Pearce £555
       30 Credit sales: L Ness £743
             Credit purchases: G Tait £1,031

Answer guide: Sales total £28,661; Purchases Returns total £1,126.

10 You are asked to make entries for credit sales, credit purchases and returns inwards and outwards relating to those transactions in a daybook listing for the purpose of writing up ledgers.

January 1 Credit purchases: P Thompson £714
           2 Credit purchases: S Brookes £206
              Credit sales: T Robson £3,817, A Willis £289
           5 Credit purchases: J Hartley £591
              Credit sales: C Richards £1,323, K Moore £2,666, C Richards £7,815
           6 Goods returned to us: A Willis £140, T Robson £522
           8 Credit purchases: D Foster £2,442, S Brookes £877
              Credit Sales: A Willis £4,850, R Waddington £6,822
         10 Credit purchases J Hartley £754, H Grass £330, P Thompson £84
         11 Goods returned by us: S Brookes £118, D Foster £56
         14 Credit Sales: T Robson £1,191
              Goods returned by us: J Hartley £297
         15 Credit purchases: N Howard £196
         16 Credit purchases: P Thompson £1,022
         17 Credit sales M Hustler £85
         18 Goods returned to us: R Waddington £383, C Richard £2,096
         20 Goods returned by us: N Howard £18
         21 Credit purchases: S Brookes £550
         23 Credit purchases H Grass £913
              Credit Sales: L Stead £2,020, A Willis £104
         24 Goods returned to us M Hustler £14
         25 Credit sales: T Robson £731, K Moore £557

28 Credit purchases: S Brookes £3,198
Goods returned to us: T Robson £1,001
29 Goods returned by us: P Thompson £136, H Grass £73
Credit sales: L Stead £2,444
30 Credit purchases: D Foster £746, P Thompson £1,672
31 Credit sales: M Hustler £1,021

The journal and adjustments to final accounts

11 The following is a list of balances in the ledgers of George Brown after preparing the trading and profit and loss account for the year ended 30 June 19-7:

Capital at 1 July 19-6		1,500
Net Profit for current year		700
Fixtures & Fittings	790	
Trade debtors	357	
Trade creditors		540
Stock at 30 June 19-7	800	
Bank balance	293	
Drawings for the year	500	
	£2,740	£2,740

After the preparation of the final accounts, the following errors were discovered:
1 Additional fixtures cost £800 had been charged to repairs account. Unrecorded depreciation on these new fixtures was estimated at £6.
2 The stock at 30 June 19-7 had been incorrectly valued. The correct valuation was £760.
3 Sales on credit on 30 June 19-7 of £54 had been completely omitted from the books.
4 Discounts allowed recorded in the cash book of £10 had not been posted to the debtors' accounts or the discount account.

Required
After correction of the above items show
a) your calculation of the true net profit and
b) the Balance Sheet at 30 June 19-7

12 A S Pire commenced trading on 1 January 19-7 with capital in the bank of £800. He did not keep any proper books of account and only had one bank account through which he passed all his transactions, business and private.

He buys an old van for £150 for use in the business and, during the month, introduces into the business extra capital of £2,000 which he won on 'Spot the ball'.

Pire provides you with the following information:
1 Invoices for goods received £2,050 of which he has paid £1,800.
2 He has drawn out of the business for his own private use £780.
3 He has paid for heating, lighting, rent, decorating etc £400 of which you estimate only £80 is attributable to the business.
4 He has had some help from his daughter during her school holidays for which Pire paid her £110.
5 Running expenses of the van amount to £200.
6 All sales are for cash which he banks daily before paying any expenses. Sales for the period were £2,055.
7 He did make the mistake during the month of allowing credit to one customer who has now been declared bankrupt – the amount involved was £15.
8 Pire's valuations at 31 January 19-7 were:
   Van   £125
   Stock £800
9 Bank balance at 31 January 19-7 was £1,400

Required:
Prepare Pire's cash book, trading and profit and loss accounts for the month and balance sheet at 31 January 19-7

Answer guide: Bank balance £1,400; GP £805; NP £375; Balance Sheet balances £2,075 (vertical method).

13 The balance sheet of F McFall at 30 June, 19-6 was as follows:

F McFall – Capital Account			Fixed Assets	Cost	Depn.	W.D.V.
Balance – 1.7.19-5		9,000	Land & buildings	6,000	–	6,000
Add Net profit for year		5,000	Plant & machinery	5,000	2,000	3,000
		14,000	Motor vehicles	3,000	1,000	2,000
Less Drawings		4,000		14,000	3,000	11,000
		10,000				
Current Liabilities			*Current Assets*			
Trade creditors	5,800		Stock		4,000	
Light and heat	300		Debtors	2,500		
Bank	1,200		*Less* provision	300		
		7,300			2,200	
			Cash		100	
						6,300
		17,300				17,300

McFall had prepared his own accounts. He has asked you to check his work, and you have discovered the following items:
1 A van, purchased during the year for £1,000 had been entered in the books as plant and machinery (plant & machinery is depreciated at 20% on cost; motor vehicles are depreciated at 25% on cost).
2 A cheque payment to a supplier of £100 on 30.6.19-6 has not yet been put through McFall's books.
3 The provision for bad debts should be increased to £400.
4 Insurance prepaid amounting to £50 has not been adjusted for in the books.
5 Bank charges of £30 have been omitted.
6 McFall withdrew goods for his own use amounting to £400. No entry has been made for this.

Required
a) Journal entries to correct the above items,
b) A corrected Balance Sheet at 30 June, 19-6.

Answer guide: Journal Plant & machinery depreciation Dr £200, Profit & Loss Cr £200; Adjusted profit £5,270; Balance Sheet balances £17,200 (ledger method).

14 The following trial balance was extracted from the books of T Palmer on 31 December 19-2 (his year end).

Capital		20,007
Freehold premises at cost	10,000	
Fixtures and fittings at cost	4,500	
Provision for depreciation 1.1.19-2		1,350
Stock 1.1.19-2	4,864	
Purchases and sales	17,623	24,472
Returns inwards and outwards	119	133
Debtors and creditors	2,120	1,496
Drawings	1,500	
Staff salaries and commission	1,530	

Light and heat	115	
Rent rates and insurance	260	
Sundry expenses	108	
Discounts allowed and received	22	124
Balance at bank	2,164	
	£44,925	£47,582

After taking out the trial balance, it was found that:
1 £35 return inwards had been entered as return outwards.
2 Bank charges £40 had not been posted from the cash book.
3 Purchases had been undercast by £2,000.
4 A cheque for £100 drawn by Palmer had not been charged to his drawings account, although entered in the cash book.
5 Rates in advance £25.
6 Depreciation of fixtures and fittings – 10% on cost.
7 Wages owing £80.
8 Closing stock £5,121.

Prepare
1 Journal entries to correct 1 – 4 above, taking balances to a suspense a/c.
2 Trading and profit and loss account and balance sheet.

Section V
The extension of final accounts presentations

Unit 1 Limited company accounts
Unit 2 Partnership accounts
Unit 3 Non-profit or club accounts
Unit 4 Manufacturing accounts

Unit 1
Limited company accounts

Overview

1 The status of limited companies is outlined distinguishing:
   a) public, and
   b) private.
2 The appropriation account as an addendum to profit & loss is explained and illustrated.
3 Terminology relating to the appropriation account (in particular) and other related aspects is explained.
4 Notes are provided explaining the types of capital.
5 The layout of the 'financed by' section of the balance sheet is presented in outline.
6 It is recognized as important to be able to convey an overall picture of the representation of company affairs at and around the end of year date, hence a brief summary is provided.
7 Ownership of shares in other companies is discussed.
8 Two examples on company accounts are presented for explanation, showing many points contained in questions.
9 The effect of taxation is ignored.

Limited companies are the most important types of trading organization today. They range from the very large multinational to the small business.

Ownership

The main distinction from sole traders and partnerships is that ownership is recognized through holdings of specific types of share that provide a more flexible pattern of capital ownership and distribution.

Protection

The relatively small businessperson can avail himself or herself of the protection of limited liability through corporate status by undertaking certain administrative preconditions, the technicalities of which need not detain us but are embodied in Company law.

Public and private companies

Limited companies fall into two distinct groups so far as status is concerned, namely:

a) public, and
b) private.

There were no reporting requirements to distinguish these two until the passing of the Companies Act 1980. This Act made the distinction between public limited companies and small and medium private limited companies and was designed to make the reporting requirements relating to non-public companies less onerous. However, the detailed requirements beyond classification were left to be enacted. It has been accepted, in principle, that the larger organization is likely to have more complex accounting requirements and more diverse methods of raising capital which call for ever more stringent reporting requirements.

The Companies Act 1981 is basically aimed at enacting the EEC Fourth Directive on Company accounts. The directive itself was adopted in July 1978 and must be applied in all member states by February 1982. The Act will reduce the amount of information small and medium companies must include in accounts filed with the Registrar of Companies and lays down new rules for the form and content of these new accounting requirements. There are two groups of companies and these are defined by maximum limits of turnover, assets and employed persons, as follows:

Small: a) Turnover no more than £1.4m,
        b) Balance sheet total not exceeding £700,000, and
        c) Not more than 50 employees.

Medium: a) Turnover no more than £5.75m,
        b) Balance sheet total not exceeding £2.8m, and
        c) Not more than 250 employees.

Small companies will only file an abbreviated balance sheet and will not have to file a profit & loss account or a director's report, though shareholders will still receive audited accounts. Medium sized companies will not have to include details of turnover and gross profit in modified accounts.

Full reporting requirements are not dealt with in this section. However, it is sufficient to say, at this stage, that the published accounts of companies have traditionally placed emphasis on the balance sheet rather than the profit & loss account. Former requirements expected the publication of a less than complete profit & loss account, omitting commercially sensitive information such as the gross profit and many important expenses.

However, certain details will need to be known and will be discussed from the point of view of preparing final accounts. Explanations will be provided wherever necessary. Such an explanation now follows:

The appropriation account

The appropriation account is an intermediate step between calculating the net profit (profit & loss account) and transferring that new profit to the balance sheet.

There are no drawings in limited company accounts. This facility is not available to the owners of the business (as will become apparent), but the owners are entitled to other types of reward relative to their status as shareholders, and this is appropriated to them as an undertaking in the appropriation account.

A diagrammatic presentation in ledger format and vertical format best illustrates the importance of the appropriation account.

Ledger format

Trading and Profit & Loss Account for year ending

TRADING ACCOUNT
- Calculating gross trading surplus
- Gross profit c/d

PROFIT & LOSS ACCOUNT
- Spending gross profit to pay expenses.
- Net profit c/d

Gross profit b/d
plus subsidiary income

APPROPRIATION ACCOUNT
- Spending net profit to pay for ownership transfers.
- Unappropriated profit c/f (or undistributed) (or retained).

Net profit b/d
Unappropriated profit b/f
(or undistributed)
(or retained).

Note
1 The appropriation account is really a continuation of the profit & loss.
2 The closing balance − transferred to the balance sheet, is called the:
   a) unappropriated profit c/f in the profit & loss account (above) or alternatively (undistributed or retained), and
   b) profit & loss account balance c/f in the balance sheet.
3 It is usual to have an unappropriated profit carried forward (abbreviated c/f) and brought forward (abbreviated b/f).

A more specific look at the appropriations by description will now be helpful.

			Net profit b/d	X
Transfer to general reserve		X		
Ordinary dividend				
Final	X			
Interim	X	X		
Preference dividend		X		
Unappropriated profit c/f		X		
		X		X

Vertical format

Income statement for year ending

Sales				X
Less cost of sales				
			X	
			X	
			X	X
Gross profit				X
Less expenses				
			X	
			X	
			X	
			X	
			X	X
Net profit				X
Add unappropriated profit b/f				X
				X
Less appropriations				
Ordinary dividend: final		X		
Interim		X	X	
Preference dividend			X	
Transfer to general reserve			X	X
Unappropriated profit c/f				£ X

Note The terminology income statement to describe the combined trading profit & loss account (including appropriation account) is used as a more modern description. It is useful, and is used in this way, particularly to distinguish this statement from a listing of year end balances which would be called the position statement (the balance sheet renamed).

Explanation of terminology

An important point is to note the interrelationship of definitions.

Ordinary dividend – is paid to ordinary shareholders (equity holders) – the owners of the business. It is paid in two forms:

> a) *Final (or proposed)* – paid at the end of the accounting period, after the Annual General Meeting of members (ordinary shareholders) who, as an important part of the business, approve the payment of the final dividend that has been recommended by the Directors.
> Therefore final or proposed dividend is shown as an expense to appropriation and a liability in the balance sheet.
> b) *Interim* – as the name suggests, a part payment, made during the course of the trading year, a payment on account to maintain a 'market' (Stock Exchange) interest in the shares. A connection with the Stock Exchange confers a particular distinction (in this respect) for public as opposed to private companies.
> Payment is made by the Directors without prior approval of shareholders and has already been paid by the time of the Annual General Meeting.

Note
Since an interim dividend is usually a device used by the directors of public companies to maintain investors' interest in the share price, the Stock Exchange Council pay more close attention and require the publication of interim accounts.

Preference dividend – is paid to fixed interest shareholders who are not the owners of the business. Many characteristics of preference shares are similar to other fixed interest holdings. Although they are classed as shares and the owners receive a dividend that may be subject to interim and final payment arrangements, such shareholders do not participate in the management (members voting rights) and do not therefore approve the final dividend. This can be contrasted with debenture holdings (see below) where interest is a fixed debt, is not an appropriation item and is therefore accounted for in the main part of the profit and loss account, prior to the calculation of net profit.

Transfer to general reserve – is a sum removed from profits to restrict its distribution to shareholders. The decision, presented to members as a recommendation, is taken by the Directors, who as the owner's representatives, decide how much of the profits shall be distributed, to whom and how much shall be retained. A transfer from the profit and loss appropriation account to the balance sheet will either
a) create, or
b) supplement

the figure entitled general reserve in the owner's capital section of the balance sheet. The balance sheet (Position Statement) can be usefully introduced at this point, showing the lower half of a vertical presentation as follows:

Financed by
Ordinary share capital
Preference share capital
General reserve

Unappropriated profit – is the remaining balance after appropriation that will also be transferred to the owner's capital section of the balance sheet and represented as the profit and loss account balance. Balance sheet extract (to date)

Financed by
Ordinary share capital	X
Preference share capital	X
General reserve	X
Profit and loss balance c/f	X

However, unlike the general reserve its distribution as profit to the owners is *not* restricted. It is a continuing balance that is added to and depleted from year to year as the case may be:

Appropriation Account	Balance Sheet	Appropriation Account	Balance Sheet
Year 1 ⟶	Year 1 ⟶	Year 2 ⟶ adjusted ⟶	Year 2 ⟶
Unappropriated Profit c/f	Unappropriated Profit b/f	Unappropriated Profit c/f	

Thus the unappropriated profit carried forward for one year (and utilized in the balance sheet) becomes the unappropriated profit brought forward in the following year, therefore it is either created or adjusted in the appropriation account and transferred to the balance sheet. In its second presentation it will be shown in the main body of the trial balance and adjusted in the appropriation account – being added to the net profit (as illustrated above).

General reserve and unappropriated profit have the common feature that, where retained, both belong to the owners of the business.

Debenture interest – is *not* an appropriation account item, but is a charge to profit & loss and is recorded as an expense.

Type of capital

Ordinary share capital
This is the capital of the owners (equity) divided into shares of nominal amounts that may be fully or partly paid. In all but exceptional circumstances, the return (if any) is determined by the Directors and voted on in General Meeting by the members.

Preference share capital
This is the share capital that is on loan to the business divided into shares of nominal amounts that are usually fully paid. Normally the return is of a fixed interest nature, with cumulative and occasionally participative rights, depending on the terms of issue.

Cumulative rights – refers to dividend rights accumulating should they be missed in any one year.

Participative rights – refers to rights to participate in profits over and above the fixed interest rate, should profits be abundant and equity shareholders have received a greater than minimum return.

Note
Share capital can be classified as:

    a) Authorized – that which the members will permit to be issued by the directors, without re-consideration by them (a maximum).
    b) Issued – that which is actually used by the company in the conduct of its business (currently employed).

Debenture capital
This is the fixed interest capital that is in no way connected with ownership, and is secured by a charge on the assets of the company. Should the directors default in paying interest then the debenture holders have certain rights accorded them by the debenture deed, including the right to appoint a receiver to overrule the directors and run the company for the benefit of the debenture holders (usually paying overdue interest and/or capital).

Share premium account
This is not strictly a subscribed capital amount (giving dividend rights) nor a retained revenue surplus. Arising on the issue of shares, a share premium is a bonus to the company, resulting from shareholders' confidence (a willingness to pay above the nominal value) on the basis of earlier trading successes. Only the nominal value can be used as the basis for paying dividend.

Illustration
100,000 shares fully paid issued at £1.25 with a nominal value of £1.00
share premium = £0.25 per share
               = £25,000 in aggregate, as represented in the Balance sheet.

Balance sheet extract.

Financed by

	Authorized	Issued
Ordinary shares of £1.00 each fully paid	100,000	100,000
Share Premium Account		25,000

Note The extract has illustrated a familiar presentation for authorized and issued amounts.

The presentation of capital balances in company accounts
Balance sheet extract in skeleton vertical account format.

Financed By

                                                  Authorized   Issued

Ordinary share capital

Preference share capital

Share premium account
General reserve
Profit & loss account balance
                     Shareholders' funds
Debentures

A summary illustrating year end procedure for published accounts — usually public companies.

1. An interim dividend is paid during the course of the period, subject to the preparation of interim accounts.
2. Final accounts are prepared and audited — and include a dividend recommended by the Directors.
3. The Annual General Meeting is fixed for a specific day.
4. All the business of the AGM is dealt with. One of the main points of this business is the approval of dividend payments that are at that point stated in the accounts as liabilities.
5. Dividend payments (warrants) are dispatched the same or next day to shareholders, eliminating the liability and depleting cash.

'Vertical' style accounts

As a point of passing interest, it is more usual to find the modern presentation for the profit and loss account and balance sheet used for accounts of limited companies than other types of business ownership. The final accounts as presented will however be shown in both forms (full page and ledger).

Ownership of other companies

Ownership of other companies occurs with both public and private companies, but is likely to be more substantial with public than private. Most public companies, as discussed, have access to the Stock Exchange for raising capital and buying other companies. Buying other companies through merger or take over has become a legitimate way of expanding business in this country. Both private and public companies while not necessarily engaging in merger or take-over activity may hold shares in other companies as an investment (probably on a relatively limited scale).

It is this type of situation that is frequently encountered in final accounting questions.

Employment of capital

Whether shares are held for a long or a short period, in the course of preparing final accounts they should be recognized as assets because they require funding.

There are two types of holding:

a) quoted shares, and
b) unquoted shares.

Quoted shares   are holdings of shares in companies that are quoted on the Stock Exchange, the advantage of holding these is that they can be held for a short time and disposed of – at the current market price.
Such holdings are in public companies.

Where there is a 'market' value (Stock Exchange price) for quoted shares, they should always be stated in a balance sheet at the *lower* of cost or market value. In this respect as others, the accountant feels happier using the cost figure. The company holding these shares is an investor, and just like any other investor, an important feature is to be able to dispose of these shares quickly.

Unquoted shares   are holdings of shares in companies that are not quoted on the Stock Exchange. Such holdings are in private companies.

The restriction on marketability means that the shares are more difficult to dispose of and are likely to result in a longer term investment.

Final accounting requirements

Such holdings, whether quoted or unquoted, involve two familiar aspects in final accounting:

a) revenue, and
b) capital.

Revenue   shares yield revenue in the form of dividend and this will be included in the profit & loss account (or other income statement) as follows:

Gross profit b/d			29,800
Dividend from shares			
quoted		1,200	
unquoted		450	1,650
			£31,450

Capital   the holding of shares utilizes some capital that could have been employed in the business for other purposes – a feature of most assets. The holdings of shares are recorded in the balance sheet (vertical presentation extract) below fixed assets but above net current assets as follows:

Fixed assets

	Cost	Depn	Nbv

Investments in shares
Quoted (market value £14,500)   12,000
Unquoted   3,000   15,000

Note
Where quoted investments are shown at cost, the market value is usually shown in brackets (as above).

Representation in the trial balance

In most cases the information for both asset and income accounting will appear in the main body of the trial balance as follows:

	Dr	Cr
Shares in companies		
Quoted	12,000	
Unquoted	3,000	
Income from investments		
Quoted dividend 10%		1,200
Unquoted dividend 15%		450

The following trial balance was extracted from the books of Cluriber Ltd, a trading concern, as at 31 December, 19-4:

	£	£
Share capital		100,000
Share premium		25,000
8% Debentures		10,000
Freehold land and buildings	105,000	
Motor vehicle at cost	40,000	
Provision for depreciation on motor vehicles as at 1 January, 19-4		15,000
Purchases and sales	120,000	158,000
Stock in trade at 1 January, 19-4	15,000	
Rent and rates	4,500	
Rent received		900
Salaries and wages	12,000	
General expenses	3,500	
Debenture interest to 30 June, 19-4	400	
Bad debts	500	
Advertising	3,000	
Debtors and creditors	13,000	12,500
Profit and loss account as at 1 January, 19-4		3,500
Interim dividend on Ordinary Shares at 30 June, 19-4	5,000	
Discounts allowed	800	
Discounts received		1,300
Balance at bank	3,500	
	326,200	326,000

You are given the following additional information:
(i) Stock in Trade at 31st December, 19-4   £20,000
(ii) Three months Rates have not been paid at 31st December, 19-4   £1,000
(iii) Depreciation is charged on the Motor Vehicles at the rate of 20% per annum on cost.
(iv) The directors propose to pay a final dividend on ordinary shares of 6%
(v) The share capital consists of 100,000 ordinary shares of £1 each fully paid up.
(vi) One quarter years rent is still to be received at 31st December, 19-4   £300

Prepare an Income Statement for 19-4 and a Balance Sheet as at 31 December, 19-4.

Cluriber Ltd

Trading Profit & Loss Account for year ended 31 December 19-4

Opening stock	15,000	Sales	158,000
Purchases	120,000		
	135,000		
Less closing stock	20,000		
Cost of goods sold	115,000		
Gross profit c/d	43,000		
	158,000		158,000
Rent & rates (4,500 + 1,000)	5,500	Gross profit b/d	43,000
Salaries & wages	12,000	Discount received	1,300
General expenses	3,500	Rent received (900 + 300)	1,200
Debenture interest 10,000 @ 8%	800		
Bad debts	500		
Advertising	3,000		
Discount allowed	800		
Depreciation 40,000 @ 20%	8,000		
Net profit c/d	11,400		
	45,500		45,500
Dividend on ordinary shares		Net profit b/d	11,400
Interim 5,000		Unappropriated profit b/f	3,500
Final 100,000 @ 6% 6,000	11,000		
Unappropriated profit c/f	3,900		
	14,900		14,900

Cluriber Ltd

Balance Sheet as at 31 December 19-4

Capital			Fixed Assets	Cost	Depn	NBV
Ordinary Shares – 100,000 fully paid @ £1 each		100,000	Freehold land and building	105,000		105,000
Share Premium		25,000	Motor vehicles	40,000	23,000	17,000
Unappropriated profit		3,900				
		128,900		145,000	23,000	122,000
			Current Assets			
8% Debentures		10,000	Stock		20,000	
			Debtors		13,000	
Current Liabilities			Rent due		300	
Creditors	12,500		Balance at bank		3,500	36,800
Proposed dividend	6,000					
Debenture interest due	400					
Rent owing	1,000	19,900				
		158,800				158,800

Example 2
J Best Ltd has the following balances at 31 March 19-8

	£	£
Authorized and issued capital		
175,000 ordinary shares of £1 each – fully paid		175,000
75,000 5% preference shares of £1 each – fully paid		75,000
General reserve at 1 April 19-7		7,000
Profit and loss balance b/f		3,350
5% debentures		30,000
Investments at cost (market value £25,250)	24,000	
Premises at cost	120,000	
Fixtures and fittings at cost	60,000	
Vehicles at cost	70,000	
Gross profit for year ended 31 March 19-8		180,000
Income on investments		4,200
Directors fees & salaries	18,500	
	6,350	24,850
Auditors expenses	1,500	
Maintenance expenses	21,000	
Bad debts	750	
Provision for bad debts		550
Provision for depreciation:		
fixtures and fittings		15,000
vehicles		12,000
Debtors	42,000	
Creditors		16,500
Bank & cash balances	65,000	
Interim dividend paid	9,500	
Debenture interest	750	
Administration & selling expenses	68,000	
Stock	11,250	
	£518,600	£518,600

At the end of the year the following adjustments are to be made:
a) Outstanding audit fees of £3,400
b) Provisions for depreciation are to be calculated on a straight line basis as follows:
Fixtures & fittings 10%
Vehicles 20%
c) Provision for bad debts is to be increased to £900
d) Debenture interest for the last half year is outstanding
e) The directors decide to:
  (i) transfer £10,000 to general reserve;
  (ii) declare a final dividend of 10% on the ordinary shares; and
  (iii) provide for the years' preference dividend.

You are required to prepare the company's profit and loss account for the year and balance sheet at the last date of that year, both in vertical format.

J Best Limited Profit and Loss Account for year ended 31 March 19-8

Gross profit b/d			180,000
Add: Income from investments			4,200
			184,200
Less Expenses:			
Audit fees and expenses (1,500 + 3,400)		4,900	
Directors fees and expenses		24,850	
Maintenance expenses		21,000	
Administrative and selling expenses		68,000	
Provision for depreciation:			
fixtures and fittings (10% × 60,000)		6,000	
vehicles (20% × 70,000)		14,000	
Bad debts		750	
Increased provision for bad debts (900 − 550)		350	
Debenture interest		1,500	141,350
Net profit			£ 42,850
Add: Undistributed profit b/f			3,350
			46,200
Less Appropriations:			
Transfer to general reserve		10,000	
Preference dividend		3,750	
Ordinary dividend − interim paid	9,500		
final proposed	17,500	27,000	40,750
Undistributed profit c/f			£ 5,450

J Best Limited Balance Sheet as at 31 March 19-8

Fixed Assets

	Cost	Depn	Nbv
Premises	120,000	–	120,000
Fixtures & fittings	60,000	21,000	39,000
Vehicles	70,000	26,000	44,000
	250,000	47,000	203,000

Investments at cost (market value £25,250)   24,000

Net Current Assets
Current Assets

Stock		11,250		
Debtors	42,000			
Less provision for bad debts	900	41,100		
Bank & Cash		65,000	117,350	

Less Current Liabilities

Creditors	16,500		
Audit fees outstanding	3,400		
Ordinary dividend proposed	17,500		
Preference dividend due	3,750		
Debenture interest outstanding	750	(41,900)	75,450
			£302,450

Financed By
Authorized & issued share capital

175,000 ordinary shares of £1 each fully paid			175,000
General reserve		7,000	
		10,000	17,000
Profit & loss balance			5,450
		Equity	197,450
75,000 Preference shares of £1 each fully paid			75,000
		Shareholders' funds	272,450
5% Debentures			30,000
			£302,450

It has to be mentioned that taxation is ignored for the purpose of preparing and presenting final accounts of companies at this level, although such information is of definite relevance to practising accountants and others.

Unit 2
Partnership accounts

Overview

1 A partnership is defined as a collection of individuals combining together to operate a business with rights and obligations to each other but without (in most cases) limited liability.

2 Partnership is the main type of organization that is permitted by most professional associations for their members.

3 Accounting for partnerships requires:
a) appropriation accounts, and
b) capital and current accounts.
These are explained.

4 Partnership final accounts are illustrated.

5 The explanation of formal accounting requirements is at the end of this chapter, listed as notes.

6 Taxation and matters relating to changes in partnership interests are ignored.

A partnership is a collection of individuals who combine together to form a unified business, and from this each partner has rights and obligations that flow to and from the business and other partners.

Partnerships are currently a less popular method of business operation than they used to be. This is probably due to two major factors, namely:

a) The relative ease and advantages (limited liability) to be gained from forming a limited company.
b) The intrinsic difficulties of running a partnership in terms of agreement between the partners etc.

However, the generalization above omits one important class – the professions. Many professions are prevented by the rules of their associations from forming limited liability associations. Generally such professional people do not engage in trade themselves, but offer a supportive service to business and the community. Accountants are among these, along with solicitors, architects, physicians, and dentists. While in terms of size they may not match companies, they are nevertheless very numerous.

Note Partnerships do not (except in very few cases) have the benefit of limited liability and it is considered important by the professions that members operate under these self-imposed constraints.

Development of partnership accounts

From sole trader accounts partnership accounts require two innovations, these are:

a) an appropriation account, and
b) a capital and current account for each partner.

The appropriation account

Similar to the appropriation account for companies, this account is concerned with the application of surplus revenue among the owners. The net profit is appropriated between the partners according to a recognized share each will obtain.

Items entered in the appropriation account will include:

1 the balance of profits (or loss) distributable among the partners,
2 partners' interest on capital contributed to the business,
3 partners' salaries drawn from the business, and
4 interest on partners' drawings.

The inclusion or exclusion of these items depends on the governing regulations that will be found either by reference to:

a) first the partnership deed, and
b) second the partnership act.

These administrative matters will be discussed below.

Note Drawings are again important (contrary to procedures for companies) since a partnership is a collection of individuals.

A diagrammatic presentation of the appropriation account for partnerships now follows – again this is a continuation from the profit & loss account and is only a subsidiary part of that account. The appropriation account – starting with the net profit b/d is shown in ledger format:

Interest on capital				Net profit b/d			X
Partners A	X			*Interest on drawings*			
B	X			Partners A		X	
C	X	X		B		X	
Salaries				C		X	X
Partners A	X						
B	X						
C	X	X					
Balance of profits							
Partners A	X						
B	X						
C	X	X					

Note 1 Amounts due to partners are recorded as debits and amounts due from partners as credits.
2 The residue of funds available to partners (according to the profit share of each) is the balance after more specific allocations have been made.
3 Partners are likely to receive:
   a) interest on the capital contributed by each, and/or

b) a salary, especially if certain partners carry out a disproportionate number of duties.

4 Partners drawing cash (and goods) out of the business for living are effectively withdrawing funds from the business — possibly reducing its trading potential, and are sometimes penalized by being charged interest — that is income to the business.

Capital and current accounts

All capital belongs to the owners of a business however it is expressed and presented in accounting, including surplus revenue. Thus in company accounts the capital belonging to the owners includes share premium, general reserve and profit & loss balances. In partnership accounts because of the adjustments required to revenue surplus, it is a common practice in addition to an appropriation account to maintain a capital and current account for each partner. These are distinguished as follows:

Capital account — contains the long term unadjusted capital contributed by a partner.

Current account — contains the profit & loss (unappropriated) profit for each partner, that is adjusted according to current year results and entitlements of specific partners.

A Partners Capital A/C

19-0	19-0
	Jan 1 Balance b/d

A Partners Current A/C

19-0	19-0
Dec 31 Drawings	Jan 1 Balance b/d
Interest on drawings	Dec 31 P & L Appropriation:
Balance c/d	Interest on capital
	Salary
	Share of profit
	19-1
	Jan 1 Balance b/d

Note 1 The balance b/d on current account is a credit balance, and a credit balance that remains after adjustment will supplement the capital account balance.

2 The current account could have a debit balance leading to a reduction in the partners' capital committment — that would in the long run not be considered satisfactory, especially if it is continued over a number of years.

Adjustments for current accounts can also be made within the balance sheet 'financed by' or capital section.

The effect of taxation on partnership accounts is ignored at this level. So too are other complications, for instance the intrinsic aspects of accounting for partners' interests as a result of admission of new partners, amalgamations and restructuring of partnerships. More advanced textbooks will deal with these aspects.

Example
Jenkins & Burt are in partnership sharing profits and losses equally. Interest on capital is allowed at 5%. Interest on partners drawings is to be charged as follows: Jenkins £30, and Burt £50. Burt is to be credited with a salary of £1,450.

The Partnership Trial Balance as at 30 June 19-2 is as follows:

		Dr	Cr
Capital	Jenkins		25,000
	Burt		15,000
Current account balances 1 July 19-1			
	Jenkins		350
	Burt		750
Drawings	Jenkins	800	
	Burt	1,200	
Provision for bad debts			350
Debtors & creditors		7,500	5,400
Rent & rates		350	
Insurance		200	
Carriage inwards		200	
Bank balance			1,100
Salaries		3,300	
Wages		2,850	
Discounts		240	650
Premises at cost		24,500	
Fixtures & equipment (cost £18,000)		12,000	
Bad debts		260	
Returns		250	300
Purchases & sales		31,500	41,700
Stock at 1 July 19-1		4,500	
Cash in hand		950	
		£90,600	£90,600

Adjustments required at year end.
a) Stock at 1 July 19-1 was valued at £8,300.
b) A provision for bad debts of 5% of debtors is required.
c) Fixtures & equipment are to be depreciated at 10% on cost.
d) Insurance premiums, paid monthly, remain outstanding for two months.
e) Rates prepaid £80.
f) Rent accrued £50.
g) Wages accrued £350.

From the above information, prepare for Jenkins and Burt:
(i) a trading profit & loss account for the year.
(ii) the capital & current accounts of the partners.
(iii) a balance sheet as at 30 June 19-2.

Jenkins & Burt

Trading, Profit & Loss Account for year ended 30 June 19-2

Opening stock		4,500	Sales		41,700
Add purchases	31,500		Less returns		250
less Returns	300	31,200			41,450
Carriage inwards		200			
		35,900			
Less closing stock		8,300			
Cost of goods sold		27,600			
Gross profit c/d		13,850			
		£41,450			£41,450
Discounts allowed		240	Gross profit b/d		13,850
Bad debts		260	Discount received		650
Provision for bad debts					
(5% × 7,500 = 375 − 350)		25			
Wages (2,850 + 350)		3,200			
Salaries		3,300			
Insurance (200 + $\frac{2}{10}$)		240			
Rent & rates (350 + 50 − 80)		320			
Depreciation of fixtures					
(10% × 18,000)		1,800			
Net profit c/d		5,115			
		£14,500			£14,500
Salary Burt		1,450	Net profit b/d		5,115
Interest on capital			*Interest on drawings*		
Jenkins	1,250		Jenkins	30	
Burt	750	2,000	Burt	55	85
Share of profits					
Jenkins	875				
Burt	875	1,750			
		£ 5,200			£ 5,200

Capital a/c Jenkins

19-1

	July 1 Balance b/d	25,000

Capital a/c Burt

19-1

	July 1 Balance b/d	15,000

Current a/c – Jenkins

19-2			19-1			
June 30 Drawings		800	July 1 Balance b/d			350
Profit & Loss Appropriation			June 30 Profit & Loss Appropriation			
Interest on drawings		30	Interest on capital		1,250	
Balance c/d		1,645	Share of profit		875	2,125
		2,475				2,475
			19-2			
			July 1 Balance b/d			1,645

Current a/c – Burt

			19-1			
			July 1 Balance b/d			750
19-2			19-2			
June 30 Drawings		1,200	June 30 Profit & Loss Appropriation			
Profit & Loss Appropriation			Salary		1,450	
Interest on drawings		55	Interest on capital		750	
Balance c/d		2,570	Share of profit		875	3,075
		3,825				3,825
			19-2			
			July 1 Balance b/d			2,570

Jenkins & Burt

Balance Sheet as at 30 June 19-2

Capital Account Balances			*Fixed Assets*			
Jenkins	25,000			Cost	Depn	Nbv
Burt	15,000	40,000	Premises	24,500	–	24,500
			Fixtures & equipment	18,000	7,800	10,200
				42,500	7,800	34,700
Current Account Balances						
Jenkins	1,645		*Current Assets*			
Burt	2,570	4,215	Stock		8,300	
			Debtors	7,500		
Current Liabilities			less provision	375	7,125	
Creditors	5,400		Prepayment		80	
Bank overdraft	1,100		Cash		950	16,455
Accruals (350 + 50 + 40)	440	6,940				
		£51,155				£51,155

Note In this case a vertical balance sheet has not been presented, but could well be.

Explanation of formal accounting requirements

Partnerships are governed by The Partnership Act 1890 and are defined as associations of two to twenty persons.

Exceptions (so far as the maximum rule is concerned) apply to accountants, solicitors and stock exchange members, or other professional persons approved by the Department of Trade.

Liability of each partner is joint and several. He or she is fully liable to the extent of his or her personal possessions for the whole debts of the partnership.

Written agreement there is no need for one, but it is wiser to have one, because there are then likely to be fewer possibilities for fundamental misunderstandings. Such a deed or articles can contain as much or as little as the partners desire though it does not necessarily cover every eventuality.

Usual accounting requirements are:
1 a statement of capital contributed by each partner;
2 the ratio in which profits (or losses) are to be shared;
3 the rate of interest, if any, to be given on capital before profits are shared;
4 the rate of interest, if any, to be charged on partners' drawings; and
5 the salaries, if any, to be paid to partners.

Section 24 Partnership Act 1890 applies as follows:

1 All partners are entitled to share equally in the capital and profits and must contribute to losses.
2 The firm must indemnify every partner in respect of payments made and personal liabilities incurred through:
   a) the ordinary and proper conduct of business, and
   b) anything necessarily done for the preservation of partnership assets;
3 The payment of capital beyond the subscribed amount entitles a partner to interest at 5%;
4 A partner is not entitled before the ascertainment of profits to interest on capital subscribed by him or her;
5 Every partner may take part in the management of the business (except a limited partner);
6 No partner shall be entitled to remuneration for acting in the business;
7 No person may introduce a partner without the consent of all existing partners;
8 All differences arising as to ordinary matters concerned with the partnership business may be decided by a majority of partners, but no change in the nature of the business may be made without the consent of all; and
9 Partnership books are to be kept at the place of business of the partnership (or the principal place, if there is more than one).

This summary should indicate why a formal agreement is important.

Limited Partnership Act 1907: permitted limited liability to be extended to a partner provided:

   a) he or she does not take part in the management, and
   b) there is at least one general partner.

Unit 3
Non-profit or club accounts

Overview

1 Not all organizations have the intention of making or attempting to make a profit, for example sports and social clubs, charities and similar associations.

2 Such examples require a modification of principles as they are applied to final accounts and an extension of the knowledge of adjustments.

3 The concept of income and expenditure is dealt with as a correction of receipts and payment entries in terms of:
   a) layout,
   b) presentation of the revenue balance, and
   c) adjustment to long term credit funds.

4 The adjustment to long term credit funds occurs in the statement of affairs or as it is more commonly called the balance sheet.

5 Special attention is given to adjustments for:
   a) income – subscriptions and subsidiary activities, and
   b) expenses – prepayments and accruals,
   that is a familiar aspect when preparing accounts for this type of organization.

Most accounts, it has been assumed, have been prepared by businesses engaging in activities that are intended to make a profit. Accounts also have to be prepared for many organizations that do not primarily intend to buy and sell goods or make a distributable profit. Sport and social clubs, charities and other associations are typical examples, and generally these are non-profit organizations.

But there is another reason for the popularity of using such organizations as the basis of examination questions (as they frequently arise) and this is that they can be used as a vehicle to reinforce accounting principles.

Income and expenditure account

The main purpose in accounting for revenue is to provide an accurate record of the true income and expenditure for a given period irrespective of the flow of cash – receipts and payments. Most people understand (club-secretaries among them) the procedure for paying and receiving money and keep accounts on this basis. But are ignorant or assumed to be, (or have only a vague knowledge) of accounting principles. Therefore, a familiar aspect of accounting is converting receipts and payments into income and expenditure accounts.

A receipts and payment account begins and ends with an opening and closing cash balance and this is a distinguishing feature of such accounts.

The layout for the revenue account

Authentic revenue accounts for clubs and associations broadly follow the principles for general revenue accounting, showing:

a) expenditure as a debit, and
b) income as a credit.

Income and Expenditure Account for year ending 31 December 19-5

Expenditure	Income

Apart from relevant adjustments to individual amounts; a receipts and payments account is often presented so that it requires a reversal of sides and re-designation.

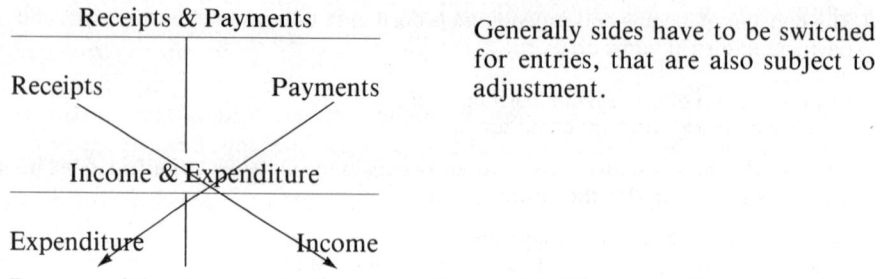

Receipts & Payments	
Receipts	Payments

Generally sides have to be switched for entries, that are also subject to adjustment.

Income & Expenditure	
Expenditure	Income

Because of the absence of adjustments for stock (with non-trading enterprises), the trading account is often redundant.

The balance

The combined revenue statement (trading account and profit & loss account) is replaced by the income and expenditure statement that shows a surplus or deficiency of revenue as the closing balance. The ledger format is used below as the basis for explanation.

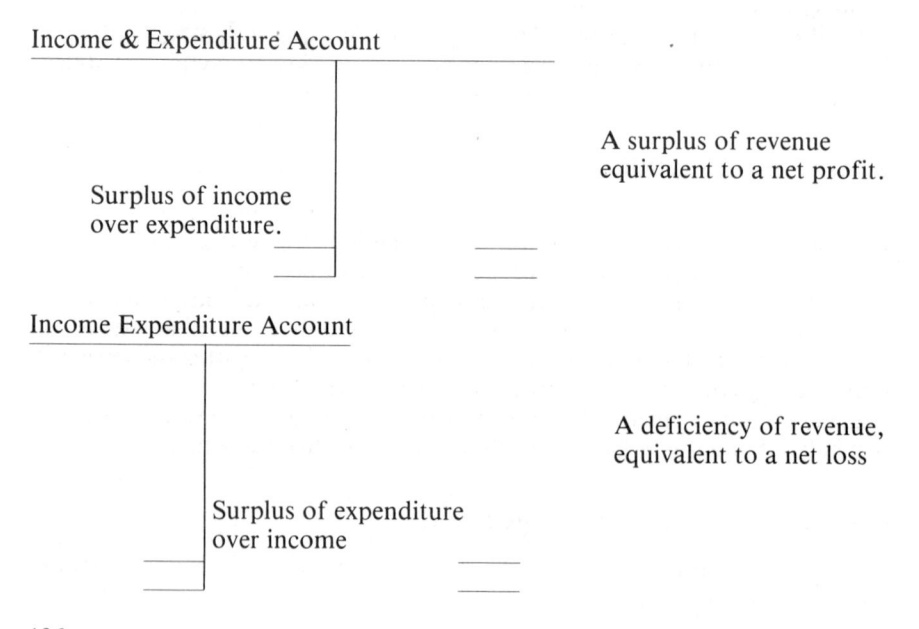

Income & Expenditure Account

Surplus of income over expenditure.	A surplus of revenue equivalent to a net profit.

Income Expenditure Account

	A deficiency of revenue, equivalent to a net loss
Surplus of expenditure over income	

Examples of income and expenditure

Expenditure	Income
Secretary's expenses	Subscriptions for year
Repairs to equipment	Surpluses from fund raising activities
Maintenance of facilities	eg Raffle
Travelling expenses	Donations received
Wages to club employees	Surplus from any trading activity
Honorariums paid to officials	eg club bar

surplus ← ──────────── → deficit

The balance sheet or statement of affairs

The balance sheet follows the conventions accepted for presentation of the closing balances (and adjustments thereto) recognizing the distinction between revenue and capital items, the only difference between trading and non-trading organizations is the description accumulated fund as a substitute for capital.

The accumulated fund is the overall surplus of the organization, belonging to members and is adjusted by the revenue surplus or deficit at the close of an accounting period. This is equivalent to capital:

a revenue surplus *increases* the Accumulated Fund

a revenue deficiency *decreases* the Accumulated Fund.

Balance Sheet

Accumulated Fund	X	
Add Surplus	X	The surplus of income over
	X	expenditure is added to the Accumulated Fund.

Adjustments for income

Membership fees & subscriptions

The collection of fees and subscriptions in many clubs and associations can be a haphazard business, especially when one considers that most of the officials are honorary. Often arrears of subscriptions and subscriptions paid in advance causes difficulty for the accountant. This difficulty can often be exploited by examiners to test a knowledge of adjustments to income.

Subscriptions paid in advance

These are equivalent to a liability of the Club; funds have been received for which no value has been given.

	Dr	Cr
double entry	I & E	BS
	(reduce credit for income).	(a liability)

ie the amount received as income for the current year should be reduced and a liability created.

Income & Expenditure	Balance Sheet
Subscriptions (current year) less advance payment in year	Capital FA CL CA Subscriptions in advance.

Subscriptions in arrears

These are equivalent to an asset of the Club (providing arrears can reasonably be expected to be received), value has been given for which no funds have been received.

	Dr	Cr
double entry	BS (an asset)	I & E (increase revenue)

ie the amount that should be received as potential income for the current year should be increased and an asset created.

Income & Expenditure	Balance Sheet
Subscriptions (current year) plus arrears for year	Capital FA CL CA Subscriptions in arrear

Life membership subscriptions (where permitted):

a) have to be apportioned over a given number of years, according to club rules; and
b) the accountant will merely take an appropriate amount as income each year, effectively treating such subscriptions as multiple payments in advance.

Calculation of the accumulated fund

A common feature of club account questions is the calculation of the accumulated fund which is only the opening capital balance at the start of an accounting period. Students will recall the equation:

    Capital   = Asset   − Liabilities

Rewritten in the context of the present unit, a similar calculation applicable to club accounts will read:

    Opening accumulated fund = Opening assets − Opening liabilities

or for the previous year:

    Closing accumulated fund = Closing assets − Closing liabilities

Thus, the accumulated fund can be calculated by adding together all assets − both current and fixed and deducting all liabilities other than long term members funds.

Illustration
The following information is taken from the closing example at the end of the unit, Roundhill Cricket Club, where the example is worked out in both the traditional and more modern layout.

Opening Accumulated Fund
= Assets − Liabilities
= 12,500 + 1,700 + 3,800 + 422 + 85 + 38 + 580 − 152 − 31 − 293
= 19,125 − 476
= 18,649

Trading activities

Clubs that engage in activities that, were it not for the fact that the profit reverts to the Club, would be regarded as business enterprises generally have to prepare accounts similar to any business enterprise eg running bars, fêtes, jumble sales etc.
This is necessary because similar problems remain even though amounts may be smaller, for example:

a) purchasing goods for resale,
b) holding stock,
c) paying wages and specific expenses, and
d) determining a net profit (or loss).

Many clubs engage in such trading activities to supplement the income from say membership subscriptions. These extra activities have to be accounted for and brought into final accounts.

Note Adjustments made to a particular side in a ledger account, by an opposite entry to the adjacent side, will be a familiar aspect of accounting. In the case of extra activities, the presentation can be done on one side, by deducting the smaller amount from the greater.

eg Sale of match refreshments   X
    less cost of refreshments   X   X

Adjustment to Expenses
Prepayments and Accruals
In many cases similar expenses have to be paid by non-profit organisations and similar periodic adjustments made for accounting purposes.
Therefore the rules for prepayments and accruals stated in an earlier section and unit apply here.
A vertical presentation can be used too:

────────── Income & Expenditure Account for year ending ──────────

────────── Balance Sheet as at ──────────

Example

The balance sheet of Little Roundhill Cricket Club at 30 September 19-4 shows the following:

Accumulated fund	18,649	Club pavillion (at cost)	12,500
Subscriptions in advance	152	Fixtures	1,700
Bar wages outstanding	31	Cricket equipment	3,800
Creditor for bar purchases	293	Bar stock	422
		Subscriptions in arrear	85
		Insurance prepaid	38
		Cash at bank	580
	£19,125		£19,125

The summary of the club cash book for the year to 30 September 19-5 shows:

Opening balance	580	Rent & rates	588
Subscriptions	1,650	Wages	932
Match fees	480	Match expenses – balls etc	133
Bar takings	2,628	Insurances	178
Locker income	107	Bar purchases	1,525
		Bar expenses	42
		Honorariums: treasurer & secretary	150
		Closing balance	1,897
	£5,445		£5,445

It is also known that:

1 The closing bar stock was valued at £650.
2 Wages for the Club are divided as follows:
  (i) groundsman   £726
  (ii) bar staff   £206.
3 Depreciation is to be provided on the basis of the written-down figures for:
  (i) cricket equipment 20%
  (ii) fixtures 10%.
4 Subscriptions paid in advance for 19-5/-6 were £205 and for 19-6/-7 were £30.
5 A bill for printing and stationery has been received for £90 that has not been put through the books.
6 Insurance prepaid £45.
7 Rent owing £70.
8 Creditors for bar purchases £380.

You are required to prepare statements for year ended 30 September 19-5 showing:

  (i) profit on the bar,
  (ii) income and expenditure, and
  (iii) closing year balances.

Little Roundhill Cricket Club
Bar Profit & Loss Account for year ended 30 September 19-5

Opening stock	422	Sales	2,628
Purchases (1,525 − 293 + 380)	1,612	Closing stock	650
	2,034		3,278
Wages (206 − 31)	175		
Expenses	42		
Surplus on bar account	1,027		
	£3,278		£3,278

Little Roundhill Cricket Club
Income & Expenditure Account for year ended 30 September 19-5

Rent & rates (588 + 70)	658	Subscriptions	
Insurances (178 + 38 − 45)	171	(1,650 − 205 − 30 − 85 + 152)	1,482
Printing & stationery	90	Bar surplus	1,027
Depreciation provision:		Locker income	107
cricket equipment (3,800 × 20%)	760	Match fees	480
fixtures & fittings (1,700 × 10%)	170		
Honorariums	150		
Groundsman's wages	726		
Match expenses − balls etc	133		
Surplus of income over expenditure	238		
	£3,096		£3,096

Little Roundhill Cricket Club
Balance Sheet as at 30 September 19-5

Accumulated Fund			*Fixed Assets*		
Balance 1st October 19-4		18,649	Pavilion at cost		12,500
Add surplus of income over expenditure		238	Pavilion fixtures (1,700 − 170)		1,530
		18,887	Cricket equipment (3,800 − 760)		3,040
					17,070
Current Liabilities			*Current Assets*		
Creditors for bar purchases		380	Barstock	650	
Creditors for printing & stationery		90	Subscriptions	−	
Subscriptions (205 + 30)		235	Insurance prepaid	45	
Rent owing		70	Cash at bank	1,897	2,592
		775			
		£19,662			£19,662

The example can be presented in the modern format, for both the profit and loss account and balance sheet, as follows:

Little Roundhill Cricket Club
Bar Profit and Loss Account for year ended 30 September 19-5

Sales		2,628
Less Cost of Sales		
Opening Stock	422	
Add: Purchases (1,525 − 293 + 380)	1,612	
	2,034	
Less: Closing stock	650	1,384
		1,244
Less: Bar expenses		
Wages (206 − 31)	175	
Expenses	42	217
Surplus on bar account		1,026
Add other income		
Subscriptions (1,650 − 205 − 30 − 85 + 152)	1,482	
Locker fees	107	
Match fees	480	2,069
		3,096
Less Expenditure		
Rent and rates (588 + 70)	658	
Insurances (178 + 38 − 45)	171	
Printing and stationery	90	
Provisions for depreciation:		
Cricket equipment (3,800 × 20%)	760	
Fixtures and fittings (1,700 × 10%)	170	
Honorariums	150	
Groundsman's wages	726	
Match expenses − balls etc	133	2,858
Surplus of income over expenditure		£ 238

Little Roundhill Cricket Club Balance Sheet as at 30 September 19-5
Accumulated Fund

Balance at 1 October 19-4			18,649
Add surplus of income over expenditure			238
			£18,887

Represented by:

Fixed Assets
Pavillion at cost			12,500
Pavillion fixtures (1,700 − 170)			1,530
Cricket equipment (3,800 − 760)			3,040
			17,070

Net Current Assets

Current Assets
Bar stock	650		
Subscriptions owing	−		
Prepayment − insurance	45		
Cash at bank	1,897	2,592	

Less Current Liabilities
Creditors for bar purchases	380		
Creditors for printing and stationery	90		
Subscriptions in advance (205 + 30)	235		
Rent owing	70	(775)	1,817
			£18,887

Unit 4
Manufacturing accounts

Overview

1 The preparation of final accounts has to incorporate the manufacturing process that is applicable to many businesses.

2 The presentation of a manufacturing account is considered as a development from the trading account.

3 The three basic stages of a manufacturing account are shown and developed as:
 a) a list, and
 b) a diagram,
   each with notes showing the treatment of raw materials, direct costs, indirect costs, work in progress, finished goods and overheads.

4 A worked example is provided showing the ledger and modern presentations — the latter is considered, in this case, to have clear advantages because of the descriptive content related to various entries.

Preparation of final accounts has so far been restricted to trading businesses which buy and sell rather than manufacture goods. The complexities of manufacture require that the standard trading account be expanded to give due recognition to the various inputs eg raw materials, labour and overheads.

Notes on manufacturing accounts have been left to this stage, not because of a lack of importance — quite the contrary, but because they:

a) serve as an introduction to aspects of manufacture and product costs, and

b) are a development from the straight-forward trading and profit & loss account.

Matters to be considered

Progressive flow from raw materials to *gross profit* overheads & *net profit*.

Raw materials:
1 opening stock
2 closing stock

Trading account A 3 materials consumed in current year

Prime cost:
1 materials used
 plus other *direct* costs:
2 direct labour
3 royalty payments

Factory indirect expenses: costs related indirectly to production but still a factory cost.
1 factory rent and rates
2 factory insurance
3 factory depreciation
4 factory power.

Work in progress:
Trading account B
1 opening stock
2 closing stock
3 production cost of completed goods.

Finished goods account:
Trading account C
1 sales
2 opening stock
3 closing stock
4 completed goods
5 *Gross profit* — the balance

Profit & loss:
overhead expenses not related to production.
Gross profit
1 administrative costs
 eg general expenses

Normal profit & loss
Expenses as they relate to non-manufacturing activity *overheads*
2 selling and distribution costs
 eg sales staff salaries
3 financial costs
 eg interest charges
4 *Net profit* — the balance.

204

Notes 1 To calculate *prime cost*, the amount of materials has to be calculated, and added to other direct costs.
Direct cost = Costs going directly into product.
2 To calculate *production cost*:
   a) add factory overhead expenses, and
   b) adjust for closing and opening work in progress.
3 Use *production cost* of goods completed to calculate gross profit – adjust for opening and closing stock of finished goods and compare against sales, as normal.
4 Use *gross profit* to calculate the net profit, as normal.

Consider the following skeleton ledger layout using what amounts to three trading accounts where there are adjustments for opening and closing balances.

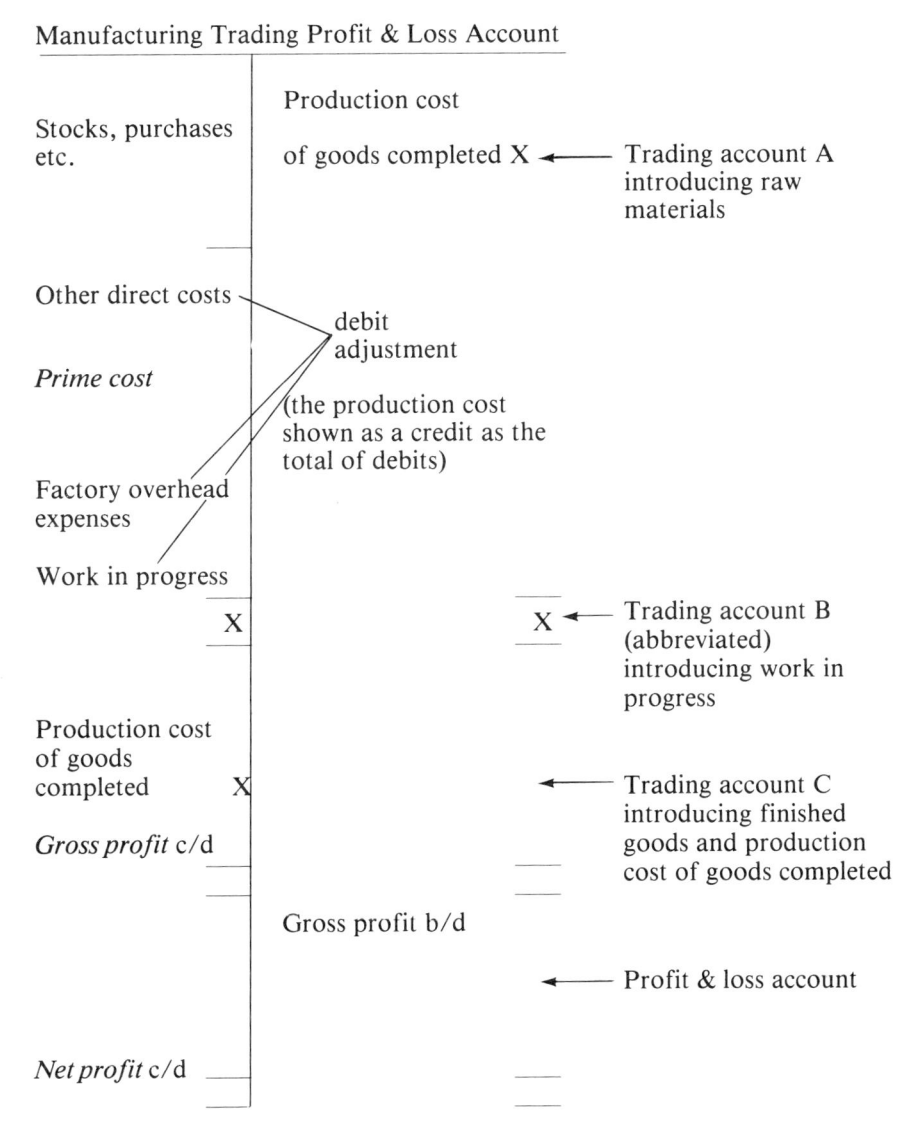

Manufacturing Trading Profit & Loss Account

Stocks, purchases etc.	Production cost of goods completed X ◄──── Trading account A introducing raw materials
Other direct costs ↘	debit adjustment
Prime cost	(the production cost shown as a credit as the total of debits)
Factory overhead expenses	
Work in progress X	X ◄──── Trading account B (abbreviated) introducing work in progress
Production cost of goods completed X	◄──── Trading account C introducing finished goods and production cost of goods completed
Gross profit c/d	
	Gross profit b/d
	◄──── Profit & loss account
Net profit c/d	

Notes 1 In the above the term *trading account* requires adjustment for stock of particular goods.
2 There are three classifications of stock that, where in existence, will also be separately represented in the Balance Sheet, these are:
  a) Raw materials
  b) Work in progress
  c) Finished goods
and they appear in the balance sheet as follows:

Balance Sheet	
Capital	Fixed assets
Current liabilities	Current assets
	Stocks of: raw materials work in progress finished goods

It is now profitable to look at a worked example of the Manufacturing Account starting with the familiar trial balance.

Example
From the following information relating to the business of F Spinners prepare a full manufacturing account, profit and loss account and balance sheet for the year ended 30 September 19-8.

	Dr	Cr
Purchases	186,100	
Sales		415,450
Opening stock of: raw materials	14,210	
work in progress	7,380	
finished goods	8,850	
Debtors	18,960	
Creditors		20,160
Discount allowed	6,680	
Discount received		8,940
Bank & cash	24,940	
General factory expenses	21,010	
Rent & rates	4,120	
Light & heat	9,630	
Factory power	15,650	
Insurance	1,250	
Sales staffs' salaries & commissions	17,990	
Royalties	18,900	
Production wages – direct	43,470	
– indirect	26,980	
Administrative salaries	14,330	
Drawings	11,000	
Capital		385,000

	Dr	Cr
Land & buildings	245,000	
Plant & machinery at cost	125,000	
Vehicles at cost	62,500	
Depreciation to date – plant & machinery		33,300
– vehicles		21,100
	£883,950	£883,950

Notes at 30 September 19-8
1. Stocks of: raw materials £16,810; work in progress £8,250; and finished goods £10,340
2. Light & heat; rent & rates; insurance are to be apportioned: factory $\frac{3}{5}$ths; administration $\frac{2}{5}$ths.
3. Depreciation provisions are to applied to cost on the basis of: plant & machinery 10%; vehicles 20%.

F Spinners

Manufacturing, Trading and Profit & Loss Account for Year Ended 30 September 19-8

Opening stock of raw materials	14,210	Production cost of goods completed c/d	342,640
Add purchases	186,100		
	200,310		
Less closing stock of raw materials	16,810		
Cost of raw materials consumed	183,500		
Production wages direct	43,470		
Royalties	18,900		
Prime cost	245,870		
Factory overhead costs			
General factory expenses	21,010		
Rent & rates ($\frac{3}{5}\times$ 4,120)	2,472		
Light & heat ($\frac{3}{5}\times$ 9,630)	5,778		
Insurance ($\frac{3}{5}\times$ 1,250)	750		
Factory power	15,650		
Production wages – indirect	26,980		
Provision for depreciation Plant & machinery (10% of 125,000)	12,500		
Vehicles (20% of 62,500)	12,500		
	343,510		
Add: Opening work in progress	7,380		
	350,890		

Less: Closing work in progress	8,250		
	342,640		342,640
Opening stock of finished goods	8,850	Sales	415,450
Add: production cost of goods completed b/d	342,640		
	351,490		
Less: closing stock of finished goods	10,340		
	341,150		
Gross profit c/d	74,300		
	£415,450		£415,450
Administration costs		Gross profit b/d	74,300
Administrative salaries	14,330	Discount received	8,940
Rent & rates ($\frac{2}{5} \times 4{,}120$)	1,648		
Light & heat ($\frac{2}{5} \times 9{,}630$)	3,852		
Insurance ($\frac{2}{5} \times 1{,}250$)	500		
Selling & distribution costs			
Sales staffs' salaries & commissions	17,990		
Financial costs			
Discount allowed	6,680		
Net profit c/d	38,240		
	£83,240		£83,240

F Spinners
Balance sheet as at 30 September 19-8

Capital				*Fixed assets*			
Opening balance			385,000		Cost	Depn	Nbv
Add: Net profit	38,240			Land & buildings	245,000	–	245,000
Less: Drawings	11,000		27,240	Plant & machinery	125,000	45,800	79,200
				Vehicles	62,500	33,600	28,900
			412,240				
					432,500	79,400	353,100
Current liabilities				*Current assets*			
Creditors			20,160				
				Stock of: Raw materials		16,810	
				Work in progress		8,250	
				Finished goods		10,340	35,400
				Debtors			18,960
				Bank & cash			24,940
			£432,400				£432,400

The example, presented in a modern format, is particularly useful in the case of a manufacturing, trading and profit and loss account where the presentation and sub-classification of information makes the account that much more readable and useful.

F Spinners, Manufacturing, Trading and Profit and Loss Account for year ended 30 September 19-8

Sales		415,450
Raw materials		
Opening Stocks		14,210
Add Purchases		186,100
		200,310
Less: Closing stocks		16,810
Cost of raw materials consumed		183,500
Production wages – direct	43,470	
Royalties	18,900	62,370
Prime cost		245,870
Factory overheads		
General factory expenses	21,010	
Rent and rates ($\frac{3}{5} \times 4,120$)	2,472	
Light and heat ($\frac{3}{5} \times 9,630$)	5,778	
Insurance ($\frac{3}{5} \times 1,250$)	750	
Factory power	15,650	
Production wages – indirect	26,980	
Provision for depreciation		
Plant and machinery (10% × 125,000)	12,500	
Vehicles (20% × 62,500)	12,500	97,640
Costs of manufacture		343,510
Add: Opening work in progress		7,380
		350,890
Less: Closing work in progress		8,250
Cost of finished goods produced		342,640
Add: Opening stock of finished goods		8,850
		351,490
Less: Closing stock of finished goods		10,340
		341,150
Sales		415,450
Gross profit		74,300
Discount received		8,940
		83,240
Administration costs		
Administrative salaries	14,330	
Rent and rates ($\frac{2}{5} \times 4,120$)	1,648	
Light and heat ($\frac{2}{5} \times 9,630$)	3,852	
Insurance ($\frac{2}{5} \times 1,250$)	500	20,330

Selling and distribution costs				
Sales staffs' salaries and commissions			17,990	
Financial costs				
Discount allowed			6,680	45,000
Net profit				£38,240

F Spinners Balance Sheet as at 30 September 19-8

Fixed assets

		Cost	Depn		Nbv
Land and buildings		245,000			245,000
Plant and machinery		125,000	33,300 12,500	45,800	79,200
Vehicles		62,500	21,000 12,500	33,600	28,900
		432,500		79,400	353,100

Net current assets
Current assets

Stock of: raw materials	16,810				
work in progress	8,250				
finished goods	10,340	35,400			
Debtors		18,960			
Bank and cash		24,940		79,300	
Less current liabilities					
Creditors		20,160		(20,160)	59,140
					£412,240

Financed By

Opening Capital			385,000
Add: Net profit		38,240	
Less: Drawings		11,000	27,240
			£412,240

Questions

Company accounts

1 The following Trial Balance was extracted from the books of N O Talot Ltd at 31 May 19-8:

Authorised, issued and fully paid capital; £1 ordinary shares		50,000
Land and buildings at cost	50,000	
Plant & machinery at cost	20,000	
Vehicles at cost	7,500	
Provisions for depreciation:		
Plant & machinery		4,000
Vehicles		3,000
Trade debtors	15,000	
Trade creditors		12,920
Discounts – net		1,300
Purchases	101,000	
Sales		151,000
Stock at 1 June 19-7	10,000	
Bad Debts written off	370	
Provision for doubtful debts		550
6% Debentures		10,500
Wages and salaries	23,455	
General expenses	11,450	
Carriage inwards	1,950	
Profit and loss account balance at 1 June 19-7		2,950
General reserve		4,750
Cash in hand	580	
Bank balance		335
	£241,305	£241,305

You are also given the following information:
1 Stock at 31 May 19-8 was valued at £11,000
2 At 31 May 1978 there were wages accrued of £245 and general expenses prepaid of £20
3 The provision for doubtful debts is to be increased to £600
4 Further depreciation is to be provided for as follows:
    10% on plant and machinery (based on cost price)
    20% on vehicles (based on cost price)
5 Provision is to be made for debenture interest
6 A further £3,000 is to be transferred to general reserve
7 The directors propose a dividend of 15% on the ordinary shares.

Required
Prepare the company's trading and profit and loss accounts for the year ended 31 May 19-8 and a balance sheet at that date.

2 The following trial balance was extracted from the books of Jonjo Ltd. a retail concern, at 31 December, 19-3:

Share capital		120,000
Freehold land and buildings at cost	80,000	
Motor vans at cost	20,000	
Provision for depreciation on motor vans at 1 January, 19-3		10,000
Sales		160,000
Rent and rates	2,500	
General expenses	7,500	

211

Wages	18,000	
Bad debts	500	
Provision for doubtful debts		600
Directors salaries	10,400	
Debtors and creditors	14,600	9,400
Profit and loss account as at 1 January, 19-3		7,000
Cost of goods sold	108,000	
Stock in trade at 31 December, 19-3	23,500	
Balance at bank	22,000	
	£307,000	£307,000

You are given the following additional information:
1. The authorized share capital is 120,000 shares of £1 each, which are all issued and fully paid.
2. Wages outstanding at 31 December, 19-3 amounted to £250.
3. The provision for doubtful debts is to be increased to £750.
4. Rent and rates amounting to £300 were paid in advance at 31 December 19-3.
5. Depreciation on motor vans is to be charged at the rate of 25 per cent. per annum on cost.
6. It is proposed to pay a dividend of £5,000 for the year 19-3.

Required
Prepare an income statement for the year 19-3 and a balance sheet as at 31 December, 19-3.

3 From the following Trial Balance and notes of Sid Stucco Ltd at 31 December 19-7, you are required to prepare:

a) Profit and loss accounts for the year, and
b) Balance sheet at 31 December 19-7.

Trial Balance at 31 December 19-7:

Ordinary share capital		120,000
5% preference share capital		20,000
Gross profit for the year		94,175
Debenture interest	700	
Stock in trade at 31 December 19-7	29,145	
Preference dividend	500	
Provision for bad debts		600
Investment income – quoted	975	
unquoted	530	1,505
Wages and salaries	22,440	
Motor vehicles – at cost	18,000	
Fixtures and fittings – at cost	11,400	
Provision for depreciation on motor vehicles		10,800
Provision for depreciation on fixtures and fittings		2,280
Debtors and creditors	31,130	22,404
Rates and insurance	4,230	
Land and buildings – at cost	128,000	
Profit and loss account balance at 1 January 19-7		6,070
Directors remuneration	16,000	
Bad debts written off	940	
Quoted investments	6,500	
Unquoted investments	5,300	
General expenses	11,920	

Balance at bank	10,629	
Share premium account		5,000
General Reserve		4,000
7% Debentures		10,000
	£296,834	£296,834

Notes
1. The directors recommend an ordinary final dividend of 10%
2. £9,000 is to be transferred to general reserve
3. The provision for bad debts is to be increased by £150
4. There is insurance prepaid of £1,245 at 31 December 19-7
5. The authorized share capital is as follows:
    130,000 ordinary shares of £1 each and
    30,000 5% preference shares of £1 each.
6. Provide for the balance of the preference dividend to be paid
7. Depreciation is to be provided:
    fixtures and fittings 10% on cost;
    motor vehicles 15% on cost.
8. The market value of the quoted investments is £10,100. The directors estimate the value of the unquoted investments at £6,500

4 A Hardaker & Co Ltd had the following Trial Balance extracted from the books at year ended 30 September 19-9

Authorized and Issued Share Capital		
150,000 Ordinary Shares £1 each fully paid		150,000
50,000 8% Preference Shares £1 each fully paid		50,000
Wages	95,820	
Salaries	18,260	
General expenses	10,500	
Carriage outward	845	
Provision for bad debts		500
Debtors & creditors	7,880	6,130
Discount received and allowed	2,110	2,440
Bad debts	660	
Provision for depreciation – machinery		8,000
vehicles		12,500
Interim dividend paid on ordinary shares	17,500	
Sales & purchases	195,000	387,500
Returns	2,500	2,085
Land and buildings at cost	185,000	
Machinery at cost	40,000	
Vehicles at cost	25,000	
Investments – quoted (market value 12,750)	10,500	
unquoted	4,500	
Stock 1 October 19-8	8,000	
Profit & loss account balance 1 October 19-8		2,870
Share premium account		15,000
General reserve		4,250
Income from investments – quoted		1,050
unquoted		900
7% debentures		10,000
Bank and cash	29,150	
	£653,225	£653,225

1. Stock at 30 September 19-8 was valued at £10,710
2. The provision for bad debts is to be increased to £750
3. The provisions for depreciation are: machinery 20%, vehicles 25% on cost
4. Wages of £1,365 are outstanding and general expenses paid in advance are £715
5. Carriage inwards outstanding £530
6. The directors have decided to transfer £5,250 to General Reserve and propose a dividend of 10%

You are required to prepare a trading and profit & loss account for year ending 30 September 19-9 and a balance sheet as at that date

Answer guide:
GP £194,265; NP £54,610; Profit & loss balance £15,730; Balance sheet totals £250,230; (vertical method).

5 The following Trial Balance was extracted from the books of Ashfalls Ltd a retail concern at 31 December, 19-6.

	£	£
Share capital		200,000
6% debentures		20,000
Share premium		40,000
Freehold land and buildings at cost	140,000	
Motor vans at cost	60,000	
Provision for depreciation on motor vans at 1 January, 19-6		20,000
Sales		316,000
Rents	4,600	600
General expenses	20,000	
Wages	37,740	
Debentures interest to 30 June, 19-6	600	
Bad debts	700	
Cost of sales	205,550	
Directors salaries	10,000	
Advertising	7,100	
Debtors and creditors	31,310	16,000
Profit and loss account as at 1 January 19-6		5,000
Stock in trade at 31 December 19-6	53,000	
Bank balance	47,000	
	617,600	617,600

You are given the following additional information:
1. Wages outstanding at 31 December 19-6 amounted to £260.
2. Rent paid in advance at 31 December 19-6 amounted to £600.
3. Depreciation is to be charged on the motor vans at the rate of 25 per cent per annum on cost.
4. The directors propose to pay an ordinary share dividend of £3,500 for 19-6.
5. The authorised share capital consists of 300,000 ordinary shares of £1 each.
6. It is proposed that £2,500 be transferred to general reserve.

Required
Prepare an income statement for 19-6 and a balance sheet at 31 December, 19-6.

6 The following Trial Balance was extracted from the books of P Cunningham & Co Ltd at 31 May 19-3.

Issued share capital		
ordinary shares fully paid £1 each		100,000
Share premium account		7,000

Profit & loss account balance at 1 June 19-2		2,950
General reserve		4,250
Cash	1,080	
Bank		835
Land & buildings at cost	94,000	
Fixtures & fittings at cost	40,000	
Vehicles at cost	24,000	
Discount allowed and received	2,150	3,250
Debtors & creditors	14,500	12,820
Purchases & sales	121,000	191,000
Returns	1,000	1,500
Stock at 1 June 19-2	10,000	
Bad debts	345	
Provision for doubtful debts		650
Provision for depreciation		
– fixtures & fittings		4,000
– vehicles		3,000
5% debentures		15,000
Debenture interest paid	750	
Wages & salaries	21,530	
Carriage inwards	1,500	
General expenses	12,650	
Loss due to flood damage	1,750	
	£346,255	£346,255

You are also given the following details:
1. Stock at 31 May 19-3 was valued at £15,000
2. Depreciation is to be provided for on a straight line basis as follows:
    20% on fixtures and fittings
    25% on vehicles
3. A provision for doubtful debts of £900 is to be carried forward
4. Salaries were accrued £465 and general expenses paid in advance £80
5. £1,500 of the flood loss is to be written off to the S G Insurance Co who have agreed to accept this amount of the claim
6. The directors have decided to transfer £5,000 to General reserve and to set aside a dividend of 15%

Required
Prepare the company's trading and profit & loss accounts for the year ended 31 May 19-3 and a balance sheet as at that date.

Answer guide:
GP £74,000; NP £24,940; Profit & loss balance £7,890; Balance sheet totals £139,140; (vertical method).

7. James Casy and Sons Ltd is a firm of wholesale grocers. Its Trial Balance at the end of 19-9 was:

	Dr	Cr
Cost of sales	602,495	
Sales		785,600
Loan interest to 31-12.-19-9	3,000	
Wages and salaries	57,110	
Rates	1,470	
Light, heat, and power	8,245	
Sundry expenses	11,030	
Travelling expenses	4,075	

215

Motor vehicle expenses		15,530	
Repairs		2,160	
Undistributed profit 19-8			49,450
Ordinary share capital (£1 shares)			150,000
5% loan (redeemable 30-6.2002)			60,000
Land and buildings at cost		75,000	
Packing machinery at cost		15,700	
Motor vehicles at cost		35,700	
Fixtures, fittings and furniture at cost		6,200	
Provisions for depreciation at 31.12.19-8			
packing machinery			4,700
motor vehicles			11,510
fixtures, fittings, furniture			2,560
Creditors			102,000
Stocks at 31.12.19-9		151,000	
Debtors		135,200	
Bank		41,905	
		£1,165,820	£1,165,820

The following adjustments have to be made:
1 Accrued charges: rates £60; wages £150; power £375.
2 Depreciation rates are: packing machinery 10% on cost; motor vehicles 20% on cost; fixtures, fittings and furniture 20% on cost.
3 The directors propose the following appropriations: taxation £30,000 dividend of 10% on the ordinary share capital.

Hint: Taxation should be treated: 1) in the Balance Sheet as a current liability; 2) in the Profit & Loss Account as an appropriation.

Partnership accounts

8 A, B, C and D are partners, sharing profits and losses 4:3:2:1 respectively. The partnership agreement states that interest on capital is to be calculated at 10% per annum, and that C is to be paid an annual salary of £400 in cash. The agreement also states that D is to be allowed an annual salary of £500, credited to his current account.

Trial Balance 31 January 19-8

Capital	A			10,000
	B			9,000
	C			8,000
	D			7,000
Drawings	A		12,000	
	B		8,500	
	C		5,900	
	D		4,000	
Current account 1.2.19-7				
	A			600
	B			1,100
	C		300	
	D			450
Net profit for the year				33,000
Salary	C		400	
Net assets			38,050	
			69,150	69,150

216

Required
1 Profit and loss appropriation account for the year ended 31 January 19-8;
2 Partners current accounts.

9 Wear and Tear are in partnership sharing profits and losses in the ratio 3:2. Under the terms of the partnership agreement the partners are entitled to interest on capital at 5% per annum and Tear is to be credited with a salary of £450 per annum. Interest is charged on all drawings but none is charged or allowed on current account balances.

The partners' capitals are: Wear £3,000 and Tear £1,000. The net profit for the year before dealing with any partners items was £2,602. At 1 January 19-6 the balances on the partners' current accounts were: Wear − credit balance of £130; Tear − debit balance of £50.

Drawings for the year: Wear £1,200; Tear £1,600
Interest on drawings: Wear £23; Tear £30.

Required
Prepare the firm's profit and loss appropriation account and the partners' capital and current accounts for the year ended 31 December 19-6

10 Big and Little are partners sharing profits and losses − Big $\frac{2}{3}$, Little $\frac{1}{3}$. The partnership agreement provides that Little should receive a salary of £600 per annum, and that interest on both Capital Accounts and Drawings should be at 6% per annum. The Trial Balance extracted at the year end 31 October, 19-3 is as follows:

Capital Accounts	− Big		15,000
	Little		10,000
Current Accounts	− Big		1,242
	Little	75	
Drawings	− Big	2,400	
	Little	1,900	
Bad debts		120	
Carriage inwards		85	
Carriage outwards		135	
Purchases and sales		16,040	25,252
Returns		222	150
Debtors and creditors		1,748	1,885
Assets at cost − land and buildings		15,000	
plant & machinery		8,000	
office equipment		3,200	
Provision for depreciation − 1.11.19-2			
plant & machinery			3,000
office equipment			1,600
Discounts		220	175
Wages and salaries		4,250	
Stock 1.11.19-2		5,289	
Insurance		280	
Cash		104	
Bank			764
		£59,068	£59,068

Note:
1 Create provision for bad debts £148.
2 Create provision for discounts − 2% of expected receipts.
3 Wages owing £300.
4 Insurance in advance £70.
5 Depreciation − Plant ⎫
  Office equipment ⎬ 10% on written down value.
  ⎭

6 Closing stock £6,151.
7 Interest on drawings – Big 72
                              Little 60

Answer guide: GP £9,917; NP £4,037; Share of profit between partners Big £1,379; Little £690 (£2,069); Balance Sheet totals £25,904; (vertical method).

11 Ewe, Mee and Hymn are partners, sharing profits and losses 5:3:2 respectively, after allowing for interest on capital at the rate of 10% pa and a salary to Hymn of £500 pa. The partnership Trial Balance at the year end, 30 June, 19-6 was as follows:

Partners' Capital Accounts	Ewe		10,000
	Mee		7,000
	Hymn		5,000
Partners' Current Accounts	Ewe		650
	Mee	440	
	Hymn		370
Partners' Drawing Accounts	Ewe	8,200	
	Mee	5,900	
	Hymn	4,600	
Sales			308,500
Purchases		244,000	
Stock 1.7.19-5		25,000	
Returns inwards		700	
Returns outwards			500
Carriage inwards		300	
Carriage outwards			450
Telephone expenses		500	
Wages, Salaries and Commissions		28,600	
Motor Expenses		2,300	
Rent, Rates and Insurance		2,100	
Bank charges		60	
Provision for Bad Debts			600
Increase in Provision for Bad Debts		200	
Debtors and Trade Creditors		26,800	28,900
Repairs and Renewals		95	
Fixtures and Fittings	Cost	3,200	
	Provision for depreciation 30.6.19-6		2,300
	Depreciation for the year	600	
Motor Vehicles	Cost	16,000	
	Provision for depreciation 30.6.19-6		4,800
	Depreciation for the year	3,200	
Cash		305	
Bank Overdraft			4,800
Suspense Account		770	
		£373,870	£373,870

Notes

1 Stock at 30 June 19-6 was valued at £22,800.
2 Hymn's 'salary' had been paid in full and included in the amount for 'Wages, Salaries and Commissions'.
3 The Sales Manager, L Porter is entitled to a commission of 1% of Gross Profit, payable 3 months after the year end.

4 Rates in advance amounted to £120.
5 Motor Expenses owing amounted to £200.
6 Included in Telephone expenses is an amount of £40 which was Ewe's own private telephone expense.
7 The Cash Book and Bank Statement had not been reconciled. The Bank Statement at 30 June 19-6 showed an overdraft of £4,972. The difference between the Cash Book and Bank Statement was the result of the following items:
   a) A lodgement of £125 made on 29 June 19-6, and entered in the Cash Book did not appear on the Bank Statement until 5 July, 19-6.
   b) Bank charges of £47 for the half year to 30 June, 19-6 had not been entered in the Cash Book.

Required
1 Trading and Profit and Loss Accounts for the year ended 30 June, 19-6.
2 Balance Sheet at 30 June, 19-6.
3 Partners Current Accounts at 30 June, 19-6.

12 You are required, using the information given below, to prepare:

a) a trading and profit and loss account and an appropriation account for the partnership for the year ended 30 June, 19-7.
b) the balance sheet at that date;
c) the partners' current accounts in columnar form.

The trial balance of the partnership T, U and V at 30 June, 19-7 was as follows:

Capital accounts:	T			10,000
	U			10,000
	V			4,000
Current accounts:	T			1,256
	U			101
	V			82
Drawings:	T		2,164	
	U		2,055	
	V		2,619	
Fixed assets at cost			50,000	
Provision for depreciation of fixed assets at 1 July, 19-6				30,000
Stock-in-trade at 1 July, 19-6			8,640	
Trade debtors and creditors			8,000	12,000
Provision for doubtful debts at 1 July, 19-6				477
Cash at bank and in hand			531	
Loan: U				5,000
Purchases and sales			81,835	97,137
Returns			1,316	623
Discounts allowed and received			2,218	1,726
Bad debts written off and recovered			336	83
Wages and salaries			7,698	
Rent, rates and insurance			1,935	
Lighting and heating			844	
Office expenses			798	
Advertising			506	
Carriage on sales			315	
Wrapping materials			334	
Van expenses			341	
			£172,485	£172,485

You are given the following information:
1. T, U and V have all agreed that:
   1. interest shall be charged on their fixed capital accounts (but not on their current accounts) at the rate of 5% per annum;
   2. V shall be entitled to a partnership salary (not included in the trial balance) of £1,200 per annum before profits or losses are divided;
   3. the balance of profits or losses shall be divided between T, U and V in the ratio 3:2:1.
2. It has been agreed between T and V (but not by U) that V's share of the balance of profits in any year shall not be less than £900.
3. U is entitled to interest at the rate of 8% per annum on his loan to the firm which has been outstanding for a year. This interest is not specifically paid in cash.
4. Fixed assets are to be depreciated at the rate of 20% per annum by the reducing balance method. No additional fixed assets have been purchased during the year.
5. Stocks at 30 June, 19-7 were:

	£
Stock-in-trade	17,925
Coke	87
Stationery	214
Wrapping materials	152

6. The provision for doubtful debts is to be made equal to 5% of the trade debtors.
7. Provisions are to be raised for discounts allowable and receivable equal to $2\frac{1}{2}$% of the trade debtors (after deducting the provision for doubtful debts) and trade creditors respectively. The provisions which existed at 1 July, 19-6 are included in the amounts shown in the trial balance for discounts allowed and received.
8. Accruals at 30 June, 19-7 were:

	£
Audit fee	300
Rent	400
Electricity	74
Coke	22
Telephone calls	29
Stationery	34
Wrapping materials	12
Repairs to van	19

9. Prepayments at 30 June, 19-7 were:

	£
Rates	127
Insurance	66
Insurance of van	53
Telephone rental	6
Road fund licence of van	20

(Institute of Cost and Management Accounts)

Income and expenditure accounts

13 The balance sheet of Skidby Young Farmers Club at 31 December 19-6 was as follows:

Accumulated fund	5,560	Clubhouse at cost	3,200
Creditors for bar purchases	400	Equipment	1,500
		Stock (bar)	780
		Subs in arrear	54
		Insurance in advance	30
		Cash in hand	396
	5,960		5,960

A summary of the club's cash book for the year to 31 December 19-7 showed the following:

Balance b/f	396	Bar purchases	3,540
Subscriptions	1,830	Rates	200
Bar takings	4,684	Insurance	180
		Bar wages	1,074
		Wages of clubhouse staff	610
		Balance c/f	1,306
	6,910		6,910

At 31 December 19-7 the following matters are to be taken into account:
1 Insurance paid in advance £ 40
2 Accrued bar wages £ 8
3 Subs in arrear £ 24
4 Creditors for bar purchases £450
5 Bar stock – value £910
6 Equipment to be depreciated by 10% on cost

Required
A bar account showing the profit or loss on the bar for the year; an income and expenditure account for the year and a balance sheet at 31st December 19-7.

14 The following information related to the Westway Social Club.

*Receipts and Payments Account
for the year ended 31 December 19-6*

Bank balance 1 January		500	Purchase of fixtures	3,000
Subscriptions 19-5	20		Bar purchases	4,000
19-6	9,750		Rates	300
19-7	30		Insurance	200
		9,800	Bar Wages and expenses	1,200
Bar takings		6,000	Entertaining fees	7,300
Donations		50	Bank balance – 31 Dec	350
		£16,350		£16,350

The club owned its own clubhouse, original cost £6,000, and also had Fixtures – cost £3,000 (Provision for Depreciation to 1st Jan 19-6 – £2,200).

	19-6 January 1	19-6 December 31
Also:		
Bar stock	2,100	2,200
Rates in advance	50	60
Bar expenses owing	30	35

Depreciation of fixtures – 10% per year on cost.

Prepare
1 Balance Sheet 1 January 19-6.
2 Income and Expenditure Account and Bar Account for the year ended 31 December 19-6.
3 Balance Sheet as at 31 December 19-6.

Answer guide: Bar profit £895; Excess of Income over Expenditure £2,305; Balance Sheet totals £11,745 (vertical method).

15

THE HIT AND TAP GOLF CLUB
Receipts and Payments Account
for the year ended 31 December 19-6

Bank balance brought forward	291	Bar purchases	4,044
Subscriptions	8,414	Barman's wages	1,150
Bar takings	6,121	Golf professionals wages	2,400
Donations	50	Cleaner's wages	450
Locker rents	220	Bar expenses	185
		Rates	420
		Repairs to clubhouse	415
		Extension to clubhouse	4,500
		Insurance	205
		Ground maintenance	400
		Balance – carried forward	927
	£15,096		£15,096

Notes

	January 1	December 31
Subscriptions owing	10	15
Subscriptions in advance	–	20
Locker rents owing	5	8
Cleaning wages owing	10	12
Insurance in advance	20	24
Bar stock	1,204	1,519

The club owned its own premises, bought ten years ago for £8,250.

Prepare
1 Balance sheet at 1 January 19-6.
2 Bar Account for year.
3 Income and Expenditure Account for 19-6 and Balance Sheet at 31.12.19-6.

16 The summarised cash account of the Woodlane Social Club for the year ended 30 June 19-4 is as follows:

Cash Account

Balance at 1 July 19-3	230	Rent of gaming machines	248
Bar takings	10,750	Bar licence fees	200
Sale of refreshments	540	Raffle prizes	197
Sale of raffle tickets	395	Cleaner's wages	434
Sale of dance tickets	188	Refreshments	289
Receipts from gaming machines	2,760	Secretary's expenses	121
Sale of old games equipment	240	General expenses	1,209
Subscriptions	412	Payment to creditors for bar supplies	8,303
		Investment in Building Society	1,600
		Barman's wages	950
		New games equipment	610
		Rates	155
		Dance expenses	270
		Balance at 30 June 19-4	929
	£15,515		£15,515

Other assets and liabilities of the club at 1 July 19-3 were:
Premises (cost)	10,500
Games equipment (cost £980)	540
Creditors for bar supplies	227
Subscriptions in advance	48
Creditors for general expenses	98
Stock of bar supplies	950

Investigation of the accounts and records of the Club revealed that:
1 The equipment sold for £240 during the year had a written down value £280 and originally had cost £350. Depreciation to be provided on the new and remaining equipment is estimated at £150 for the year ended 30 June 19-4.
2 Stocks of bar supplies at 30 June 19-4 were valued at £835.
3 The item 'subscriptions £412' in the Cash Account includes £35 in respect of the year 19-4/-5. Subscriptions in arrears at 30 June 19-4 were £28.
4 Wage owing to the barman amounted to £22 at 30 June 19-4.
5 The Building Society had notified the Club that, in respect of the £1,600 investment, interest amounting to £100 had been credited to the investment amount. No entry had been made in the books of account of the Club in respect of this item (ignore taxation).
6 Creditors for bar supplies at 30 June 19-4 amounted to £196.
7 One fifth of the rates is attributable to the bar.

Required
1 A Balance Sheet of the Woodlane Social Club as at 1 July 19-3.
2 A Bar Trading Account and the Income and Expenditure Account for the period ended 30 June 19-4, and a Balance Sheet as at that date.

(Association of Certified Accountants)

Answer guide: Bar profit £1,160; Excess of Income over Expenditure £2,612; Balance Sheet totals (vertical method) £14,459.

Manufacturing accounts

17 From the information given below relating to the WYZ Manufacturing Co Ltd for the year ended 31 December 19-1 prepare Manufacturing, Trading, Profit and Loss Accounts and Balance Sheet.

Bank charges	650
Cash at bank	10,360
Creditors	7,300
6% debentures	25,000
Debtors	11,200
Fuel and power (factory)	5,870
Furniture and fittings	8,000
General reserve	20,000
Interest on debentures	750
Interim dividend	3,600
Investments	16,000
Investment income	1,300
Land and buildings	89,000
Machinery and plant	57,000
Manufacturing wages	23,210
Office expenses	4,460
Profit and loss account surplus	7,450
Purchase of raw materials	47,550
Rates and insurance	3,740
Bad debts reserve	200
Salaries	9,460
Sales	131,400

Share capital (authorized)	150,000
Share capital (issued)	120,000
Stock at 1 January 19-1	
Raw materials	13,200
Finished goods	8,600
Stock at 31 December 19-1	
Raw materials	16,780
Finished goods	10,400

Notes

1 Increase general reserve by 20%.
2 Depreciate land and buildings by 5%, machinery and plant by 10%, and furniture and fittings by 15%.
3 Provide £10,000 for taxation (ignore all other aspects of taxation).
4 Provide for balance of year's interest on debentures.
5 Provide for a final dividend of 5%.
6 Increase bad debts reserve to 5%.

Answer guide: Price cost £67,180; Production cost of completed goods £78,750; GP £54,450; NP £29,930; Balance Sheet balances £157,780. (vertical method).

18 A L Armbells Ltd manufacture alarm clocks. At 31 March, 19-8 the following balances were extracted from the firm's books:

Stocks at 1 April, 19-7:	
Raw materials	16,000
Work in progress	8,400
Finished goods	10,500
Purchases for the year:	
Raw materials	234,000
Indirect materials	11,240
Direct power	8,420
Lighting and heating	3,160
Printing and stationery	1,690
Postage and telephones	1,300
Carriage on raw materials	1,500
Factory salaries	14,500
Administration salaries	10,500
Direct wages	86,700
Insurance	3,200
Advertising	6,500
Depreciation for the year:	
Factory machinery	13,500
Office machinery	1,700
Carriage outwards	4,800
General office expenses	2,500
Sales	477,200
Provision for bad debts	170

Notes

1 Stocks at 31 March. 19-8:
  Raw materials   18,000
  Work in progress   6,000
  Finished goods   14,700
2 Adjustments have yet to be made for:
  a) Insurance in advance £700
  b) Administration salaries accrued £500
  c) Provision for bad debts is to be increased by £200.
3 Apportionments have to be made as follows:

a) Lighting and heating – factory $\frac{1}{2}$
   general office $\frac{1}{2}$.
b) Administration salaries includes £1,800 per year for a junior clerk employed in the works manager's office.
c) Insurance to be charged – factory $\frac{3}{5}$
   general office $\frac{2}{5}$.
d) General office expenses includes £1,300 for the cleaning of the factory office.

Required
Manufacturing, trading and profit and loss accounts for the year ended 31 March, 19-8. A balance sheet is *not* required.

19 Using the information given below, which relates to a manufacturing company VR Ltd, you are required to prepare a statement to show clearly:

1 cost of raw materials used;
2 total direct cost or prime cost;
3 cost of the finished products produced;
4 cost of the finished goods sold;
5 gross profit;
6 net profit before taxation;
for the year ended 31 December 19-0

Raw materials: Stock at 1 January 19-0	78,000
Purchases	304,000
Stock at 31 December 19-0	82,000
Finished goods: Stock at 1 January 19-0	102,000
Stock at 31 December 19-0	114,000
Work in progress: at 1 January 19-0	32,000
at 31 December 19-0	36,400
Sales	800,000
Manufacturing direct wages	120,000
Manufacturing expenses	50,600
Repairs and maintenance of plant and machinery	27,000
Depreciation: Plant and machinery	76,000
General offices	10,000
Sales warehouse and offices	14,000
Delivery expenses on sales	13,200
Power	20,000
Light and heat: Factory	4,800
General offices	1,600
Sales warehouse and offices	2,600
Administration expenses	32,400
Selling and distribution expenses	52,200

Answer guide: Cost of manufacture £598,400; Gross profit £218,000.

20 Using the following balance prepare a manufacturing account for the year ended 31.10.19-4.

Stocks at 1.11.19-3	
Raw materials	11,060
Work in progress	6,210
Indirect wages	8,340
Factory lighting, heating and power	2,100
Factory rent and rates	2,600
General factory expenses	2,550
Direct wages	25,640
Factory insurance	1,500
Royalties	1,000
Carriage in	700
Raw material purchases	40,610
Plant and machinery at cost	55,000

Stocks at 31.10.19-4
   Raw materials   4,010
   Work in progress   3,800

The plant and machinery is to be depreciated at 10% per annum on cost.
In your account show clearly
1) Cost of raw materials consumed.
2) Prime cost.
3) Factory cost of finished goods produced.

If 50,000 units were produced during the year what was the manufacturing cost per unit.

21 The following trial balance was extracted from the books of T Manning (manufacturer) as at 31.12.19-2.

	£	£
Capital		77,160
Stocks – raw materials	20,820	
– finished goods	2,900	
Factory plant and machinery (at cost)	24,000	
Office furniture and fittings (at cost)	2,000	
Vehicles (at cost)	3,000	
Provision for depreciation		
Plant and machinery		9,000
Vehicles		2,000
Furniture and fittings		1,000
Freehold buildings – (at cost)	30,000	
Manufacturing wages	34,900	
Sales		299,640
Purchases of raw materials	183,280	
Factory fuel	8,640	
Factory general expenses	3,600	
Debtors and Creditors	12,840	6,540
Rent		330
Office Salaries	23,750	
Rates and Insurance	2,000	
Motor expenses	2,440	
Office expenses	1,000	
Advertising	5,000	
Repairs to plant and machinery	12,460	
Discount allowed and received	840	220
Bad debts	600	
Cash in hand	560	
Cash at bank	10,860	
Provision for bad debts		600
Drawings	9,000	
	£396,490	£396,490

Prepare manufacturing, trading and profit and loss account for the year ended 31.12.19-2 and a Balance Sheet as at that date after taking the following matters into consideration
a) Stocks at 31.12.19-2 – raw materials £25,040
                         finished goods £ 3,700
b) Manufacturing wages accrued due at 31.12.19-2 £860
c) Rent receivable due £30.
d) Rates paid in advance £150
e) Increase the provision for bad debts by £100
f) Depreciat on is to be provided at the following rates:
   plant and machinery   10% on cost
   vehicles   15% on cost
   furniture and fittings 20% on cost

Section VI
Account controls

Unit 1 Control accounts
Unit 2 Bank reconciliation
Unit 3 Incomplete records

Unit 1
Control accounts

Overview

1 Control accounts can be defined as ledger accounts presenting condensed summaries of composite ledger entries.
2 They permit the location of errors to specific time periods, or sections of the books.
3 The principles are illustrated through:
   a) sales ledger control accounts – total debtors account, and
   b) purchase ledger control accounts – total creditors account.
4 Complications related to the principles of accounting generally and control accounts are discussed.
5 The overall aim of control accounts is to ensure the composite balances balance to reduce the chance of error or omission passing unnoticed.
6 Examples of total debtor and total creditor accounts are given.

Control accounts are periodic summaries (say monthly) of inter-related transactions, connected to a major business activity.
Examples are:
1 Credit sales and related adjustments eg returns and discounts;
2 Credit purchases and related adjustments eg returns and discounts;
3 Remuneration and related payments for employees.
  Now the above definition may be cumbersome, that is why some examples have been given immediately but the important words are:
a) summaries, and
b) inter-related transactions.
For the purpose of appreciating the principles, the explanation that follows will be confined to examples 1 and 2 – credit sales and credit purchases.
  Control accounts are an important part in the system to check and supplement the trial balance. The basic function is the location of errors to particular periods in time and sections of books. **Location to:**

227

a) time periods – months; where control accounts are prepared monthly, and
b) sections of the books; where there are alphabetic divisions.

The control account is the check on the ledger to which it relates, but for this purpose is contained in the general ledger.

Replication and duplication

The control account is a summary of related information. It is not necessarily part of the double-entry system but reproduces information in aggregate on the same side as the original.

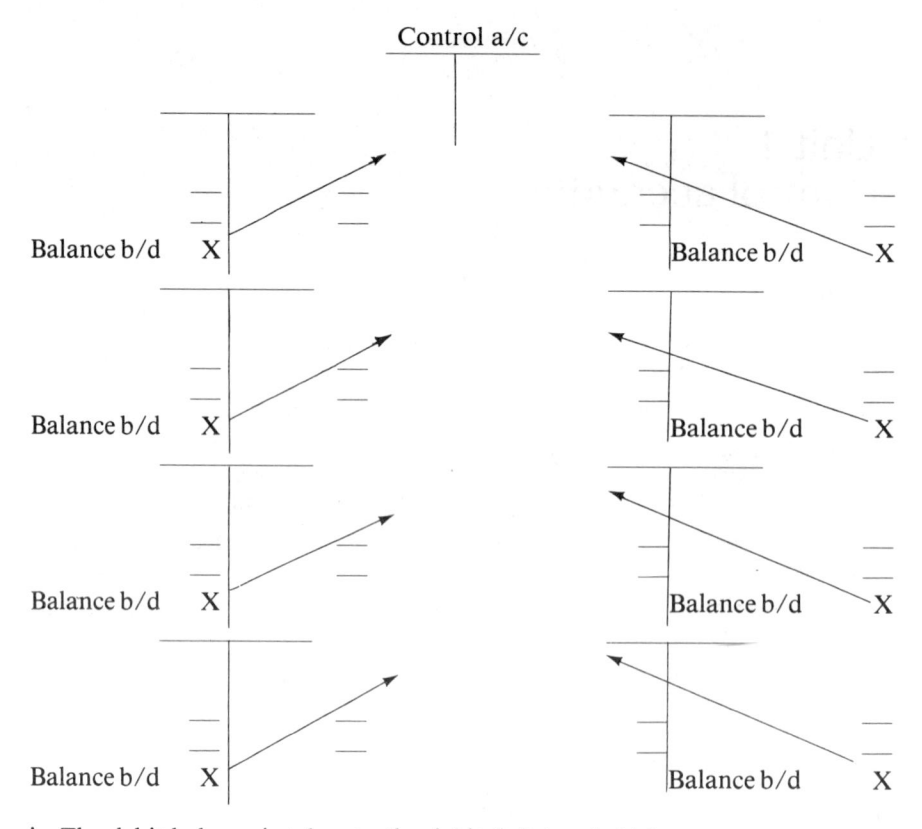

Control a/c

Balance b/d   X   Balance b/d   X

Balance b/d   X   Balance b/d   X

Balance b/d   X   Balance b/d   X

Balance b/d   X   Balance b/d   X

ie The debit balance is taken to the debit (left-hand side),
   the credit balance is taken to the credit (right-hand side).

Credit sales and purchases

Credit entries are those contained in the personal account of debtors and creditors, although of course the entries are on opposite sides; and reproduced in the control accounts for debtors – debtors control account or sales ledger control account and for creditors – creditors control account or purchase ledger control account.

The opening balances are adjusted by similar general personal ledger entries leading to the closing balances:

Total creditor control a/c   Total debtors control a/c
Additional creditors   Additional debtors
Discount received   Discount allowed
Returns outward   Returns inward
Payments   Receipts

but certain figures can also come from sources other than ledgers:
1 Daybooks — initial transaction and returns,
2 Cashbook — receipts, payments and discounts,
acting as a further check of the sufficiency of the book-keeping system.

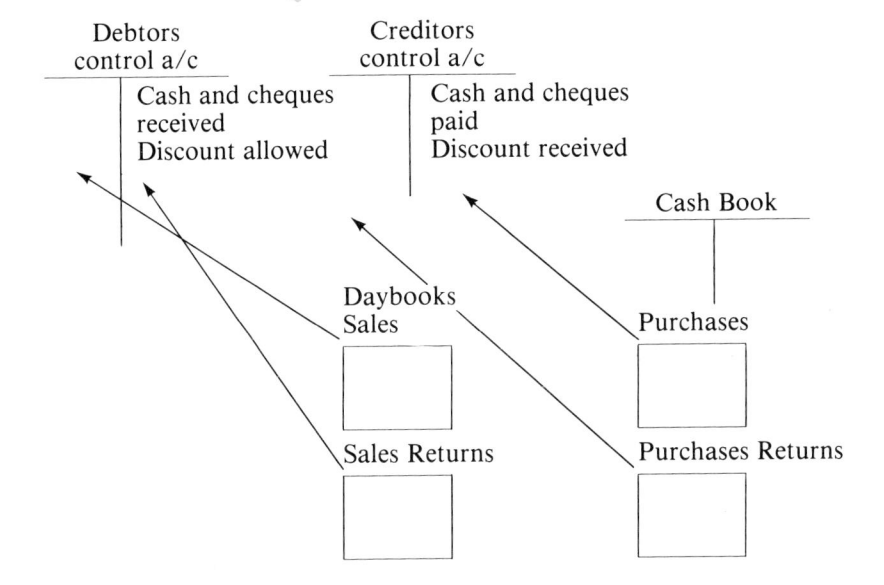

```
        Debtors              Creditors
       control a/c          control a/c
            | Cash and cheques  | Cash and cheques
            | received          | paid
            | Discount allowed  | Discount received
                                                    Cash Book
                                                        |
                           Daybooks
                           Sales              Purchases

                           Sales Returns      Purchases Returns
```

Some complications

Dishonoured cheque — where a payment by cheque has been passed through the internal system (and entered in the Cash Book), it is subsequently disallowed by the paying bank because of its customer's credit status. The position prior to the recognition of payment should be restored.

Sales Ledger Control a/c

Dishonoured cheque   1,290   Cheques and cash   £204,860

The debit for the dishonoured cheque re-establishes the earlier position, effectively nullifying the record of payment.

Set-offs — instead of a cash or bank payment goods are exchanged by offsetting an amount owed for an amount due between mutual customers. This requires adjustment in both the sales ledger and purchase ledger control accounts.

         Purchases Ledger   Sales Ledger
           Control a/c   Control a/c

Set-off sales ledger X
                                        Set-off purchases ledger X

Thus the need for a cash or bank settlement has been bypassed.

Cash sales and purchases – should be ignored since control accounts are only for credit transactions. But payment for credit sales and purchases can be through cash or bank.

Bad debts and provisions for bad debts – bad debts written off are an expense of trading and therefore should be included in a total debtors account, since they reduce the amount of cheques or cash likely to be received.

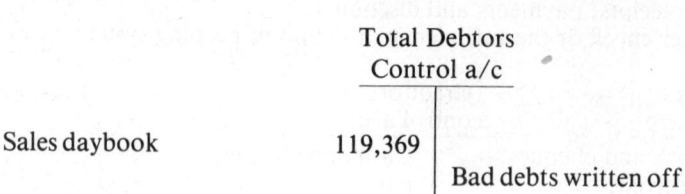

Total Debtors Control a/c

Sales daybook	119,369	Bad debts written off	204

Provisions for bad debts are merely a book transaction and do not affect the amount of cash or cheques likely to be received and should be ignored.

Points such as the above are included in questions to test the knowledge of control account themselves and accounting principles.

Balancing – off

Control accounts should:

a) balance in total, and
b) closing balances should equal the total of personal account balances in the ledger.

Where this does not occur there is likely to have been an error or omission and the matter should be investigated.

Examples

1 Sales ledger control account
   From the following information prepare a control account for the month of November 19-3.

		£
November 1	Opening balances	38,984
	Totals for November	
	Sales daybook	209,612
	Returns inward daybook	1,320
	Cheques and cash received	214,841
	Bad debts written off	855
	Discount allowed	19,502
	Balances in sales ledger set-off against balances in the purchase ledger.	
November 30 closing balances		30,359

Total Debtors Control a/c

Nov 1	Balance b/f	38,984	Nov 30	Returns inward daybook	1,320
30	Sales daybook	209,612		Cheques and cash paid	194,841
				Discount allowed	19,502
				Bad debts written off	1,855
				Set-offs	719
				Balance c/d	30,359
		£248,596			£248,596

2 Purchases ledger control account
From the following information prepare a control account for the month of November 19-3

	£
November 1 Opening balances	32,717
Totals for November	
Purchases daybook	135,410
Returns outward daybook	846
Cheques and cash paid	125,363
Discounts received	15,224
Cash refund	117
Balances in purchase ledger set off against balances in the sales ledger	719
November 30 Closing balances	26,092

Total Creditors Control a/c

Nov 30	Returns outward daybook	846	Nov 1	Balances b/f	32,717
	Cheques & cash paid	125,363	30	Purchases daybook	135,410
	Discount received	15,224		Cash refund	117
	Set-offs	719			
	Balance c/f	26,092			
		£168,244			£168,244

Note Opening balance − is the sum of personal account opening balances.
Closing balance − is the sum of personal account closing balances.
Set-offs in the two ledgers have to be for identical amounts.

To illustrate the use of control accounts in a system, an example now follows for the control of sales and associated balances. A similar example could be applied to purchases. Unlike the above (conventional example) the following, dealing only in simple accounts, rather more clearly illustrates the principles of control (a function of control accounts) that is as much a reason for keeping double-entry records as any other.

Example

On 1 August 19-9 D Adams had the following balances in her sales ledger accounts.

Bounds	86
Hirons	440
Kolkowski	125
Lane	53
McGrath	761
Seddon	28
Rackham	115
Clarke	56
Linnell	78
Brewster	83
Scott	19
Workman	42

During August the following credit sales were made:

Aug 2	Hirons	60
3	Bounds	46
5	Brewster	173
8	Linnell	86
11	Brewster	419
	Scott	30
13	Hirons	41
17	Workman	57
19	Linnell	32
23	McGrath	223
25	Brewster	16
25	Scott	48
27	Rackham	20
30	McGrath	155
31	Rackham	93

The following returns were made during the month:

August 11	Linnell	24
17	Hirons	15
26	Brewster	3
31	Rackham	74

During August the following cash was received:

August 8	Hirons	55	(discount £5)
	Brewster	83	
16	Brewster	200	
20	Hirons	26	
21	Scott	35	(discount £4)
23	Workman	42	
	Linnell	62	
26	Linnell	29	(discount £3)
27	Scott	48	
31	McGrath	500	

On 31 August it was decided to write off Bounds as a bad debt.

Required

1 The written up sales ledger, sales daybook, sales returns daybook, cash book, discount allowed account, returns account and bad debts account.

2 A complete sales ledger control account at 31 August.

Daybooks

Sales Daybook
Aug	2	Hirons	60
	3	Bounds	46
	5	Brewster	173
	8	Linnell	86
		Transfer to ledger	365
Aug	11	Brewster	419
		Scott	30
	13	Hirons	41
	16	Transfer to ledger	490
Aug	17	Workman	57
	19	Linnell	32
	23	McGrath	223
	24	Transfer to ledger	312
Aug	25	Brewster	16
		Scott	48
	27	Rackham	20
	30	McGrath	155
	31	Rackham	93
		Transfer to ledger	332

Sales Returns Daybook

Aug	11	Linnell	24
	16	Transfer to ledger	24
	17	Hirons	15
	24	Transfer to ledger	15
Aug	26	Brewster	3
	31	Rackham	74
		Transfer to ledger	77

Sales Ledger

Bounds
Aug	1	Balance b/d	86	Aug 31	Bad Debts		132
	3	Sales	46				
			132				132

233

				Hirons			
Aug	1	Balance b/d	440	Aug	8	Cash	55
	2	Sales	60			Discount	5
	13	Sales	41		17	Returns	15
					20	Cash	26
					31	Balance c/d	440
			541				541
Sept	1	Balance b/d	440				

				Kolkowski			
Aug	1	Balance b/d	125	Aug 31	Balance c/d		12
Sept	1	Balance b/d	125				

				Lane			
Aug	1	Balance b/d	53	Aug 31	Balance c/d		53
Sept	1	Balance b/d	53				

				McGrath			
Aug	1	Balance b/d	761	Aug 31	Cash		500
	23	Sales	223				
	30	Sales	155		Balance c/d		639
			1,139				1,139
Sept	1	Balance b/d	639				

				Seddon			
Aug	1	Balance b/d	28	Aug 31	Balance c/d		28
Sept	1	Balance b/d	28				

				Rackham			
Aug	1	Balance b/d	115	Aug 31	Returns		74
	27	Sales	20				
	31	Sales	93		Balance c/d		154
			228				228
Sept	1	Balance c/d	154				

				Brewster			
Aug	1	Balance b/d	83	Aug	8	Cash	83
	5	Sales	173		16	Cash	200
	11	Sales	419		26	Returns	3
	25	Sales	16		31	Balance c/d	405
			691				691
Sept	1	Balance b/d	405				

Scott

Aug	1	Balance b/d	19	Aug 21	Cash	35
	11	Sales	30		Discount	4
	25	Sales	48	27	Cash	48
				31	Balance c/d	10
			97			97
Sept	1	Balance b/d	10			

Clark

Aug	1	Balance b/d	56	Aug 31	Balance c/d	56
Sept	1	Balance b/d	56			

Linnell

Aug	1	Balance b/d	78	Aug 11	Returns	24
	8	Sales	86	23	Cash	62
	19	Sales	32	26	Cash	29
					Discount	3
				31	Balance c/d	78
			196			196
Sept	1	Balance b/d	78			

Workman

Aug	1	Balance b/d	42	Aug 23	Cash	42
	17	Sales	57	31	Balance c/d	57
			99			99
Sept	1	Balance b/d	57			

General Ledger

Discount Allowed

Aug	8	Hirons	5	Aug 31	Balance c/d	12
	21	Scott	4			
	26	Linnell	3			
			12			12
Sept	1	Balance b/d	12			

Bad Debts

Aug 31	Bounds	132	Aug 31	Balance c/d	132
Sept 1	Balance b/d	132			

Returns Inward

Aug 11	Linnell	24	Aug 31	Balance c/d	116
	17	Hirons	15			
	26	Brewster	3			
	31	Rackham	74			
			116			
Sept	1	Balance b/d	116			116

Cash

Aug 8	Hirons	55	Aug 31	Balance c/d		1,080
	Brewster	83				
16	Brewster	200				
20	Hirons	26				
21	Scott	35				
23	Workman	42				
	Linnell	62				
26	Linnell	29				
27	Scott	48				
31	McGrath	500				
		1,080				1,080
Sept 1	Balance b/d	1,080				

Sales

Aug 31	Balance c/d	1,499	Aug 8	Transfers from S.D.		365
			16	Transfer from S.D.		490
			24	Transfer from S.D.		312
			31	Transfer from S.D.		332
		1,499				1,499
Sept 1	Balance b/d	1,499				

Sales Ledger Control A/c

Balance b/d	1,886	Cash		1,080
Sales	1,499	Returns		116
		Discount		12
		Bad Debts		132
		Balance c/d		2,045
	3,385			3,385
Balance b/d	2,045			

Unit 2
Bank reconciliation

Overview

1 Control of a business current account is an important aspect in the management of any firm.
2 Reconciliation itself requires comparison of balances as they appear in:
   a) the bank statement, and
   b) the cash book
3 Differences arise through the timing of entries, largely as a result of:
   a) bank clearing of cheques, and
   b) the necessity to post cheques.
4 The bank and client look at the same transaction from a different accounting viewpoint: a business debit becomes a credit to the bank and vice versa.
5 The principle of reconciliation is straightforward and it is probably relatively easy to reconcile balances in practice, but theoretical problems do appear to cause difficulty for students.
6 Therefore it is worthwhile to study the method of working and examples, and to practice questions to get used to the terminology.
7 Examples are provided.

Control of cash and/or bank balances is an important part of any business. Most businesses conduct the majority of their transactions through a bank via the use of a current account because it is more convenient to pay and receive money by cheque. Therefore such businesses need to:
a) monitor the bank funds, and
b) have an accurate record of the state of the current account balance.

It so happens that banks aid this process by preparing bank statements that are sent to customers periodically or on request, and contain a listing of cheques 'cleared' as taken from the banks' records. (Mechanized accounting stationery has a similar format.)

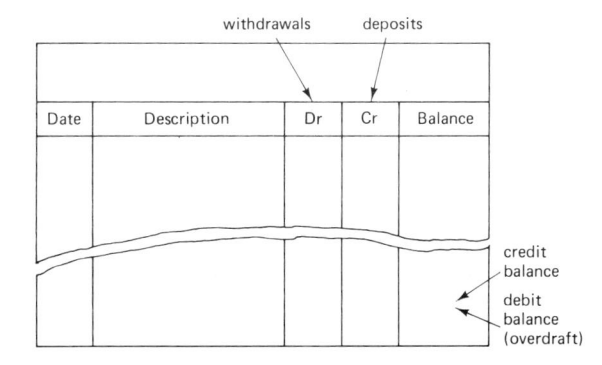

Date	Description	Dr (withdrawals)	Cr (deposits)	Balance

credit balance
debit balance (overdraft)

237

But the bank balance as printed on the bank statement rarely agrees with the internal figure produced by the business as shown in the cash book (bank column).

This is the three column cash book as contained on ledger account stationery.

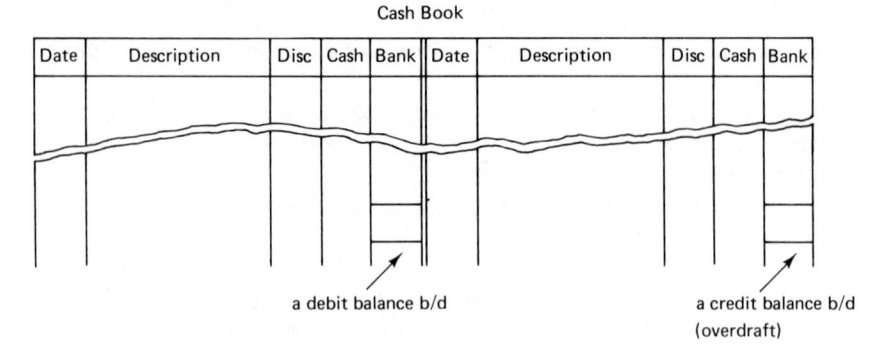

Cash Book

Date	Description	Disc	Cash	Bank	Date	Description	Disc	Cash	Bank

a debit balance b/d

a credit balance b/d (overdraft)

The difference can be accounted for as:

1 the timing of entries in the records of bank and business, and
2 the status of the initiator – the bank can initiate the entries for direct transactions and charges.

Timing of entries

Depending on the direction of flow there is a delay between entering on one record and on another record, this is caused by one or both of:

a) the bank clearing system, and
b) postal delays.

Bank clearing system

Without entering into the technicalities of this, once a payment by cheque is made it is received by the supplier and paid into the bank, and passes through the bank system to form the basis for adjustment of the payer's account. There is an average clearing period of about three days.

Postal delays

Sending a cheque by post is going to cause a time lag because the payer will write up the books (including cash book) at the time the cheque is sent.

Status of initiator

Usually the business prepares its own cheques. It is the originator of payment and receives cheques paid to it. Modern business conditions have determined that banks make and receive payment on behalf of their customers. Thus the bank has earlier knowledge of a transaction and adjusts its records before the business. This is the case with many payments that have a regularity about them eg standing orders, direct debits, credit transfers and bank commissions and charges.

A further complication arises here because the bank designs its accounting system for its own business use, and not that of its clients. Therefore the two organizations are looking at the same transaction from different accounting positions.

Take the straight-forward example of a bank balance from the point of view of:

a) the business, and
b) the bank.

The business regards its funds as a debit balance in the cash book
ie the bank owes the business its money on demand.
The bank regards the business funds as a credit balance in its accounts
ie the bank owes the business money.
Thus all entries will appear as opposites between the bank and business books. ie debits in the business will appear as credits in the bank and vice versa.

In summary, the following appear as:

1 *Business payments*
    credit in the cash book
    debit in the bank statement

2 *Business receipts*
    debit in the cash book
    credit in the bank statement

3 *Bank surplus*
    debit balance b/d in the cash book
    credit balance in the bank statement

4 *Bank overdraft*
    credit balances b/d in the cash book
    debit balance in the bank statement

A difficulty and its solution

The principles of bank reconciliation usually appear clear enough, but the main problem occurs with the mechanics of preparing statements.

To solve this problem requires:

a) a clear understanding of the terminology used, since this can sometimes be confusing;
b) an understanding of the effect a transaction will have; and
c) a method of working.

A suggested resolution of points a), b) and c):

(i) can be obtained by good practical commercial knowledge,
(ii) a knowledge of your own bank account,
(iii) an understanding of debit and credit, that should have already been obtained, and
(iv) a precise method of working that will be discussed.

Method of working

1 The majority of entries will be included in both the bank and business records, the actual reconciliation comprises of those (six to ten entries) that are not.
2 A record will often appear on one or other document. (Some questions are more complicated.)

3 Mark the statement or ledger entry in which each of the entries appear just once, this can be done by exception — ticking off those that do appear on both (see example).
4 The entries so discovered will be those required for the reconciliation.
5 The correct arrangement of these will provide (in most questions) a reconciliation, and
6 Figures are arranged to be either additions to or deductions from the opening balance.

Where a reconciliation is not arrived at, and there is no immediate error in the reconciliation itself, then this amounts to:

a) an error in recording, or
b) an omission in recording.

In either case there has been a failure in the accounting system that the exercise has been designed to reveal.

A reconciliation statement can be prepared working from:

a) cash book balance to bank statement balance, or
b) bank statement balance to cash book balance.

In practice it is frequently the case to work as in b) because this is a known figure from outside the organization that should confirm the internal figure. Usually it is best to 'write up' one or other document taking the missing information for one off the other, since the information will be there. Invariably, the question asks for one or other document to be written up. This is usually the cash book because in practice if not complete, the information can be obtained from cheque 'stubs'.

A simple example now follows

Cash Book
(bank columns)

19-5			19-5		
March 28	Total b/fwd	4,950	March 28	Total b/fwd	3,210
31	F Bower	380	29	B Billington	270
	P Child	1,930		R Porter	440
			30	S Wiles	92
			31	J Merrills	128
			31	Balance c/d	3,120
		7,260			7,260

19-5
April 1 Balance b/d 3,120

Bank statement

		Dr	Cr	Balance
March 28				1,740
29	B Billington	270		1,470
30	S Wiles	92		1,378
31	J Merrills	128		
	A Turnbull	86		
	F Bower		380	
	P Child		1,930	
	Charges	22		3,452

240

Write up the cash book (continuation).

March 31 Balance b/d	3,120	March 31	A Turnbull	22
			Bank charges	86
			Bank c/d	3,012
	3,120			3,120

The amended balance is £3,012.

The reconciliation statement would be:
bank statement to cash book
Bank reconciliation statement

bank statement balance	3,452
less R Porter	440
amended cash book balance	£3,012

Suppose the cash book March 31 had a further entry (cheque received, but not recorded on the bank statement) say to G Stanley for £660, the changes would have been:

G Stanley	660			
			Balance c/d	3,780
	7,920			7,920
April 1 Balance b/d	3,780			

the amended cash book balance would have been 3,120 − 22 − 86 + 660 = £3,672

The reconciliation statement would be:
Bank reconciliation statement

bank statement balance	3,452
less R Porter	440
	3,012
Plus G Stanley	660
amended cash book balance	£3,672

Cash Book to Bank Statement
The above statements work from the Bank Statement to the Cash Book, but it is also possible that this method of working be reversed to work from the Cash Book to the Bank Statement.

The above two reconciliation statements are now rewritten according to the suggested reversal, but note the adjustments will be reversed. Where they were added they will be deducted and vice versa.

Bank reconciliation statement
Amended cash book balance		3,012
Add R Porter		440
Bank statement balance		3,452

and the amendment

Bank reconciliation statement
Amended cash book balance		3,672
Add R Porter		440
		4,112
Less G Stanley		660
Bank statement balance		3,452

Thus it is a matter of adopting a method and sticking to it. A further example now follows, using the guidelines suggested above.

Example

Cash Book (Bank a/c only)

March	24	Balance b/f	5,319	March	25	R Spotit	80
	26	T Jones	376			L Varney	44
		F Perry	251			P Hadman	18
	29	N Queens	198		26	K Carman	409
	30	P West	15		27	P Stewart	312
		F Lake	740			B F Barclay	72
		J Garner	126			J Black	50
					29	F Brown	54
						K S Green	29
						M Palmer	35
						S Coleman	14
					30	T Fuller	10
						A Smart	8
						Balance c/f	5,890
			7,025				7,025

Bank statement

	Dr	Cr	Balance
March 24 Balance b/f			5,319
25 R Spotit	80		
L Varney	44		
S Barnes	63		
P Hadman	18		5,114
26 F Perry		251	5,365
27 P Stewart	312		5,053
B Russell		642	5,695
29 G Day	97		
F Brown	54		
K S Green	29		
M Palmer	35		5,480
30 F Lake		740	
J Garner		126	
R Coutts		3	
T Fuller	10		
A Smart	8		6,331
31 S Barnes	484		5,847

Prepare a bank reconciliation statement, writing up the cash book first,

a) Checking off items in the cash book with those in the bank statement, circling those without a corresponding entry.
b) Checking off items in the bank statement with those in the cash book circling those without a corresponding entry.
c) Updating the cash book.
d) Preparing a bank reconciliation statement as at 31 March 19-5.

Cash Book (Bank a/c only)

March 24	Balance b/f	5,319	March 25	R Spotit	80
26	T Jones	ⓐ376		L Varney	44
	F Perry	251		P Hadman	18
29	N Queens	ⓐ198	26	K Carman	ⓐ409
30	P West	ⓐ15	27	P Stewart	312
	F Lake	740	28	B F Barclay	ⓐ72
	J Garner	126	29	J Black	ⓐ50
				F Brown	54
				K S Green	29
				M Palmer	35
			30	S Coleman	14
				T Fuller	10
				A Smart	8
			March 31	Balance c/f	5,890
		7,025			7,025

Bank statement		Dr	Cr	Balance
March 24 Balance b/f				5,319
March 25 R Spotit		80		
L Varney		44		
S Barnes		⑥③		
P Hadman		18		5,114
March 26 J Barclay			251	5,365
March 27 P Stewart		312		5,053
March 28 B Russell			⑥④②	5,695
March 29 G Day		⑨⑦		
F Brown		54		
K S Green		29		
M Palmer		35		5,480
March 30 F Lake			740	
J Garner			126	
R Coutts			③	
T Fuller		10		
A Smart		8		6,331
March 31 S Barnes		④⑧④		5,847

Write up cash book – enter items shown in bank statement that have *yet to adjust* cash book.

March 31	Unadjusted balance b/f	5,890	March 25	S Barnes	63
27	B Russell	642	29	G Day	97
30	R Coutts	3	31	S Barnes	484
			31	Balance c/f	5,891
		6,535			6,535

Bank reconciliation statement
Cash book to bank statement (5,891 — 5,847)

Balance per cash book (amended)			5,891	
Add K Carman			409	
B F Barclay	⎫ cash book	72		Add back items that
J Black	⎬ credits not in	50		have *yet to reduce*
	⎪ bank statement			bank balance
S Coleman	⎭	14	545	
			6,436	
Less T Jones	⎫	376		
	⎬ cash book			Deduct items that
N Queens	⎪ debits not	198		have *yet to increase*
	⎪ in bank			bank balance
P West	⎭ statement	15	589	
Balance per bank statement			£5,847	

Bank reconciliation statement
Bank statement to cash book (5,847 — 5,891)

Balance per bank statement				5,847
Add T Jones		376		
N Queens	cash book debits not in bank statement	198		Add back items that have yet to *increase* bank balance.
P West		15	589	
			6,436	
Less K Carman		409		
B F Barclay	cash book credits not in Banks statement	72		Deduct items that have yet to *reduce* bank balance
J Black		50		
S Coleman		14	545	
Balance per cash book			£5,891	

A more difficult example now follows, but the principles are still the same. Some questions seek to test principles of double entry, using bank reconciliation as a vehicle for this purpose.

Example

The bank statement of Misbal Ltd for the period ended 31 August, 19-1, showed an overdrawn balance of £4,792 which did not agree with the company's cash book.

The following discrepancies came to light during an examination of the cash book and the bank statement:

1 Two credit transfers amounting to £149 and £526 had been posted to the bank statement on 15 August from sources unknown to the company. Subsequent enquiry revealed that the credit belonged to another customer of the bank with a similar name.
2 A deposit of £2,906 had been sent to the bank on 28 August, but not credited by the bank until 1 September, 19-1.
3 An annual subscription to a trade association amounting to £27 had been paid by the bank but had not been entered in the cash book.
4 The bank had credited the company's account with £679 being the proceeds of a foreign bill. No entry had been made in the cash book.
5 A debit of £26 appeared on the bank statement for an unpaid cheque which had been returned marked 'customer's signature required'. The cheque had been signed by the customer and paid into the bank again on 3 September, 19-1.
6 On 1 July, 19-1 the company had entered into a hire-purchase agreement to pay by banker's order a sum of £57 on 28 of each month commencing July. The bank had debited the account of another customer.
7 Cheques issued amounting to £4,972 had not been presented to the bank for payment until after 31 August, 19-1.
8 Bank charges amounting to £16 had not been entered in the cash book.

9 Dividends amounting to £326 had been credited by the bank but not entered in the cash book.
10 A cheque issued to a supplier for £167 had been entered twice in the cash book.

After correcting the discrepancies detailed above, the bank statement reconciled with the balance in the cash book.

You are required to:
a) prepare a bank reconciliation statement as on that date, and
b) show the necessary adjustments in the cash book of Misbal Ltd bringing down the correct balance on 31 August, 19-1.

Misbal Limited
Bank Reconciliation Statement as at 31 August 19-3

Balance as per bank statement (overdraft)		4,792
Add: Credit transfers (149 + 526)	675	
Hire purchase instalment (2 × 57)	114	
Unpresented cheques	4,972	5,761
		10,553
Less: Deposit not credited	2,906	
Bank debit error	26	2,932
Balance amended (overdraft)		7,621

Misbal Cash Book (Amended)

Credit transfer	679	Balance b/d – *omitted*	8,750
Dividends	326	Trade association subscription	27
Supplier	167	Bank charges	16
Balance c/d	7,621		
	8,793		8,793

Unit 3
Incomplete records

Overview

1 Incomplete records are a further test of accounting systems as presented in a standard form.

2 Cases are given when information can be missing making records incomplete so far as double-entry principles are concerned.

3 Profit or capital to date can be calculated by establishing a surplus of assets above liabilities.

4 Standard accounts are usually prepared from the information provided.
5 Information used has to be checked for its correctness, in the case of bankings, with outside sources, bank statements can be used.
6 A statement of affairs assumes the function of a balance sheet without the reliability that all information used is correct (and therefore balances).

Incomplete records, so far as double entry is concerned, are often used as a further test of accounting knowledge, ie preparing accounting statements from limited or concealed information.

Reasons for missing information

1 Choice of a limited system — maintenance of a cash book as the prime or only source of entry.
2 Inefficiency — documents may be lost and not recorded.
3 Destruction (or part destruction) — books and records destroyed by fire or some other catastrophe.

Calculation of capital and/or profit

Given knowledge of the full valuation of assets and liabilities, then profit can be deduced. Remember the equation:

Profit + Liabilities = Assets
Profit = Assets − Liabilities
(surplus) (given   (known
         valuation)   liabilities)

Just as profit for the current year can be calculated as the surplus from the year's revenue earning activities, so too can capital as the surplus (including initial funds) from all previous years' revenue earning activities.

Capital   = Assets − Liabilities
(initial funds   (total   (total
   +   assets)   liabilities)
accumulated
surplus)

In incomplete records it is likely that one or other of these equations will have to be used. A proviso to this is that no new unspecified cash or resources have been introduced during the period for which the formulae are to apply.

Cash and/or bank records

Cash or bank accounts may have to be compiled from the information given in the standard method applicable to double-entry book-keeping. In this way missing information becomes recognizable. The next step is to know how to find it.

Where only one piece of information is missing it is usual to take this as the missing figure and deduce it from the rest of the information provided, as with a balancing figure in a standard account. A proviso is that other information calculated or re-presented in the course of preparing a recognized statement is assumed to have been done correctly. In practice the accuracy of other information may be open to question so this course may not be acceptable. If the information is relevant to a bank account, then a check can be made by using the bank statement prepared by the bank.

Statement of affairs

The balance sheet implies a degree of certainty about items balancing. As this cannot be guaranteed with incomplete records, the terminology used to head such a listing is statement of affairs.

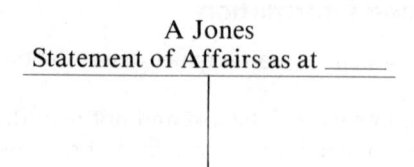

A Jones
Statement of Affairs as at _____

A useful procedure (to follow when working on incomplete records) bearing in mind that information may have to be deduced at any stage, is to:

1 prepare an opening statement;
2 open or complete a cash book, taking account of receipts and payments through the bank or by cash;
3 prepare control accounts for totals of debtors and creditors (and related information);
4 open other ledger accounts for missing information, where these are required; and
5 prepare final accounts comprising:
   a) trading account,
   b) profit & loss, and
   c) statement of affairs.

More than one piece of missing information

Where this is reliably the case and in examination questions it would be worth checking that nothing has been overlooked, a problem arises. Assumptions or deductions have to be made, with possibly one estimate based upon another, this situation would be most unsatisfactory in practice because it undermines the principles of double-entry accounting.

Single entry

Many systems are based on single entry and usually consist primarily of the cash book, with additional rulings to classify receipts and payments. Where this is the case with small businesses the accountant will want to go back to source documents, and will expect the client to retain these.

Note
Where profitability, cost of sales figures or sales figures appear to be missing, refer to Section 7 Unit 1 p 265.

Example

P Metters keeps her books on a single entry basis. The following balances and account relate to her business for the year ended 31 December 19-5.
You are required to prepare final accounts from the information provided.
A summary of Metters' cash book for the year is as follows:

Bank balance	1.1.19-5	1,036	Payments for purchases on credit	11,731
Cash balance	1.1.19-5	142	Cash purchases	1,073
Cash sales		885	Wages	10,010
Receipts for sales on credit		27,927	Salaries	1,462
			General expenses	872
			Rent	489
			Rates	258
			Drawings	1,420
			Light & heat	912
			Bank balance 31.12.19-5	1,554
			Cash balance 31.12.19-5	209
		£29,990		£29,990

A list of closing balances is as follows:	31.12.19-4	31.12.19-5
Land & buildings	28,400	28,400
Fixtures & fittings	6,520	5,868
Plant & machinery	10,980	9,882
Debtors	8,210	10,996
Prepayments for rent	88	128
Creditors	6,334	8,113
Accruals for rates	45	85
Stock	5,130	6,280

Adjustments
1 Fixtures & fittings, and plant & machinery have been depreciated by 10%.
2 Discount received and allowed were estimated at £960 and £1,030 respectively.
3 A provision for bad debts is to be made for £500.
To find opening capital

P Metters
Statement of Affairs 31.12.19-4

Capital balance 1.1.19-4		54,127	Fixed assets		
			Land & buildings		28,400
			Fixtures & fittings		6,520
			Plant & machinery		10,980
					45,900
Current liabilities			Current assets		
Creditors	6,334		Stock	5,130	
Accruals	45	6,379	Debtors	8,210	
			Prepayments	88	
			Bank	1,036	
			Cash	142	14,606
		60,506			60,506

To find total sales and purchases on credit

Total Debtors

Balance 1.1.19-5	8,210	Cash received	27,927
Credit sales (?)	31,743	Discount allowed	1,030
		Balance 31.12.19-5	10,996
	39,953		39,953

Total Creditors

Cash paid	11,731	Balance 1.1.19-5	6,334
Discount received	960	Credit purchases (?)	14,470
Balance 31.12.19-5	8,113		
	20,804		20,804

To find gross and net profit

P Metters
Trading & Profit & Loss Account for year ended 31 December 19-5

Opening stock		5,130	Sales cash		885
Add purchases cash	1,073		credit		31,743
credit	14,470	15,543			32,628
		20,673			
Less closing stock		6,280			
Cost of goods sold		14,393			
Gross profit c/d		18,235			
		32,628			32,628
Discount allowed		1,030	Gross profit b/d		18,235
Provision for depreciation			Discount received		960
Fixtures & fittings	652				
Plant & machinery	1,098	1,750			
Provision for bad debts		500			
Wages		10,010			
Salaries		1,462			
General expenses		872			
Light & heat		912			
Rent (489 + 88 − 128)		449			
Rates (258 − 45 + 85)		298			
Net profit c/d		1,912			
		19,195			19,195

To produce the statement of affairs

P Metters
Statement of Affairs 31.12.19-5

Capital balance 1.1.19-5		54,127	*Fixed assets*			
Add net profit	1,912		Land & buildings			28,400
Less drawings	1,420	492	Fixtures & fittings			5,868
		54,619	Plant & machinery			9,882
						44,150
Current liabilities			*Current assets*			
Creditors	8,113		Stock		6,280	
Accruals	85	8,198	Debtors	10,996		
			less			
			provision	500	10,496	
			Prepayment		128	
			Bank		1,554	
			Cash		209	18,667
		62,817				62,817

Questions

Control accounts

1 From the following information prepare a purchases ledger control account for the month of August 19-2.

Aug 1	Balance b/f	40,915
	Totals for August	
	Purchases daybook	155,720
	Returns outward	1,268
	Payments to suppliers	165,889
	Discount received	2,384
	Cash refund	56
Aug 31	Balance c/f	27,150

From the following information prepare a sales ledger control account for the month of August 19-2.

August 1	Balance b/f	50,214
	Totals for August	
	Sales daybook	320,446
	Returns inward	1,580
	Receipts from customers	305,233
	Bad debts written off	892
	Discounts allowed	4,140
August 31	Balance c/f	58,815

2 From such of the following information as is relevant, prepare the sales ledger control account at 31 December 19-2.

Sales ledger balances 1 December 19-2	Cr	1,500
	Dr	39,754
Cash sales		5,482
Credit sales		291,962
Returns inwards		2,176
Returns outwards		1,994
Receipts from sales ledger customers		283,976
Discount allowed		6,490
Discount received		5,950
Bad debts written off		410
Increase in provision for bad debts		800
Sales ledger balances 31 December 19-2	Cr	1,204
	Dr	?

P Brown a credit customer had a debit balance on the sales ledger account of £810, and a credit balance on the purchases ledger account of £594, at the end of December. By agreement such balances were set off one against the other on the last day of the month, the balance being settled by a cheque mid-way through the following month.

3 You are required to prepare from the information below the sales ledger control account and purchases ledger control account for the quarter July – September 19-7.

Sales ledger balance 1 July 19-7	Dr	10,020
	Cr	28
Purchase ledger balance 1 July 19-7	Dr	6
	Cr	7,430

Payment to trade creditors	46,843
Receipts from credit customers	59,965
Purchases on credit	47,790
Sales on credit	62,300
Bad debts written off	102
Discounts allowed	1,740
Discounts received	1,425
Returns inward	531
Returns outward	120
Sales ledger credit balance 30 September 19-7	18
Purchase ledger debit balance 30 September 19-7	13

4 The following information has been extracted from the books of Bowler Limited and relates to purchases and sales information. All amounts have been entered in the respective ledger accounts for the month of January 19-6.

Sales ledger debtor balances at 1 January	30,828
Purchases ledger creditor balances 1 January	21,643
Sales daybook	104,210
Purchases daybook	68,188
Receipts from customers (cheques and cash)	101,063
Payments to suppliers (cheques and cash)	59,390
Returns inwards	718
Returns outwards	349
Bad debts written off during the month	207
Provision for bad debts	650
Discount allowed	1,580
Discount received	2,320
Salesmen's commission	1,042
Set-off in sales and purchases ledgers	1,986
Customers' cheques dishonoured	632
Amount overpaid to suppliers and refunded	415
Uncleared cheque returned as incomplete (not signed)	154

You are asked to confirm the following closing balances:
Purchases ledger control £26,355
Sales ledger control £30,116

Answer guide: Purchases ledger control (total) £90,400; Sales ledger control (total) £135,670.

5 From the following transactions of Gambol Ltd prepare the Debtors and Creditors Control Accounts in the General Ledger for the year ended 31 December 19-1.

	£	
Cash received	110,712	
Purchases	79,948	
Bills of exchange received		
of which £526 were dishonou ed	8,114	
Inward returns	2,004	
Bad debts written off	652	
Cash paid	74,614	
Sales	127,456	
Discount received	2,950	
Outward returns	1,070	
Discounts allowed	4,656	
Debtors ledger balance 1 January 19-1	16,048	Dr
Debtors ledger balance 1 January 19-1	114	Cr
Creditors ledger balance 1 January 19-1	12,470	Cr

Creditors ledger balance 1 January 19-1   210   Dr
Allowances to customers on damaged goods sold   424

Notes
a) The cash received included £100 in respect of debit balances on the creditors ledger and £188 in respect of debts previously written off.
b) The sum of £868 owing to a customer for goods supplied by him was set off against his debt.

6 The trial balance of Keats & Co revealed a difference in the books. In order that the error(s) could be located it was decided to prepare purchase and sales ledger control accounts.

From the following prepare the control accounts and show where an error may have been made:

	£
Jan 1 Purchase ledger balances	11,874
Sales ledger balances	19,744
Totals for year:	
Purchase day book	154,562
Sales day book	199,662
Returns outwards day book	2,648
Returns inwards day book	4,556
Cash paid to suppliers	78
Cheques received from customers	185,960
Discounts allowed	5,830
Discounts received	2,134
Bad debts written off	396
Customers' cheques dishonoured	30
Cheques paid to suppliers	150,000

Dec 31 The list of balances from the purchase ledger gave a total of £15,566 and that from the sales ledger a total of £22,694.

Control accounts in the accounting system

7 Prepare or complete the following:

1   *Wages A/c*

Dec 31 Bank	7,700	Jan 1 Accrual b/d	135
Accrual b/d	160	Dec 31 Profit & Loss A/c	
	£		£

| | | Jan 1 Accrual b/d | 160 |

2   *Insurance A/c*

Jan 1 Prepayment b/d	100	Dec 31 Profit & Loss A/c	430
April 6 Bank		Prepayment c/d	110
	£		£

| Jan 1 Prepayment b/d | 110 |

3   *Debtors Control A/c*

Jan 1 Balance b/d	4,815	Dec 31 Bank	35,700
Dec 31 Sales		Discount allowed	790
		Sales returns	200
		Bad debts	145
		Balance c/d	5,100
	£		£

| Jan 1 Balance b/d | 5,100 |

```
                            Creditors control a/c
    4 Opening creditors            ?
      Credit purchases         29,800
      Purchase returns            120
      Payments to credit suppliers 27,600
      Discount received           695
      Contra-Sales Ledger A/c     200
      Closing creditors         3,900
                            Rates a/c
    5 Prepaid rates 1 Jan          80
      Rates paid in year          400
      Profit & Loss A/c (Rates)   385
      Prepaid rates – 31 Dec       ?
```

8 On 1 November 19-5, D Brown had balances on Sales Ledger of £1,126, made up of the following debtors.
Peacock £461, Richards £318, Adamson £115, Swales £185 and Wilson £47.
During November goods were sold on credit as follows:

```
November   6  to Peacock    £ 86
           7  to Richards   £195
          15  to Wilson     £ 67
          21  to Swales     £123
          26  to Pickles    £454
          28  to Casson     £213
Returns during November  9  from Richards  £73
                        20  from Wilson    £16
```

Cash was received from the following customers:
```
November  10  Peacock   £234  (after allowing discount of £26)
          14  Richards  £257
          17  Wilson    £ 98
          25  Swales    £166  (after allowing discount of £19)
          29  Pickles   £198  (after allowing discount of £22)
```
On 30 November it was decided to write off Adamson as a debt considered to be irrecoverable.
You are required to:
1 Write up the sales daybook, sales returns daybook, sales account, cash account, discount allowed account and bad debts account.
2 Prepare a list of sales ledger balances at 30 November.
3 Prepare a sales ledger control account for November.

Answer guide: Pickles Balance b/d £234; Richards Balance b/d £183; Sales Ledger Control Balance b/d £1,040.

9 On February 1 19-7, P Richards had balances on the Purchases Ledger of £910, made up of the following creditors:
Robson £400, Saunders £180, Brookes £200, Waudby £40
Hartley £90.
During February goods were purchased on credit as follows:
```
February   5  from Robson    300
           9  from Saunders   80
          18  from Brookes   120
          23  from Hartley   100
          28  from Howard     20
          30  from Moore      40
Returns during February  9  were from Robson   £20
                        19  were from Brookes  £40
```
Cash was paid to the following customers:

255

February 10 to Robson   £390 (after receiving discount of £10)
         13 to Saunders £180
         20 to Brookes   £196 (after receiving discount of £4)
         28 to Hartley   £186 (after receiving discount of £4)

Required
1 Write up the purchases daybook, purchase returns daybook, purchases account, purchases returns account, cash account and discounts received account.
2 Prepare a list of purchase ledger balances at 28 February.
3 Prepare a purchases ledger control account for February.

10 One June 1 19-5 J Gregory had balances on sales ledger of £721 made up of the following:
T Hales £126, P Barham £245, C Roache £79, K Downs £90 and R Salinger £181
During June goods were sold on credit as follows:

June 6 to T Hales   £156
      8 to P Barham   £232
     12 to K Downs   £ 29
     19 to R Salinger £ 43
     23 to P Barham   £194
     28 to L Johnson   £ 86

Returns during June — June 10 from T Hales   £24
                             23 from K Downs   £5

Cash was received from the following customers:
June 11 from T Hales   £140 (after allowing a discount of £16)
     12 from P Barham   £209 (after allowing a discount of £23)
     21 from R Salinger £163 (after allowing a discount of £18)
     27 from K Downs   £114

On June 30 it was decided to write off C Roache as a debt considered to be irrecoverable.

Required
1 Write up the sales daybook, sales returns daybook, sales account, cash account, discounts allowed account and bad debts account.
2 Prepare a list of sales ledger balances at 30 June.
3 Prepare a sales ledger control account for June.

Bank reconciliation statements

11   *High Street Bank Ltd*

J Wilson
25 Old Street
Hull.   Dr   Cr   Balance
19-3
June 1 Balance   1,427 CR
     3 Cash/cheques   220   1,647 CR
     3 Cash/cheques   150   1,797 CR
     3   0127   80   1,717 CR
     4   0130   100   1,617 CR
     5 Cash/cheques   45   1,662 CR
     5   0128   145   1,517 CR
     6   0131   40   1,477 CR
     6 Charges   55   1,422 CR
     6 Standing order — insurance   25   1,397 CR
     7 Cash/cheques   58   1,455 CR

J'Wilson Cash Book (Bank column only)

June 1	Balance b/fwd	1,427	June 2	Rent	80
2	J Watkins	220	2	B Jones	145
2	A Hardcastle	150	3	Hull Corporation	125
4	J Wade	45	3	Cash	100
6	O Green	172	4	D Robinson	40
6	N Clark	58	5	S Perkins	310
			7	Balance c/fwd	1,272
		£2,072			£2,072

Prepare J Wilson's bank reconciliation statement at 7 June 19-3.

12 The cash book and bank statement of the Goodhelp Charity for the period to the end of June 19-6 are given below.

Complete the cash book by showing the additional entries necessary to arrive at the correct cash book balance at 30 June 19-6 and prepare a bank reconciliation statement at the same date.

Cash book

			£			cheque no	£
June 25	Balance b/f		569.50	June 25	Advertising	101	3.35
	25	Playgroup fees	27.00	25	Salaries	102	101.55
	28	Grant	500.00		Cash	–	5.00
	28	Donations	11.50		Salary	103	15.75
	29	Subscriptions	3.15		Salary	104	20.45
	30	Playgroup fees	14.40	28	Postages	105	6.60
				28	Inland Revenue	106	27.30
				28	Stationery	Cash	2.00
				29	Rent	107	35.00
				29	Equipment	108	8.35
				30	Postages	109	2.20
				30	Pension fund	110	18.00
				30	Balance c/f		880.10
			£1,125.55				£1,125.55

Bank account

Date		Detail	Payments £	Deposits £	Balance £
June 25		Balance			585.65
	28	100	16.15		
		Cash		22.00	
		Charges	7.50		
		Interest		26.00	
		Bank giro		500.00	1,110.00
	29	101	3.25		
		102	101.55		
		275	55.40		
		104	20.45		
		Cash		9.50	938.85
	30	105	6.60		
		Bank giro-tax refund		34.20	
		107	35.00		
		Cash		3.15	934.60
July 1		106	27.30		
		Cash		14.40	921.70

257

13 J Thomas, a sole trader, has prepared the following balance sheet as at 31 March 19-2.

Capital account		23,000	Fixed plant		8,000
Current account			Motor vehicles		2,500
			Fixtures and fittings		450
As at 1.4.19-1	4,850				10,950
Profit for the year	2,235				
	7,085		Less: due to hire-		
Drawings for the year	1,270	5,815	purchase company		700
		28,815			10,250
Current liabilities			Current assets		
Trade creditors	15,590		Stock	21,150	
Accruals	1,100	16,690	Debtors	13,530	
			Bank balance	535	
			Cash	40	35,255
		£45,505			£45,505

The balance on the bank statement of J Thomas at the 31 March 19-2, showed a credit balance of £3,915.

On checking the bank statement with the cash book for the year ended 31 March 19-2, you find that the following items have not been recorded in the cash book:

1 Bank charges at 30 June 19-1 £360.
2 Standing order payments to a hire-purchase company of £110 per month: £10 per month representing interest charges. Seven instalments were paid during the year.
3 A cheque of £65 received from a debtor was returned to the bank as the drawer had insufficient funds. Enquiries reveal that the debtor is now bankrupt, and the cheque will not be met.
4 Four payments direct into the bank account of £65 each, representing rent received for letting part of the premises.
5 Several personal cheques drawn by Thomas for his private use amounting to £1,120.
6 Cheques amounting to £5,435 drawn in favour of suppliers, and entered in the cash book, had not been presented to the bank until after 31 March 19-2.

Required
a) Prepare a statement to show the adjustments you consider necessary to the bank balance in the above balance sheet, and reconcile that with the Bank statement.
b) Prepare a revised balance sheet incorporating the adjustments made necessary by the discovery of the omitted items.

14 On 31 May 19-4 the cash book of Andrews Ltd showed a balance at bank of £5,250 overdrawn.

From the following information prepare a statement showing the necessary adjustments to the cash book and a bank reconciliation statement.

1 An unidentified credit transfer amounting to £250 which appeared on the bank statement on 29 May was found to belong to another customer of the same bank.
2 Bank charges of £50 shown on the bank statement had not been entered in the cash book.
3 Cheques drawn amounting to £2,550 had not been presented to the bank for payment at 31 May.
4 A cheque for £120 paid into the bank had been credited in the cash book in error.
5 A cheque for £30 banked on 12 January was returned marked 'refer to drawer' and entered in the cash book. The cheque was re-presented one week later without

re-entry in the cash book and was paid.
6 The bank statement does not include cheques paid into the bank on 31 May 19-4 and entered in the cash book on that day £1,525.
7 A cheque payment of £120 in May had been entered in the cash book as £12.
8 The receipts side of the cash book had been over-added by £100.

Answer guide: Adjusted cash book balance £5,238 (overdraft).

Incomplete records

15 Angela Abbott records her transactions in a haphazard manner, and when asking you to prepare her annual accounts and a balance sheet at 30 June, 19-4, provides you with the following information:

	1.7.19-3 £	30.6.19-4 £
Plant and machinery at cost	8,000	7,000
Stock	6,000	7,500
Sales debtors	400	450
Purchase creditors	395	405
Bank (in hand)	100	
Bank (overdrawn)		125
Wages owing	30	50

Angela Abbott keeps a rough book in which she has recorded the following:
Credit sales for the year £20,500.
Credit purchases for the year £14,305.
Cheques paid for wages £2,200.
Cheques paid for general expenses £1,800.

She also informs you that the proceeds of plant and machinery sold amounted to £850, and that she keeps no record of cheques drawn for herself. After some discussion it is agreed to provide for depreciation on plant and machinery at 15% pa based on cost at the year end.

Required
Prepare the accounts as required by Angela Abbott.

16 T Marfleet has asked you to prepare the accounts for his business from the following information:
1

	1.1.19-7 £	31.12.19-7 £
Stock at cost	5,700	6,650
Debtors	3,100	3,600
Trade creditors	2,460	2,515
Wages owing	90	105
Insurance in advance	60	70

2 Bank summary for the year ended 31 December, 19-7.

Opening balance	875	Trade creditors	24,800
Cash from debtors	35,100	Shop rent	520
		Wages	5,100
		General expenses	310
		Insurance	280
		Drawings	4,300
		Closing balance	665
	£35,975		£35,975

259

3. The only fixed assets of the business are shop fixtures, purchased 1 January 19-5 for £2,000 and depreciated at 10% pa on cost.
4. Discounts allowed in 19-7 amounted to £800, and discounts received £610.
5. Marfleet took goods with a selling price of £300 for his own use during the year.
6. All purchases and sales are credit transactions; all receipts are banked, and all payments are by cheque.

Required

Marfleet's trading and profit and loss account for the year ended 31 December 19-7, and a balance sheet at that date.

Answer guide: Debtors control £3,600; Creditors control £2,515; Gross profit £12,185; Net profit £5,580; Balance Sheet totals £12,385 (ledger method).

17 Mr Parsons employed a student to run the boat hire business which he operated from his cafe by the river Trent. He had found in previous years that it was worth operating only for ten weeks. The student was paid a wage of fifteen pounds a week for the season plus and end of season bonus equal to one third of the profit before charging the bonus. The opening stock of tickets would last for two weeks and the order printed would last for two full seasons. The net takings were handed over to Mr Parsons daily and his cash records totalled £621. He paid the following accounts:

	£
Birthday present for Mrs Parsons	20
Petrol	127
Varnish, paint, etc	32
Replacement oars	48
Printing of tickets	60
Rowing boat	90
Annual river licence	50
New percolator for cafe	100

The student had paid the following accounts from the daily takings

	£
Varnish, paint, etc	27
Wages (to student)	120

The accounts for last year showed stocks at the end of that period of:

	£
Varnish, paint, etc	25
Spare equipment	41
Boats	1,200
Printing	4

Closing stocks this year were:

	£
Varnish, paint	21
Spare equipment	88
Petrol	10

Required

a) Prepare a profit and loss account and closing balance sheet for the boat hire business after allowing depreciation at 10% of the reducing balance of fixed assets.
(15 marks)
b) What changes would you make to the above accounts if the student worked a further two five day weeks after the end of the season repainting the boats including 3 days on the new boat (which was not used that season). (Ignore paint costs.)
(4 marks)
(Total 19 marks)
(Association of Certified Accountants)

18 T B purchased an existing business on 1 December 19-5 for the sum of £20,000. The assets acquired included: premises £13,000, fixtures and equipment £1,400 and trading stock £3,600. He did not keep any accounting records in the first year but from documents produced by him the following facts were ascertained:

1 All payments were made by cheque and all receipts banked immediately.
2 On 1 December 19-5, he opened a bank account with £1,200 and on 31 August 19-6 he deposited a further sum of £500 as working capital.
3 During the year he received £20,470 in respect of cash sales and payments from debtors. At 30 November 1976 customers owed the sum of £1,656.
4 At the financial year end 30 November 19-6 he was not able to produce details of amounts paid to suppliers of goods during the year. The only information available was a file of unpaid invoices from suppliers, which produced the amount owing to suppliers at 30 November 19-6 of £1,188.
5 Payments made from his business bank account during the year included Rates £260, of which £52 was prepaid, advertising £284, fixtures and equipment £220, wages £1,568, general expenses £386, drawings £2,080, and £164 for household expenses.
6 At 30 November 19-6, the selling price of the trading stock was £6,400. TB normally expects to sell all goods which will produce for him a gross profit of 25 per cent on selling price. His closing bank balance was £884.
7 Fixtures and equipment are to be depreciated at 10 per cent.

Required
a) A summarised cash account for the year ended 30 November 19-6.
b) The trading and profit and loss accounts for the year, and a balance sheet as at 30 November 19-6, and
c) Comment on the first year of trading under the management of TB.
(Institute of Chartered Secretaries and Administrators)

19 Maurice Crumb has recently commenced business as a second-hand dealer. He has no knowledge of accounting and, at the end of his first year of trading, asks you for advice. He provides the following information:

'On 1st July 19-3 I started in business as a second-hand dealer, giving up my job as a salesman for which I had been paid £1,500 per year. I had recently inherited £4,000 from an aunt, and this, together with a loan of £2,000 from a friend, provided me with sufficient capital to commence my business. I leased some premises for which I paid £3,000 for a five year lease, and paid the balance of my capital into the bank.

'I needed some transport so I bought an old van for £900, paying by cheque. I think the van was a real bargain — it would have cost me at least £1,200 from another dealer — and having run it for a year it will last me for four more years.

'My first deal was to buy five hundred army greatcoats for £5 each. I paid £1,000 on account and, after I had sold three hundred of them for £10 each and received the cash, I settled the account and paid the balance into the bank. I've sold another fifty as a job lot for £9 each, but I haven't been paid yet. I think I can sell the remaining greatcoats for at least £9 each, so I've made a very good profit there.

'My second deal was to buy fifty old transistor radios for £400, which I paid for by cheque. My hobby is electronics, so by using some spare parts which I had at home — which must have cost me about £40 a year or so ago — I was able to repair forty of them, and sell them at £15 each. The other ten seem to be beyond repair, but I should be able to take them to pieces and sell the usable parts for £20.

'My final deal was to buy some office furniture at an auction sale — eighty desks which cost me £560, and eighty chairs for an additional £240. I've only paid £600 of the cost so far, but I've promised to pay the balance as soon as possible. I've found various buyers for this furniture, and have sold fifty desks and chairs for £750; I've received all the money for this. I actually sold another four desks for £40, but I haven't been paid for those yet. I'm rather concerned about that sale, however,

261

because I have been told that the customer is in considerable financial difficulties.

'There was not much else happened during the year. I paid a few odd expenses in cash — about £170, I think — but all other monies I paid into the bank, where the balance at 30th June 19-4 was £1,128. I draw money out for my own spending whenever I needed it'.

Required

a) Tabulate clearly, for each of the deals made by Maurice Crumb, the sales value, the cost of purchases and the value of the closing stock. Explain clearly the reason for the value you have placed on the closing stock.

b) Prepare a trading, profit & loss account for the year ended 30 June 19-4 and a balance sheet as at that date, stating clearly any assumptions you have made.

c) What financial considerations are relevant in helping Mr Crumb to decide whether or not he should continue in business?

(Association of Certified Accountants)

Section VII
Additional information and statements from final accounts

Unit 1 Accounting ratios (including mark-up & margin)
Unit 2 Funds flow statements (including SSAP 10)
Unit 3 Cash budgeting

Unit 1
Accounting ratios (including mark-up and margin)

Overview

1 Accounting ratios provide the means of comparing figures in final accounts by percentages, fractions and ratios.
2 Comparisons are usually between different businesses and for different years and require care in use.
3 Comparisons can be misleading.
4 An example to be used as the basic illustration is set out.
5 Examples of ratios are presented under the headings:
sales,
profitability,
turnover,
working capital.
6 The trading account for the illustration is presented for your information.
7 Investment ratios are finally discussed but these are not relevant to the business unless it holds shares outside. They are also treated separately because they cannot be served by the illustration given.
8 An example is given to combine ratios with an understanding of final accounts.
9 Sufficient examples of accounting ratios are examined to enable the student to develop his or her own ideas in conjunction with more advanced textbooks.

What are commonly referred to as accounting ratios not only include arithmetic ratios but other arithmetic relationships for the purpose of comparison. Accounting ratios are expressed as:

a) fractions,
b) percentages, and
c) ratios.

It is conventional to adopt one or other for a specific purpose. The comparisons made are usually between:

(i) other businesses for the same accounting period, and
(ii) the same business but for earlier accounting periods.

Comparisons are often made between figures contained in earlier or current final accounts, such comparisons have to be made with care and in practice some knowledge of trading conditions affecting the firm(s) under review and industry generally are required – so far as is possible.

Hints about comparisons

1 There is a tendency for figures to be out of date when based on final accounts since the latest of these usually begins at least twelve months earlier.
2 Sometimes there is a shortage of complete figures and estimates have to be devised.
3 Accounting periods of different businesses do not always exactly coincide.
4 An intelligent estimate can often act as a good substitute. What is important is to attempt to look beyond the figures and develop some understanding of the business.

Ratios under review

Although there are many ratios, these can be limitless within the constraints of accounting information. The major ones will be discussed leaving the search for further ratios to:
a) more advanced texts, and
b) the student's initiative.

The ratios to be discussed are as follows:

A Sales ratios

1 Mark-up ⎫
2 Margin   ⎬ and conversion from one to the other, and
3 Sales to capital employed (at start of trading period).

B Profitability ratios

1 Net profit to sales,
2 Net profit to capital employed (at start of trading period), and
3 Net profit to owner's capital (at start of trading period).

C Turnover ratios

1 Rate of stock turnover,
2 Collection period for debtors, and
3 Collection period to creditors.

D Working capital ratios

1 Current ratio, and
2 Liquid (or acid test) ratio.
And finally others not confined to final accounts.

E Investment ratios

1 Dividend yield, and
2 Price/earnings ratio.

These ratios will now be discussed and the following example used to illustrate those ratios appropriate to the sole trader's account (excluding investment ratios).

Example

Balance Sheet as at 30 April 19-7

Capital 1 May 19-6	90,000	*Fixed assets*		
Net profit for year	20,000	Land & buildings at cost		55,000
	110,000	Fixtures & equipment at cost		
Less drawings	12,000	less depreciation		15,000
	98,000	Vehicles at cost less depreciation		9,500
				79,500
Loan (long term)	16,000	Investments		2,000
Current liabilities		*Current assets*		
Creditors	30,000	Stock	28,500	
		Debtors	24,000	
		Bank & cash	10,000	62,500
	£144,000			£144,000

Other details for year ending 30 April 19-7
Sales   360,000
Purchases   307,000
Opening stock   21,500
Gross profit   60,000

From the above calculate the following ratios:

1 Mark up and margin.
2 Sales to capital employed.
3 Net profit to sales.
4 Net profit to capital employed.

265

5 Net profit to owners capital.
6 Rate of stock turnover.
7 Collection period for debtors.
8 Payment period to creditors.
9 Current ratio.
10 Liquid (acid test) ratio.

A Sales ratios

The mark-up and margin compare gross profit to:

a) Cost price and
b) Selling price respectively.

Figures will be obtained from the trading account to derive a collective figure for all transactions.

Note
1 that it is the same gross profit, compared on a different basis.
2 gross profit = sales − cost of sales.

1 The mark-up compares the profit to the cost price of goods and is expressed as a percentage.

$$\frac{\text{Gross profit}}{\text{Cost price}} \times 100\%$$

Imagine that a retailer buys goods for resale at cost price and then adds profit to cover costs and service capital − this is mark-up.

2 The margin compares the profit to the selling price of goods and is expressed as a percentage.

$$\frac{\text{Gross profit}}{\text{Selling price}} \times 100\%$$

This same retailer buys goods at cost to sell at a known selling price (the manufacturers recommended retail price), thus profit can be calculated on the selling price.

Example

$$\text{Margin} = \frac{\text{GP}}{\text{Sales}} \qquad \text{Mark up} = \frac{\text{GP}}{\text{Cost of sales}}$$

$$= \frac{60,000}{360,000} \qquad = \frac{60,000}{(360,000 - 60,000)}$$

$$= 16.6\% \ (\tfrac{1}{6}) \qquad = 20\% \ (\tfrac{1}{5})$$

Note conversion rule (see following heading).

$\tfrac{1}{6}$ ←─────────────────────────────→ $\tfrac{1}{5}$

3 Sales to capital employed is illustrated by the definition (below) for capital employed.

$$\text{Sales to CE} = \frac{\text{Sales}}{\text{Capital employed}} \times 100\%$$

$$= \frac{360{,}000}{106{,}000}$$

$$= 339.6\%$$

This means that the business turns over its long-term capital more than three times (3.39) in the year to produce sales.

Conversion of mark-up to margin – there is a relationship between mark-up and margin, namely that they both measure the same gross profit, and there is a common rule to be applied for converting one to the other. Accounts examiners frequently expect students to appreciate the relationship (between these two ratios) and be able to use them, say in incomplete records questions.

A diagrammatic illustration showing a 25% mark-up (profit on cost) and a 20% margin (profit on sales) is as follows:

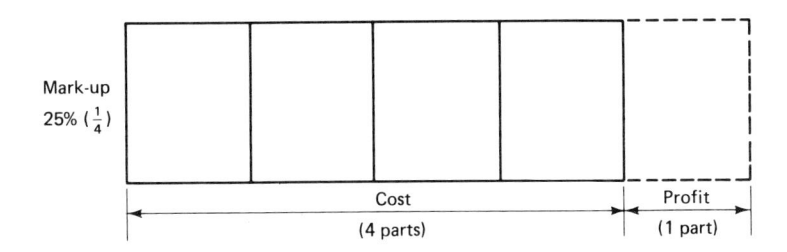

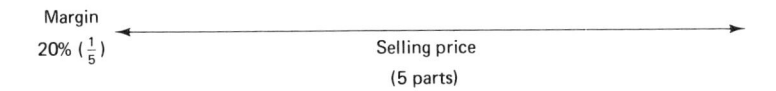

Mark-up 25% ($\frac{1}{4}$)

Cost (4 parts) | Profit (1 part)

Margin 20% ($\frac{1}{5}$)

Selling price (5 parts)

The mark up can be illustrated as 25% or $\frac{1}{4}$ ie the cost comprises of four parts then an equal or fifth part (denoted by the dotted line) is added to provide the profit.

Alternatively the margin can be illustrated as 20% or $\frac{1}{5}$ ie the selling price comprises of five equal parts including the profit (dotted line).

Therefore the same profit is represented by the fraction:

(i) a $\frac{1}{4}$ in the case of the mark-up
(ii) a $\frac{1}{5}$ in the case of the margin.

Thus by a simple rule (that applies generally) the following conversions can be made – the usefulness of which will be discovered in numerous types of exercise.

mark-up to margin = $\frac{1}{4}(+1) = \frac{1}{5}$
margin to mark-up = $\frac{1}{5}(-1) = \frac{1}{4}$

Take a mark up of 100%, a figure currently used in certain retail sectors.

```
Mark-up
100%
```

Cost	Profit
(1 part)	(1 part)

Selling price
(2 parts 100 + 100)

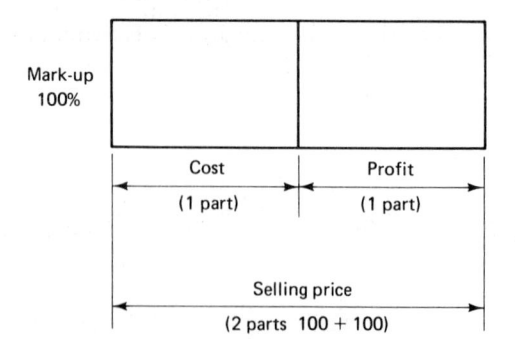

Mark-up to margin

$$\text{Mark-up} = \frac{\text{Profit}}{\text{Cost price}} = \frac{100}{100} = 1 = 100\%$$

$$\text{Margin} = \frac{\text{Profit}}{\text{Selling price}} = \frac{100}{100+100} = \frac{100}{200} = \frac{1}{2} = 50\%$$

Margin to mark-up

$$\text{Margin} = \frac{\text{Profit}}{\text{Selling price}} = 50\% = \frac{1}{2\,(-1)}$$

$$\text{Mark-up} = \frac{\text{Profit}}{\text{Cost price}} = 1 = 100\%$$

Now return to the discussion in the example ($\frac{1}{6}$ to $\frac{1}{5}$ and vice versa).

B Profitability ratios

Gross profit to sales (the margin) is the basic measure of trading efficiency and will have to be adjusted upwards if the figure is insufficient to meet the requirement of the business, assuming no other method is available, eg reducing expenses. The mark-up is another way of expressing the same profit.

1 Net profit to sales is the measure of profitability after expenses have been deducted. Out of this comes the reward to owners and they will expect the net profit to be sufficient for the risk and amount invested.

$$\text{NP to sales} = \frac{\text{Net profit}}{\text{Sales}} \times 100\%$$

Example

$$\text{NP to sales} = \frac{20{,}000}{360{,}000} \times 100\%$$
$$= 5.56\%$$

2 Net profit to capital employed is a better comparison of relative profit since it takes this as a ratio to capital. Capital employed has several definitions according to accounting opinion. I am going to proceed on the basis that it is long-term capital, ie Owner's capital (at start of period) plus any other long-term loans

$$\text{NP to CE} = \frac{\text{Net profit}}{\text{Capital employed}} \times 100\%$$

for the purpose of this example:

Capital 1 May 19-6	90,000
Loan (long term)	16,000
	106,000

Example

$$\text{NP to CE} = \frac{20,000}{106,000} \times 100\%$$
$$= 18.87\%$$

3 Net profit to owner's capital is the basis for calculating the return earned by the business. This measure takes only the funds (at the start of the period) belonging to the owners with which to compare net profit.

$$\text{NP to OC} = \frac{\text{Net profit}}{\text{Owner's capital}} \times 100\%$$

Example

$$\text{NP to OC} = \frac{20,000}{90,000} \times 100\%$$
$$= 22.22\%$$

Remember it is the same profit figure that is being compared against different bases and it is important to be clear about which base is used. Accountants as a rule pay great attention to consistency and the base for evaluating profit is no exception to this. So the same basis should be used when making comparisons, of one measure to another.

C Turnover ratios

Ratios which measure the turnover of critical assets and liabilities of the business are now discussed. Such measures indicate trends for working capital movement (current assets − current liabilities) and are vital indicators for business success.

1 Rate of stock turnover is probably the most vital indicator for any business and represents the rate at which potential sales (stock) is turned into actual sales and profit earned.

$$\text{RST} = \frac{\text{cost of goods sold}}{\text{average stock held}}$$

The resulting measure is not a percentage but either expressed as

a) times per year, or
b) days,

ie the period of time in which it takes an average amount of stock to be turned round (sold).

The ratio times per year is probably the most used but can be converted to days by using the result as a divisor.

Average stock held can be a monthly average but because figures are extracted from final accounts, it is more usual that an average of opening and closing stock should be taken ie a yearly average.

ie ASH as the denominator $= \dfrac{\text{opening stock} + \text{closing stock}}{2}$

therefore the usual presentation is:

Rate of stock turnover $= \dfrac{\text{cost of goods sold}}{\dfrac{\text{opening stock} + \text{closing stock}}{2}}$

The information for the closing stock and cost of goods sold is more usually found in the trading account, except that in the example given has to be deduced since there is no trading account (but see p 272)
ie Cost of goods sold = Cost of sales = Sales − Gross profit
Closing stock (in this case) is found in the balance sheet.

Example

$\text{RST} = \dfrac{\text{CGS}}{\dfrac{\text{OS} + \text{CS}}{2}}$

$= \dfrac{300{,}000}{\dfrac{21{,}500 + 28{,}500}{2}}$

$= \dfrac{300{,}000}{25{,}000}$

= 12 times a year (or one month)

converted to days $= \dfrac{365}{12} = 30.4$

A similar process is applied to debtors and creditors for respective turnover figures. Where these are not provided, assumptions have to be made about the amount of sales and purchases respectively that are made for credit, unless suggestions about the type of business indicate otherwise. In the example I think it is fair to regard them all as made by credit − disregarding any minor inaccuracy.

2 Collection period for debtors − the success a business has in collecting its debts regularly and maintaining an effective policy for managing its debts will contribute to the success or failure of its operations.

A calculation similar to that for rate of stock turnover applies:

Collection period $= \dfrac{\text{credit sales in period}}{\text{average debtors}}$

and considerations similar to rate of stock turnover apply to these average figures.

Example
Assuming the debtors figure to be the average and all sales to be in credit.

$\text{CP} = \dfrac{360{,}000}{24{,}000}$

= 15 times a year

3 Collection period for creditors – just as a business may wish to collect its debts as soon as possible, so can other businesses be expected to pursue the same policy.

A calculation similar to the above applies:

Collecting period $= \dfrac{\text{credit purchases in period}}{\text{average creditors}}$

Example
Assuming the creditors figure to be the average and all purchases to be on credit.

$\text{CP} = \dfrac{307{,}000}{30{,}000}$

$= 10.23$ times a year

It would be difficult in these cases to apply an overall rule for turnover figures since much depends on:

a) the type of business,
b) the customs and practice that have been accepted over the years,
c) the effect credit has on trading activity, and
d) what competitors are doing.

But it is important to note that a sound policy or all three fronts prevents illiquidity, recourse to borrowing, and perhaps worse.

D Working capital ratios

Such ratios reflect the balance within working (or circulating) capital between current assets and current liabilities. Ratios here are usually expressed in the recognized format for arithmetic ratios as relative parts to the base of one.

1 Current ratio compares all current assets to current liabilities and an accepted normal level is recognized as being 2:1, ie two parts current asset to one part current liability anything less (where current liabilities exceed half the current assets) is regarded as harmful, subject to the limitations about generalizations.
Current assets: Current liabilities

Example
```
        CA:     CL
= 52,500:   30,000
=   2.08:        1      – is satisfactory
```

2 Liquid (acid test) ratio again compares current assets to current liabilities, but this time the listing of current assets omits closing stock. This reduces the accepted normal level to 1:1, ie one part liquid current asset to one part current liabilities; anything less (where current liabilities exceed current assets less stock) is generally regarded as harmful.

Current assets – Stock: Current liabilities

Example
```
        CA – stock:    CL
= 62,550 – 28,500:  30,000
= 1.13:1               – is satisfactory
```

Stock (goods available for sale) is regarded as critical to the continuance of a business and cannot be easily reduced to produce liquid funds. Therefore a sensible measure of liquid assets (those regarded as near cash) would rightly exclude stock, since were the business in difficulties it would not be helpful to sell stock and prejudice its future further (assuming not too much surplus stock was held).

Stock is usually valued at cost, but if a forced sale means that many of the same items are sold collectively in the same place, then the price falls, and sales may be made for less than cost. The sale (sometimes by auction) of bankrupt stock has probably not gone unnoticed by students, and is usually disposed of at knock-down prices.

Liquid or near liquid assets generally include cash, bank balances, and various debtor balances.

The reconstructed trading account

As a footnote, the trading account for the above example, has been written up, just to satisfy any doubts about the genuineness of figures and would be as follows:

	Trading Account		
Opening stock	21,500	Sales	360,000
Add purchases	307,000		
	328,500		
Less closing stock	28,500		
Cost of goods sold	300,000		
Gross profit c/d	60,000		
	£360,000		£360,000

Investment ratios

The discussion that concludes this topic does not use the above example to illustrate the ratios used, because comments about the type of investment that require this type of information would not be relevant to the above mode of business — namely the small sole trader. But they are nevertheless important basic ratios used by investors in public companies, to determine alternative measures of success from Stock Exchange information.

Dividend yield is a measure of the real rate of return on shares, usually in public companies that are quoted on the Stock Exchange, by evaluating the dividend declared (on the nominal value) against the current market value, that for public companies is quoted daily. Formula is as follows:

$$\frac{\text{Dividend per share}}{\text{Market price per share}} \times 100\%$$

and is another percentage ratio.

Example
Company X Ltd declares a 20% dividend on its £1 ordinary shares, that are valued at £2.50 on the market.

$$\frac{£1 \times 20}{£2.50} \times 100\%$$
$$= \frac{20p}{250p} \times 100$$
$$= 8\%$$

Price/earnings ratio is a measure of the time period (say years or as many dividends as are paid annually), that it would take to recoup the initial outlay — usually at market value, given the current dividend. Formula is as follows:

Market price

Earnings per share

Example
Company X Ltd using the same information

$$\frac{£2.50}{£1 \times 20\%}$$
$= 12\frac{1}{2}$ years

is a ratio of time, but similar in principle to the yield.

Using ratios to construct final accounts

Questions are set not only to test knowledge of the ratios themselves but to apply ratio analysis to other uses, in this case preparation of final accounts. The question below is given as an example, students should complete the final accounts from the information (ratio) given. The answer is progressive, so that the answer procedure can be followed rather than being presented as a fait accompli.

Example
Magna Limited
Calculations for:
1 closing stock required using rate of stock turnover formula

$$RST = \frac{C \text{ of } S}{ASH}$$

$$10 = \frac{70,000}{\frac{6,000 + CS}{2}}$$

CS = £8,000

2 current assets required given ratio

CA:CL = 2:1
CA = £32,400

3 the ordinary share capital from the proposed dividend

ie if $12\frac{1}{2}\%$ = £7,500 then find 100%
    OSC = £60,000

The question

Magna Limited

Trading and Profit & Loss Account for the year ended 31 December 19-3

Stock 1 Jan 19-2	6,000	Sales	120,000
Purchases			
Less Stock 31 Dec 19-2	....		
Cost of Sales	70,000		
Gross profit c/d	....		
	....		....
General expenses	8,370	Gross profit b/d	....
Rent & rates	....	Discount received	....
Selling & distribution expenses	....		
Advertising	....		
Wages & salaries	....		
Insurance & maintenance	....		
Discount allowed	2,550		
Net profit c/d	....		
	....		....
Transfer to general reserve	2,500	Net profit b/d	11,300
Proposed dividend	....	Balance b/fwd	3,300
Balance c/fwd	....		
	....		....

Magna Limited
Balance Sheet as at 31 December 19-3

Authorised & issued capital		*Fixed assets*	
Ordinary shares of £1 each		Premises	38,300
fully paid	....	Machinery	....
General Reserve	....		
Profit & loss balance	....	*Current assets*	
		Stock	....
		Debtors	13,500
Current liabilities		Bank & cash	....
Creditors	8,700		
Proposed dividend	7,500		
	83,300		83,300

Other information

1. Gross profit to sales ?%
2. Net profit to sales ?%
   as a percentage of sales
   3) to 6)
3. Rent & rates $3\frac{1}{2}$%
4. Advertising expenses 4%
5. Insurances maintenance 2%
6. Selling & distribution 6%
   expenses
7. Rate of stock turnover 10
8. Return on owners capital ?%
9. Ordinary dividend pro- $12\frac{1}{2}$%
   posed
10. Current ratio 2:1
11. During the year the
    average rate of discount
    on purchases has been $2\frac{1}{2}$%

Part answer

Magna Limited

Trading and Profit & Loss Account for the year ended 31 December 19-3

Stock 1 Jan 19-2	6,000	Sales	120,000
Purchases			
Less stock 31 Dec 19-2	8,000		
Cost of sales	70,000		
Gross profit c/d	50,000		
	120,000		120,000
General expenses	8,370	Gross profit b/d	50,000
Rent & rates	4,200	Discount received	
Selling & distribution expenses	7,200		
Advertising	4,800		
Wages & salaries			
Insurance & maintenance	2,400		
Discount allowed	2,550		
Net profit c/d	11,300		
Transfer to general reserve	2,500	Net profit b/d	11,300
Proposed dividend	7,500	Balance b/fwd	3,300
Balance c/fwd			

275

Magna Limited

Balance sheet as at 31 December 19-3

Authorised & issued capital		*Fixed assets*	
Ordinary shares at £1 each full paid	60,000	Premises Machinery	38,300
General reserve	2,500		
Profit & loss balance		*Current assets*	
		Stock	8,000
		Debtors	13,500
Current liabilities		Bank & cash	
Creditors	8,700		
Proposed dividend	7,500		
	83,300		83,300

The complete answer

Magna Limited

Trading and Profit & Loss Account for the year ended 31 December 19-3

Stock 1 Jan 19-2	6,000	Sales	120,000
Purchases	72,000		
	78,000		
Less stock 31 Dec 19-2	8,000		
Cost of sales	70,000		
Gross profit c/d	50,000		
	120,000		120,000
General expenses	8,370	Gross profit b/d	50,000
Rent & rates	4,200	Discount received	1,800
Selling & distribution expenses	7,200		
Advertising	4,800		
Wages & salaries	10,980		
Insurance & maintenance	2,400		
Discount allowed	2,550		
Net profit c/d	11,300		
	51,800		51,800
Transfer to general reserve	2,500	Net profit b/d	11,300
Proposed dividend	7,500	Balance b/fwd	3,300
Balance c/fwd	4,600		
	14,600		14,600

Magna Limited

Balance sheet as at 31 December 19-3

Authorised & issued capital		*Fixed assets*	
Ordinary shares of £1 each fully paid	60,000	Premises	38,300
		Machinery	11,000
General reserve	2,500		47,600
Profit & loss balance	4,600	*Current assets*	
	67,100	Stock	8,000
Current liabilities		Debtors	13,500
Creditors	8,700	Bank & cash	10,900
Proposed dividend	7,500		
	83,300		83,300

Other information

1. Gross profit to sales — 41.6%
2. Net profit to sales as a percentage of sales — 9.4%
3. Rent & rates — $3\frac{1}{2}$%
4. Advertising expenses — 4%
5. Insurance maintenance — 2%
6. Selling & distribution expenses — 6%
7. Rate of stock turnover — 10
8. Return of owner's capital* — 18.8% or 16.8%
9. Ordinary dividend proposed — $12\frac{1}{2}$%
10. Current ratio — 2:1
11. During the year the average rate of discount on purchases has been — $2\frac{1}{2}$%

* 11.3/60 = 18.8%
  11.3/67.1 = 16.8%

Unit 2
Funds flow statements

Overview

1 Funds flow statements summarize changes in the financial structure of the firm that have arisen between the preparation of two consecutive sets of accounts, namely a trading period.
2 Final accounts show two different positions but not the changes themselves.
3 Changes are expressed in terms of sources and applications of funds.
4 The net result of such changes in the structure of the business is given in terms of either:
   a) Bank and cash, or
   b) Working capital
   and different types of statement are prepared to reflect these.
5 The skeleton layout of both types of statement is given.
6 Examples of the classification of changes are given, showing the division into sources and applications.
7 The distinction between cash and working capital statements is illustrated diagrammatically.
8 Specific points of difficulty are recognized and explained, eg contribution to trading – provisions for depreciation.
9 A final summary is provided.
10 An example is presented on pp 284–6 showing two types of statement, together with explanatory notes.
11 The working capital statement is represented according to advice given by the Accountants' Institutes to their members as set out in the 1975 Statement SSAP 10.
12 The example provided is reworked according to Statement of Standard Accounting Practice No 10.

These are statements prepared by accountants to indicate the changes in funding that have arisen between the preparation of one set of final accounts and the next set. Usually a statement is prepared for the previous period (just completed) to show the difference between the previous set of accounts and the current set.

The idea can be best illustrated diagrammatically.

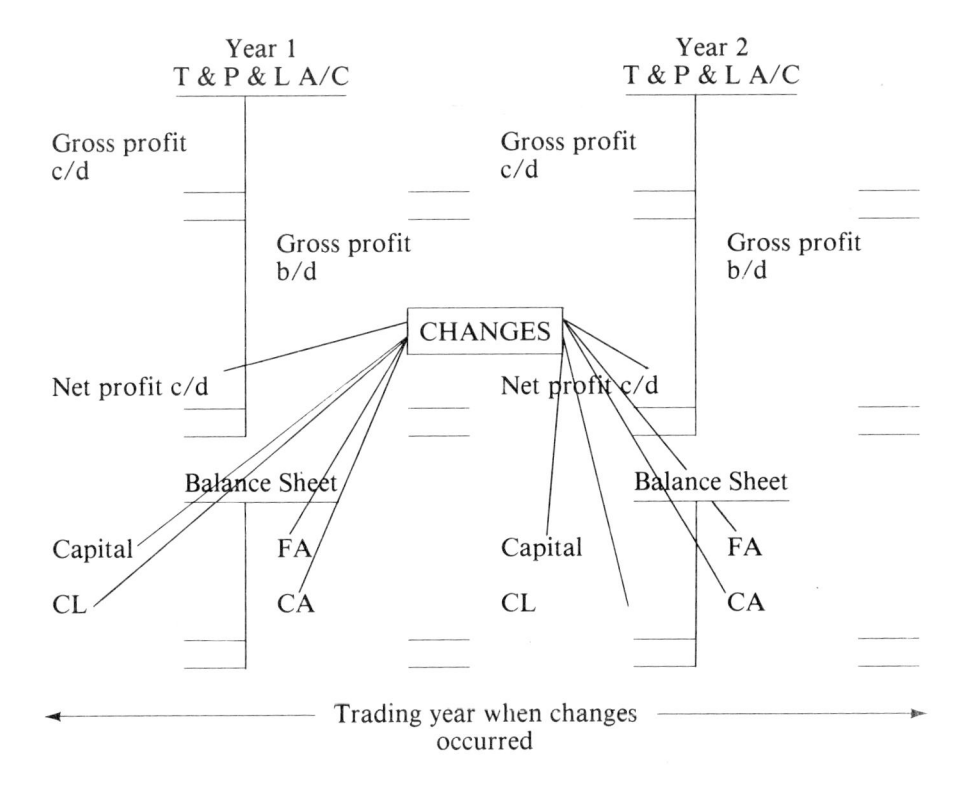

[Diagram showing Year 1 and Year 2 T & P & L A/C and Balance Sheets, with arrows from Gross profit b/d, Net profit c/d, Capital, CL, FA, CA of both years pointing to a central "CHANGES" box. Below: "Trading year when changes occurred"]

Changes

The funds flow statement incorporates these **changes** and presents them as an intelligible statement in the form of:

1 Sources – generally additions to funds (amounts received), and
2 Applications – generally deductions from funds (amounts paid out).

The statement produces its figures as **differences** between amounts contained in:

a) balance sheets, and
b) profit & loss accounts,
   for years 1 & 2.

Incidentally, it has to be mentioned that the majority of figures come from the balance sheet.

Cash or bank

Changes ultimately affect the medium of exchange – **cash or bank** – and it has been common for changes in the flow of funds to be reduced to a difference between opening and closing cash and bank balances.

Working capital

However, a better (and often more difficult) method to appreciate that is preferred by accountants ie that of working capital. As will have been noted

earlier the expression includes, not only cash and/or bank, but also the net difference between all current assets and current liabilities.
ie Working capital = Current assets − Current liabilities
   (net current assets)

Thus two types of funds flow statements are frequently produced, the latter being technically superior, these are:

a) cash, and
b) working capital.

The basic layout of statements

The two types are illustrated

1 cash flow, and
2 working capital − that has two sections:
   a) adjustments to working capital, and
   b) adjustments within working capital

1 Cash flow

X Ltd Cash Flow Statement for year ending

Sources and applications

Sources
                                              X
                                              X
                                              X
                                              X   X

Applications
                                              X
                                              X
                                              X
                                              X
                                              X   (X)

Increase or decrease in cash and/or bank

The balance will be:

a) an increase (positive) sources *greater* than applications, or
b) a decrease (negative) sources *less* than applications.

The change will be the difference between the two balance sheet figures, for cash and/or bank.

2 Working capital − a two part statement:

a) Looks at longer term adjustment to working capital, in terms of sources and applications, that is presented in a manner similar to the cash flow statement.

X Ltd Working Capital Flow Statement for year ending ─────

Sources & Applications

Sources

	X	
	X	
	X	X

Applications

	X	
	X	
	X	
	X	(X)

Increase or decrease in working capital

The balance will be
 (i) an increase (positive) sources greater than applications,
 (ii) a decrease (negative) sources less than applications.

b) Looks at the shorter term adjustments to working capital itself in terms of
 (i) increases,
 (ii) decreases.

Increase in working capital

	X	
	X	
	X	X

Decrease in working capital

	X	
	X	
	X	X

Net change in working capital

Both concluding figures (in parts a, and b) should equal the difference between opening and closing working capital figures found from the respective balance sheets. This serves as a check on the accuracy of the statement. See 'check' presented as a footnote on p 286.

It can probably be seen that working capital statements are a development from cash statements.

Examples of sources and applications

A straight-forward listing of some familiar considerations is now presented:

Sources	**Applications**
Raising of funds:	*Reducing funds*:
Capital – from owners	Capital – paying off loans
from others	

Sale of fixed assets – even if for a nominal amount (disposal proceeds)	Purchase of fixed assets including buildings plant & machinery etc.
Net profit (plus adjustments – from profit & loss	Payment to owners – Drawings, dividend etc
Increase in current liabilities (Creditors provide funds) eg increase in overdraft	*Increase in current assets* (Debtors utilize funds) eg increase in stock
Decrease in current assets eg reduction of stock	*Decrease in current liabilities* eg reduction of overdraft

Below is shown the distinction between cash & working capital.

Cash

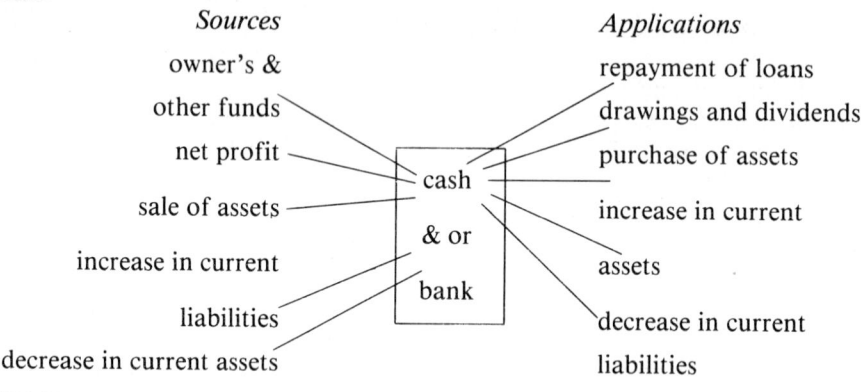

Sources		*Applications*
owner's & other funds		repayment of loans
		drawings and dividends
net profit		purchase of assets
sale of assets	cash & or bank	increase in current assets
increase in current liabilities		
decrease in current assets		decrease in current liabilities

Working capital
Sources   *Applications*

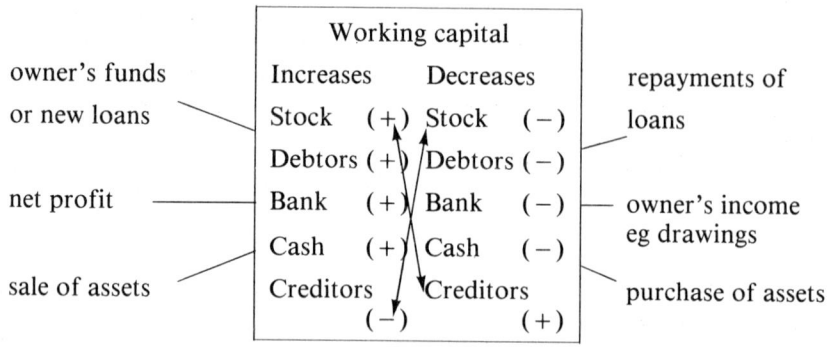

	Working capital		
owner's funds or new loans	Increases Decreases		repayments of loans
	Stock (+) Stock (−)		
	Debtors (+) Debtors (−)		
net profit	Bank (+) Bank (−)		owner's income eg drawings
	Cash (+) Cash (−)		
sale of assets	Creditors Creditors		purchase of assets
	(−) (+)		

Funds circulate within working capital more frequently.

Accountants prefer working capital statements because frequent changes in the composition of working capital do not necessarily affect this critical figure as a whole, whereas in the cash statement cash as the resultant figure is more easily variable. In particular stock cannot be manipulated to improve liquidity, since any increase in cash or bank through a reduction of stock is purely an adjustment internal to working capital.

General points

1 The statement examines the differences between the figures contained in previous year's final accounts and the following year's final accounts.
2 The difference represents the total changes that have occurred during the year.
3 The breakdown of statements consists of sources and applications collected together and listed.

Specific problems

Contribution from trading is comprised primarily of profit for the year, since profit is a source of funds that the business itself generates, ie profit as a source is available to owners or managers.

However, contribution does not only consist of net profit as recorded in the final accounts. It also includes book adjustments such as provisions, that do not directly affect funding (save in restricting profit) these have to be added back to restore the profit to a sum reduced by monetary expenses but not provisions.

Contribution then comprises of:

a) net profit, and
b) adding back non-monetary adjustments.

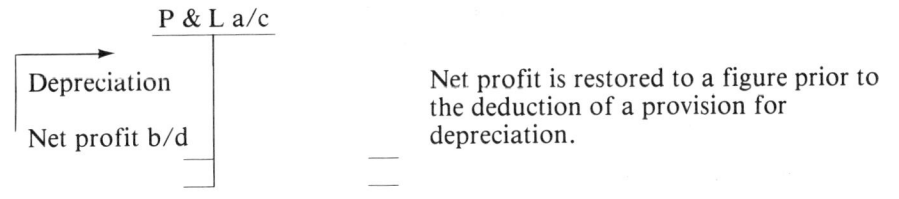

```
         P & L a/c
┌──────────────┐
│ Depreciation │         Net profit is restored to a figure prior to
│              │         the deduction of a provision for
│ Net profit b/d│         depreciation.
└──────────────┘
```

Drawings are a withdrawal of funds, money is applied to them to pay proprietors, they are:

a) paid during the year, and
b) restrict the amount of profit that can be used to fund the business from internal sources.

Dividend — There are two classifications:
a) dividend paid, and
b) dividend proposed.
Dividend paid is an expense and has already adjusted the net profit, in common with most expenses. Dividend proposed is a source, recorded as a liability and not paid until the following period (see pp 178 and 288).

Cumulative items — Profit can be recorded as cumulative profit in respect of a number of years results (note unappropriated profit). However, only the current period profit should be taken to a funds statement, the point is to read the narrative carefully:
profit for the year — Is what it says.
balance of profit — May not be just for the year.
Remember: drawings are for the year.
Depreciation (like profit) is also sometimes recorded as a cumulative figure (see example p 284) and a similar identification process is required.

General rule: The fund flow figure required (the difference) is a deduction of the earlier from the later figure, in the case of cumulative amounts.

Note The adjustment of a provision for doubtful debts is achieved by taking a net debtors figure in the working capital section of a balance sheet.

A summary

Where there is an opportunity to spend, use or consume funds, there is likely to be an application. Ask: 'Are funds being applied to . . .' eg the depletion of the cash and bank figure – then this can be recorded as an application. Likewise where a contribution is made then it is likely to be a source Ask: 'Are funds coming from somewhere . . .' eg the owners – then there is a source.
Remember: the answer is always provided in the statement presented as:
a) cash and bank, or
b) working capital (that is more difficult to compute).

Example
The following details refer to the business of J A Thompson.

	19-5	19-6			19-5		19-6	
Capital -1 May (19-4)	80,000 (19-5)	84,000	*Fixed assets*					
Net profit	12,000	18,000	Freehold premises		45,000		52,000	
	92,000	102,000	Fixtures & fittings (cost)	18,000		25,000		
Less drawings	8,000	12,000	less dep'n	5,000	13,000	7,000	18,000	
	84,000	90,000	Vehicles (cost)	21,500		24,000		
Loan from P Stevens	9,000	12,500	less dep'n	4,000	17,500	8,000	16,000	
Current liabilities								
Creditors	15,000	17,500	Investment @ cost		3,500		4,000	
					84,000		90,000	
			Current assets					
			Stock	10,200		11,800		
			Debtors	8,300		10,900		
			Bank & cash	5,500	24,000	7,300	30,000	
	108,000	120,000			108,000		120,000	

Prepare: 1) a Cash flow statement
2) a Working capital

J A Thompson Cash Flow Statement for year ending 30 April 19-6
Sources & Applications

Sources
Contribution from trading (18,000 + 2,000 + 4,000)	24,000	
Loan P Stevens (12,500 – 9,000)	3,500	
Reduction of investment (8,500 – 4,000)	4,500	
Increase in creditors (17,500 – 15,000)	2,500	34,500

Applications
Increase in freehold premises (52,000 – 45,000)	7,000	
Increase in fixtures & fittings (25,000 – 18,000)	7,000	
Increase in vehicles (24,000 – 21,500)	2,500	
Drawings	12,000	
Increase in stock (11,800 – 10,200)	1,600	
Increase in debtors (10,900 – 8,300)	2,600	32,700
Bank & cash (increase)		£ 1,800

Example: (repeated) to clearly show the origin of entries for the Cash Statement, before moving on to the Working Capital arrangement.

The following details refer to the business of J A Thompson.

	19-5	19-6		19-5	19-6
Capital-1 May (19-4)	80,000 (19-5)	84,000	Fixed assets		
Net profit (1)	12,000	18,000	Freehold premises	45,000	52,000
	92,000	102,000	Fixtures & fittings (cost)		
Less drawings	8,000	12,000		18,000	25,000
	84,000	90,000	(2) less dep'n	5,000 13,000	7,000 18,000
			Vehicles (cost)	21,500	24,000
			(2) less dep'n	4,000 17,500	8,000 16,000
Loan from P Stevens	9,000	12,500			
Current liabilities					
Creditors	15,000	17,500	Investments at cost	8,500	4,000
				84,000	90,000
			Current assets		
			Stock	10,200	11,800
			Debtors	8,300	10,900
			Bank & cash	5,500 24,000	7,300 30,000
	108,000	120,000		108,000	120,000

J A Thompson Cash Flow Statement for year ending 30 April 19-6

Sources & applications

Sources
Contribution from trading *(18,000 + 2,000 + 4,000)   24,000
Loan P Stevens *(12,500 − 9,000)   3,500
Reduction of investment *(8,500 − 4,000)   4,500
Increase in creditors *(17,500 − 15,000)   2,500   34,500

Applications
Increase in freehold premises *(52,000 − 45,000)   7,000
Increase in fixtures & fittings *(25,000 − 18,000)   7,000
Increase in vehicles *(24,000 − 21,500)   2,500
Drawings   12,000
Increase in stock *(11,800 − 10,200)   1,600
Increase in debtors *(10,900 − 8,300)   2,600   32,700

                                                   £1,800 (3 see notes)
Bank & cash (increase)

* Workings are shown in brackets for every adjustment.

J A Thompson Working Capital Statement for year ending 30 April 19-6
Sources & applications

Sources		
Contribution for trading* (18,000 + 2,000 + 4,000)	24,000	
Loan P Stevens* (12,500 − 9,000)	3,500	
Reduction in investment* (8,500 − 4,000)	4,500	32,000
Applications		
Increase in freehold premises* (52,000 − 45,000)	7,000	
Increase in fixtures & fittings* (25,000 − 18,000)	7,000	
Increase in vehicles* (24,000 − 21,500)	2,500	
Drawings	12,000	28,500
Working capital (increase)		£ 3,500
Working capital adjustment		
Increase in working capital 4 (see notes)		
Debtors* (10,900 − 8,300)	2,600	
Stock* (11,800 − 10,200)	1,600	
Bank & cash 3 (see notes)	1,800	6,000
Decrease in working capital 4 (see notes)		
Creditors (17,500 − 15,000)		2,500
Net increase in working capital		£ 3,500

```
Check        WC    = CA  -  CL
  19-5     9,000 = 24,000 - 15,000
  19-6    12,500 = 30,000 - 17,500
Net increase  3,500
```

* Workings are shown in brackets for every adjustment.

Note
1. The net profit figure is for the year.
2. The depreciation figures (fitting & vehicles) are cumulative − £2,000 (£7,000 − £5,000) + £4,000 (£8,000 − £4,000) respectively are the figures added back to contribution from trading.
3. Bank & cash is itself an application to cash & bank, but is used as the residual (and balancing) item in the cash statement.
4. The working capital adjustment in the statement bearing the name looks differently at the working capital effect *only*.
ie debtors and bank when they increase, *increase* working capital creditors when they increase *decrease* working capital.

Development of the working capital statement

The Accounting Standards Committee developed a revised practice for preparing working capital statements − Statement of Standard Accounting Practice 10. The aim of the standard on source and application of funds is to establish standard classification to aid user comparisons of various company statements.

The suggested layout is as follows:

X Limited Statement of Source & Application of Funds for year ending

Source of funds
Net profit (before tax)*			X
Adjustments for items not involving the movement of funds			
Depreciation			X
Total generated from operations			X

Funds from other sources
Issues of shares for cash		X	
Issue of loan capital		X	X
			X

Application of funds
Dividends paid		X	
Tax paid*		X	
Purchase of fixed assets		X	X
			X

Increase/decrease in working capital
Increase/decrease in stock		X	
Increase/decrease in debtors		X	
Decrease/increase in creditors (excluding taxation and proposed dividend)		X	
		X	

Movement in net liquid funds
Increase/decrease in cash	X			
Increase/decrease in short term investments	X		X	X

* At the level of statement preparation in this text, taxation is ignored.

In all parts of the text, tax levied on income and profits is ignored to avoid introducing complications to a basic text. Tax paid is shown in this statement layout, in line with the original, since it is after all an application of funds.

Note
1. The statement layout (above) is concerned with corporate enterprise and therefore owners receive dividend unlike payments to sole proprietors and partners.
2. The change in working capital does not treat increases and decreases separately, as in the main explanation given and there will be a possible aggregate of positive and negative figures.

Suppose the above layout is applied to the worked example J A Thompson, recognising that he is a sole trader, creating minor differences.

The statement can be re-written as follows:

J A Thompson Statement of Source & Application of Funds for year ending 30 April 19-6

Source of funds
Net profit before tax			18,000
Add depreciation			6,000
Total generated from operations			24,000
Funds from other sources			
Additional loan from P Stevens		3,500	3,500
			27,500
Applications			
Drawings by proprietor		12,000	
Purchases of fixed assets:			
Freehold premises	7,000		
Fixtures & fittings	7,000		
Vehicles	2,500	16,500	28,500
			(1,000)
Increase/decrease in working capital			
Increase in stocks		1,600	
Increase in debtors		2,600	
Increase in creditors		(2,500)	
		1,700	
Movement in net liquid funds			
Increase in cash	1,800		
Decrease in short term investments	(4,500)	(2,700)	(1,000)

Proposed dividend and taxation (companies)

Where included in accounts that require a flow analysis, a problem is created when the flow of funds statement is presented through an analysis of working capital. A payment should be regarded as an application of funds, but any verification of such changes within the statement should exclude the liability (if any) recorded in the Balance Sheet.

Adjusted profit (companies)

Be sure that profit used is that prior to adjustment for appropriations eg dividend paid, if not then appropriations should be added back at the contribution stage.

Unit 3
Cash budgeting

Overview

1 The 'cash' budget is concerned with the immediate flow of receipts into and payments out of the business (not to be confused with funds flow).

2 The term 'cash' includes cash & bank.

3 The cash budget is merely part of a more comprehensive budgeting system.

4 Receipts and payments are classified.

5 A diagrammatic skeleton layout of a cash budget is provided, together with notes.

6 Aspects of examination questions are discussed.

7 An example is provided together with explanatory notes.

Business cash requirements can be projected by a simple cash budget, showing:
receipts — money into the business, and
payments — money out of the business,
over a period of time, say six months.
Such a method enables an owner or manager to plan ahead and budget for the requirements of a business, having reasonable knowledge of the position — particularly if a shortage is likely to occur, so that remedial action may be taken.

Most business activities involve the receipt and payment of liquid funds, and thus affect the balances:
either

a) bank, or
b) cash.

A full system will contain budgets for sales, production and overheads etc and will ultimately incorporate a cash budget that will in some way be affected by these other budgets. However, a full discussion of budgeting procedures is more appropriately dealt with in a management accounting textbook, and is beyond the scope of this book.

Most cash budgets provide information on a monthly basis and are arranged as follows:

```
                     Months              Cash or Bank a/c
Receipts _ _ _ _ _ _ _ _ _ _ _ _ _ _ Debits  |  Credits
  ↓                  _ _ _ _ _ _ _ _
Payments _ _ _ _ _ _
  ↓
                                     the ledger account is
                                     merely illustrated.
```

Think of it as a ledger cash account rearranged and stretched horizontally over the months receipts and payments actually occur, so that a straight forward cash account will verify a closing balance. A more complete layout diagram will be shown below.

Receipts
Cash sales
Credit sales (when money received)
Other receipts eg
loans received
sale of assets

Payments
Cash purchases
Credit purchases (when money paid)
Purchase of assets
Wages & salaries ⎱
Rent & rates   ⎬ Expenses
Light & heat   ⎰
Other payments eg
drawings & dividend

Items included have to increase or decrease cash or bank and are taken when they actually occur. When a business is starting capital introduced should be brought into the cash budget because this is a cash injection. Book transactions ie provisions do not affect cash & bank and are not included in the cash budget eg depreciation.

Layout of a budget

	Jan	Feb	March	April	May	June
Opening balance		x	x	↗	↗	↗
Plus receipts						
Cash sales	x	x				
Credit sales	x	x	x			
		x	x			
Less payments						
Cash purchases	x	x				
Credit purchases	x	x				
Wages & salaries	x	x	x	x		
Closing balance		x	x			x

Note
1 Each closing balance becomes the opening balance for the next month.
2 It is better to record each month's information in two columns, insetting the additions to be sub-totalled.
3 The closing balances form the projected cash in hand and/or bank balance or overdraft.
4 An overdraft at the bank will produce a negative running balance until it is repaid ie payments have exceeded receipts and a reversal of this must occur:
   a) for a reasonably long period of time, and
   b) by a large enough amount, sooner or later to satisfy the bank.

Questions
Examination questions set on budgeting can combine other aspects of accounting eg ratios – mark-up and margin, and preparation of projected final accounts (as example). To prepare projected final accounts, a closing bank/cash balance

is required, if only for the purpose of producing a budget statement. Overall, the preparation of cash budgets in this form provides a useful test of accounting knowledge.

Example

Peta Jones starts a trading business on 1 July 19-0 by introducing £10,000 into the business bank account. The following are her plans and estimates for the next six months.

(i) Sales are expected to be:

	July	Aug	Sept	Oct	Nov	Dec
Cash	1,650	1,750	1,800	2,450	2,700	2,950
Credit	1,500	1,850	1,950	2,600	3,100	2,850

Selling prices (calculated from cost) require adding 50%.
Debtors are allowed one month's credit from invoice date.

(ii) Purchases are expected to be:

July	Aug	Sept	Oct	Nov	Dec
3,700	2,900	3,100	3,700	3,400	3,450

All purchases are on credit and Jones is allowed two months from invoice date.

(iii) Expenses are payable when they occur and are estimated at £450 a month.
(iv) Rent & rates (payable on 15th) will be £250 per month.
(v) Jones plans to draw £300 a month on the last business day of the month.
(vi) Jones intends buying a delivery van off D Wyke in October at a cost of £4,200 to be paid for in November, December and January by three equal instalments.
(vii) A depreciation policy for the delivery van is adopted to make depreciation £1,000 over a full year and Jones suggests you consider the van owned for the whole trading period.

You are required to prepare:
a) A cash budget for six months to 31 December 19-0.
b) A projected set of final accounts: (i) trading profit & loss, and
    (ii) balance sheet.

Cash Budget for period 1st July 19-0 to 31 December 19-0

See Notes (below)		July	Aug	Sept	Oct	Nov	Dec
Opening balance	(1)	10,000	10,700	13,000	12,000	12,550	12,400
Receipts							
Cash sales		1,650	1,750	1,800	2,450	2,700	2,950
	(2)						
Credit sales		—	1,500	1,850	1,950	2,600	3,100
		1,650	3,250	3,650	4,400	5,300	6,050
		11,650	13,950	16,650	16,400	17,850	18,450
Payments	(3)						
Purchases		—	—	3,700	2,900	3,100	3,700
Expenses		450	450	450	450	450	450
Rent & rates		200	200	200	200	200	200
Drawings (9)		300	300	300	300	300	300
						(4)	
Delivery van		—	—	—	—	1,400	1,400
		950	950	4,650	3,850	5,450	6,050
Closing balance		10,700	13,000	12,000	12,550	12,400	12,400
						(8)	

292

P Jones

Trading & Profit & Loss Account
For year ended 31 December 19-0

Opening stock (6)	–	Sales cash		13,300
Purchases (10)	20,250	Sales credit (10)		13,850
	20,250			27,150
Less closing stock (7)	2,150			
Cost of goods sold	18,100			
Gross profit c/d	9,050			
	£27,150			£27,150
Expenses	2,700	Gross profit b/d		9,050
Rent & rates	1,200			
Depreciation (5)	500			
Net profit c/d	4,650			
	£9,050			£9,050

P Jones
Balance sheet as at 31 December 19-0

Capital			*Fixed assets*		
		(1)			
Balance 1 July 19-0		10,000	Delivery Van		4,200
Add profit	4,650		Less dep'n		500
	(9)				
Less drawings	1,800	2,850			3,700
		12,850	*Current assets*		
				(7)	
Current liabilities			Stock	2,150	
	(3)			(2)	
Trade creditors	6,850		Debtors	2,850	
	(4)			(8)	
D Wyke	1,400	8,250	Cash & bank	12,400	17,400
		£21,100			£21,100

Notes
1. The balance is capital introduced, since the business has just commenced.
2. There is a one month period for receiving debts.
3. There is a two month period for paying creditors.
4. At the end of the period a liability remains on the delivery van.
5. Depreciation (6 months) is required for the delivery van.
6. Opening stock is nil since the business has just commenced.
7. The closing stock has to be calculated by deriving the margin and gross profit, and then working back.
8. The cash and bank figure is the closing balance from the budget.
9. Drawings affect the budget because cash is taken out monthly and the balance sheet shows a reduction of profit.
10. Purchases and sales are the full invoiced amounts.

Questions

Accounting ratios

1

B Tarbitten

Balance Sheets as at 31 June 19-1

Capital 1 July 19-0	131,200	Land & buildings at cost	83,500
Net profit	11,280	Fixtures & equipment	
	142,480	at cost *less* depreciation	16,410
Less drawings	9,150	Vehicles at cost *less*	
	133,330	depreciation	23,135
Loan (long term)	30,000	Investments (market price £2,570)	2,100
Creditors	40,560	Stock	56,350
		Debtors	17,712
		Bank and cash	4,683
	203,890		203,890

Other details for year ending 31 June 19-1
Sales 250,600
Opening stock 52,250
Rate of stock turnover four times.

Required
From the above information a calculation and explanation of the significance of the following:
1 Gross profit to sales as a percentage
2 Net profit to sales as a percentage
3 Total expenses to sales as a percentage
4 Working capital
5 Current ratio
6 Liquid (acid test) ratio
7 Return on owners capital 1 July 19-0
8 Return on capital employed 1 July 19-0
9 Mark-up
10 Margin
11 Debtors ratio
12 Creditors ratio

2

K Harmer

Balance Sheets as at 31 July 19-2

Capital 1 Aug 19-1	243,600	Land & buildings at cost	110,550
Net profit	54,700	Fixtures & equipment	
		at cost *less* depreciation	40,180
	298,300		
Less drawings	38,840	Vehicles at cost *less*	
		depreciation	69,283
	259,460		
Loan (long term)	36,500	Investments (market price £9,812)	7,000
Creditors	105,940	Stock	65,256
		Debtors	89,419
		Bank and cash	20,212
	401,900		401,900

Other details for year ending 31 July 19-2
Sales   512,200
Opening stock   58,624
Rate of stock turnover six times.

Required
From the above information a calculation and explanation of the significance of the following:
1. Gross profit to sales as a percentage
2. Net profit to sales as a percentage
3. Total expenses to sales as a percentage
4. Working capital
5. Current ratio
6. Liquid (acid test) ratio
7. Return on owners capital 1 August 19-1
8. Return on capital employed 1 August 19-1
9. Mark-up
10. Margin
11. Debtors ratio
12. Creditors ratio

Answer guide: Cost of sales £371,640; Liquid ratio 1.03:1; GP to Sales 27.4%.

3

a) You are required to prepare a trading and profit and loss account and a balance sheet for the year from the following information:

Year ended 30 June, 19-8

Sales for the year	£90,000
Gross profit margin	25% of sales
Opening stock	£24,000
Fixed assets	?
Current ratio	3:1
Creditors	£18,000
Balance at bank	?
Reserves	?
Closing stock	?
Current assets	?

295

Rate of stock turnover   3
Overheads   10% of sales
Net profit for the year was equal to 10% of the equity at the *beginning* of the year.
Average debtors collection period — two months.
At the beginning of the year share capital represented 80% of the equity.

b) Assuming the company in part a) is a retail food concern — make brief comments on *two* of the above ratios.

4 The balance sheets and trading and profit and loss accounts for the year ended 30 June 19-0 of Q Ltd and R Ltd are given below:

Balance Sheets as at 30 June 19-0

	Q Ltd		R Ltd	
Fixed assets at cost	120,000		60,000	
Less: Provision for depreciation	40,000	80,000	20,000	40,000
Current assets				
Stocks	114,000		60,000	
Debtors	44,000		40,000	
Bank	22,000		20,000	
	180,000		120,000	
Less: current liabilities	60,000	120,000	60,000	60,000
Net assets employed		£200,000		£100,000
Ordinary share capital fully paid		190,000		90,000
Revenue reserve				
Profit & loss account balance		10,000		10,000
		£200,000		£100,000

Trading and Profit and Loss Account for year ended 30 June 19-0

	Q Ltd		R Ltd	
Sales		320,000		240,000
Stock at 1 July 19-9	78,000		40,000	
Add: Purchases	228,000		170,000	
	306,000		210,000	
Less Stock at 30 June 19-0	114,000	192,000	60,000	150,000
Gross profit		128,000		90,000
Less: General expenses		112,000		78,000
Net profit		16,000		12,000
Add: Balance brought forward		6,000		2,000
		22,000		14,000
Less: Dividends paid		12,000		4,000
Balance carried forward		£10,000		£10,000

You may assume that stocks have increased evenly throughout the year.

a) Calculate the following ratios separately for each company:
   (i) net profit for the year as a percentage of net assets employed at 30 June 19-0;
   (ii) net profit for the year as a percentage of sales;
   (iii) gross profit for the year as a percentage of sales;
   (iv) current assets to current liabilities at 30 June 19-0;

(v) debtors and bank to current liabilities at 30 June 19-0;
(vi) cost of sales to average stock held during the year.
b) Comment on *two* of the ratios you have calculated.
c) Consider any reservations you may have about the use of ratio analysis.

Accounting ratios and final accounts

5 From the following outline and additional information you are asked to complete the final accounts and any missing information.

Train and Wilson Limited
Trading and Profit and Loss Account for year ended 31 March 19-9

Opening stock	35,630	Sales	
Add purchases			
Less closing stock			
Cost of sales	38,270		
Gross profit c/d			
General expenses		Gross profit b/d	
Rent and rates		Discount received	
Selling & distribution expenses			
Advertising			
Wages and salaries	6,712.2		
Insurance & maintenance			
Discount allowed			
Net profit c/d			
Transfer to general reserve		Net profit b/d	
Proposed dividend	10,400	Balance b/fwd	
Balance c/fwd			

Train and Wilson Limited
Balance Sheet as at 31 March 19-9

Authorisation & issued capital		*Fixed assets*	
Ordinary shares of £1 each fully paid		Premises	49,240
General reserve 10,000		Machinery	
2,500			
Profit & loss balance	5,640	*Current assets*	
Current liabilities		Stock	
Creditors	40,105	Debtors	51,158
Proposed dividend		Bank and cash	

Other information – as a percentage of sales

1 Gross profit	$16\frac{2}{3}$	
2 Net profit	$7\frac{1}{2}$	
3 Rent & rates	$1\frac{1}{2}$	
4 Advertising expenses	1	
5 Insurance & maintenance	$\frac{1}{2}$	
6 Selling & distribution expenses	2	

not as a percentage of sales

7 Rate of stock turnover	4	
8 Return on owners capital	?	
9 Ordinary dividend proposed	10%	
10 Current ratio	2:1	
11 During the year the discount on purchases has been	£2,408	
12 During the year the discount on sales has been	£1,540.8	

6 From the following outline and additional information you are asked to complete the final accounts and any missing information.

Boston and Boyers Limited

Trading and Profit and Loss Account for year ended 31 August 19-7

Opening stock	45,780	Sales	416,960
Add purchases			
Less closing stock			
Cost of sales			
Gross profit c/d			
General expenses	15,357	Gross profit b/d	
Rent and rates		Discount received	
Selling & distribution expenses			
Advertising			
Wages and salaries	30,382		
Insurance & maintenance			
Discount allowed			
Net profit c/d			
Transfer to general reserve		Net profit b/d	31,272
Proposed dividend		Balance b/fwd	
Balance c/fwd			

Boston and Boyers Limited

Balance Sheet as at 31 August 19-7

Authorised & issued capital			*Fixed assets*	
Ordinary shares of £1 each fully paid		120,520	Premises	
General reserve	15,500		Machinery	35,740
		18,750		
Profit & loss balance				
Current liabilities			*Current assets*	
Creditors			Stock	
Proposed dividend			Debtors	13,380
			Bank and cash	3,160
		195,400		

Other information — as a percentage of sales

1 Gross profit	25	7 Rate of stock turnover	6
2 Net profit	?	8 Return on owners capital	?
3 Rent and rates	5	9 Ordinary dividend proposed	12.5%
4 Advertising expenses	1	10 Current ratio	2.5:1
5 Insurance & maintenance	0.5	11 During the year the discount on purchases has been	5%
6 Selling & distribution expenses	2.5	12 During the year the discount on sales has been	?

Decimal parts will require rounding up to the nearest whole pound.

7 From the outline and information given below you are asked to complete the final accounts.

Hughes and Co Limited

Trading and Profit and Loss Account for year ended 30 April 19-4

Sales		600,000
Less cost of sales		
Opening stock		
Add purchases	_____	
Less closing stock		
Gross profit	47,500	_____
Other revenue		
Discount received		
Rent received	_____	_____
Expenses		
General expenses	16,750	
Depreciation of fixed assets		
Selling & distribution expenses		
Debenture interest	7,000	
Wages and salaries		
Provision for doubtful debts		
Insurance & maintenance		
Discount allowed	_____	
Net profit		
Add profit & loss account balance brought forward		22,500
Less appropriations		
Transfer to general reserve		
Dividend: interim		
final	_____	_____
Profit & loss account balance carried forward		£ _____

Hughes & Company Limited Balance Sheet as at 30 April 19-4

		Cost/Depn		Nbv
Fixed assets				
Land and buildings				
Plant and machinery		63,120		37,540
Fixtures and fittings		61,950		33,820
Investments at cost				
Net current assets				
Current assets				
Stock				
Debtors	52,300			
Less provision for doubtful debts	_____			
Bank				
Cash		3,510		
Less current liabilities		_____		
Creditors		65,330		
Proposed dividend	_____	_____	(_____)	_____
				£ _____

	Authorised	Issued
Financed by		
Ordinary share capital	======	_____

Share premium
General reserve
Profit & loss account balance 25,525
                Shareholders' funds
10% debentures
                                          £253,025

Additional information
1. On formation of the Company 400,000 shares of 25p each were issued
2. On 1 May 19-3 the Company issued a further 100,000 shares at 40p per share, of exactly the same type as was issued on formation
3. On 1 May 19-3 the Company's reserves were £12,500
4. By 1 May 19-3 the Company's provision for doubtful debts stood at £1,950, the provision is to be maintained at 5% of debtors
5. Discount received was 2.5% of purchases and discount allowed £15,280
6. The rate of stock turnover is 10
7. Investments which cost £14,900 currently stand at a market value of £16,350
8. Current ratio is 1.5 to 1
9. Depreciation of fixed assets is at:
    Plant and machinery 25% per annum on cost
    Fixtures and fittings 20% per annum on cost
10. On 1 May 19-3 fixed assets were valued at:
    Plant & machinery £47,340
    Fixtures & fitting £49,560
11. Gross profit to sales 25%
12. Expenses given as percentages of turnover were:
    Wages and salaries 10.25
    Insurance and maintenance 0.3
13. Other income and expense figures are:
    Rent received £15,100
    Selling distribution £18,535
14. The directors declare a mid-year dividend of 5% and a final dividend of 10%

8 From the outline and information given below, you are asked to complete the final accounts.

R L Atkinson Limited

Trading and Profit and Loss Account for year ended 28 February 19-8

Sales		
Less cost of sales		
Opening stock	63,400	
Add purchases	_____	
Less closing stock		520,000
	_____	
Gross profit		
Other revenue		
Discount received		
Rent received	_____	_____
Expenses		
General expenses	16,630	
Rent and rates		
Selling & distribution expenses		
Advertising		
Debenture interest	4,800	
Wages and salaries		
Insurance & maintenance		

Discount allowed
Net profit
Add profit & loss account balance b/fwd | | | 26,810

Less appropriations
Transfer to general reserve
Dividend: 15% preference paid | 7,500
          ordinary | 37,000

Profit & loss account balance c/fwd

R L Atkinson Limited, Balance Sheet as at 28th February 19-8

Fixed assets
Land and buildings   147,500
Plant and machinery   54,500
Fixtures and fittings   39,250

Investments at cost
Net current assets
Current assets
Stock
Debtors   71,190
Bank
Cash
Less current liabilities
Creditors
Proposed dividend   (_____)

Financed by
                     Authorised   Issued
Ordinary share capital   200,000
Preference share capital   100,000

Share premium
General reserve
Profit & loss account balance
             Shareholders' funds
8% Debentures

Additional information
1. Percentages related to turnover
    Discount allowed   1.0
    Insurance & maintenance   0.5
    Wages and salaries   7.5
    Advertising   0.3
    Selling & distribution   1.3
    Net profit   8.0
    Margin   20.0
2. Discount received 1.0% of purchases
3. Ordinary dividend proposed 20%
4. The last issue of shares (of same type as previously) £15,000 was issued at a price of £1.25

5   A transfer of £20,000 from profits was made to create a general reserve
6   Creditors total £54,180
7   Stock turnover is eight times
8   Rent received is £16,113
9   Cash figure is one-third of liquid funds ie bank and cash
10 Investments costing £13,500 were currently valued at £16,200

Funds flow statements

9   D Larter has the following balance sheets as at 31 December:

	19-1			19-2	
Fixed assets at cost		16,000			18,500
Less depreciation		2,500			3,000
		13,500			15,500
Net current assets					
Current assets					
Stock	7,500			8,250	
Debtors	8,300			9,720	
Cash at bank	1,400	17,200		1,580	19,550
Less current liabilities					
Creditors	6,950	(6,950)	10,250	7,850 (7,850)	11,700
		£23,750			£27,200
Financed by:					
Capital 1 January		22,500			23,750
Add net profit for the year		7,850			10,900
		30,350			33,650
Less drawings		6,600			7,450
		£23,750			£27,200

You are asked to prepare his funds flow statements by the
a) Cash method, and
b) Working capital method

Answer guide:
a) Cash (increase) £180
    Total sources £12,300
    Total applications £12,120

b) Working capital (increase) £1,450
    Total sources   £11,400
    Total applications   £9,950
    Increase   £2,350
    Decrease   £900

10 V Handy has the following Balance Sheet as at 30 September

	19-5		19-6	
Fixed assets				
Land & buildings at cost		60,600		90,100
Fixtures & fittings at cost less depreciation		35,400		28,200
Machinery at cost less depreciation		32,800		24,000
		128,800		142,300
Net current assets				
Current assets				
Stock	15,160		18,230	
Debtors	27,910		25,480	
Cash at bank	14,880	57,950	–	43,710

Less current liabilities							
Creditors	30,370				26,220		
Bank overdraft	–	(30,370)	27,580		540	(26,760)	16,950
			£156,380				£159,250

Financed by		
Capital: 1 October	130,000	156,380
Add net profit	40,570	12,130
	170,570	168,510
Less drawings	14,190	19,260
	156,380	149,250
Loan (repayable 19-9)	–	10,000
	£156,380	£159,250

Note
1 The only new investment in fixed assets during the year to 30 September 19-6 was for land and buildings in preparation for new products.
2 Fixed assets other than land and buildings are depreciated.
From the above prepare, for year ending 30 September 19-6, the following funds flow statements:
a) cash, and
b) working capital.

11

J R Wilkins

Balance Sheet as at 31 December for years 19-5 and 19-6

	19-5	19-6		19-5	19-6
Owners capital			*Fixed assets*		
Opening balance	95,100	102,200	Land & buildings at		
Net profit	22,400	28,500	cost	55,000	70,000
	117,500	130,700	Fixtures & equipment at cost	*33,000*	*40,000*
Less drawings	15,300	19,200		*10,000*	*15,000*
	102,200	111,500		*23,000*	*25,000*
Long term loan	15,000	25,000	Motor vehicles at		
Current liabilities			cost	*12,500*	*16,200*
Creditors	30,100	35,700	Less depreciation	*4,600*	*8,100*
				7,900	*8,100*
				85,900	103,100
			Investments at cost	15,100	20,400
			Current assets		
			Stock	*25,000*	*27,300*
			Debtors	*16,800*	*14,500*
			Bank & cash	*4,500*	*6,900*
				46,300	48,700
	£147,300	£172,200		£147,300	£172,200

J R Wilkins

Profit and Loss Account for years ended 31 December

	19-5	19-6		19-5	19-6
Administration, advertising, distribution & selling exps	50,320	48,150	Gross profit	80,520	81,150
			Rent from sub-letting	–	4,000
Provision for depreciation					
Fixtures & equipment	4,600	5,000			
Motor vehicles	3,200	3,500			
Net profit	22,400	28,500			
	£80,520	£85,150		£80,520	£85,150

Sales are: 19-5 £122,600   19-6 £138,500

From the above information for J R Wilkins prepare funds flow statements showing the following:
1 Cash changes,
2 Working capital changes and
3 Working capital changes according to SSAP 10

Calculate the following ratios for the two years; also from the above information:
1 Net profit to sales,
2 Net profit to capital employed (owners fund plus long term loans),
3 Current ratios, and
4 Liquid ratios.
   Ignore taxation.

12 From the statements set out below of R Jones Limited, you are required to a) present a cash flow statement, b) comment on cash flow statements generally and c) indicate any deficiencies in this type of statement.

Profit and Loss Accounts for Year ended 31 December

	19-7		19-8	
Gross Profit		68,100		97,280
Less: Depreciation	4,600		5,500	
General expenses	38,200		42,100	
Interest on debentures	2,000	43,800	1,000	48,600
		24,300		48,680
Add: Balance brought forward		17,750		22,750
		42,050		71,430
Less: Proposed ordinary dividend	9,300		10,700	
Transfer to general reserve	10,000	19,300	12,000	22,700
		£22,750		£48,730

Balance Sheets as at 31 December

	19-7		19-8	
Fixed Assets at cost		164,000		228,000
Less: Depreciation to date		17,000		22,500
		147,000		205,500
Current assets				
Stock	17,200		31,330	
Debtors	11,150		16,200	
Bank	8,700	37,050	15,650	63,180

Less: Current Liabilities							
Creditors	15,000			25,150			
Proposed Dividend	9,300	(24,300)	12,750	10,700	(35,850)		27,330
			£159,750				£232,830
Financed by							
Ordinary share capital			83,000				105,000
General reserve			28,000				40,000
Profit & loss account			22,750				48,730
Shareholders' funds			133,750				193,730
5% debentures			26,000				39,100
			£159,750				£232,830

13

Rooker and Skinner Limited

Profit and Loss Accounts for Year ended 31 December

		19-6			*19-7*
Gross Profit		67,300			95,250
Less depreciation	5,500		8,000		
General expenses	34,800		37,000		
Interest on debentures	1,000	41,300	1,250		46,250
Net profit		26,000			49,000
Add balance b/fwd		20,000			29,500
		46,000			78,500
Less proposed ordinary dividend	6,500		8,500		
Transfer to general reserve	10,000	16,500	15,000		23,500
		£29,500			£55,000

Rooker and Skinner Limited

Balance Sheets as at 31 December

	19-6				*19-7*		
Fixed Assets at cost			135,000				211,000
Less depreciation to date			16,000				24,000
			119,000				187,000
Current assets							
Stock	21,000			28,000			
Debtors	11,000			14,000			
Bank	8,000			15,000			
	40,000			57,000			
Less current liabilities							
Creditors	13,000			22,000			
Proposed dividend	6,500	19,500	20,500	8,500	30,500		26,500
			£139,500				£213,500

Financed by

Ordinary share capital	65,000	87,000
General reserve	25,000	40,000
Profit & loss account	29,500	55,000
Shareholders' funds	119,500	182,000
5% debentures	20,000	31,500
	£139,500	£213,500

You are required from the above information to produce:
  (i) a cash flow statement, and
  (ii) a working capital statement according to SSAP 10,
  (iii) a calculation of the following ratios for each years 19-6 and 19-7; sales were £201,900 and £285,750 respectively,
    a) Net profit to sales
    b) Net profit to capital employed
    c) Net profit to owner's equity
    d) Current ratio
    e) Liquid ratio.

14

Balance Sheets of Narrow Waters Ltd as at 31 December

	19-7		19-8	
	£	£	£	£
Fixed assets				
Plant at cost	42,000		59,500	
Less depreciation	14,850	27,150	20,240	39,260
Transport vehicles at cost	5,100		6,800	
Less depreciation	1,700	3,400	2,650	4,150
		30,550		43,410
Current assets				
Stock	9,179		11,421	
Debtors	7,241		8,219	
Bank	6,118		–	
	22,538		19,640	
Less current liabilities				
Creditors	8,864		10,712	
Dividend	3,000		3,000	
Bank overdraft	–		3,184	
	11,864		16,896	
Working capital		10,674		2,744
		£41,224		£46,154
Represented by				
Share capital		30,000		30,000
Profit & loss account		11,224		16,154
		£41,224		£46,154

Required   A flow of funds statement according to SSAP 10.

Cash budgeting

15 C Kidner started a trading business on 1 November 19-6, by introducing £10,000 into the business bank account. Kidner's plans for the first six months of trading are as follows:

1 Purchase of goods from suppliers:

	Nov	Dec	Jan	Feb	March	April
£	2,150	1,700	1,800	1,700	1,800	1,700

Kidner plans to pay suppliers two months after purchase

2 Sales (all on credit) are expected to be:

	Nov	Dec	Jan	Feb	March	April
£	1,000	1,250	1,250	1,500	2,000	2,000

Selling prices (as shown) are determined by adding 50% to the cost price of the goods. Debtors are expected to pay one month after invoice date

3 Rent of premises will be £250 per month payable on the first day of each month.
4 Kidner plans to buy a delivery van in January at a cost of £3,900 to be paid for in equal instalments over the months of January, February and March.
5 Trading and general expenses are payable as they arise and are expected to be £450 per month.
6 Depreciation of the delivery van is expected to be £300 by the end of April 19-7.

Required
a) A cash budget for the six months to 30 April 19-7,
b) a projected trading and profit and loss account for period ended 30 April 19-7, and
c) a projected balance sheet as at 30 April 19-7.

16

Brian Marson

Balance Sheet as at 31 March 19-5

Capital			Fixed assets		
Opening balance		198,680	Land & buildings		156,800
Add net profit		28,630	Fixtures & equipment		38,300
			(Cost £55,000)		
		227,310			195,100
Current liabilities			*Current assets*		
Creditors Feb	23,180		Stock at cost	47,150	
March	24,920		Debtors (March)	24,330	
Accrued exps March	8,290	56,390	Bank balance	17,120	88,600
		283,700			283,700

The following estimates are given for the six months to 30 September 19-5

	April	May	June	July	August	September
Sales	30,000	35,000	35,000	40,000	40,000	40,000
Purchases	20,000	25,000	25,000	20,000	15,000	10,000
General expenses	6,500	6,500	6,500	8,500	8,500	9,500

Notes
1 One fifth of sales are for cash
2 Debtors normally pay one month after sale
3 Creditors are paid two months after purchase (all purchases are for credit)
4 Accrued expenses for March are paid in the month of April the expenses incurred are all paid one month after the month during which they arise.

5 Selling price is calculated at cost plus 100%
6 Fixtures and equipment are to be depreciated by 20% per annum
7 Buildings are to be extended at a cost of £100,000 to be paid for equally in the months of July – October
8 Drawings are made to the extent of £1,050 a month
9 A loan is made by G Bright for £35,000 in July
10 More fixtures costing £6,500 are purchased at the end of September and are therefore not regarded as depreciating during this current period

Required
(i) a cash budget for the period,
(ii) a projected trading and profit and loss account, and
(iii) a projected balance sheet.

17 A Rose starts trading on 1 January 19-1 by introducing £15,000 into the business bank account. The following are Rose's plans and estimates for the next six months:

(i) Sales are expected to be:

	Jan	Feb	March	April	May	June
Cash	2,500	2,750	3,000	3,250	3,500	3,750
Credit	4,500	5,000	5,500	6,000	7,500	7,500

Selling prices (calculated from cost) require adding 50%.
Debtors are allowed one month's credit from invoice date.

(ii) Purchases are expected to be:

Jan	Feb	March	April	May	June
5,000	6,000	7,000	8,000	10,000	12,000

All purchases are on credit and Rose is allowed two months from invoice date.
(iii) Expenses are payable when they occur and are estimated at £1,550 a month.
(iv) Rent and rates (payable on the first day of each month) will be £1,330 a month.
(v) Rose intends to draw £950 a month for personal use.
(vi) A plan to purchase a motor van is proposed at a cost of £6,800 payable by four equal instalments April – July.
(v) The depreciation policy for the delivery van is adopted to make depreciation of £2,000 over a full year, and Rose suggests you consider the van owed from the start of the trading period.

You are required to prepare:
a) A cash budget for the six months to 30 June 19-1,
b) A projected set of final accounts: (i) trading profit and loss, and (ii) balance sheet.

Answer guide: Closing cash balance £8,170; gross profit £18,250; Net Loss £30; balance sheet balances £9,270 (vertical method).

18 Capt Hampson, RNVR (retired) has a small business selling boating supplies and, to enable him to plan ahead for the six months July to December 19-9, he provides you with the following information:

Balance Sheet as at 30 June, 19-9

Capital		21,500	*Fixed assets*			
Add net profit		2,000		Cost	Depn.	NBV
		23,500	Premises	7,500	–	7,500
			Fixtures	3,000	500	2,500
			Motor vehicles	2,500	500	2,000
Long-term loan		7,250		13,000	1,000	12,000

Current liabilities			Current assets		
Creditors		3,500	Stock		4,500
			Debtors	2,250	
				3,750	6,000
			Prepayments		250
			Bank		11,500
					22,250
		£34,250			£34,250

Capt. Hampson estimates

Sales to be	July	Aug.	Sept.	Oct.	Nov.	Dec.
	£5,000	£4,500	£5,500	£4,400	£6,000	£3,500

Payable two months after delivery

Purchases to be	July	Aug.	Sept.	Oct.	Nov.	Dec.
	£6,500	£4,250	£5,000	£5,250	£4,500	£3,000

Payable one month in arrears.

Rent payable one month in advance £250 per month.

Administrative expenses are to be £150 for each month July, August and September and thereafter £200 per month payable as they arise.

The mark-up is estimated to be 50%.
Depreciation is to be taken on the cost of assets at the close of the accounting period
    fixtures 10% per annum
    van   20% per annum.
Additional premises are in the process of being built and are to be completed in December, payment in full is to be made in three stages October to December at £1,500 per month.

He buys a motor van in August for £2,000, payments to be made; September £1,000 and October £1,000.
Old fixtures costing £500 were disposed of in October for £300. The fixtures had been out of use during the period and it was agreed that no depreciation should be taken. The fixtures were valued in the books at £400. All receipts and payments are to be made through the bank account.

Required
a) Produce a cash budget for July to December.
b) Produce a projected trading and profit and loss account for the period.
c) Comment briefly on the changes you have discovered.

19 J Phillipson provides the following details and asks you to show the projected bank balance and net profit.

Balance sheet as at 31 August 19-0

Owner's capital			Fixed assets	
Opening balance		115,000	Land & buildings	85,000
Add net profit		39,989	Motor vehicles	17,170
		154,989		102,170
Less drawings		22,500		
		132,489		

Current liabilities			Current assets		
Creditors July	6,560		Stock	33,090	
August	7,212		Debtors (August)	8,713	
Accrued expenses	1,196	14,968	Bank and cash	3,484	45,287
		£147,457			£147,457

1 Planned capital expenditure:
   a) extension to premises totalling £30,000 is to be carried out in stages and paid for in three monthly instalments commencing in October;
   b) purchase of new delivery vehicle at a cost of £6,130, to be paid for by deposit £2,130, in February and two instalments of £2,000 in each month of March and April.

2 Planned purchases

	Sept	Oct	Nov	Dec	Jan	Feb
(units)	550	600	650	700	750	750

3 Goods to be purchased on credit and paid for two months after purchase
4 Cost of goods £15 per unit
5 Planned sales

	Sept	Oct	Nov	Dec	Jan	Feb
(units)	750	750	850	850	900	950

6 Selling price to be cost plus 50%
7 Half the sales are for cash, debtors are expected to pay within one month of sale
8 General expenses to be paid at £1,120 per month, payable one month after they are incurred
9 Wages to be paid are £560 per month, payable immediately
10 Existing motor vehicles are expected to depreciate by £500 per month. The new motor vehicle will not be affected by this policy
11 Drawings of £1,875 per month are expected to continue during the six months
12 A provision for bad debts is to be created as 5% of end of period debtors

To meet Phillipson's requirements you should prepare:
a) a cash budget for the period,
b) a revenue statement for the period, and
c) a balance sheet as at 28 February 19-1.

20 D Woodhouse provides the following details and asks you to show the projected bank balance and net profit.

Balance Sheet as at 31 January 19-7

Owner's capital			Fixed assets		
Opening balance		33,360	Land & buildings		25,000
Add net profit		12,130	Motor vehicles		6,550
			Fixtures & fittings		1,420
		45,490			32,970
Less drawings		10,019			
		35,471			
Current liabilities			Current assets		
Creditors December	3,202		Stock	4,794	
January	4,716		Debtors	3,313	
Accrued expenses	347	7,725	Bank & cash	2,119	10,226
		£43,196			£43,196

1 Planned purchases

	Feb	March	April	May	June	July
(units)	450	500	500	550	550	600

Purchases are made on credit and paid for two months after the month in which they are invoiced.

2 The cost of goods is £10 per unit and selling price is to be cost plus 50%
3 Planned sales

	Feb	March	April	May	June	July
(units)	300	375	375	600	825	825

Two-thirds of the sales are made on credit and paid for one month after the month in which they are invoiced. The balance are for cash.
4. General expenses are to be £350 a month, payable one month after they arise.
5. Drawings by the proprietor are expected to be £950 a month commencing in April.
6. Wages to be paid are £430 per month, payable on the last business day of the month in which they arise.
7. Depreciation policy is as follows:
Motor vehicles 25%
Fixtures and fittings 50%

To meet the requirements of Woodhouse, you should prepare the following:
a) a cash budget for the period,
b) a revenue statement for the period, and
c) a balance sheet as at 31 July 19-7.

21 As a practising consultant, you are approached by a recently established business enterprise. This enterprise is seeking financial accommodation from its bankers, who are prepared to provide overdraft facilities, but before final approval can be given the figure for maximum overdraft is required, and the time in the year when this will arise. The forecast cash balance at the end of the first period of trading is also required. The following facts and forecasts are obtained from your client:

(i) Trading will commence on 1 March 19-5, when £8,000 cash will be introduced into the business.
(ii) Business premises costing £22,000 will be paid for at the commencement of trading. A mortgage of the business premises has been negotiated for the sum of £12,000, receivable on 31 March 19-5. This amount is to be repaid over ten years at quarterly intervals by equal instalments of capital plus interest at the rate of 12 per cent. per annum on the balance outstanding at the end of each quarter. The first repayment plus interest will be made on 30 June 19-5.
(iii) A part of the premises will be let on a five year tenancy at £200 per calendar month (inclusive of property rates), payable quarterly in advance as from 1 April 19-5.
(iv) Sales are estimated at £8,000 per month for the first quarter, £12,000 per month for the second quarter, and thereafter £24,000 per month. All sales are on credit and will be paid for by the end of the month following that in which the sales have taken place.
(v) A minimum stock of goods to the value of £12,000 will be purchased in March 19-5 and will be maintained throughout the period.
(vi) Trade creditors will allow accounts to be settled in the month following that in which the goods are supplied.
(vii) Gross profit margin on cost is expected to be 25 per cent throughout the period.
(viii) Insurances are estimated to be £240 per annum payable in 1 March 19-5 in advance.
(ix) Property rates are estimated to be £360 per annum payable half-yearly in advance on 1 April and 1 October.
(x) Other business expenses are expected to be £1,000 per month to be paid at the end of the month following that in which they are incurred.
(xi) Private drawings are estimated to be £400 per month, except in the months of July and October when additional drawings of £200 in each month will be made.

Required
a) A monthly cash flow forecast for the period 1 March 19-5 to 31 December 19-5;

b) Forecast trading and profit and loss account in respect of the above period;
c) Forecast balance sheet as at 31 December 19-5; and
d) Forecast flow of funds statement in respect of the above period, reconciling the opening and closing cash balances.

(Institute of Chartered Accountants.)

Section VIII
Regulatory matters

Unit 1 Statute
Unit 2 Accounting concepts, conventions & standards
Unit 3 Auditing & auditors

Unit 1
Statute

Overview

1 Statutes affecting companies and partnerships are given in outline.

2 A reference is made to partnership legislation contained in the main text.

3 Briefly, the developing aspects of legislation affecting companies is given.

Companies

The basic (consolidating) Act regulating the affairs of companies, containing the legal provisions as expressed in Company Law is The Companies Act 1948. Other Acts are:

The Companies Act   1967
The Companies Act   1976
The Companies Act   1980
The Companies Act   1981

All these Acts interest accountants as far as the publication of final accounts is concerned.

The Registration of Companies requires the issue of a Certificate of Incorporation at commencement, issued under the Acts.

There are three methods of maintaining companies:

1 Unlimited – having corporate powers, but not providing limited liability to members (these are quite rare).
2 Companies limited by guarantee – formed on a subscription basis by members, that is not regarded as suitable for trading organizations.
3 Companies limited by shares – the familiar method of operation adopted by trading companies.

There are two types of company:

1 Private – the small corporate enterprise whose members benefit through limitation of their liability but there are restrictions on the transferability of shares.
2 Public – subject to the main rigours of legislation, stock exchange and accounting requirements, listed companies are able to maintain a market for shares and increase the potential for raising capital. Members again have limited liability.

Company legislation

The Companies Act 1948

This Act is the major aspect of legislation that has governed company affairs for over thirty years and followed recommendations made by the Cohen Committee. Later Acts are primarily amendments to this where it has been recognized that changes have been required.

The Act is a development from earlier legislation, laying emphasis on:

a) publication of information relating to the issue of shares,
b) accounts of holding companies and subsidiaries,
c) publicity relative to company affairs, and
d) powers of control given to the then Board of Trade (Department of Trade), its agent the Registrar, and the Courts.

Companies Act 1967

This had the following three major aspects:

1 Laid down specific requirements for insurance companies;
2 Applied to Companies in general as follows:
   a) ending the status of exempt private company – requiring equal filing regulations for public and private companies,
   b) enabled the limited company to change status to unlimited, and vice versa (but once only during its existence), and
   c) required full information about subsidiaries, associated companies and directors shareholdings; political contributions; and details about profit and turnover;
3 Laid down requirements for the publication of company accounts.

Companies Act 1976

This had important sections concerning the obligations and rights of auditors and cleared up technical deficiencies in the 1948 Act. Such matters primarily related to notification of meetings; attendance at meetings; the right to be heard on matters concerning the auditor; the protection of members should the auditor resign. Matters not related to auditors included stricter rules concerning accounting periods and tighter definitions for accounting records.

Companies Act 1980

This makes a significant distinction between public and private companies in

2 A listing of concepts and conventions is provided and each rule is briefly discussed.
3 A listing of accounting standards and exposure drafts is given.

Accounting concepts and conventions are basically the rules followed by accountants in order to prepare accounts. The classification of these particular rules as either concepts or conventions need not concern us in this text, since taken together they amount to the principles under which accountants work.

Accounting standards, for financial accounts, have been formulated in this country in recent years (as Statements of Standard Accounting Practice) to provide a concensus as to which rules are acceptable in the case of specific circumstances.

Until the formulation of standards (and the process is still incomplete), accountants could apply concepts and conventions in different ways, so that with different assumptions the same trading results could be represented differently.

Concepts and conventions

Money measurement – Money is the common method of expressing value in accounts so that unlike items can be compared according to their monetary worth. But this means that the only assets that are brought into accounts are those that can be valued in money terms, eg employees cannot be brought in – although many authorities would regard them as important assets of any business or organization.

Stable monetary unit – Accounting statements are at the present time (even with the recent standard) largely prepared on the basis that the monetary unit is stable. However, money values change which affect price levels and purchasing power, and this is currently recognized under SSAP 16, although many accountants disagree with this specific remedy (see Appendix I).

Entity – Accounting records are kept only from the point of view of the business and not the owners. Only those economic events which affect the business are recorded.

Going concern – It is assumed that unless there is other evidence the business will continue to operate. Were this not the case the assets, especially those of little use outside the business, would be unlikely to retain their stated value.

Periodicity – The surplus generated by the business is accounted for at given intervals, when accounts are prepared – usually one year. One period follows from another, but many accounting problems relate to a decision about which period should a particular item of revenue be accounted for.

Matching (or accruals) – This is an attempt to ensure that revenues recorded in a period are matched with the expenses incurred in earning them.

Consistency* – Accounting information should be prepared on a consistent basis within and between periods as there are sometimes alternative bases for different situations.

Cost – This requires that inputs are recorded at acquisition price, supported by evidence of the transaction. This provides for uniformity, and a reliable basis under conditions of stable prices. Under other than stable price conditions, serious distortions can arise, ie historic and current values may not be distinguished.

terms of the name, noting that the title of the public company should distinguish it from the private company. But more fundamentally the Act tightens the rules for raising capital and the calculation of profit; loans to and directors contracts; and 'insider dealing' (directors and others using knowledge for personal gain)

Companies Act 1981

This implements the EEC Fourth Directive on reporting requirements, intr ducing uniform presentations for companies in member states. The Act includ the outcome of the distinctions between small, medium and large companies reporting and filing requirements. Certain quite radical changes are also m in the context of raising capital, share premiums and redemptions, and co panies buying their own shares.

Partnerships

The basic Act is The Partnership Act 1890 and the Limited Partners Act Both these Acts are of particular importance to auditors who should h working knowledge of them.

The emphasis in this section is to reinforce aspects of accounting and illu changes that have occurred. It is in the area of corporate legislation that has exercised much of its influence and this is a natural consequence importance and development of corporate enterprise over the last h years.

Partnership legislation has remained stable over recent decades, and dealt with in Unit 2 Section 5.

The law and accounting

The link between legislation and accounting practice is strong. Usua leaves the technical accounting considerations of implementati accountancy profession and itself concentrates on the principles. cases that have come before the Courts legal judgements have, how times run counter to accounting opinion.

Unit 2
Accounting concepts, conventions standards

Overview

1 The rules under which the profession operates can be regarded c discussed as:

   a) concepts and conventions, and
   b) standards.

Dual aspect – The essence of double-entry book-keeping ensures that all entries are recorded twice, once as debits and once as credits.
Conservatism* – A cautious or prudent approach is taken towards estimating valuations (a pessimistic view). Accountants have traditionally taken this view to counter over-optimistic opinions of managers and/or owners.
Materiality* – Accountants will not necessarily make a record in final accounts of items which are regarded as not material relative to the business and its size.
Objectivity – Accounting information should be based as far as possible on objective evidence, free from bias, that is capable of independent verification.
Realization – Increases in the value of assets should not be recognized in accounting statements until a legitimate transaction takes place, exchanging one type of asset for another. However, the realization is not always clearly definable, eg value for the sale of an item on credit, is usually taken when invoiced.
Note* denotes accounting conventions.

Accounting standards

Statements of Standard Accounting Practice are recognized as the standard authoritative internal rules of the accounting profession and can be illustrated by the example SSAP 14: Group Accounts. A full listing (in numerical) order now follows:

1. Accounting for the results of associated companies
2. Disclosure of accounting policies
3. Earnings per share
4. The accounting treatment of government grants
5. Accounting for Value Added Tax
6. Extraordinary items and prior year adjustments
7. Accounting for changes in the purchasing power of money (this provisional standard was replaced in January 1976 by an Interim Recommendation)
8. The treatment of taxation under the imputation system in the accounts of companies
9. Stocks and work in progress
10. Statements of source and application of funds
11. Accounting for deferred taxation (replaced in October 1978 by SSAP 15)
12. Accounting for depreciation
13. Accounting for research and development
14. Group accounts
15. Accounting for deferred taxation
16. Current cost accounting
17. Accounting for post balance sheet events
18. Accounting for contingencies

Concepts, conventions and standards are included here with the minimum of comment. The professional student of accounting will need to build up his or her own knowledge of such matters. Other students should know about the existence of these rules and statements.

All practising accountants and auditors will have knowledge of these matters since concepts and conventions will inevitably be learned through training and practice. But, more often than not, standards will have to be learned by keeping up-to-date, since they are a relatively new innovation and change with some regularity (see listing).

Further difficulties arise from the consideration and acceptance of these rules by the membership of accounting bodies, because as democratic, self-regulatory associations (with some statutory controls) all standards have to be accepted by the membership and follow an administrative procedure prior to formulation. The standards usually start as exposure drafts for consideration. A list of exposure drafts is presented as for standards. Exposure drafts pre-empt standards and can be recognized (as the example):

ED 8 'Accounting for changes in the purchasing power of money'.
The full set now follows (listed in numerical order):

ED 1 Accounting for the results of associated companies
     2 Disclosure of accounting policies
     3 Accounting for acquisitions and mergers
     4 Earnings per share
     5 Extraordinary items and prior year adjustments
     6 Stocks and work in progress
     7 Accounting for extraordinary items (replaced ED 5)
     8 Accounting for changes in the purchasing power of money
     9 The accounting treatment of grants under the Industry Act 1972
    10 Accounting for VAT
    11 Accounting for deferred taxation
    12 The imputation system of taxation in company accounts
    13 Statements of source and application of funds
    14 Accounting for research and development
    15 Accounting for depreciation
    16 Supplement to extraordinary items and prior year adjustments
    17 Accounting for research and development – revised
    18 Current Cost accounting
    19 Accounting for deferred taxation
    20 Group accounts
    21 Accounting treatment of foreign currency transactions
    22 Accounting for post balance sheet events
    23 Accounting for contingencies
    24 Current cost accounting
    25 Accounting for the results of associated companies

In many cases (even without detailed investigation) the link between exposure drafts and standards can be seen from the above listings.

Unit 3
Auditing and auditors

Overview

1 The work of the auditor has traditionally been concerned with stewardship.

2 There are two types of auditor:

a) the professional auditor, and
b) the internal auditor.

3 Current statute and standards (for accounting and auditing) have superimposed obligations on to those traditionally undertaken by auditors.

4 The complexities of modern business require the auditor to have a high standard of skill and judgement.

5 The auditor in the main still examines books and accounts as the prime area of responsibility, in order to decide whether they show a 'true and fair view'.

6 The student (as his or her studies progress) should be aware of modern developments, just as the auditor has to be.

Reference has been made elsewhere in this book to the work of the auditor. The auditor primarily checks on the stewardship of the business, on behalf of the owners, who leave part or all of the management of the business to employees.

The professional external auditor is part of a team working as a partner of, or under a partnership, and should have no other association with the organization beyond that for which he or she is engaged. The internal auditor also performs similar duties, making similar checks, but without the same degree of authority and responsibility. The internal auditor is usually an employee in a larger organization and is responsible to management for his or her (often more regular) checks.

Statute and current professional rules place additional obligations on the external auditor when carrying out duties. As well as adhering to accounting standards the auditor has a personal set of standards also published by the professional Institutes.

The work of the auditor cannot be discussed in a few paragraphs. It is a complex undertaking that requires accounting skill and judgement of a high standard, together with a flexible understanding of the conditions and difficulties under which various businesses operate. Although the professional auditor has traditionally been concerned with a periodic review (following the preparation of final accounts), the nature of new responsibilities and the size of business effectively means that his or her relationship with the business is on more of a continual basis.

Specifically, the professional auditor examines the evidence from which the final accounts of a business are prepared. This can be very broad spanning work with books of accounts and vouchers of various types to the examination of assets and a working knowledge of computing systems. The conclusion of this investigation requires the auditor to decide whether the accounts show 'a true and fair view' and to do this the underlying records and books must be accepted as accurate.

It is not the responsibility of the external auditor to produce information unless he or she is specifically employed to do so ie in a different capacity. The auditor only reports on the accuracy and state of the information. Management has the responsibility for preparation.

One of the aims of this text, as it has progressed, has been to keep students in touch with important aspects of basic financial accounting, and to give them an appreciation of the modern profession. The auditor/accountant has to be aware of developments in standards and statute in order to update knowledge and experience, and to respond to changes in business that are causing the profession to change its attitudes and ideas.

Conclusion

The text has been designed to help the student overcome some initial difficulties with financial accounting problems that confront most, but deter others from gaining at least a minimal knowledge of the subject.

The emphasis has been to direct students to attempt examples from this and other text books. A willingness by the student to undertake examples of increasing difficulty is important. To continue the studies he or she must also look to more advanced text books, of which there are many from which to select on the market. There may, alternatively, be a need to use this basic book in conjunction with advanced texts currently being used, if so, then so much the better. Both I think have their place.

It has to be recognized that the diagrammatic approach, novel though it may be, has its limitations. The object has been, however, to provide a secure basis of knowledge appropriate to double entry book-keeping and financial accounting from which the student can advance.

One important point is that most accounting problems can be reduced to the basic *debit* and *credit* entries. A complex set of adjustments or specialized entries can often be solved in this way. It may help to draw small ledger 'T' accounts to assist in this process – the diagrammatic approach is then useful in this respect!

Appendix 1
Accounting for price level changes

1 Introduction

2 The aim of inflation accounting

3 Working towards an acceptable solution – a standard

4 The type of index calculations required

5 Statement of Standard Accounting Practice No 16

6 Example

Introduction

This Appendix provides an insight into some of the ideas and methods behind accounting for price level changes. What should be said is that the double entry approach is still perfectly valid, it is just that certain assumptions relating to the principles have to be revised eg historic cost valuation. Some aspects of accounting for price level changes are presented to give an idea of current developments, that will need to be studied at least by those seeking a professional qualification, but only after the basic principles of double-entry have been mastered. Accounting for price level changes has been included in this manner because, it is not part of the basic theory of financial accounting, but rather a part that, at the current state of practice has been grafted on to historically prepared information.

This Appendix is by no means a complete coverage of the subject, and were it so, would require as many pages of text as have already been written to fully explain it. Accounting for price level changes has to be seen mainly in the context of accounting for inflation (rising prices) rather than deflation (falling prices), although the principles would be the same, whatever movement takes place the direction of changes and effects are clearly opposites.

However, the road towards acceptance of ideas has been far from easy and there have been two schools of thought that have become (and to some extent still are) irreconcilable. These differences appear to depend essentially on the background and experience of the accountant, making the decision. In the Introduction there was an early discussion about the accounting professions and the role of the auditor. The two views about inflation accounting appear to reflect these positions. The auditors and others are ultimately responsible to, and concerned with, the protection of shareholders' interests, whereas internal accountants are concerned with the business as a unit (or entity) and not just the interests of one selected group. For the time being the two theories can merely be stated:

1 Current Purchasing Power (CPP),
2 Current Cost Accounting (CCA).

It is the second of these two that is now more widely accepted since this method of accounting tends to protect the interest of the business as a whole and will still protect the shareholders.

The aim of inflation accounting

Inflation has been a feature of the modern capitalist economic system for decades. What is today regarded as a moderate amount would be between 2% and 4% as occurred in the late 1950s and early 1960s. In the late 1960's and early 1970's the rate ranged from 5% to 10%. In recent years, however, there have been more dramatic increases in general prices as can be seen by the following figures extracted from the index of retail prices:

Year	Prices increase (%)
1975	24.2
1976	16.5
1977	15.8

Later figures have been slightly better especially when considered against the 1975 figure of 24.2% and are generally acknowledged to be falling.

Year	Price increase (%)
1978	8.3
1979	13.4
1980	18.0
1981	11.9

The increasing rate of inflation among industrialized countries has been a general problem but the United Kingdom appears to have been less successful in controlling inflation compared with other countries. It is against this background of inflation that interest in accounting for price level changes has, more than any other single factor, concerned the profession in the 1970's. Although the subject is not new and there has been published criticism of accounting methods, it is probably fair to say that in those days the profession and its leaders tended to give the subject less than the full consideration it required.

Deficiencies in accounting statements in a period of inflation

Not taking into account inflation, there would still be many faults that could be found in accounting statements some of which have been resolved or reduced through the standard setting process. One such problem would be the method of stock valuation, an asset of major importance constituting a high percentage of the assets of many major public companies.

However, the presence of inflation has caused the following major problem areas to be recognized in both the profit and loss account and the balance sheet.

1 Depreciation

A principle of accounts has been to match current costs against current revenue for a period in which accounts are prepared. Depreciation has always been a problem in this context. Accountants have chosen therefore to solve it by making assumptions about the life expectancy of long term assets applying these consistently by introducing non-cash costs as a charge on profits at the end of the accounting period, that also serve to reduce the 'cost' of any asset held in the balance sheet. But the charge to profit and loss has been traditionally based on historic cost. This historic cost figure will comprise assets purchased at different times and therefore at different relative pounds. The asset purchased in 1971, will be invoiced in 1971 pounds, the asset purchased in 1975 will be invoiced in 1975 pounds (with lower purchasing power in an inflationary period). But they previously would have been depreciated (without adjustment) as though the pounds of 1971 and 1975 maintained the same purchasing power. This is contrary to the purpose of a provision for depreciation, the charge for use of assets against current profits will be insufficient neither will sufficient funds be provided to replace assets. Viewed in another way, too high a profit may encourage excessive distribution.

2 Cost of goods sold

The effect of inflation is not limited to relative changes in the purchasing power of money outside a specific accounting period, especially during periods of high inflation. Prices increase continually throughout an accounting period and therefore, stock held at the start, or goods purchased early on would appear to be 'cheaper' than those purchased at or towards the close of an accounting period. Therefore a calculation is required to 'equalize' these costs and the resulting effect upon profit, ensuring that profit is not overstated, leading to an imaginary trading success.

3 Monetary items

In a period of inflation purchasing power losses will be incurred by holding monetary and near monetary assets eg debtor, bank and cash balances. Such changes can occur both within and between accounting periods, eg 10% inflation during a year will cause the purchasing power of money to decrease by 10%, other things being equal. Conversely, gains can be achieved by getting into debt; eg a bank overdraft, held over the course of the same year will produce a purchasing power gain, as the amount eventually repaid will not have the same purchasing power as the amount originally borrowed.

In periods of high inflation it usually follows that high interest rates will, at least to some extent, compensate for any loss incurred by lenders, although this is by no means certain.

4 Lenders of long-term funds

They may also be at an even greater disadvantage than short term lenders since their initial investment is held by a business over a number of periods and may be repaid in pounds of substantially less purchasing power than the original loan. What is worse is that these loans may be contracted at historic (low) rates of interest and may not be compensated for. However, most authorities now consider that the benefits of long-term borrowing should not be included with that of short-term borrowing.

5 Ordinary share capital raised

This is generally expressed in purchasing power terms at the date of acquisition. If prices have increased since the original funds were raised the ordinary shareholders will require their funds to have increased by a similar amount, to break even in purchasing power terms. Holders of equity are at an advantage over other long term financiers in that the dividend is variable (hopefully upwards) and should maintain its relative purchasing power to the general price of goods and services. The price of shares (in listed companies) should also increase to benefit ordinary shareholders, producing a capital gain on realization.

6 Long term assets and stocks

These have been expressed in terms of historical cost, with no attempts made to adjust costs to current terms. The most usual departure was land and buildings to be revalued on the basis of a qualified valuer's report.

The degree and effect of errors in profit measurement

The degree of error cannot be assessed until there is complete agreement on the methods of adjustment. It is generally expected that a much reduced profit will be shown after price level adjustments have been made. This may not be the case if gains in respect of long term debt are included in the distributable profit – the CPP method.

The main effect of these errors is probably related to corporate taxation and dividend policy. Without adjustment, many companies are almost certainly paying extremely high rates of taxation on real profit, and dividends may be distributed in excess of real profit, thus damaging the capital of a company.

It cannot be expected that the problems of taxation will be solved until those accounting methods concerned with price level changes that precede the calculation of taxation are changed first. What is probably the case is that some businesses are paying more tax than they otherwise would, and some are paying less. Current measures such as accelerated capital allowances, writing off the cost of plant, generous stock relief, reducing the increasing cost of stock, are only crude alternatives to a fully inflation-proofed profit.

However, where wage claims are also related to published profit figures excessive pay increases may be negotiated as the employees' share of this imaginery success. This is verified by the fact that some unions acknowledge the use of published financial information in the negotiation process. The problem is not only of interest so far as the revenue statement is concerned eg the overstatement of profit by under recording depreciation and the like but also the balance sheet, through the under-recording of asset values, producing a capital employed figure that is historically low. Note that the combined effect on both high profit and low capital will have produced over-optimistic rate of return ratios in all business statements for the last twenty or thirty years.

One argument against inflation accounting has been that prices will inevitably be increased when company directors realize what poor returns are being made on invested capital. This is a debatable point if the effects of competition, both national and international, are considered. For instance, the current depressed economic climate has shown competition to be a powerful weapon against increasing prices.

Incomplete and partial adjustments

A number of partial methods have been suggested, these are:

1 Additional transfers to reserve

A reserve designed to accumulate funds, specifically for replacement of assets, eg a fixed asset replacement reserve, shown in the financed by section of the balance sheet.

2 Replacement cost accounts

In the revenue account sales are matched, as far as possible, against purchase costs at the time of sale. Depreciation is based on current not historic asset costs. Provision may also be made for losses or gains on monetary items. In the balance sheet, fixed assets are valued at current replacement costs, with the aid of appropriate price indices regarded as a fore runner of full CCA.

3 Stock valuation based on LIFO principles

This approach has been used much more in the United States of America than in the United Kingdom where it is not acceptable for taxation purposes. Contrary to FIFO (first in first out) as predominantly used in this country, LIFO (last in first out) uses a method of stock valuation to calculate profit, by matching sales against the most recent purchases of stock that are admitted to the production process. In the balance sheet, however, stock will be shown at historic purchase prices – many months or possibly years out of date, and therefore while this method may depress profits (in terms of rising prices), it will mislead as far as the balance sheet is concerned and will inflate prices in times of falling prices. Little more will be said about this but a good cost accounting book will quickly explain these very important differences between FIFO and LIFO, even without considering price level changes.

More comprehensive methods

Current purchasing power (CPP)

The theory is based on the principles that monetary elements in an historical cost valuation statement can be converted by application of a common purchasing power unit to that of stable purchasing power. The problem is that the prices of goods and services in any one period do not change by uniform amounts and frequently move up or down relative to each other. Therefore a uniform average applicable to all transactions does not exist.

The proponents of this method appeared to accept that the Index of Retail Prices (or some similar index) was a suitable basis for adjusting relative prices over time, as did PSSAP 7. But the problem lies in the construction of this (and other similar indices) in that it is based on consumer prices charged which affect 'middle income' households that are clearly dissimilar from those of business. In particular, a consumer price index has been suggested for adjusting the final accounts of quoted companies. A problem here is that a general consumer index will not usually accurately reflect changes in company purchasing power. Consider for example, an adjustment for specific fixed assets that have few, if any, characteristics common to the goods in the 'average' shopping basket.

This method is very different from replacement cost accounting as historical cost adjusted figures by a general price index do not generally produce the equivalent of current replacement costs. Furthermore, there is frequently some delay in production of such indices, since much reliance is placed on external sources for information ie the Government Statistical Service, that cannot be expected to produce information in line with individual corporate requirements, eg at year end.

Current cost accounting (CCA)

This is not so much an overall method for containing price changes (inflation) by application of a comprehensive index, but a method for revaluing specific assets and liabilities (or classes of these) in line with changes in specific indices maintained for the purpose. Such indices may be available from the Government Statistical Service, Trade Associations etc or may have to be specifically constructed.

Replacement cost accounts (for CCA aims to record all costs in current values — so far as is possible) match sales against the current cost of these sales in the revenue account. Depreciation is based on current specific asset costs (as indexed or taken from current price lists) not historic, nor some disassociated index. Provision may also be made for losses or gains on monetary items. Stock and work in progress is also valued at current cost, with the aid of price lists, invoices or indexes etc. The double entry in these cases is made through a capital reserve account or capital adjustment account.

As was stated earlier CPP has been closely identified with the protection of shareholders and their purchasing power, whereas CCA is more concerned with the protection of the entity via its assets, through the facility of charging an up-to-date amount for their use, but also ensuring that they are retained at an up-to-date price, relative to each specific asset or group of assets. Those who formerly opted for CPP have only probably recently been converted to the superiority of CCA, because they looked on a business only from the point of view of protecting owners, without seeing that CCA did this coupled with other benefits that were not available under the CPP method.

Working towards an acceptable solution — a standard

The road towards a standard

January 1973	ED8	Accounting for Changes in the Purchasing Power of Money
January 1974		Appointment of the inflation accounting committee — the Sandilands Committee
May 1974	PSSAP7	Accounting for Changes in the Purchasing Power of Money
September 1975		Report of the Inflation Accounting Committee
December 1975	PSSAP7	Withdrawn
November 1976	ED18	Current cost accounting
July 1977	ED18	Rejected by member of the ICAEW
November 1977		Hyde guidelines published
April 1979	ED24	Current cost accounting
March 1980	SSAP16	Current cost accounting

ED8 proposed that companies should publish supplementary statements along side their conventional accounts. The additional statement would revise historically prepared accounts according to CPP principles. ED8 formed the basis of PSSAP7 (the only statement prefixed by the word provisional) that requested companies comply with its recommendations, and its requested implementation fitted in with doubts in the profession about its acceptability.

In the meantime, between the publication of the exposure draft and provisional standard, the Government intervened and the Department of Trade appointed the Committee on Inflation Accounting, shortly to become known as the Sandilands Committee. The Committee took an independent course and recommended a system of Current Cost Accounting. As a result of this the Accounting Standards Committee moved away from its own provisional standard and set up a working party, the Inflation Accounting Steering Group (IASG) to investigate the Sandilands proposals. The result of this was ED18. The exposure draft supporting current cost accounting was considered to be unnecessarily complicated and was rejected by members of the Institute of Chartered Accountants for England and Wales. The Government, reaffirmed its support for current cost accounting in its discussion document issued in July 1977 'The Future of Company Reports'. Following these peculiar circumstances, the accountancy profession issued a set of interim proposals The Hyde guidelines (named after the committee chairman). A further exposure draft was then issued by the ASC (ED24) that became the current standard SSAP 16.

The type of index calculation required

The problem of accounting for inflation in practice is quite complex because of the difficulty in developing and applying an appropriate basis from which to work. Inflation accounting adjustments are based on the recorded monetary amounts taken from historically-based information that are adjusted according to the appropriate index. The basic principles of double entry apply equally to the adjustments as they have done to the historic data that they are used to convert.

Indexation

The index is prepared on a points basis, relative to 100, ie whatever number the index stands at currently. Sometime in the past (either months or years) it stood at 100, therefore the index is applied in a calculation according to the number of points it has increased (or decreased) by in a given period. There can be few or many indices but the principle is still the same.

The basic formula consists of a numerator and denominator that act as a 'weight' on a given monetary amount that is then revised up or down according to the arrangements (relative size) of the numerator and denominator.

To calculate a new amount

ie Amount $\times \dfrac{\text{Numerator}}{\text{Denominator}}$ = Result

eg 180 $\times \dfrac{100}{130}$ = 138

180 $\times \dfrac{130}{100}$ = 234

To calculate a difference
ie   Amount × (Numerator/Denominator − Numerator/Denominator) = Result

eg   630   (130/100 − 110/90) = 49

     700   (100/100 − 110/100) = (70)

The numerator and denominator have already been related to index numbers, but what is important is to appreciate what these index numbers represent, and how they affect the specific adjustment under consideration. In an accounting context, this requires an understanding of the accounting principles behind the adjustment.

Index information may be presented in the following (summarized) way:

	Specific index industrial buildings (of type used)	*General index* retail prices
1975	100	100
1976	110	117
1977	115	135
1978	145	146
1979	160	166
1980	180	196

Note that CCA is concerned with specific indices as they affect specific assets.

Example

Take buildings that were purchased ten years ago for £50,000 when the index stood at 100, the index is currently stated to be at 150. What is the recognized real monetary value? Not £50,000 less a calculation of depreciation on that figure but:

£50,000 × 150/100 = £75,000

ie   £75,000, less a calculation of depreciation on that figure.

Therefore the monetary price of the buildings has risen in current terms to £75,000, in other words, given today's values, were we to sell them, the buildings would fetch £75,000 or thereabouts. Now that is entirely what we would expect to happen during a period of inflation, the movement would be upwards.

ie   the index would be 150/100

          and not 100/150

Application of an index (CCA)

There are three types of information that could be subject to adjustment, these are:

1 opening balances (from previous period accounts),
2 changes occuring during the year, and
3 closing balances.

Invariably closing balances do not have to be adjusted by indexing because they are stated at end of year figures eg debtors and cash.
Items that require adjustment are as follows:

The revenue account

1 *Stock*: would have to be adjusted according to the method of recording current cost that is adopted eg perpetual inventory recording new purchase prices as they occur, on a continuous basis. At the close of the year a stock figure for the period would be calculated on the basis of the current (revised) costs at the end of that period.
2 *Cost of sales*: in most businesses there is a significant delay between the date on which goods are purchased and the date when they are eventually sold. As a result, the sales in a profit statement for 1980 will usually be matched against a mixture of 1979 and 1980 purchase costs although in a period of inflation the later will normally be stated at a greater monetary amount. The current cost of stocks sold or consumed in production would be taken at the period they were converted from the perpetual records.
3 *Depreciation*: the charge for depreciation in each year's accounts is based on asset costs. In many cases these asset costs, and hence the depreciation charge, will represent a completely different purchasing power position from that which is in existence today. An age analysis will have to be prepared for all fixed assets, showing fixed assets purchased in a particular year and adjustments made for depreciation. This may be complex and time consuming, at least, on the first occasion since much of the information may not be readily available. However the process may be shortened by going back for a limited period of time, all assets deemed to have been purchased within that period.

The balance sheet

1 *Monetary items*: including bank balances, cash on hand, debtors, prepayments, creditors and accruals. While conventional accounting always reports monetary items in the balance sheet, it does not account for the effect of purchasing power gains and losses in the profit calculation. It is necessary to show there are losses to be made from holding such assets, just as there are gains from not holding. The problem is to find or calculate indexes relevant to which the liquid funds are to be used.
2 *Fixed assets*: the preparation of schedules applicable to depreciation applies, because assets should be shown at an up-to-date value as part of the process for ensuring adequate provisions are made.
3 *Stock*: requires an adjustment to protect the short term purchasing power to ensure that it can be replaced, usually at higher prices.
4 *Long term liabilities*: there are considerable differences of opinion regarding the treatment of gains on long term liabilities not least the differences between CPP and CCA, but a concentration on CCA still reveals differences, and many would feel that these should be dealt with as a non-distributable reserve, instead of being placed within the profit statement.

Current Cost Accounting Standard – SSAP 16

General application
1 Accounting periods beginning on or after 1 January 1980.

2 Applies to listed companies and large non-listed companies (larger than defined reporting minimum in the EEC Fourth Directive).
3 Specifically excludes insurance or property companies, investment or unit trusts, 'non-profit' companies, wholly owned subsidiaries of the United Kingdom or Irish origin.

Main requirements
1 Profit and loss account and balance sheet should be prepared on the basis of current cost accounting.
2 Current cost accounts should be supported by notes.
3 Current cost of earnings per share should be stated for listed companies.

Balance sheet
1 Assets stated at their value to the business (usually net current replacement cost).
2 Liabilities stated at historical amounts.
3 Capital stated at historic cost (difference between historic cost and value to the business of assets to be transferred to reserves.)

Profit & loss account
1 Current cost operating profit is the historic cost accounting profit reduced by:
   a) Extra depreciation − to allow for higher current costs of fixed assets.
   b) Cost of sales adjustment (COSA) − to allow for higher current costs of stocks.
   c) Monetary working capital adjustment (MWCA) − to allow primarily for the effect of higher prices on capital included in debtors less creditors.
2 A gearing adjustment then increases the above total to allow for any benefit from net borrowing to a company's shareholders.
3 The result is the *current cost profit* that is not necessarily distributable.

Voluntary disclosure
1 Change in shareholders' equity, after allowing for the change in the general purchasing power of money.
2 Funds flow statement, prepared on the current cost accounting basis.
3 Gearing adjustment, calculated by alternative means.

Index requirements for SSAP 16
Various classes of fixed assets: buildings, and plant and machinery etc.
Debtors ⎫
Creditors ⎬ similar.
Stock
Other calculations for SSAP 16:
cost of sales adjustments, monetary working capital adjustment, and gearing adjustment.

Explanation

Extra depreciation: increases the historic cost figure, so that combined, the full charge for depreciation will reflect the value to the business of fixed assets consumed during the year. Because of the absence of a profit and loss account provision for earlier depreciation on the part of an asset recently (currently) revalued a charge for 'backlog' depreciation may have to be raised, to fully provide for replacement at the end of the useful life of an asset.

Cost of sales adjustment (COSA): stocks consumed are often held at historic cost relative to their value to the business at time of sale. A charge is therefore made against revenue, sufficient to finance replacement of stocks at higher prices. There are complications, however, for it would be impossible to account for all stock items separately, taking account of special purchases, seasonal prices, future trading and the like, so an overall average is permitted to be employed.

$$\text{COSA} = (C - O) - Ia\left(\frac{C}{Ic} - \frac{O}{Io}\right)$$

Where
- C = historical cost value of closing stock
- O = historical cost value of opening stock
- Ic = price index when closing stock was acquired
- Io = price index when opening stock was acquired
- Ia = average price index for period.

This adjustment can similarly be used for the monetary working capital adjustment to compile figures for adjusted debtor and creditor balances, given that relevant index and historic cost figures are inserted.

Monetary working capital adjustment (MWCA): complementing the cost of sales adjustment, this reflects the changes in capital requirements, arising from the effect of changes in specific prices on debtor and creditor balances. Overdrafts and cash are treated somewhat subjectively and the comparability of this adjustment may be affected.

Note that taken together MWCA and COSA are the two adjustments that revise the historically prepared figures for working capital.

The overall aim is to closely reflect price changes experienced by a company, and relevant price indices are produced by the Government Statistical Service for use by the accountant or alternatively the accountant can construct his or her own.

Current cost operating profit: is the figure left after subtracting extra depreciation, cost of sales, monetary working capital and related interest adjustments from the historic cost profit before interest and tax. It is a measure of how well the business has performed before allowing for the effect of long term financing not included in the monetary working capital adjustment. The balance remaining is available to pay interest on long term finance, taxation and dividend, and finance growth.

Gearing adjustment: is the gearing proportion of the sum of extra depreciation, cost of sales and monetary working capital adjustments that relate to assets that have been financed by net borrowing rather than ordinary shareholders.
As used in SSAP 16:

$$\text{Gearing adjustment} = \frac{L}{L + S} \times A$$

where
- L = Liabilities
- S = average shareholder's interest.
- A = current cost adjustments to allow for the impact of price changes on net operating assets.
- A = extra depreciation on fixed assets
  + extra loss on sale of fixed assets
  + cost of sales adjustment
  + monetary working capital adjustment.

Current cost profit attributable to shareholders: is the current cost operating profit plus the gearing adjustment less related interest. It can only be distributed as a cash dividend where one or more of the following occur:

1 unused cash from a previous year is utilized,
2 borrowing has been increased to at least the gearing adjustment, or
3 the operating capability of the business has been reduced.

Example

The following are the income statements and position statements of a company expressed in historical cost terms for the first two years trading.
Illustration

Income Statements

	Year 1	Year 2		Year 1	Year 2
Opening stock	1,500	2,000	Sales	13,500	18,850
Purchases	10,000	15,000			
	11,500	17,000			
Closing stock	2,000	5,000			
Cost of sales	9,500	12,000			
Gross profit	4,000	6,850			
	13,500	18,850		13,500	18,850
Expenses	2,000	3,000	Gross profit	4,000	6,850
Depreciation	500	650			
Net profit	1,500	3,200			
	4,000	6,850		4,000	6,850

Position Statements

	Opening	End Year 1	End Year 2
Fixed assets – Cost			
book value	5,000	4,500	5,850
Stock	1,500	2,000	5,000
Debtors	500	6,000	9,000
Bank	5,000	3,000	450
	12,000	15,500	20,300
Capital	12,000	12,000	12,000
Undistributed profit	–	1,500	4,700
Loan	–	1,600	1,600
Creditors	–	400	2,000
	12,000	15,500	20,300

1 *Details of fixed assets*	–	Cost 1	5,000
		Depn 1	500
			4,500
		Cost 2	2,000
			6,500
		Depn 2	650
			5,850

2 *Indices*
   A) *Retail Price Index*
      Year 1   Beginning   100
                    Purchases, sales,
                        expenses & loan   110
                    End of year   120
      Year 2   Purchase of asset   120
                    Purchases, sales
                        & expenses   130
                    End of Year   140

   B) *Specific indices*
      Year 1   Stock
                        Beginning & acquired   100
                        Closing stock bought   120
                        End of year   130
                        Average index   110
                  Assets
                        Beginning & acquired   100
                        End of year   130
      Year 2   Stock
                        Closing stock bought   160
                        End of year   170
                        Average index   150
                  Assets
                        Bought in year   150
                        End of year   180

The first year results would be adjusted as follows:

CPP accounts
Workings
   A) *Fixed assets*
      Cost $5{,}000 \times \dfrac{120}{100} = 6{,}000$
      Depreciation at 10%   600
   B) *Holding gains/losses*
      (i) *Monetary items*

	Year 0	1
Monetary assets (debtors and bank)	5,500	9,000
Monetary liabilities	0	400
Net monetary assets	5,500	8,600

NMA at beginning of year

      Loss $= \left(5{,}500 \times \dfrac{120}{100}\right) - 5{,}500$
                 $= 6{,}600 - 5{,}500 = 1{,}100$

During year, NMA increased by
      $8{,}600 - 5{,}500 = 3{,}100$
Assuming the increase occurred at an even rate, apply average index of 110

$$\text{Loss} = \left(3{,}100 \times \frac{110}{100}\right) - 3{,}100$$
$$= 3{,}410 - 3{,}100 = 310$$

The total loss of purchasing power by holding monetary assets = 1,410

(ii) *Long term liabilities*

Acquired – index 110; now 120

$1{,}600 \times \dfrac{120}{110} = $ 1,745

Actual value still 1,600

Gain to firm by having fixed long term liability   145

CPP Accounts

Income Statement

Sales	$13{,}500 \times \dfrac{120}{110}$			14,727
Opening stock	$1{,}500 \times \dfrac{120}{100}$	1,800		
Purchases	$10{,}000 \times \dfrac{120}{110}$	10,909		
		12,709		
Closing stock	$2{,}000 \times \dfrac{120}{120}$	2,000	10,709	
Gross profit			4,018	
Expenses	$2{,}000 \times \dfrac{120}{110}$	2,181		
Depreciation		600	2,781	
Net profit			1,237	
Loss on monetary items		(1,410)		
Gain on long term liability		145	1,265	
Net loss			28	

Position Statement

Fixed assets		6,000 − 600	5,400
Stocks			2,000
Debtors			6,000
Bank			3,000
			16,400
Creditors		400	
Loan		1,600	2,000
			14,400

			Updated
Capital		$12,000 \times \dfrac{120}{100}$	14,400
Loss for year		28	
		11,972	
CPP reserve − balancing figure		2,428	
			14,400

CCA accounts
Workings
A) *Cost of sales adjustment*

Opening Stock	1,500
Closing Stock	2,000
increase	500

Volume change
 A) Move closing stock back to average of year
  $2,000 \times \dfrac{110}{120}$ 1,833
 B) Move opening stock forward to average of year
  $1,500 \times \dfrac{110}{100}$ 1,650
 A) − B) = 183
∴ Price change =
   Total change 500
   Less volume change 183 = 317

Balance sheet stock value
1) Update opening stock to value at 1 Jan
   it is at 1 Jan value   0
2) Update closing stock to value at 31 Dec
    $2,000 \times \dfrac{130}{120}$ = 2,166
   Balance sheet   2,166
   Transfer to unrealised
   revaluation reserve
   (2,166 − 2,000) − 0 = 166

B) *Monetary working capital adjustment*
Note, unlike the CPP monetary adjustment this method excludes cash — covered by gearing adjustment

	Debtors	Creditors	Net
Opening	500	0	500
Closing	6,000	400	5,600
1) Increase in net MWC			5,100

2) Volume change
   A) Closing NMWC backdated to average
   $$5,600 \times \frac{110}{130} \qquad\qquad 4,738$$
   B) Opening NMWC forward dated to average
   $$500 \times \frac{110}{100} \qquad\qquad 550$$
   $$\qquad\qquad 4,188$$

   A) − B)
   ∴ Price change
   Total change 5,100
   Less volume change 4,188 = 912

C) *Gearing adjustment*
No adjustment since bank balance exceeds borrowing

D) *Fixed assets*
Acquisition 100
End of year 130

$5,000 \times \dfrac{130}{100}$ = 6,500   Depreciation   650
                                        H C depn   500

                                        Adjustment   150

Current cost reserve
C O S A   317
Stock at year end   166
M W C A   912
Fixed assets   1,500
                  ─────
                  2,895

CCA Accounts

Income statement
Historical cost profit   1,500
Current cost adjustments
   C O S A   317
   M W C A   912
   Depreciation   150   1,379
                                     ─────
Current cost operating profit   121

337

Position Statement

Fixed assets	6,500	
	650	5,850
Stock		2,166
Debtors		6,000
Bank		3,000
		17,016
Creditors	400	
Loan	1,600	2,000
		15,016
Capital		12,000
Undistributed profit		121
Current cost reserve		2,895
		15,016

Appendix 2
Accounts documents and flow of documents

Uses

1 To illustrate the flow of documents,
2 To illustrate basic documents,
3 To provide a reference point for 1 and 2 for use throughout the text.

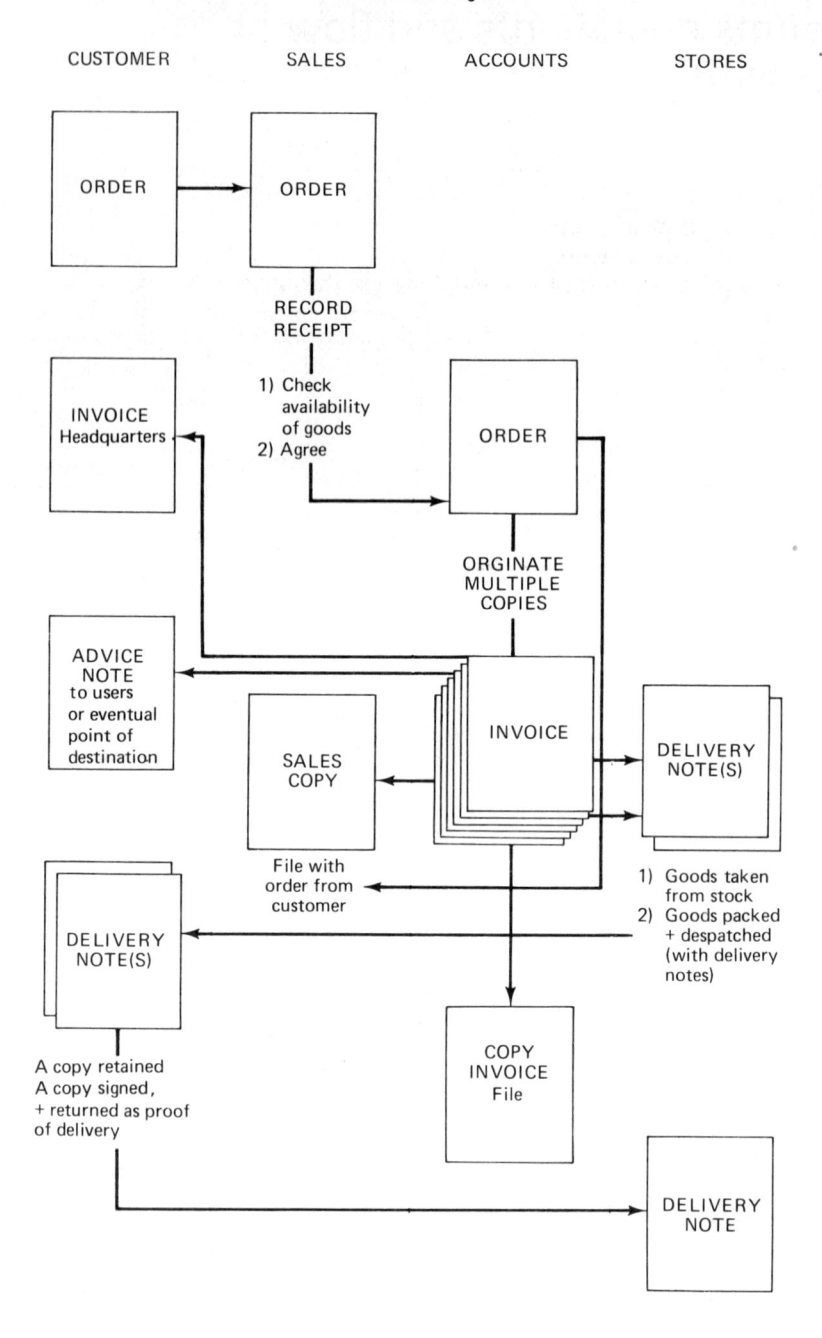

Flow of documents in credit sale of goods

CUSTOMER	SALES	ACCOUNTS	STORES

ORDER (Customer) → **ORDER** (Sales)

RECORD RECEIPT
1) Check availability of goods
2) Agree

→ **ORDER** (Accounts)

ORGINATE MULTIPLE COPIES

INVOICE (multiple copies)

- **INVOICE Headquarters** (to Customer)
- **ADVICE NOTE** to users or eventual point of destination
- **SALES COPY** — File with order from customer
- **DELIVERY NOTE(S)** (Stores)
  1) Goods taken from stock
  2) Goods packed + despatched (with delivery notes)
- **COPY INVOICE File** (Accounts)

DELIVERY NOTE(S) (Customer)
A copy retained
A copy signed, + returned as proof of delivery

→ **DELIVERY NOTE** (Stores)

340

**Flow of documents
in credit purchase of goods**

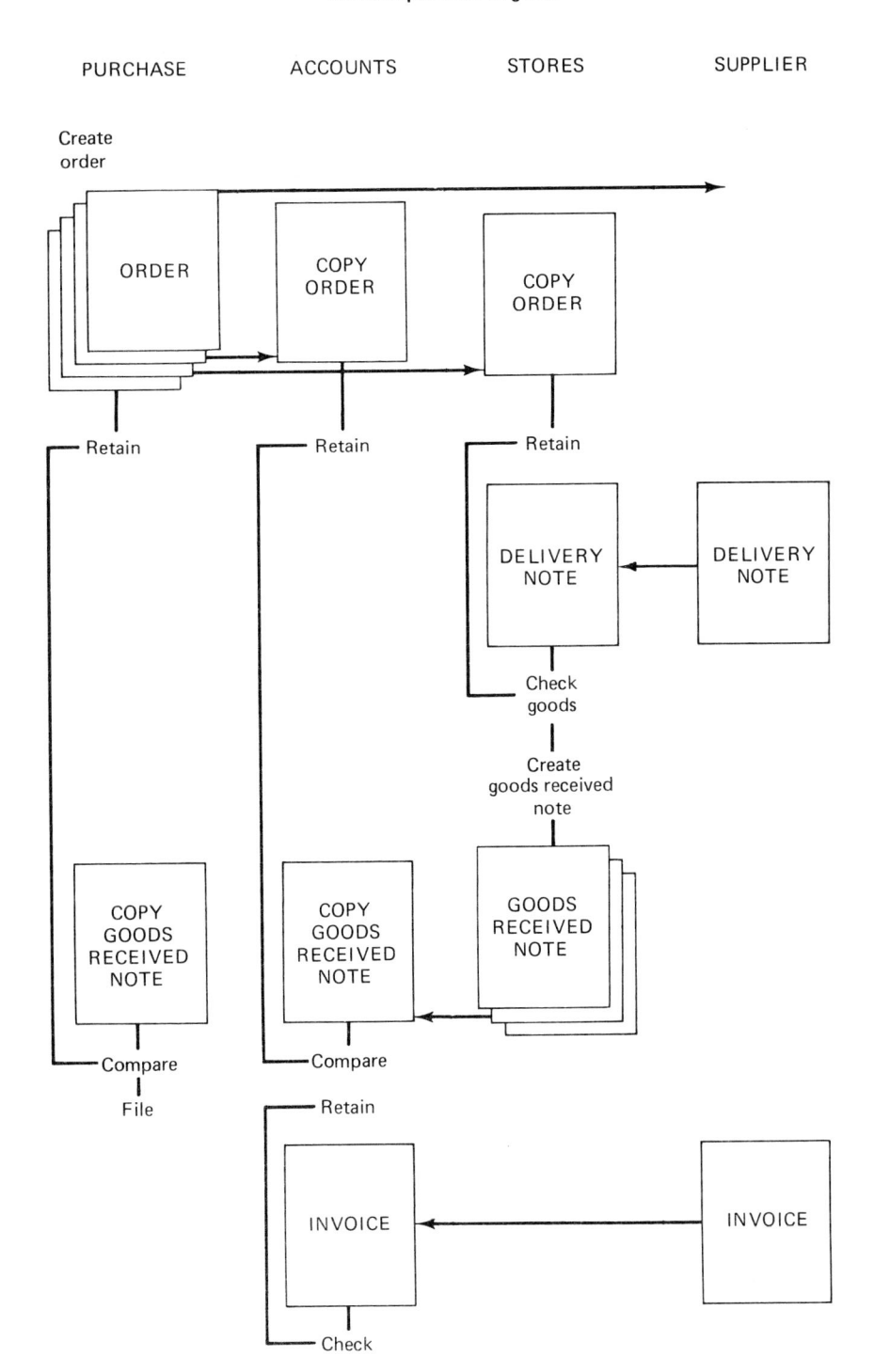

| PURCHASE | ACCOUNTS | STORES | SUPPLIER |

Create order

ORDER → COPY ORDER → COPY ORDER → (Supplier)

- Retain (Purchase)
- Retain (Accounts)
- Retain (Stores)

DELIVERY NOTE ← DELIVERY NOTE (from Supplier)

Check goods

Create goods received note

GOODS RECEIVED NOTE → COPY GOODS RECEIVED NOTE (Accounts) → COPY GOODS RECEIVED NOTE (Purchase)

- Compare / File (Purchase)
- Compare (Accounts)

Retain

INVOICE ← INVOICE (from Supplier)

Check

341

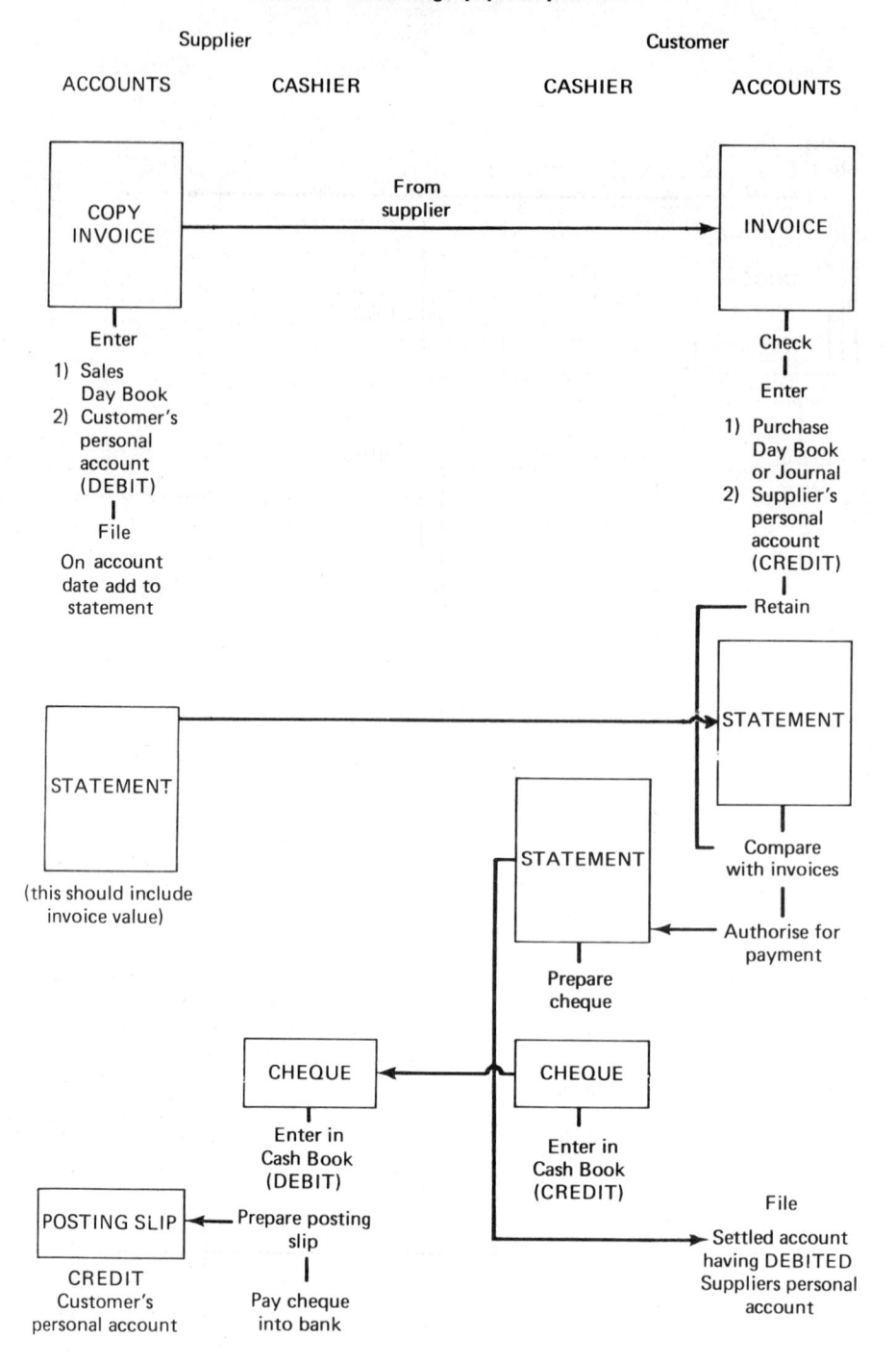

**Purchase + sale of goods
on credit − accounting + payment procedures**

Supplier		Customer	
ACCOUNTS	CASHIER	CASHIER	ACCOUNTS

```
┌─────────┐      From supplier       ┌─────────┐
│  COPY   │ ───────────────────────► │ INVOICE │
│ INVOICE │                          │         │
└─────────┘                          └─────────┘
```

Supplier ACCOUNTS (COPY INVOICE):
Enter
1) Sales Day Book
2) Customer's personal account (DEBIT)

File
On account date add to statement

Customer ACCOUNTS (INVOICE):
Check
Enter
1) Purchase Day Book or Journal
2) Supplier's personal account (CREDIT)

Retain

```
┌──────────┐                         ┌──────────┐
│STATEMENT │ ──────────────────────► │STATEMENT │
└──────────┘                         └──────────┘
```

(this should include invoice value)

Compare with invoices

Authorise for payment

```
              ┌──────────┐
              │STATEMENT │
              └──────────┘
              Prepare cheque
```

```
   ┌────────┐         ┌────────┐
   │ CHEQUE │ ◄────── │ CHEQUE │
   └────────┘         └────────┘
```

Enter in Cash Book (DEBIT)

Enter in Cash Book (CREDIT)

File
Settled account having DEBITED Suppliers personal account

```
┌──────────────┐   Prepare posting slip
│ POSTING SLIP │ ◄──
└──────────────┘
    CREDIT
  Customer's        Pay cheque
personal account    into bank
```

342

Specimen order

			No. AP. 3721

ORDER

Date	Delivery by:	Terms:

Please send to: ....
....
....
....

To:

Quantity	Description	Price

(For conditions of ordering, see overleaf)

Specimen delivery note

				No AC1498
	DELIVERY NOTE		Date	

Customer Order No.	Part No.	Quantity	Description	Price per item

Delivery Instructions
(address) ....
....
....
....
....

Carrier ....

Received by:
(signature) ....
(status) ....

Business stamp

Date ....

Specimen invoice

No P.I.1796

INVOICE

VAT No. . . . .   Date: . . . .

Customer's Order No.	Quantity	Description	Price	£

Delivered to: . . . .

£

VAT 15%

£

Specimen goods received note

No. DC4886

GOODS RECEIVED NOTE

Received from: Date: ....

....
....
....
....
....
....

Carrier

No. of prices or cases ....   Condition ....

Quantity	Description of goods

Received by: ....

Specimen statement

Order No.	Quantity	Description	VAT	Debit	Credit	Balance

STATEMENT

No. JY6785

Date . . . .

REMITTANCE SLIP

No. JY6785

Amount Outstanding £ . . . .

FOR OFFICE USE
Received by . . . .   Date . . . .

Appendix 3
Business final accounts — first six years trading for a fashion shop

Uses

1 To present a full set of authentic business accounts over a period.
2 To illustrate how a business can develop over the years.
3 To show the completed work so far as the financial accountant is concerned.
4 To provide material for ratio analysis.
5 To provide material for funds flow analysis.

Mr R Trend and Mrs B Trend t/a Rainbow Boutique
Trading & Profit & Loss Account for 21 weeks ending 31 March 19-2

Sales		4,164
Purchases	3,565	
Less stock at 31.3.-2	889	
		2,676
Gross profit		1,488
Gross profit percentage		(35.8%)
Less overhead expenses		
Rent	312	
Rates	70	
Insurance	10	
Heat & light	37	
Telephone	33	
Motor & travelling	68	
Casual labour	11	
Advertising	44	
Postage & stationery	14	
Repairs & renewals	41	
Accountancy fees	32	
Cleaning	30	
Bank charges	3	
Sundry expenses	16	
Depreciation	5	
Interest on loan re lease	16	
Total overhead expenses		742
Net profit for the period		746
Divisible between partners		
Mr R Trend	373	
Mrs B Trend	373	746

Mr R Trend and Mrs B Trend t/a Rainbow Boutique
Balance Sheet as at 31 March 19-2
Joint partners capital account

Cash introduced			182
Profit for the period			746
			928
Less income tax		30	
drawings		240	
			270
Balance at 31 March, 19-2			658

Represented by:			
Fixed assets	Cost	Depreciation	Net
Lease – 20A High St Newcutlynes	800		800
Cassette tape recorder	34	5	29
Total fixed assets			829
Current assets			
Stock	889		
Cash in hand	12		
Total current assets		901	
Current liabilities			
Creditors & accrued charges	230		
Loan re lease	716		
Bank overdraft	48		
Loar a/c – M Lender	78		
Total current liabilities		1,072	
Working capital deficit			(171)
Net worth at 31 March, 19-2			658

Signed:
    R Trend
    B Trend

We have prepared the foregoing Accounts from the books and vouchers of the business and from information supplied to us and certify the same to be in accordance therewith.

18 July, 19-2
Addit and Charge
15 Bristol Street
Newcutlynes   Addit and Charge
                                          Chartered Accountants

Mr R Trend and Mrs B Trend t/a Rainbow Boutique
Trading & Profit & Loss Account for year ended 31 March 19-3
31.3.19-2
(21 weeks)

19-2				19-3
4,164	Sales			17,144
–	Stock 1 April 19-2	889		
3,565	Purchases	14,124		
3,565		15,013		
889	Less stock 31 March 19-3	3,202		
2,676	Cost of sales			11,811
1,488	Gross profit			5,333
(35.8%)	Gross profit percentage	(31.1%)		
	Overhead expenses (including depreciation)			
–	Wages	837		
312	Rent	631		
70	Rates	160		
10	Insurance	71		
37	Heat & light	148		
33	Telephone	114		
68	Motor & travelling	259		
11	Casual labour	24		
44	Advertising	154		
14	Postage & stationery	32		
41	Repairs & renewals	51		
32	Accountancy fees	45		
30	Cleaning	133		
3	Bank charges	50		
16	Sundry expenses	77		
16	Interest on loan re lease	52		
5	Depreciation	63		
742	Total overhead expenses (including depreciation)			2,901
746	Profit for the year			2,432
	Divisible between partners			
373	Mr R Trend			1,216
373	Mrs B Trend			1,216
746				2,432

350

Mr R Trend and Mrs B Trend t/a Rainbow Boutique
Balance Sheet as at 31 March 19-3

31.3.19-2				
	Joint partners capital account			
–	Balance 1 April 19-2			658
–	Loan account – M Lender			567
182	Cash introduced			–
746	Profit for the year			2,432
928				3,657
30	*Less* income tax		224	
240	drawings		1,143	1,367
658	Balance 31 March 19-3			2,290
	Represented by:			
	Fixed assets			
800	Lease 20A High Street, Newcutlynes			800
29	Fixtures, fittings & machinery			257
–	Motor vehicle			52
829	*Total fixed assets*			1,109
	Current assets			
889	Stock	3,202		
–	Debtors	120		
12	Cash in hand	185		
–	Prepayments	32		
901	*Total current assets*		3,539	
	Current liabilities			
230	Creditors & accrued charges	1,726		
716	Loan (re lease acquired)	443		
48	Bank overdraft	189		
78	Loan account – M Lender	–		
1,072	*Total current liabilities*		2,358	
(171)	*Working capital*			1,181
658	*Net worth as at 31 March 19-3*			2,290

Signed: R Trend
B Trend
Partners

We have prepared the foregoing Accounts from the books and vouchers of the business and from information supplied to us and certify the same to be in accordance therewith.

24 July 19-3

Addit and Charge
Chartered Accountants

Mr R Trend and Mrs B Trend t/a Rainbow Boutique
Trading & Profit & Loss Account for the 18 months ended 30 September 19-4

19-3		19-4
17,144	Sales	24,993
889	Stock 1 April 19-3	3,202
14,124	Purchases	15,204
15,013		18,406
(3,202)	Less stock 30 September 19-4	1,894
11,811	Cost of sales	16,512
5,333	Gross profit	8,481
31.1%	Gross profit percentage 30%	
	Overhead expenses (including depreciation)	
861	Wages	1,683
631	Rent	2,059
160	Rates	538
71	Insurance	102
148	Heat and light	475
114	Telephone	213
259	Motor and travelling	277
154	Advertising	252
32	Postage and stationery	38
51	Repairs and renewals	135
45	Accountancy fees	119
133	Cleaning	189
50	Bank charges	154
–	Bad debts	24
77	Sundry expenses	67
52	Interest on loan re lease	42
–	Legal fees	65
63	Depreciation	286
2,901	Total overhead expenses (including depreciation)	6,718
2,432	Profit for the period	1,763

Mr R Trend and Mrs B Trend t/a Rainbow Boutique
Balance Sheet as at 30 September 19-4

1.4.19-3			
	Joint partners capital account		
658	Balance 1 April 19-3		2,290
567	Loan account		–
2,432	Profit for the period (18 months)		1,763
3,657			4,053
224	*Less* income tax	540	
1,143	drawings	1,918	2,458
2,290	*Balance as at 30 September 19-4*		1,595
	Represented by:		
	Fixed assets		
800	Lease & goodwill 20A High Street, Newcutlynes		600
257	Fixtures, fittings and machinery		557
52	Motor vehicles		225
1,109	*Total fixed assets*		1,382
	Current assets		
3,202	Stock in trade	1,894	
120	Debtors	–	
185	Cash in hand	85	
32	Prepayments	–	
3,539	*Total current assets*		1,979
	Current liabilities		
1,726	Creditors & accrued charges	1,298	
443	Loan (re: lease acquired)	85	
189	Bank overdraft	383	
2,358	*Total current liabilities*		1,766
1,181	*Working capital*		213
2,290	*Net worth as at 30 September 19-4*		1,595

Signed: R Trend
B Trend
Partners

We have prepared the foregoing Accounts from the books and vouchers of the business and from information supplied to us and certify the same to be in accordance therewith.

11 February 19-5
Addit and Charge
15 Bristol Street
Newcutlynes

Addit and Charge
Chartered Accountants

Mr R Trend t/a Rainbow Boutique
Trading & Profit & Loss Account for year ended 30 September 19-5

(18 months)

19-4			
24,993	Sales (including Market Sales £8,652)		27,526
3,202	Stock 1 October 19-4	1,894	
15,204	Purchases	17,211	
18,406		19,105	
1,894	Less stock 30 September 19-5	2,091	
16,512	Cost of sales		17,014
8,481	Gross profit		10,512
(33.9%)	Gross profit percentage (38.2%)		
	Overhead expenses (including depreciation)		
1,683	Wages	1,094	
–	Commission payable (Smith)	800	
2,059	Rent (includes market stall £840)	2,730	
538	Rates	368	
102	Insurance	55	
475	Heat and light	380	
213	Telephone	198	
277	Motor and travelling expenses	363	
252	Advertising	125	
38	Postage and stationery	66	
135	Repairs and renewals	154	
119	Accountancy fees	101	
189	Cleaning	65	
154	Bank charges	79	
24	Bad debts	–	
67	Sundry expenses	22	
–	Interest on loan	222	
42	Interest on loans re: lease	12	
65	Legal fees	–	
286	Depreciation	208	
–	Loss on motor vehicle	34	
6,718	Total overhead expenses (including depreciation)		7,076
1,763	Profit for the year		3,436

Mr R Trend t/a Rainbow Boatique
Balance Sheet as at 30 September 19-5

19-4			
	Capital account		
2,290	Balance as at 1 October 19-4		1,595
1,763	Profit for the year		3,436
4,053			5,031
540	*Less* income tax	328	
1,918	drawings	1,731	2,059
1,595	Balance as at 30 September 19-5		2,972
	Represented by:		
	Fixed assets		
600	Lease & goodwill, 20A High Street, Newcutlynes		600
557	Fixtures, fittings and machinery		898
225	Motor vehicles		143
1,382	*Total fixed assets*		1,641
–	Goodwill		2,000
	Current assets		
1,894	Stock in trade	2,091	
–	Debtors	17	
–	Bank account	1,266	
85	Cash in hand	90	
1,979	*Total current assets*	3,464	
	Current liabilities		
1,298	Creditors & accrued charges	2,161	
85	Loan (re: lease acquired)	–	
383	Bank overdraft	–	
–	Loan account Mrs B Trend	1,972	
1,766	*Total current liabilities*	4,133	
213	*Working capital*		(669)
1,595	*Net worth as at 30 September 19-5*		2,972

We have prepared the foregoing Accounts from the books and vouchers of the business and from information supplied to us and certify the same to be in accordance therewith.

23 January 19-6
Addit Charge
15 Bristol Street
Newcutlynes

Addit and Charge
Chartered Accountants

Mr R Trend t/a Rainbow Boutique
Trading & Profit & Loss Account for year ended 30 September 19-6

WE 30.9.19-5			
27,526	Sales		26,293
1,894	Stock 30 September 19-5	2,091	
17,211	Purchases	16,393	
19,105		18,484	
2,091	Less stock 25 September 19-6	2,524	
17,014	Cost of sales		15,960
10,512	Gross profit		10,338
38.2%	Gross profit percentage 39.3%		
	Add sundry income		
–	Deposit interest		1
–	Rent received		12
10,512			10,351
	Overhead expenses (including depreciation)		
1,094	Wages	1,539	
600	Commission payable	–	
2,730	Rent	977	
368	Rates	367	
55	Insurance	62	
360	Heat and light	418	
198	Telephone	222	
363	Motor and travelling expenses	438	
125	Advertising	212	
66	Postage and stationery	73	
154	Repairs and renewals	278	
–	Burglar alarm installation & rental	293	
101	Accountancy fees	110	
65	Cleaning	48	
79	Bank charges	140	
22	Sundry trade expenses	39	
222	Interest on loan	122	
12	Interest on loans – re: lease	–	
242	Depreciation	177	
7,076	Total overhead expenses (including depreciation)		5,515
3,436	Profit for the year		4,836

Mr R Trend t/a Rainbow Boutique
Balance Sheet as at 30 September 19-6

30.9.19-5				
	Capital account			
1,595	Balance 30 September 19-5			2,972
3,436	Profit for the year			4,836
5,031				7,808
–	*Less* loss on lease surrendered & legal costs		766	
328	Income tax		330	
1,731	Drawings		3,681	4,777
2,972	Balance as at 25 September 19-6			3,031
	Represented by:			
	Fixed assets			
600	Lease & goodwill, 20A High Street, Newcutlynes			
898	Fixtures, fittings & machinery			796
143	Motor vehicles			107
1,641	*Total fixed assets*			903
2,000	Goodwill			2,000
	Current assets			
2,091	Stock in trade	2,524		
17	Debtors & prepayments	16		
1,266	Bank account	249		
90	Cash in hand	337		
–	Bank deposit account	266		
3,464	*Total current assets*		3,392	
	Current liabilities			
2,161	Creditors & accrued charges	2,009		
1,972	Loan account – Mrs B Trend	1,255		
4,133	*Total current liabilities*		3,264	
669	*Working capital*			128
2,972	*Net worth as at 25 September 19-6*			3,031

We have prepared the foregoing Accounts from the books and vouchers of the business and from information supplied to us and certify the same to be in accordance therewith.

16 December 19-6
Addit and Charge
15 Bristol Street   Addit and Charge
Newcutlynes   *Chartered Accountants*

Mr R Trend t/a Rainbow Boutique
Profit & Loss Account for the year ended 25 September 19-7

Shop 1			19-7		19-6
Sales	100%		32,884	100%	26,298
Stock as at 26 September 19-6		2,524			2,091
Purchases		22,499			16,393
		25,023			18,484
Less stock 25 September 19-7		5,538			2,524
Cost of goods sold			19,485		15,960
Gross profit	40.7%		13,399	39.3%	10,338
Add other income					
Deposit account interest			11		1
Rent received			—		12
			13,410		10,351
Overhead expenses (including depreciation)					
Wages		1,958			1,539
Rent		1,092			977
Rates		399			367
Insurance		130			62
Light and heat		491			418
Telephone		204			222
Motor and travelling expenses		714			438
Advertising		455			212
Postage and stationery		194			73
Repairs and renewals		119			278
Burglar alarm rental		39			293
Accountancy fees		140			110
Cleaning		51			48
Bank charges		225			140
Sundry trade expenses		77			39
Loan interest		92			122
Depreciation		409			177
Total overhead expenses (including depreciation)	20.6%		6,789	20.9%	5,515
Profit for the year	20.1%		6,621	18.4%	4,836

Mr R Trend t/a Rainbow Boutique
for the 12 weeks from 2 July 19-7 to 25 September 19-7
Shop 2

Sales	100%		8,796
Purchases		8,908	
Less stock 25 September 19-7		3,482	
Cost of goods sold			5,426
Gross profit			3,370
Gross profit percentage	38.3%		
Overhead expenses (including depreciation)			
Wages		703	
Rent		476	
Rates		209	
Heat and light		145	
Telephone		60	
Motor and travelling expenses		13	
Advertising		79	
Postage and stationery		119	
Repairs and renewals		54	
Accountancy fees		40	
Cleaning		5	
Bank charges		80	
Sundry trade expenses		35	
Loan interest		23	
Depreciation		195	
Total overhead expenses (including depreciation)	25.4%		2,236
Profit for the period (12 weeks)	12.9%		1,134

Mr R Trend t/a Rainbow Boutique
Balance Sheet as at 30 September 19-7

			25.9.19-6
Capital account			
Balance as at 26 September 19-6		3,031	2,972
Add profit for the year – Shop 1	6,621		4,836
profit for the period – Shop 2	1,134	7,755	–
		10,786	7,808
Less Loss on lease	–		766
Income tax	1,234		330
Drawings	2,587	3,821	3,681
Balance as at 25 September 19-7		6,965	3,031
Represented by:			
Fixed assets			
Fixtures, fittings & machinery		1,937	796
Motor vehicles		793	107
Lease & goodwill, 58 Lower Street Newcutlynes		3,557	–
Goodwill – 29 High Street Newcutlynes		2,000	2,000
Total fixed assets (including goodwill)		8,287	2,903
Current assets			
Stock in trade	9,020		2,524
Debtors & prepayments	1,703		16
Bank current account	–		249
Bank deposit account	7		266
Cash in hand	806		337
Total current assets	11,536		3,392
Current liabilities			
Creditors & accrued charges	6,970		2,009
Loan account Mrs B Trend	507		1,255
Loan account Mrs C Brown	1,000		–
Loan account Mr T Brown	1,913		–
Bank overdraft	1,068		–
Bank loan account	1,400		–
Total current liabilities	12,858		3,264
Working capital (deficit)		(1,322)	128
Net worth as at 25 September 19-7		6,965	3,031

We have prepared the foregoing Accounts from the books and vouchers of the business and from information supplied to us and certify the same to be in accordance therewith.

3 March 19-8
Addit and Charge
15 Bristol Street
Newcutlynes   Addit and Charge
                Chartered Accountants

Mr R Trend t/a Rainbow Boutique
Balance Sheet as at 30 September 19-8

		30.9.19-8	25.9.19-7
Capital account			
Balance as at 26 September 19-8		6,965	3,031
Add profit for the year – Shop 1		6,334	6,621
profit for the year – Shop 2		1,770	1,134
		15,069	10,786
Less Income tax	736		1,234
Drawings	4,268	5,004	2,587
Balance as at 30 September 19-8		10,065	6,965
Represented by:			
Fixed assets			
Fixtures, fittings & machinery		3,488	3,437
Motor vehicles		535	793
Lease & goodwill, 58 Lower Street, Newcutlynes		2,057	2,057
Goodwill – 29 High Street, Newcutlynes		2,000	2,000
Total fixed assets (including goodwill)		8,080	8,287
Current assets			
Stock in trade	9,040		9,020
Debtors & prepayments	1,449		1,703
Bank deposit account	166		7
Cash at bank	1,711		–
Cash in hand	85		806
Total current assets	12,451		11,536
Current liabilities			
Creditors & accrued charges	7,163		6,970
Loan account Mrs B Trend	–		507
Loan account Mrs C Brown	1,000		1,000
Loan account Mr T Brown	1,366		1,913
Bank overdraft	–		1,068
Bank loan account	937		1,400
Total current liabilities	10,366		12,858
Working capital		1,985	(1,322)
Net worth as at 30 September 19-8		10,065	6,965

We have prepared the foregoing Accounts from the books and vouchers of the business and from information supplied to us and certify the same to be in accordance therewith.

4 January 19-9
Addit and Charge,
15 Bristol Street,
Newcutlynes   Addit and Charge
                                Chartered Accountants

Mr R Trend t/a Rainbow Boutique
Profit and Loss Account for the year ended 29 September 19-9
Shop 1

					19-8
Sales	100%		47,039	100%	32,671
Less cost of sales					
Stock 1 October, 19-8		5,418			5,538
Purchases		29,931			18,602
		35,349			24,140
Less stock 29 September 19-9		7,132			5,418
Cost of goods sold			28,217		18,722
Gross profit	40.0%		18,822	42.7%	13,949
Add other income					
Deposit account interest	0.1%		47		6
	40.1%		18,869	42.7%	13,955
Overhead expenses (including depreciation)					
Wages		2,961			2,086
Rent		471			1,092
Rates		486			416
Insurance		243			92
Light and heat		879			733
Telephone		273			218
Motor & travelling expenses		729			515
Advertising		763			300
Postage and stationery		219			337
Repairs and renewals		469			659
Burglar alarm rental		5			51
Accountancy fees		180			160
Cleaning		139			69
Bank charges		506			180
Sundry trade expenses		190			166
Depreciation		378			547
Total overhead expenses (including depreciation)	18.9%		8,891	23.3%	7,621
Profit for the year	21.2%		9,978	19.4%	6,334

Mr R Trend t/a Rainbow Boutique
Profit and Loss Account for the year ended 29 September 19-9
Shop 2

					19-8
Sales	100%		33,114	100%	28,357
Less cost of sales					
Stock 1 October, 19-8		3,622			3,482
Purchases		20,633			17,051
		24,255			20,533
Less stock 29 September 19-9		4,947			3,622
Cost of goods sold			19,308		16,911
Gross profit	41.7%		13,806	40.3%	11,446
Overhead expenses (including depreciation)					
Wages		4,900			4,360
Rent		2,250			2,250
Rates		649			913
Light and heat		538			533
Telephone		205			155
Motor & travelling expenses		28			23
Advertising		147			141
Postage and stationery		126			60
Repairs and renewals		222			160
Burglar alarm rental		77			–
Accountancy fees		130			118
Cleaning		77			43
Bank charges		176			405
Sundry trade expenses		172			123
Loan interest		73			113
Depreciation		444			279
Total overhead expenses (including depreciation)	30.8%		10,214	34.1%	9,676
Profit for the year	10.9%		3,592	6.2%	1,770

Mr R Trend t/a Rainbow Boutique
Balance Sheet as at 29 September 19-9

			30.9.19-8
Capital account			
Balance as at 1 October 19-8		10,065	6,965
Add profit for the year − Shop 1		9,978	6,334
profit for the year − Shop 2		3,592	1,770
		23,635	15,069
Less income tax	906		736
Drawings	4,967	5,873	4,268
Balance as at 29 September 19-9		17,762	10,065
Represented by:			
Fixed assets			
Freehold property − 29 High Street, Newcutlynes		10,071	−
Shop fittings and equipment		3,167	3,488
Motor vehicles		3,710	535
Lease & goodwill − 58 Lower Street, Newcutlynes		2,057	2,057
Goodwill − 29 High Street Newcutlynes		2,000	2,000
Total fixed assets (including goodwill)		21,005	8,080
Less bank loan account		9,534	−
		11,471	8,080
Current assets			
Stock in trade	12,079		9,040
Debtors and prepayments	903		1,449
Bank deposit account	1,334		166
Cash at bank	202		1,711
Cash in hand	60		85
Total current assets	14,578		12,451
Current liabilities			
Creditors and accrued charges	7,508		7,163
Bank loan account	−		937
Loan account − Mrs B Trend	−		1,000
Loan account − Mrs C Brown	779		1,366
Total current liabilities	8,287		10,466
Working capital		6,291	1,985
Net worth as at 28 September 19-9		17,762	10,065

Accountants report
We have prepared the foregoing Accounts from the books and vouchers of the business and from information supplied to us and certify the same to be in accordance therewith.

29 January 19-0
Addit and Charge
15 Bristol Street
Newcutlynes

Addit and Charge
Chartered Accountants

Note Schedules of fixed assets are not presented here.

Appendix 4
Professional questions and answers — foundation level

ACCA questions

	Numbers
Journal adjustments and suspense account	1 – 4
Depreciation	5 – 7
Limited company	8 – 10
Partnership	11 – 13
Income and expenditure	14 – 17
Control accounts	18 – 19
Bank reconciliation	20 – 22
Incomplete records	23 – 26

1 The balance sheet of J Thompson, a sole trader, as at 31 March, 1975 was as follows:

J Thompson
Balance sheet as at 31 March, 1975

Capital at 1 April, 1974	£18,900	Land and buildings		
Profit for the year ended		(at valuation)		£15,500
31 March, 1975 £4,500		Machinery (cost)	£13,000	
Less drawings 1,500	3,000	Less depreciation	7,500	5,500
Creditors	6,300	Stock at cost	5,700	
Overdraft	2,700	Debtors	4,200	9,900
	£30,900			£30,900

Further investigation reveals the following information:
  (i) The closing stock includes damaged goods which, although they had cost £100, have an estimated sale value of £75.
  (ii) Debtors include £200 in respect of a customer who has gone bankrupt. A doubtful debt provision of $2\frac{1}{2}$% is also required.
  (iii) The machinery was acquired five years ago, and is being depreciated down to its scrap value on a straight line basis over eight years. A more realistic estimate indicates that the life span will be ten years.
  (iv) The land and buildings were revalued in December 1974 by Mr Thompson. The original cost was £13,500 and the surplus was credited to the profit and loss account for that year.
  (v) Wages owing at 31 March, 1975 amounted to £95, but this has not been reflected in the accounts.
  (vi) Charges for the bank overdraft, amounting to £80, have not been recorded in the accounts.
  (vii) In arriving at the profit for the period, a salary of £1,000 paid to

Mr Thompson had been deducted as an expense.
(viii) £200 rent owing to Mr Thompson for the letting of part of his business premises had not been received, and no entry had been made in the books in respect of this item.

Required

a) Prepare journal entries to reflect such corrections as you consider necessary.
(12 marks)
b) Draw up a statement of revised profit for the period, and prepare a new balance sheet as at 31 March, 1975. (8 marks)
(20 marks)
(ACCA Foundation 1975)

2 After the preparation of a trial balance, an unexplained difference of Dr £218 remains, and a suspense account is opened for that amount. Subsequent investigations reveal:

(i) £35 received from A Jones and credited to his account has not been entered in the Bank Account.
(ii) The owner of the business has taken goods which cost £69 for his own use. No entries have been made for this at all.
(iii) A payment of £47 to M Smith has been credited to that account.
(iv) Discounts allowed (£198) and discounts received (£213) have been posted to the discount accounts as credits and debts respectively.
(v) Bank interest received of £111 has not been entered in the bank account.
(vi) £211 owing by A Able has been debited incorrectly to B Able.
(vii) The carriage outwards (£98) has been treated as a revenue.

Required

a) Prepare the suspense account making the entries necessary to eliminate the debit balance there is. Indicate clearly how you would deal with *all* of the errors discovered. (9 marks)
b) To what extent is the balancing of a trial balance evidence of absence of error? (5 marks)
(Total 14 marks)
(ACCA Foundation 1977)

3
a) An inexperienced bookkeeper has drawn up a trial balance for the year ended 30 June 1977:

	Dr £	Cr £
Provision for doubtful debts	200	
Bank overdraft	1,654	
Capital		4,591
Creditors		1,637
Debtors	2,983	
Discount received	252	
Discount allowed		733
Drawings	1,200	
Office furniture	2,155	
General expenses		829

Purchases	10,923	
Returns inwards		330
Rent and rates	314	
Salaries	2,520	
Sales		16,882
Stock	2,418	
Provision for depreciation of furniture	364	
	£24,983	£25,002

Required
Draw up a 'corrected' trial balance, debiting or crediting any residual error to a suspense account. (4 marks)
b) Further investigation of the suspense account, ascertained in *a*) above, reveals the following errors.
  (i) Goods bought from J Jones amounting to £13 had been posted to his account as £33.
  (ii) Furniture which had cost £173 had been debited to the general expense account.
  (iii) An invoice from Suppliers Ltd, for £370 had been omitted from the purchase account, but credited to Suppliers Ltd account.
  (iv) Sales on credit to A Hope Ltd, for £450 had been posted to the sales account, but not to the debtors' ledger.
  (v) The balance on the capital account had been incorrectly brought forward in the ledger, and should have been £4,291.
  (vi) An amount of £86 received from A Blunt, a debtor, in settlement of his account had been treated as a cash sale.
  (vii) Discount allowed has been undertotalled by £35.

Required
Prepare journal entries correcting each of the above errors and write up the suspense account. (12 marks)
c) There are several types of error which will not affect the balancing of a trial balance; these include errors of omission, commission and principle. Explain what is meant by these terms and give an example of each. (5 marks)
(Total 21 marks)
(ACCA Foundation 1977)

4 After completing a draft profit and loss account for the year ended 30 April 1980 of ABC Limited the following balances remained and a suspense account entry was required for the difference which had arisen:

Fixed assets: at cost	60,000	
provision for depreciation		31,000
Ordinary share capital		35,000
Retained earnings		12,000
Stock in trade, at cost	14,000	
Sales ledger control account	9,600	
Purchases ledger control account		6,500
Balance at bank	1,640	

Difference on balances suspense account   740

                                        £85,240   £85,240

After investigation the following discoveries were made:
   (i) A rent payment of £350 in March 1980 had been debited in the sales ledger control account.
  (ii) Although instructed to do so, the accounts clerk had not set a debt due from B Bell of £1,560 in the sales ledger control account against an amount due to B Bell in the purchases ledger control account.
 (iii) Discounts allowed of £500 during the year ended 30 April 1980 had not been recorded in the company's accounts.
 (iv) No entry had been made for the refund of £2,620 made by cheque to L Green in March, 1980, in respect of defective goods returned to the company.
      Note: The correct entries had been made previously for the return of the goods to ABC Limited.
  (v) The purchases day book for February 1980 had been undercast by £300.
 (vi) A payment of £1,000 to K Bloom in January 1980 for cash purchases had been debited in the purchases ledger control account.
      Note: The company does not maintain a credit account with K Bloom.
 (vii) No entries had been made in the company's books for cash sales of £2,450 on 30 April 1980 and banked on that date.
(viii) No entries had been made in the company's books for bank charges of £910 debited in the company's bank account in December 1979.
 (ix) The company's cash book (bank debit column) had been overcast by £1,900 in March 1980.
  (x) A cheque payment of £8,640 for new fixtures and fittings in April 1980 had not been recorded in the company's books.
 (xi) A payment by cheque of £1,460 in June 1979 for stationery had not been posted to the appropriate nominal account.

Required
a) The journal entries for items 1, 6, 9 above.
   Note: Narratives are required.
b) The corrected list of balances at 30 April 1980.   (18 marks)
c) Explain briefly the reasons for preparing bank reconciliation statements.
                                                                        (4 marks)
                                                                        (22 marks)
                                                              (ACCA Foundation 1980)

5 On 1 January, 1973, a manufacturer acquired two identical machine tools at a cost of £5,000 each, and a reprographic machine for the office at a cost of £2,000. The machine tools are depreciated at 20% per annum on a declining balance basis, and the reprographic machine, which has an estimated residual value of £200 and a life of 6 years, is depreciated on a straight line basis. On 1 January, 1974 one of the machine tools was sold for £2,750, and a new one acquired for £8,000.

Required
a) Prepare the relevant asset accounts, the provision for depreciation accounts, and the sale of asset account, for the year ended 31 December, 1974.
                                                                        (9 marks)

b) The manufacturer, observing the sale of asset account and the cost of the new machine, notes that 'in future we must increase the depreciation rate because we underestimated the amount of cash needed to replace the asset'. Discuss this statement. (7 marks)

(16 marks)

(ACCA Foundation 1975)

6

a) At 1 March 1976, the following balances appeared on the ledger accounts of Hill and Co. Ltd:

	£
Van A a/c	1,550
Van B a/c	1,500
Office equipment a/c	2,100

Each asset account had a corresponding 'provision for depreciation account', the respective balances on each being £1,388, £960, and £780. Van A was originally acquired in December 1972, and it was considered that it would last six years with a residual value of £50. It is company policy to provide a full year's depreciation in the year of acquisition, and depreciation of 40% per year is calculated on a declining balance. Van B was acquired in June 1974 (depreciation at 40% per year on a declining balance) and was sold in December 1976 for £230. A new van C was obtained for £1,800 (less trade discount 10%), and was expected to have a five year life, and is to be depreciated on a declining balance at 40% per year.

The Office Equipment is depreciated on a straight-line basis at 10% on cost.

Required

Prepare all the necessary ledger accounts relevant to the above information for the year ended 28 February 1977). (8 marks)

b) An employee, observing the depreciation balances on the above accounts, notes with relief that 'the company has plenty of funds for replacement'.

Required

Comment briefly on the validity of this observation. (6 marks)

(Total 14 marks)

(ACCA Foundation 1977)

7 Greenacres Limited, a well-established company, specialising in the distribution of agricultural buildings, equipment and fertilisers, commenced a machinery repair service on 1 January 1977.

From the beginning of the new venture, the repair service used a prefabricated building which the company bought originally with the intention of selling it. In fact, the building was included in trading stock at cost at 31 December 1976, at £10,000 and was then displayed for retail sale at £13,000.

In preparing the building for use as a workshop on 1 *January* 1977, the following expenditure was incurred:

	£
Foundations and erection costs	1,000
Interior and exterior painting	600
Heating and lighting systems	3,000

On 1 January 1978, further work was undertaken on the repair service building's heating system at a total cost of £1,400, half of which related to repairs and the rest concerned the installation of additional thermostatic controls.

On 30 June 1978, the following work was completed on the workshop building:

	£
Installation of partition walls	1,600
Renewal of wooden window frames	1,000

Early in 1979, following the closure of the machinery repair service, the workshop building, including the heating and lighting systems, was sold for £8,000. It is company policy to provide depreciation annually on prefabricated buildings at the rate of 10% of cost at the end of each financial year (31 December).

Required
a) The following ledger accounts as they would appear in the books of Greenacres Limited for each of the financial years ended 31 December 1977, 1978 and 1979:
   (i) Repair service workshop building;
   (ii) Repair service workshop building provision for depreciation.
   Note: The balances on accounts should be brought down at the end of each financial year.
b) The repair service workshop building disposal account.   (17 marks)
(ACCA Foundation 1979)

8 The following list of balances was extracted from the books of the Howton Company Ltd at 31 December, 1974.

£1 ordinary shares		150,000
8% £1 preference shares		50,000
7% debentures		100,000
General reserve		65,000
Land and buildings at cost	111,000	
Plant and machinery at cost	382,000	
Undistributed profit at 1 January, 1974		35,000
Share premium account		20,000
Stock at 1 January, 1974	35,000	
Sales		290,000
Discounts allowed and received	3,200	4,600
Debtors and creditors	48,000	27,000
Provision for depreciation – plant and machinery		85,500
Bank	7,500	
Carriage inwards	1,100	
Purchases	165,000	
Suspense account		400
Wages	23,500	
Lighting and heating	2,900	
Office salaries	8,600	
Debenture interest	7,000	
Directors' fees	12,800	
Interim dividends		
ordinary (5%)	7,500	

preference (4%)		2,000
Provision for doubtful debts		1,500
General expenses	11,900	
	£829,000	£829,000

Inspection of the books and records of the company yields the following additional information.
  (i) On 31 December, 1974, the company issued bonus shares to the ordinary shareholders on a 1 for 10 basis. No entry relating to this has yet been made in the books.
  (ii) The authorised share capital of the company is 200,000 £1 ordinary shares and 50,000 8% £1 preference shares.
  (iii) Stock at 31 December, 1974 was valued at £41,000.
  (iv) The suspense account (£400) relates to cash received for the sale of some machinery on 1 January, 1974. This machinery cost £2,000 and the depreciation accumulated thereon amounted to £1,500.
  (v) The directors, on the advice of an independent valuer, wish to revalue the land and buildings at £180,000, thus bringing the value into line with current prices.
  (vi) Wages owing at 31 December, 1974 amount to £150.
  (vii) Depreciation is to be provided on plant and machinery at 10% on cost.
  (viii) General expenses (£11,900) includes an insurance premium (£200) which relates to the period 1 April, 1974 to 31 March, 1975.
  (ix) The provision for doubtful debts is to be reduced to $2\frac{1}{2}$% of debtors.
  (x) The directors wish to provide for:
      (1) A final ordinary dividend of 5%
      (2) A final preference dividend
      (3) A transfer to general reserve of £15,000.

Required
Prepare, *in vertical form*, the trading and profit and loss accounts of the Howton Company Ltd for the period ended 31 December, 1974 and a balance sheet as at that date. Ignore taxation. (20 marks)
(ACCA Foundation 1975)

9

a) The following balances have been extracted from the books of the Nemesis Company Limited as at 30 September, 1977:

Creditors	6,300
Sales	80,000
Land at cost	18,000
Buildings at cost	38,000
Furniture and fittings at cost	22,000
Bank (credit balance)	6,000
Depreciation – buildings	6,000
– furniture and fittings	10,000
Discounts received	1,764
Unappropriated profit at 1 October 1976	2,000
Provision for doubtful debts	816
Goodwill	16,400

Cash in hand	232
Stock at 1 October 1976	14,248
Interim dividend on preference shares	600
Rates	2,124
Wages and salaries	8,000
Insurance	1,896
Returns inward	372
General expenses	436
Debtors	12,640
Purchases	43,856
Debenture interest	400
Bad debts	676
5% debentures	16,000
6% £1 preference shares	20,000
£1 ordinary shares	20,000
General reserve	10,000
Share premium	1,000

Additional information:
  (i) Stock on hand at 30 September 1977 was £15,546.
  (ii) Insurance paid in advance — £100.
  (iii) Wages owing — £280.
  (iv) Depreciation is to be provided at 10% on cost of buildings, and at 20% on the written down value of furniture and fittings.
  (v) Provision for doubtful debts is to be reduced to 5% of debtors.
  (vi) Debenture interest outstanding of £400.
  (vii) The directors propose to pay a 5% Ordinary Dividend and the final Preference Dividend, and to transfer £8,000 to General Reserve.

Required
Prepare the trading, profit and loss and appropriation account for the period ended 30 September 1977 and a Balance Sheet as at that date. (22 marks)
b) Examine the accounts you have prepared in *a*) above and then answer the questions below:
  (i) How did the share premium account arise?
  (ii) How could the goodwill account have arisen?
  (iii) What is the rate of return on net capital employed, and what is the significance of this figure?
  (iv) Which of the reserves are capital reserves and which are revenue reserves, and what, in principle, is the difference between the two?
  (v) The company is relatively highly geared: what does this mean? (8 marks)
(Total 30 marks)
(ACCA Foundation 1977)

10 Shortly after the end of the accounting year on 30 November 1979, the following relevant information was obtained from the records of Greystone Limited:

	£
Capital: authorised	35,000
issued and fully paid – ordinary shares of £1 each	25,000
8% redeemable preference shares of £1 each	6,000
Loan capital – 9% debentures	8,000
Retained earnings at 30 November 1978	19,900
Land and buildings	
at 30 November 1979: at cost	20,000
at 30 November 1978: provision for depreciation	6,000
Fixtures and fittings	
at 30 November 1979: at cost	40,000
at 30 November 1978: provision for depreciation	8,000
Sales	50,600
Stock in trade – at 30 November 1978	9,000
Purchases	30,500
Establishment expenses	2,700
Administrative expenses	6,000
Discounts allowed	600
Discounts received	400
Trade debtors	12,900
Provision for doubtful debts	400
Trade creditors	5,000
Balance in hand at bank	7,600

Additional information:
  (i) Depreciation is provided at the following annual rates on the cost of fixed assets held at the relevant accounting year end:
      Land and buildings $2\frac{1}{2}$%
      Fixtures and fittings   10%
  (ii) It is now estimated that 5% of the amount due from trade debtors at 30 November 1979, will never be paid; it is proposed that the provision for doubtful debts should be adjusted accordingly.
  (iii) The interest on the debentures for the year ended 30 November 1979, has been paid and recorded correctly in the cash book, but it was debited to various personal accounts in the debtors ledger. In every case, the debenture interest paid was the only entry in the personal account.
  (iv) The following information is given concerning the value of the company's stock in trade at 30 November 1979:

	£
At net realisable value it was	13,800
At cost to the company it was	13,000
At selling price it was	19,000

  (v) During the year under review, certain fixtures and fittings, which had cost £2,000 and whose written down value at 30 November 1978, was £1,600, were sold for £600. The only entry concerning the sale of these fixtures and fittings related to the sale proceeds which had been paid into the company's bank account and credited to sales.
  (vi) The directors propose to pay the dividend on the preference shares and a dividend on the ordinary shares of 10% for the year ended 30 November 1979.

Note: Ignore ACT

Required
a) The trading and profit and loss account for the year ended 30 November 1979, and a balance sheet as at that date. (19 marks)
b) Explain briefly the reasons determining your choice of stock valuation at 30 November 1979. (3 marks)
(Total 22 marks)
(ACCA Foundation 1979)

11 Smith and Jones formed a partnership on 1 April, 1974, sharing profits and losses in the ratio 2:1. The partnership was formed to manufacture and sell a new type of tin-opener developed and patented by Smith. Smith contributed capital of £8,000 and Jones of £5,000, and it was agreed to pay interest on capital of 6% per annum. As Jones had the business acumen, it was agreed that he was to be responsible for most of the day to day work of the partnership, and therefore was to receive a salary of £1,000 per annum.

The initial capital was paid into a bank account. The partnership acquired a ten year lease of suitable business premises for £6,000. The manufacturing process was relatively simple, and involved stamping out a plastic mould and inserting the patented cutting and opening device which was made under licence by Blades Ltd. The machines for producing the plastic moulds cost £5,000, and were to be paid for on an instalment basis of 10 quarterly payments of £500. This machinery, made by Synthetics Ltd., was estimated to have a working life of 5 years.

Sales made through mail order were on a cash basis and all such cash received was paid immediately into the bank. Some local retailers collected the tin-openers for themselves and were allowed a trade discount of 20% (on the normal price of £1) and a cash discount of 5% if the accounts were settled promptly. These local sales provided a cash float from which some miscellaneous payments were made by cash. These were –

wages	£600
postage	2,582
petrol and oil	248
motor repairs	170

At the end of March 1975, the partnership had £48 cash in hand.

A summary of the bank statement for the year to 31 March, 1975 showed:

Deposits	£
Capital introduced	13,000
Other bankings	23,590
Payments	
Lease	6,000
Blades Ltd. (Purchases)	5,400
Purchases of plastic	3,800
Synthetics Ltd.	2,000
Gas and electricity	150
Van (bought 1 July, 1974)	800
Insurance	150
Wages	1,500
Packaging material	1,627
Advertising	620
Telephone	760

Drawings – Smith 2,140
– Jones 1,520

A cheque sent out on 31 March, 1975 for electricity (£35) had not been cleared by the bank.

Of the tin-openers sold during the year, 5,000 were sold to local retailers, and of these 4,800 had been paid for by the end of the year and had been allowed the appropriate trade and cash discounts. The insurance included £40 for motor insurance which expired on 30 June, 1975. Blades Ltd. were owed £250 at 31 March, 1975.

At 31 March the partnership had stock valued at £660.

Required
a) Prepare a Cash Account and Bank Account for the period ended 31 March, 1975. (6 marks)
b) Prepare a Trading and Profit and Loss Account for the period ended 31 March, 1975 and a Balance Sheet as at that date. State clearly (by way of notes) any assumptions you make. (16 marks)
c) Advise the partners on the success (or otherwise) of their first year of business. (6 marks)

(28 marks)
(ACCA Foundation 1975)

12 On 30 September, 1977, Alexander and Arnold completed their first year of trading in partnership. They shared profits and losses in the ratio Alexander $\frac{2}{3}$, Arnold $\frac{1}{3}$, and were entitled to 5% per annum interest on capital. Arnold was also entitled to a salary of £1,490 per annum. They kept a debtors' ledger, a creditors' ledger for goods purchased, and a single entry record of all other transactions.

A summary of their cash transactions for the year ended 30 September 1977, is given below:

	£
Receipts:	
Cash float for till	20
Cash sales	12,800
Receipts from debtors	44,900
Payments:	
Creditors – goods purchased	2,600
Drawings – Alexander	1,400
– Arnold	1,200
Lodgements with Bank	52,190

A summary of the partnership bank account for the year ended 30 September 1977 is also available.

	£
Bankings:	
Capital paid in – Alexander	8,400
– Arnold	7,200
Banked from business	52,190
Cheques drawn:	
Premises	11,000
Cash float	20
Creditors for goods	50,200
Van	1,600
Sundry expenses	4,720

The partners also supplied the following details: £
(i) Stock in hand at 30 September 1977   6,000
(ii) Debtors at 30 September 1977   5,400
(iii) Bad debts written off (already excluded from debtors balance)   200
(iv) Creditors at 30 September 1977   3,000
(v) Depreciation is to be provided for the van at 10% on cost.
(vi) Sundry expenses accrued   150

Required
Prepare the trading, profit and loss and appropriation account for the period ended 30 September 1977 and a balance sheet as at that date. (21 marks)
(ACCA Foundation 1977)

13 Webb and Guy are partners sharing profits and losses in the ratio 3:1, and the partnership agreement provides for Guy to receive a salary of £2,000 per annum, and for interest on capital at 5% per annum. The partners' current accounts for the year ended 31 December 1978 were as follows:

	Webb £	Guy £		Webb £	Guy £
Drawings	4,280	3,950	Balance at 1 Jan		
Goods		100	1978	900	100
			Salary		2,000
			Interest on capital	480	300
			Share of profit	4,500	1,500
Balance at 31 Dec			Balance at 31 Dec		
1978	1,600		1978		150
	£5,880	£4,050		£5,880	£4,050

The balance sheet as at 31 December 1978 was:

	£	£		£	£
Capital accounts			Premises at cost		10,400
Webb	8,000		Equipment at cost	4,000	
Guy	5,000	13,000	*Less*: depreciation	2,400	1,600
					12,000
Current Accounts					
Webb	1,600		Stock	2,800	
Guy	(150)	1,450	Debtors	1,100	
			Cash	200	4,100
Creditors and Accruals		1,650			
		£16,100			£16,100

Investigation of the accounts revealed the following information:
(i) The goods taken by Guy had been charged at selling price rather than at cost (£65).
(ii) The interest on capital had been provided at 6% per annum.
(iii) The closing stock included some items which had been valued at original cost (£550), but which had deteriorated badly while in store and were considered to have a market value of £200.
(iv) The equipment had been depreciated in 1978 at 10% on original cost, but

coming year, but that costs will rise by 25% from 1 April, 1975. Bar stocks are normally held at the level of one half of one month's purchases. The bar makes a gross profit margin of 20% on all sales. Bar sales are for cash which is banked daily. The bar steward, who is paid £100 per month, receives a commission of 5% of the gross profit for the year. This is paid with his final wage cheque.

(v) The club runs monthly social evenings, and charges members £1 per head admission. An average of 200 members attend each of these evenings. Expenses usually amount to 70 pence per head.

(vi) Other expenditure is estimated at:

Insurance	£80
Bar licence	50
Rates	500
Heat and light	250
Miscellaneous	70

The rates are paid on 1 July in respect of the following twelve months, and the insurance payment is for the period 1 October, 1975 to 30 September, 1976. All payments are made by cheque, except for the miscellaneous expenses which are paid from the imprest cash fund, which is reimbursed immediately.

Required

a) Prepare the estimated bank account for the year ending 31 March, 1976.
(6 marks)
b) Construct an estimated bar trading and profit and loss account for the year ending 31 March, 1976. (4 marks)
c) Prepare an income and expenditure account for the year ending 31 March, 1976, and a balance sheet as at that date. (10 marks)
(20 marks)
(ACCA Foundation 1975)

15 The assets and liabilities of the Berley Sports Club at 31 December, 1974 were as follows:

	£
Pavilion at cost *less* depreciation	13,098
Bank and cash	1,067
Bar stock	291
Bad debtors	231
Rates prepaid	68
Contributions owing to Sports Club by users of sports club facilities	778
Bar creditors	427
Loans to Sports Club	1,080
Accruals – water	13
electricity	130
miscellaneous	75
loan interest	33
Contributions paid in advance to Sports Club by users of sports club facilities	398

The treasurer has analysed the cash book for the year, and produced the following receipts and payments account for the year ended 31 December, 1975.

should have been depreciated at 15% per year of the written down value at 1 January 1978.
(v) The partnership agreement had been amended on 1 July 1978 to increase Guy's annual salary to £2,700, with effect from 1 July, but this had not been reflected in the accounts.
(vi) No provision had been made for doubtful debts, but a provision of 3% of debtors is now considered desirable.
(vii) £82 owing for electricity had not been accrued.

Required
a) a statement showing the revised net trading profit for the year ended 31 December 1978; (8 marks)
b) the amended current accounts of the partners; (6 marks) and
c) a revised balance sheet as at 31 December, 1978. (8 marks)
(Total 22 marks)
(ACCA Foundation 1978)

14 The Alway Social Club had the following assets and liabilities as at 31 March, 1975.

Assets	£
Clubhouse (at cost)	8,400
Equipment (cost £2,300)	1,200
Bar stocks	400
Rates prepaid	100
Insurance prepaid	35
Subscriptions in arrears	16
Cash at bank	980
Cash in hand	10
Liabilities	
Creditors for bar purchases	800
Subscriptions in advance	8
Electricity account owing	30

The treasurer seeks your assistance in preparing a forecast income and expenditure account for the period ending 31 March, 1976 and a balance sheet as at that date, and supplies you with the following information.
(i) The club has 300 members, and it is intended to raise the subscriptions from the current £4 per annum to £5 per annum. The members who have paid advance will be allowed subscriptions at the old rates. It is anticipated t the members currently in arrears with their subscriptions will pay arrears during the coming year.
(ii) Extensions to the clubhouse are planned which will cost an estim £1,500. Of this sum it is anticipated that £1,000 will be paid during the
(iii) Some of the club's sports equipment (which cost £250 and has a v down value of £100) will be sold for an estimated £50, and replace new equipment costing £340. All equipment is depreciated on a strai basis over four years, and none of the equipment is more than thr old.
(iv) Bar purchases are made monthly on credit and paid for in th following delivery. It is anticipated that the same volume of b which is fairly constant on a monthly basis — will be done

	£		£
Opening balance	1,067	Bar purchases	2,937
Bar sales	4,030	Repayment of loan capital	170
Telephone	34	Rent of ground	79
Contributions from users		Rates	320
of club facilities	1,780	Water	38
Socials	177	Electricity	506
Miscellaneous	56	Insurance	221
		Repairs to equipment	326
		Expenses of socials	67
		Maintenance of ground	133
		Wages of groundsman	140
		Telephone	103
		Bar sundries	144
		Loan interest	97
		Miscellaneous	163
		Closing balance	1,700
	£7,144		£7,144

The treasurer also provides the following information as at 31 December, 1975:

	£
Bar stock	394
Bar debtors	50
Bar creditors	901
Rent prepaid	16
Water charges owing	23
Electricity owing	35
Creditors for bar sundries	65
Contributions by users of sports club facilities –	
owing to sports club	425
paid in advance to sports club	657
Rates prepaid	76

Depreciation on the Pavilion for the year was £498.

Required
a) Ascertain the balance on the accumulated fund as at 1 January, 1975
(3 marks)
b) Prepare a statement showing the gross and net profit earned by the bar
(6 marks)
c) Prepare an Income and Expenditure Account for the year ended 31 December, 1975 and a Balance Sheet as at that date. (12 marks)
(21 marks)
(ACCA Foundation 1976)

16 The Brydding Sports Club had, for many years, provided sporting facilities for cricket, tennis, hockey and bowls. Each sport was managed by a separate section, and each section was required to make an annual contribution to the parent Sports Club which provided, managed and maintained the clubhouse and grounds. Up till 1978, the Club's financial records had been confined to a cash and bank account, backed by such documentary evidence as members

remembered to hand to the treasurer. However, at the end of 1977, it was evident that the sections' contributions together with growing sales in the club bar would require the Club to register for the purposes of VAT, and thus maintain financial records in a more formal manner. In order to prepare for this, it was decided to ask a club member (who, fortuitously, was an accountant) to elicit such information as was necessary to enable him to draw up a set of accounts for the year ended 31 December 1977.

Alex Ander, the accountant, first sought the assistance of the treasurer, who was able to supply summaries of the bank and cash accounts for 1977, as follows:

Bank Account
for the period 1 January 1977 – 31 December 1977

Receipts	£	*Payments*	£
Cash banked	4,500	Electricity	290
Contributions from sections –		Water rates	90
1976 – 77	400	Maintenance of clubhouse	430
1977 – 78	900	Maintenance of machinery	75
Sundry income	90	Improvements to bar	950
Bank interest	50	Rent of ground	180
		Loan repayment and interest	250
		Petrol	135
		Bar purchases	3,160

Cash Account

Receipts	£	*Payments*	£
Bar sales	5,950	Bar purchases	970
Donations	10	Wages of cleaner	100
		Sundry light fittings	30
		Lodgements at bank	4,500
		Miscellaneous expenses	80

It was evident from the records and bank statement that the balance in the bank current account had been £1,100 on 1 January 1977, and that the cash in hand at that date had been £200. The bank interest proved attributable to a bank deposit account of £490, which had remained constant at that level during the period.

The bar sales were listed daily in a 'bar book', and the bar maintained a strict control on prices in order to ensure a gross margin on sales of $33\frac{1}{3}\%$. The bar chairman explained that although he had not taken stock during 1977, he had done so on 1 January 1977 when the bar stock, at cost, had been valued at £530. All bar sales were for cash, although at the end of the period there were 'IOU's' in the till which amounted to £50. Up till 1 January 1977, all bar purchases had been for cash, but, with growing sales volume, credit facilities had been granted, and at 31 December 1977, bar creditors were owed £240.

The Club Secretary was also able to provide some information based on the club minutes. The clubhouse, he explained, had been built in 1971, for a cost of £10,000, and, given the type of construction, it was considered to be suitable for use for 25 years. The building had been made possible, in part, by a loan from a National Sports Association of £2,000, which was repayable at £200 per year. Interest for the year to 31 December 1977 was £50. The club had acquired some new mowing machinery at a cost of £600, which, with luck and careful use, would last 6 years, ie until 31 December 1979.

The contributions or levy from the sections was based on a financial year which ran from April to March — to align with the playing seasons. The levy for 1976 – 77 (which had been completely paid) had been £1,200, and for 1977 – 78 £1,400. The sections were required to complete their levies by the end of March each year, but had no fixed time for paying any instalments during the year.

Alex sought copies of all invoices from the treasurer, and, in so far as they were available, concluded that at 31 December 1977 the club owed a further £30 for electricity and the annual charge for the rent of the ground was £240. Both these accounts were paid up to date at 1 January 1977. Armed, therefore, with information from the secretary, treasurer and bar chairman together with his own findings, he prepared the accounts for the year ended 31 December 1977.

Required
a) Prepare the income and expenditure account at the Brydding Sports Club for the year ended 31 December 1977 and a balance sheet as at that date. Show clearly all your workings, and state as a footnote to the accounts any assumptions you have made. (22 marks)
b) The secretary, having received the accounts, comments that he finds it difficult to understand how the club's bank balance has only risen by a few hundred pounds while there is a healthy surplus on the income and expenditure account. Explain to him why this has occurred. (6 marks)

(28 marks)
(ACCA Foundation 1978)

17 The treasurer of the Bamford Country Dancing and Rambling Society has prepared the following receipts and payments account for the year ended 31 December 1978:

Receipts	£	Payments	£
Opening balance	1,760	Purchase of amplifier	
Subscriptions (*see note* (i)):		(bought 1 July 1978)	700
Country dancing	2,410	Country dancing:	
Rambling	1,690	Musicians' fees	900
Annual dinner – ticket sales	340	Coaching fees	820
Sales of hut	670	Hall – Rent	330
Country dancing festival –		Rates for year to	
Admissions	940	31 December 1978	800
Sales – clothes	2,100	Decorating	110
refreshments	8,300	Cleaning	160
		Annual rambling expedition	1,320
		Annual dinner – hotel and catering	410
		Country dancing festival:	
		Prizes	170
		Adjudicator's fee	90
		Purchases – clothes	1,800
		refreshments	7,000
		Closing balance	3,600
	£18,210		£18,210

383

Additional information:

(i) a) Subscriptions

	Country Dancing £	Rambling £
Received in 1977 for 1978	130	60
Received in 1978 for 1977	10	140
for 1978	2,300	1,520
for 1979	100	30
	£2,410	£1,690

b) It is not the policy of the Society to take into account subscriptions in arrear until they are paid.

(ii) The hut which was sold during 1978 had been valued at £800 on 31 December 1977, and was used for the Society's activities until sold on 30 June 1978.

(iii) Immediately after the sale of the hut, the Society rented a new hall at £330 per annum.

(iv) The above receipts and payments account is a summary of the Society's bank account for the year ended 31 December 1978; the opening and closing balances shown above were the balances shown in the bank statement on 31 December 1977 and 1978 respectively.

(v) All cash is banked immediately and all payments are made by cheque.

(vi) A cheque for £200 drawn by the Society on 28 December 1978, for stationery was not paid by the bank until 4 January 1979.

(vii) The Society's assets and liabilities at 31 December 1977 and 1978, in addition to those mentioned earlier, were as follows:

31 December	1977 £	1978 £
Stocks of goods for resale, at cost:		
Clothes	1,300	1,100
Refreshments	310	600
Sundry creditors – Annual dinner (catering)	–	70
Purchases – Clothes	600	400
Refreshments	300	500

The Society has now instructed its treasurer to prepare an income and expenditure account for the year ended 31 December 1978, and a balance sheet at that date.

It is proposed to provide for depreciation on the amplifier at the rate of 20% per annum on cost, pro rata to time.

Required

a) The Society's income and expenditure account for the year ended 31 December 1978, and balance sheet as at that date. Comparative figures are not required. (18 marks)

b) Outline the advantages of income and expenditure accounts as compared with receipts and payments accounts. (4 marks)

(Total 22 marks)
(ACCA Foundation 1979)

18 The following transactions relate to a sales ledger for the year ended 31 December, 1974:

	£
Balance on sales ledger control 1 January, 1974	8,952
Sales as per posting summaries	74,753
Receipts from debtors	69,471
Discounts allowed	1,817

The clerk in charge had prepared from the ledger cards a list of balances outstanding on 31 December, 1974 amounting to £9,663 but this did not agree with the balance of the sales ledger control account. There were no credit balances on the ledger cards.

Investigation of the differences revealed:
 (i) The bank statement showed credit transfers of £198 which had been completely overlooked.
 (ii) Journal entries correctly posted to the ledger cards had been overlooked when posting control account: debts settled by set-off against creditors' accounts £2,896, bad debts £640.
 (iii) When listing the debtor balances three ledger cards with debit balances of £191 had been incorrectly filed and consequently had not been included in the list of balances.
 (iv) The machine operator when posting a ledger card had incorrectly picked up an old balance of £213.50 as £13.50 and had failed to check her total balances.
 (v) £1,173 entered in the cash book as a receipt from J Spruce had not been posted as no account under that name could be traced. Later it was discovered it was in payment for a car which had been used by the sales department and sold to him second-hand.

Required
 a) Prepare the sales ledger control account for the year ended 31 December, 1974 taking into account the above adjustments. (10 marks)
 b) Reconcile the clerks' balance of £9,663 with the corrected balance on the sales ledger account. (5 marks)
 c) Explain the benefits that accrue from operating control accounts. (6 marks)
 (21 marks)
 (ACCA Foundation 1975)

19 A business maintains a manual record of debtors' accounts, posting entries to the sales ledger from copies of invoices and credit notes. Cheques and discounts allowed are posted to the sales ledger from copies of daily cash sheets. Copy invoices and credit notes and daily cash sheets are totalled to provide for entries in the control account. All transfers into and out of the sales ledger are recorded through a transfer journal, which is totalled to provide for further entries in the control account.

At the end of March 1975, the balances appearing in the sales ledger totalled to Dr £9,275, and the balance in the sales ledger control account was Dr £9,905.

An investigation of the difference revealed the following errors:
 (i) A copy invoice for £80 has been posted to a customer's account as £8.
 (ii) A copy credit note for £22 has been debited to a customer's account.
 (iii) Discounts allowed of £14 shown on the daily cash sheets have not been posted to the customer's accounts.
 (iv) An invoice for £135 for J Brown has been posted to the debit of R Brown's account.

(v) Two debit balances of £45 and £27 have been omitted from the list extracted from the sales ledger.
(vi) An account for £110 in the sales ledger has been settled by contra entry to the purchase ledger, but no record has been made of this in the transfer journal.
(vii) A balance of £59 in a sales ledger account has been written off as irrecoverable, but has not been entered through the transfer journal.
(viii) The copy invoices were over-added by £325.
(ix) Cash of £25 paid in settlement of a customer's credit balance has been entered on the wrong side of the customer's account.

Required
a) Prepare a statement reconciling the sales ledger total with the sales ledger control account. (16 marks)
b) List the main benefits to be derived from the use of control accounts.
(6 marks)
(Total 22 marks)
(ACCA Foundation 1977)

20 According to the cash book of Rex Ltd the company has a credit balance at the bank of £380 on 30 June, 1975, but this is *not* borne out by the bank of the same date. An investigation into the difference yields the following information.
(i) A standing order for a charitable subscription of £40 had been paid by the bank on 29 June but no entry had been made in the cash book.
(ii) A cheque paid for advertising on 10 June for £179 had been entered in the cash book as £197.
(iii) Cheques for £1,037 sent to creditors on 30 June were not paid by the bank until 6 July.
(iv) Cheques received from customers amounting to £1,680 were paid into the bank on 30 June but were not credited by the bank until 1 July.
(v) On 20 June a cheque for £114 was received from a customer in settlement of an invoice for £120. An entry of £120 had been made in the cash book.

Required
a) Prepare a statement reconciling the cash book balance with the bank statement. (8 marks)
b) Explain how a company may have reduced its bank balance during an accounting period but still have earned a profit for that same period.
(8 marks)
(16 marks)
(ACCA Foundation 1975)

21
a) The cash book of a business shows a favourable bank balance of £3,856 at 30 June 1977. After comparing the entries in the cash book with the entries on the related bank statement you find that:
(i) Cheques amounting to £218 entered in the cash book, have not yet been presented for payment to the bank.
(ii) An amount of £50 entered on the debit side of the cash book has not been banked.

(iii) An amount of £95 has been credited by the bank to the account in error.
(iv) The bank has credited and then debited the bank statement with an amount of £48, being A Jones' cheque which it forwarded on 1 July 1977 marked 'insufficient funds — return to drawer'.
(v) Interest of £10 has been charged by the bank, but not yet entered in the cash book.
(vi) A cheque from a customer entered in the cash book as £88 had been correctly entered by the bank as £188.

Required
a) (i) Show the additional entries to be made in the cash book and bring down the corrected balance.
   (ii) Prepare a bank reconciliation statement.
                                                                              (8 marks)
b) Explain the reasons for preparing a bank reconciliation statement.
                                                                              (6 marks)
                                                                       (Total 14 marks)
                                                                (ACCA Foundation 1977)

22 On 15 May 1978, Mr Lakes received his monthly bank statement for the month ended 30 April 1978. The bank statement contained the following details.

Mr Lakes
Statement of Account with Baroyds Limited
(*Balance indicates account is overdrawn)

Date	Particulars	Payments	Receipts	Balance
		£	£	£
1 April	Balance			1,053.29
2 April	236127	210.70		842.59
3 April	Bank Giro Credit		192.35	1,034.94
6 April	236126	15.21		1,019.73
6 April	Charges	12.80		1,006.93
9 April	236129	43.82		963.11
10 April	427519	19.47		943.64
12 April	236128	111.70		831.94
17 April	Standing Order	32.52		799.42
20 April	Sundry Credit		249.50	1,048.92
23 April	236130	77.87		971.05
23 April	236132	59.09		911.96
25 April	Bank Giro Credit		21.47	933.43
27 April	Sundry Credit		304.20	1,237.63
30 April	236133	71.18		1,166.45

For the corresponding period, Mr Lakes' own records contained the following bank account:

387

Date	Detail	£	Date	Detail	Cheque No.	£
1 April	Balance	827.38	5 April	Purchases	128	111.70
2 April	Sales	192.35	10 April	Electricity	129	43.82
18 April	Sales	249.50	16 April	Purchases	130	87.77
24 April	Sales	304.20	18 April	Rent	131	30.00
30 April	Sales	192.80	20 April	Purchases	132	59.09
			25 April	Purchases	133	71.18
			30 April	Wages	134	52.27
			30 April	Balance		1,310.40
		£1,766.23				£1,766.23

Required
a) Prepare a statement reconciling the balance at 30 April as given by the bank statement to the balance at 30 April as stated in the bank account.
(10 marks)
b) Explain briefly which items in your bank reconciliation statement would require further investigation. (4 marks)
(Total 14 marks)
(ACCA Foundation 1978)

23 A Neal, a haulage contractor, seeks your assistance in calculating his profit for the year ended 30 June, 1975 and also requires a balance sheet as at that date. He submits the following data:

	£
Cash balance at 1 July, 1974	3,740
Cash balance at 30 June, 1975	2,950
Drawings for the year	1,780
Receipts from debtors	10,354
Debtors at 1 July, 1974	2,511
Debtors at 30 June, 1975	3,114
Drivers' wages (including £200 owing)	4,111
Rent of business premises (£1,600 per year)	1,200
Miscellaneous payments	2,134

Required
a) Ascertain the profit for the year ended 30 June, 1975, and draw up a balance sheet as at that date *making any assumptions you think reasonable*.
List the additional data you would require from Mr Neal in order to undertake the task more completely. (12 marks)
b) Explain to Mr Neal the benefits which would accrue if his accounts were kept in a 'double entry' form. (4 marks)
(16 marks)
(ACCA Foundation 1975)

24 Mr Wilson, a retailer, has his accounts prepared for the year ending on 30 June. On the morning of 1 July, 1976, however, his shop and most of the business records were destroyed by fire. At the beginning of the year, 1 July, 1975, Mr Wilson's assets and liabilities had been as follows:

	£
Fixtures at cost less depreciation	1,000
Stock	950
Debtors	160
Prepayment for rates	30
Bank (asset)	2,565
Cash	90
Creditors – Goods	610
electricity	25
accountancy fees	65

Mr Wilson's bank was able to provide copies of his bank statements, and an analysis of these revealed the following information for the year to 30 June, 1976:

	£
Cash and cheques paid in	16,456
Payments for:	
Goods	16,781
Rates	180
Electricity	110
Income tax (Mr Wilson)	830
Rent	650
Accountancy fees	65
Caribbean Holidays Ltd	490

A letter was sent to all the known customers and suppliers requesting information about monies owed and owing. A summary of their replies indicated that at 30 June, 1976, the position was as follows:

	£
Creditors for goods	979
Electricity owing	47
Accountancy fees owing	125
Rent owing	150
Rates prepaid	40
Trade debtors	360

Wilson's insurance company agreed to pay £1,250 for the stock destroyed by the fire (none of which could be salvaged) and £750 for the loss of the fittings. The money in the till on 30 June amounting to £190 had survived the fire. Mr Wilson had banked his cash takings after the payment of certain expenses which he estimated at:

Sundry expenses	£2 per week	(*50* week year)
Purchase of goods	£15 per week	
Shop assistant's wages	£30 per week	

He was uncertain of his personal drawings which he thought were 'usually between £55 and £65 per week'. Mr Wilson was somewhat inflexible in his business practice, and consistently sold his goods at a 25% mark up on cost of goods sold.

Required

Prepare a trading and profit and loss account for the year to 30 June, 1976 and a balance sheet as at that date. Show all your workings and assumptions.

(28 marks)
(ACCA Foundation 1976)

25

Dear Mr Guy,

   I am most relieved that you have agreed to assist me by sorting out the financial affairs of my second-hand business, which as you know commenced on 1 January 1976. Such records as I have kept are, unfortunately, to be found on now rather scruffy scraps of paper stored in a large cardboard box. Doubtless you will want to examine these records for yourself, but I thought it might assist you if I were to summarise my business dealings up to 31 December 1976 as I recall them.

   In December 1975 I was lucky enough to win £5,000 on the football pools, and this, together with £1,000 loaned to me by a friend − I agreed, incidently, to pay him 10% per year interest − formed the initial capital of £6,000. I put £5,500 into the bank immediately − in a separate business account. I needed a lorry to enable me to collect and deliver the second-hand goods, and I'm pleased to say I made a profit of £460 here; a dealer was asking £1,300 for a second-hand lorry, but, I beat him down to £840. I've only paid by cheque £200 of this so far, but as I will finish paying the full £840 in three years, it will be mine before it falls to pieces in another five years from now.

   I rent some business premises, and, as they are fairly dilapidated, I only pay £350 a year. I've paid by cheque this year's rent and also £50 in respect of next year.

   My first bit of business was to buy a job lot of 2,000 pairs of jeans for £6,000. I've paid a cheque for £4,000 so far, and my supplier is pressing me for the balance. To date, I've sold 1,500 pairs, and received £5,800, but I reckon I'm still owed £500, most of which I should be able to collect. I promptly banked the £5,800 as it was all in cheques.

   I bought 800 T-shirts for £1,200 out of my bank account. I've sold 700 of these for cash − £1,500 in all − but as the remainder have got damaged I'd be lucky if I get £50 for them.

   I managed to get some pocket-calculators cheaply − 50 of them only cost me £400, but I'm rather pleased I haven't paid for them yet, as I think there is something wrong with them. My supplier has indicated that he will in fact accept £200 for them, and I intend to take up his offer, as I reckon I can repair them for £1 each and then sell them at £8 a time − a good profit.

   I haven't paid my cash into the bank at all, as the cash I got for the T-shirts and my initial float enabled me to pay for my petrol − £400 − and odd expenses − £250. Also it enabled me to draw £20 per week for myself. As I've done so well I also took my wife on holiday − it made a bit of a hole in the bank account but it was worth all £600 of it.

   Perhaps, from what I've told you, you can work out what profit I've made − only keep it as small as possible as I don't want to pay too much tax!

Yours sincerely,
Bert Huggins.

Required

a) From the data provided by Mr Huggins prepare a business trading, and profit and loss account for the period ended 31 December 1976, and a balance sheet as at that date. Show clearly all your workings and assumptions as notes to the accounts. (22 marks)

b) Write a short report to Mr Huggins highlighting what you consider to be the most important features revealed by the accounts you have prepared.
(6 marks)
(Total 28 marks)
(ACCA Foundation 1977)

26 Since commencing business several years ago as a cloth dealer, Tom Smith has relied on annual receipts and payments accounts for assessing progress. These accounts have been prepared from his business bank account through which all business receipts and payments are passed. Tom Smith's receipts and payments account for the year ended 31 March 1980 is as follows:

	£		£
Opening balance	1,680	Drawings	6,300
Sales receipts	42,310	Purchases payments	37,700
Proceeds of sale of		Motor van expenses	2,900
grandfather clock	870	Workshop: rent	700
Loan from John Scott	5,000	rates	570
Closing balance	1,510	Wages – John Jones	3,200
	£51,370		£51,370

Additional information:
a) The grandfather clock sold during the year ended 31 March 1980 was a legacy received by Tom Smith from the estate of his late father.
b) The loan from John Scott was received on 1 January 1980; interest is payable on the loan at the rate of 10% per annum.
c) In May 1980 Tom Smith received from his suppliers a special commission of 5% of the cost of purchases during the year ended 31 March 1980.
d) On 1 October 1979, Tom Smith engaged John Jones as a salesman. In addition to his wages, Jones receives a bonus of 2% of the business's sales during the period of his employment; the bonus is payable on 1 April and 1 October in respect of the immediately preceding six month's period.
Note: It can be assumed that sales have been at a uniform level throughout the year ended 31 March 1980.
e) In addition to the items mentioned above, the assets and liabilities of Tom Smith were as follows:

At 31 March	1979	1980
	£	£
Motor van, at cost	4,000	4,000
Stock in trade, at cost	5,000	8,000
Trade debtors	4,600	12,290
Motor vehicle expenses prepaid	–	100
Workshop rent accrued due	–	200
Trade creditors	2,900	2,200

f) It can be assumed that the opening and closing balances in the above receipts and payments account require no adjustment for the purposes of Tom Smith's accounts.
g) As from 1 April, 1979, it has been decided to provide for depreciation on the motor van annually at the rate of 20% of the cost.

Required

The trading and profit and loss account for the year ended 31 March 1980, and a balance sheet at that date of Tom Smith.

(17 marks)
(ACCA Foundation 1980)

ACCA summary answers

Note: No answer is supplied to descriptive questions, or descriptive parts to calculative questions. Final accounts use the vertical format for presentation, unless the contrary is stated.

1 a *Journal* Dr Profit 25, Profit 200, Profit 100, Machinery 1,200, Machinery 300, Profit 2,000, Profit 95, Profit 80, Drawings 1,000, Debtors 200.
Cr Stock 25, Debtors 200, Provision for DD 100, Opening capital 1,200, Profit 300, Capital 2,000, Wages accrued 95, Bank 80, Profit 1,000, Debtors 200.

b *Statement* Balance sheet profit 4,500. Add: Overprovision 300, Salary 1,000, Rent due 200. Deduct: Stock deterioration 25, Bad debt 200, Provision DD 100, Unrealised profit 2,000, Wages 95, Bank interest 80. Revised net profit 3,500

Balance sheet Assets: Land and buildings 15,500, Machinery (cost) 13,000, Depreciation 6,000, Stock 5,675, Debtors (less provision) 3,900, Rent owing 200. Liabilities: Capital 20,100, Revaluation 2,000, Profit 3,500, Drawings 2,500, Creditors 6,300, Accruals 95, Overdraft 2,780.

2 *Suspense account* Dr Balance per trial balance 218, Discounts received 426, Balance 188. Cr Bank 35, Discount allowed 396, M Smith 94, Bank 111, Carriage outward 196.

3 a *Trial balance* Suspense account − 1,175 entered as a debit.

b *Journal* Dr J Jones 20, Furniture 173, Purchases 370, A Hope 450, Capital 300, Sales 86, Discount allowed 35. Cr Suspense 20, General expense 173, Suspense 370, Suspense 450, Suspense 300, A Blunt 86, Suspense 35.

Suspense Dr Balance 1,175, Cr J Jones 20, Purchases 370, A Hope 450, Capital 300, Discount allowed 35.

4 a *Journal* Dr Rent payment 350, Retained earnings 1,000, Suspense 1,900. Cr Sales ledger control 350, Purchases ledger control 1,000, Cash book 1,900.

b *Corrected list of balances* Dr Fixed assets at cost 68,640, Stock in trade at cost 14,000, Sales ledger control 9,810. Cr Fixed asset − depreciation 31,000, Ordinary share capital 35,000, Retained earnings 10,230, Purchases ledger control 6,240, Bank 9,980.

5 a *Ledgers* Office equipment: Dr Balance 2,000. Cr Balance 2,000.
Provision for depreciation − office machinery: Dr Balance 600. Cr Balance 300, Profit and Loss 300.
Machine Tools: Dr Balance 10,000, Cash 8,000, Cr Sale of Machine 5,000, Balance 13,000.
Provision for depreciation − machine tools: Dr Sale of machine 1,000, Balance 3,400. Cr Balance 2,000.
Profit and Loss 2,400.
Sale of Machine: Dr Machine tool 5,000. Cr Provision 1,000, Cash 2,750, Profit and Loss 1,250.

6 a *Ledgers*
Vehicle A: Dr Balance 1,550. Cr Balance 1,550.
Vehicle B: Dr Balance 1,500. Cr Sale of asset 1,500.
Sale of asset: Dr Vehicle B 1,500. Cr Provision 960, Bank 230, Profit and Loss 310.
Vehicle. Dr Bank 1,620. Cr Balance 1,620
Office equipment: Dr Balance 2,100. Cr Balance 2,100.
Provision for depreciation – Vehicle A: Dr Balance 1,453. Cr Balance 1,388, Depreciation 65.
Provision for depreciation – Vehicle B: Dr Sale 960. Cr Balance 960.
Depreciation: Dr Office equipment 210, Vehicle C 648, Vehicle A 65, Cr Profit and Loss 923.
Provision for depreciation – Vehicle C: Dr Balance 648. Cr Depreciation 648.
Provision for depreciation – office equipment: Dr Balance 990. Cr Balance 780, Depreciation 210.

7 *Ledgers*
(i) Repair service workshop building – cost, 1977, Dr Prefabricated building 10,000, foundation and erection 1,000, Painting 600, Heating and lighting 3,000. Cr Balance 16,900.
1978: Dr Balance 14,600, Heating additions 700, Partition walls 1,600. Cr Balance 16,900.
1979: Dr Balance 16,900. Cr Disposal 16,900.
(ii) Repair service workshop building – depreciation: Dr 1978 Balance 3,150; 1979 Disposal 3,150. Cr 1977 Profit and Loss 1,460; 1978 Profit and Loss 1,690; 1979 Balance 3,150.
b Repair service workshop building – disposal 1979: Dr Cost 16,900. Cr Provision 3,150, Bank 8,000, Profit and Loss 5,750.

8 *Trading account* Sales 290,000, Opening stock 35,000, Purchases 165,000, Carriage inwards 1,100. Closing stock 41,000, Cost of sales 160,100, Gross profit 129,900.
Profit and Loss Account Revenue: Reduced provision 300, Discounts received 4,600.
Expenditure: Discounts allowed 3,200, Loss on sale of machinery 100, Wages 23,650, Lighting and heating 2,900, Office salaries 8,600, Depreciation provision 38,000, Debenture interest 7,000, Director's fees 12,800, General expenses 11,850. Totals 108,100. Net Profit 26,700.
Appropriations: Undistributed profit b/f 35,000, Dividend – Ordinary interim 7,500, final 8,250, Preference interim 2,000, final 2,000, General Reserve 15,000, Undistributed profit c/f 26,950 – total 61,700.
Balance Sheet Share capital – ordinary, authorised 200,000, issued 165,000, preference, authorised 50,000, issued 50,000, Share premium 5,000, Revaluation reserve 69,000, General reserves 80,000, Undistributed profit 26,950 – totals 180,950, Debentures 100,000, Total 495,950; Land and building 180,000, Plant and machinery (cost) 380,000 less depreciation 122,000, Stock 41,000, Debtors (net) 46,850, Bank 7,500, Creditors 27,150, Proposed dividend – ordinary 8,250, preference 2,000, Total 495,950.

9 *Trading account* Sales 80,000, Returns 372, Stock 1.10.76 14,248, Purchases 43,856, Stock 30.9.77 15,546, Cost of sales 42,558, Gross profit 37,070. Profit and Loss account – vertical format: Income: Provision

not required 184, Discount received 1,764. Expenses: Rates 2,124, Wages and salaries 8,280, Insurance 1,796, General expenses 436, Bad debts 676, Depreciation – building 3,800, fixtures and fittings 2,400, Debenture interest 800 – Total 20,312. Net profit: 18,706. Appropriations: Unappropriated profit b/d 2,000, Dividend paid – interim preference 600, Dividend proposed – final preference 600, ordinary 1,000, Transfer to general reserve 8,000, Unappropriated profit c/f 10,506.
Balance Sheet Issued share capital – ordinary 20,000, preference 20,000, Share premium 1,000, General reserve 18,000, Unappropriated profit 10,506, Debentures 16,000, Total 85,506. Land 18,000, Buildings (cost) 38,000 less depreciation 9,800, Furniture and fittings (cost) 22,000 less depreciation 12,400, Stock 15,546, Debtors 12,008 (provision 632), Prepayments 100, Cash 232, Creditors 6,300, Accruals 680, Dividends proposed 1,600, Overdraft 6,000, Other assets – Goodwill 16,400.

10 *Trading account* Sales 50,000, Cost of sales 26,500, Gross profit 23,500. Profit and Loss account – vertical format: Expenses: Establishment 2,700, Depreciation – land and buildings 500, fixtures and fittings 3,800, Loss on sale 1,000, Administration 6,000, Debenture interest 720, Provision for DD 209, Discount allowed 600 – Total 15,529. Income: Discount received 400. Net profit: 8,371. Appropriations: Proposed dividend – preference 480, ordinary 2,500 Retained earnings b/f 19,900, Retained earnings c/f 25,291.
Balance sheet Lands and buildings (cost) 20,000 less depreciation 6,500, Fixtures and fittings (cost) 38,000 less depreciation 11,400, Stock 13,000, Trade debtors 11,571, Bank 7,600, Trade creditors 5,000, Proposed dividends 2,980, Total 64,291. Share capital (authorised 35,000) issued and fully paid – ordinary 25,000, preference 6,000, Retained earnings 25,291, Debentures 8,000, Total 64,291.

11 *Cash account* Dr Sales 364. Cr Wages 600, Postage 2,582, Petrol and oil 248, Motor repairs 170, Balance 48.
Bank account Dr Capital – Smith 8,000, Jones 5,000, Mail order 23,590. Cr Lease 6,000, Blades Ltd. 5,400, Purchases 3,800, Synthetics Ltd 2,000, Gas and electricity 185, Van 800, Insurance 150, Wages 1,500, Packaging 1,627, Advertising 620, Telephone 760, Drawings – Smith 2,140, Jones 1,520, Balance 10,088.
Trading, profit and loss and appropriation Sales 27,590, Purchases 9,450, Closing stock 660, Cost of sales 8,790, Gross profit 18,800. Depreciation 1,000, Amortisation 600, Telephone 760, Discount allowed 192, Gas and electricity 185, Depreciation 160, Wages 2,100, Petrol and oil 248, Motor repairs 170, Postage 2,582, Packaging material 1,627, Advertising 620, Insurance 140, Total 10,384, Net profit 8,416. Appropriations: Salary – Jones 1,000, Interest on capital – Smith 480, Jones 300, Share of profit – Smith 4,424, Jones 2,212.
Balance sheet Capital – Smith 8,000, Jones 5,000, Current Accounts – Smith 2,764, Jones 1,992, Total 17,756. Leasehold premises (cost) 6,000 less depreciation 600, Machinery (cost) 5,000, Van (cost) 800 depreciation 160, Stock 660, Debtors and prepayments 170, Bank 10,088, Cash 48, Creditors 250, Total 17,756.

12 *Trading, profit and loss and appropriation* Sales 63,300, Purchases 55,800, Closing stock 6,000, Cost of sales 49,800, Gross profit 13,500. Sundry expenses 4,870, Bad debts 200, Depreciation 160, Net profit

8,270. Appropriations: Interest on capital – Alexander 420, Arnold 360, Salary 4,000, Share of profits – Alexander 4,000, Arnold 2,000, Total 8,270.

Balance sheet Capital – Alexander 8,400, Arnold 7,200, Current accounts – Alexander 3,020, Arnold 2,650, Total 21,270. Premises 11,000, Vans (cost) 1,600 less depreciation 160, Stock 6,000, Debtors 5,400, Bank 250, Cash 330, Creditors and accruals 3,150, Total 21,270.

Cash book Dr Cash – Bank 20, Sales 12,800, Debtors 44,900, Total 57,720. Bank – Capital – Alexander 8,400, Arnold 7,200, Cash 52,190, Total 67,790. Cr Cash – Bank 52,190, Creditors 2,600, Drawings: Alexander 1,400, Arnold 1,200, Balance 330. Bank – Premises 11,000, Cash 20, Creditors 50,200, Van 1,600, Sundry 4,720, Balance 250.

Debtors/Sales. Cr Bad debts 200, Cash 12,800, Bank 44,900, Debtors 5,400.

Creditors/Purchases. Dr Cash 2,600, Bank 50,200, Creditors 3,000.

13 *Profit statement* Share of profit 6,000, Interest on capital 780, Salary 2,000, Total 8,780. Goods at cost 35, Overvaluation of stock 350, Provision for DD 33, Accrual 82, Over depreciation 100, Total 8,380.

Appropriations: Dr Webb – Drawings 4,280, Balance 1,055, Guy – Drawings 3,950, Stock 65, Balance 30. Cr Webb – Balance 900, Interest on capital 400, Share of profit 4,035, Guy – Balance 100, Salary 2,350, Interest on capital 250, Share of profit 1,345.

Balance sheet – ledger format: Capital – Webb 8,000, Guy 5,000, Current accounts – Webb 1,055, Guy 30, Creditors 1,732, Total 15,817. Premises (cost) 10,400, Equipment (cost) 4,000 less depreciation 1,700, Stock 2,450, Debtors (less provision 33) 1,067, Cash 200, Total 15,817.

14 *Bank account – estimated* Dr Balance 980, Subscriptions – arrears 16, current 1,490, Sale of equipment 50, Bar sales 14,875, Proceeds from socials 2,400. Cr Club house extension 1,000, Equipment 340, Purchases 11,800, Wages 1,200, Commission 149, Social expenses 1,680, Insurance 80, Imprest Cash – miscellaneous 70, Bar licence 50, Rates 500, Heat and light 250, Balance 2,692.

Bar trading, profit and loss – estimated: Sales 14,875, Opening stock 400, Purchases 12,000, Closing stock 500, Cost of sales 11,900, Gross profit 2,975, Bar licence 50, Wages 1,200, Commission 149, Net profit 1,576.

Income and expenditure – estimated – ledger format: Dr Insurance 75, Miscellaneous 70, Depreciation 597, Rates 475, Light and heat 220, Loss on equipment 50, Surplus 2,307.

Cr Subscriptions 1,498, Bar profit 1,576, Surplus on social 720.

Balance Sheet – estimated – ledger format: Cr Accumulated fund 10,303, Surplus 2,307, Creditors 1,000, Total 13,610. Dr Clubhouse (cost) 9,900 less owing 500, Equipment (cost) 2,390 less depreciation 1,547, Stock 500, Prepayment 165, Bank 2,692, Cash 10, Total 13,610.

15 *Bar trading and profit and loss* Sales 3,849, Opening stock 291, Purchases 3,411, Closing stock 394, Cost of sales 3,308, Gross profit 541, Bar Sundries 209, Net profit 332.

Income and expenditure Net profit from bar 332, Contribution from users 1,168, Socials (net) 110, Miscellaneous 56, Ground rent 63, Rates 312, Water 48, Electricity 411, Loan interest 64, Miscellaneous 88, Insurance 221, Repairs 326, Maintenance 133, Wages 140, Telephone (net) 69, Depreciation 498, Deficit 707.

Balance sheet Accumulated fund 13,377, Deficit 707, Loans 910, Total 13,580. Pavilion at cost less depreciation 12,600, Bar stock 394, Bar debtors 50, Prepayments 92, Cash at bank and in hand 1,700, User contributions owing 425, Bar creditors 901, Accruals 123, User contributions in advance 657, Total 13,580.

16 a *Income and expenditure* Bar sales 6,000, Cost of sales 4,000, Gross profit 2,000, Contributions from sections 1,350, Donations 10, Sundry income 90, Bank interest 50. Depreciation − Clubhouse 450, Machinery 100, Loan interest 50, Electricity 320, Water rates 90, Maintenance − Clubhouse 430, Machinery 75, Rent of ground 240, Petrol 135, Light fittings 30, Wages 100, Miscellaneous 80, Surplus 1,400.
Balance Sheet − ledger format. Cr Accumulated fund 9,250, Surplus 1,400, Loan 600, Creditors 240, Accruals 90, Total 11,850. Dr Clubhouse (cost) 10,950 less depreciation 2,850, Machinery (cost) 600 less depreciation 400, Stock 900, Debtors 200, Deposit account 490, Bank 1,480, Cash 480, Total 11,850.

b *Cash flow statement − net 380* Surplus 1,400, Depreciation 550, Accruals 90, Creditors 240, Total 2,280, Sales 50, Contributions (net) 50, Capital expenditure 950, Loan repayment 200, Cash 280, Stock 370, Total 1,900.

17 *Income and expenditure − ledger format* Dr Accommodation − Hut, loss on disposal 130, Hall expenses 1,235, Depreciation 70, Stationery 200, Loss on Annual dinner 140, Country dancing 1,720, Annual rambling expedition 1,320, Excess income over expenditure 1,715, Total 6,530. Cr Subscriptions − Country dancing 2,440, Rambling 1,720, Country dancing festival 680, Sales − Clothes 300, Refreshments 1,390, Total 6,530.
Balance sheet − ledger format Cr General fund 3,080, Excess income over expenditure 1,715, Trade creditors 970, Prepaid subscriptions 130, Total 5,895. Dr Amplifier (cost) 700 less depreciation 70, Stock 1,700, Prepayments 165, Bank 3,400, Total 5,895.

18 a *Sales ledger control (1)* Dr Balance 8,952, Sundry debtors 74,753. Cr Bank 69,471, Discount allowed 1,817, Balance 12,417.
Sales ledger control (2) Dr Balance 12,417, Car 1,173.
Cr Credit transfers 198, Contras 2,896, Bad debts 640, Balance 9,856.

b *Reconciliation* Balance before adjustment 9,663, Add: Debit balances 191, Corrections 200. Less: Credit transfers 198, Total 9,856.

19 a *Correction of sales ledger control* Sales ledger control 9,905. Less: Bad debts 59, Contra entry 110, Addition error 325, Total 9,411. Sales Ledger balances 9,275. Add: Incorrect credit (2 × 25) 50, Ommissions 72, Underposting 72. Less: Discount 14, Incorrect debit (2 × 22) 44, Total 9,411.

20 a *Balance per cash book (380)* Cr Receipts 1,680, Sanding order 40, Error 6. Dr Error 18, Payments 1,037.

21 a *Cash book* Dr Balance 3,856, Debtor 100. Cr A Jones 48, Interest 10, Balance 3,898.
Bank reconciliation Cash book 3,898, Add: Cheques not presented 218, Amount credited in error 95, Less: Cash in transit 50.

22 a *Balance per bank statement* 1,166.4 Add: Payments not recorded in bank account − Charges 12.80, Cheque 19.47, Standing order 32.52, Receipt in bank account 192.80.
Less: Payments not on bank statement − Rent 30, Wages 52.27, Recorded error (87.77 − 77.87) 9.90.

23 *Estimated trading and profit and loss* Sales 10,957, Fuel 2,119, Wages 4,111, Gross profit 4,727, Rent 1,600, Miscellaneous 2,134, Net profit (before depreciation) 993. Calculation of sales: Closing debtors 3,114, Receipts 10,354, Opening debtors 2,511, Total 10,957. Difference on cash account, treated as oil and petrol etc. No information provided about haulage fleet.
Incomplete balance sheet Cr Profit 993, Drawings 1,780. Dr Debtors 3,114, Cash 2,950.

24 *Trading, profit and loss* Sales 22,000, Cost of sales 17,600, Gross profit 4,400, Rates 170, Electricity 132, Rent 800, Accountancy fees 125, Expenses 100, Wages 1,500, Loss on fixtures 250, Net profit 1,323.
Balance Sheet Capital 4,095, Profit 1,323, Drawings 4,214, Total 1,204, Fixtures at cost less depreciation 750, Stock 1,250, Debtors 360, Prepayments – rates 40, Cash 190, Creditors (goods 979, electricity 47, rent 150, fees 125) 1,301, Bank overdraft 85, Total 1,204.

25 *Trading, profit and loss* Sales 7,800, Purchases 7,400, Closing stock 1,750, Cost of sales 5,650, Gross profit 2,150, Provision for DD 50, Rent 350, Petrol 400, Other expenses 250, Interest on loan 100, Depreciation on lorry 140, Net profit 860.
Balance sheet Capital 5,000, Profit for year 860, Drawings 1,640, Loan 1,000, Total 5,220.
Lorry (cost) 840 less depreciation 140, Loan outstanding 640, Stock 1,750, Debtors less provision 450, Prepayment 50, Bank 4,900, Cash 310, Creditors 2,200, Accruals 100, Total 5,220.

26 *Trading, profit and loss – ledger format* Dr Cost of sales 34,000, Gross profit 16,000, Total 50,000.
Cr Sales 50,000. Dr Workshop – rent 900, rates 570, Wages 3,200, Bonus 500, Loan interest 125, Motor vehicle – expenses 2,800, depreciation 800, Net profit 8,955, Total 17,850. Cr Gross profit 16,000, Commission 1,850.
Balance sheet – ledger format Capital 12,380, Addition 870, Net profit 8,955, Drawings 6,300, Loan 5,000, Bank overdraft 1,510, Trade creditors 2,200, Accrued charges 825, Total 25,440. Motor van (cost) 4,000 less depreciation 800, Stock 8,000, Trade debtors 12,290, Commission due 1,850, Amounts prepaid 100, Total 25,440.

ICMA questions

	Numbers
Journal, ledger accounts and adjustments	1 – 3
Prepayments, accruals and depreciation	4 – 6
Manufacturing accounts	7 – 9
Incomplete records	10 – 12
Cash flow	13
Cash budget	14

1 From the information given below you are required to compile the following accounts, separately, as they would appear in the ledger of PES Limited

during the year ended 31 December, 1976:
a) Cash at bank
b) Sundry debtors
c) Materials stock
d) Sundry creditors
e) Plant and machinery (at cost)
f) Provision for depreciation of plant and machinery
g) Profit or loss on the sale of plant and machinery
h) Creditor for VAT
j) Wages control
k) Provision for bad debts
l) Creditor for PAYE
m) Creditor for national insurance, etc

The balances on the above accounts at the beginning and end of the year were as follows:

	1 January 1976	1 January 1977
Debit balances:		
Bank	5,000	29,000
Sundry debtors	40,000	43,000
Materials stock	54,000	58,000
Plant and machinery	200,000	219,000
	£299,000	£349,000
Credit balances:		
Sundry creditors	22,000	23,000
Provision for depreciation of plant and machinery	81,800	94,000
Creditor for VAT	4,100	4,400
Wages accrued	1,900	1,400
Provision for bad debts	2,000	2,150
Creditor for PAYE	1,600	1,100
Creditor for national insurance	600	700
	£114,000	£126,750

The following information is given of transactions that took place during the year in respect of the accounts which you are required to show:

	£
Invoiced sales less returns, including VAT	396,000
Discount received	5,000
Discount allowed	9,100
Issues of materials to factory	180,000
Deficit on stocktaking	6,000
Depreciation of plant and machinery for the year	20,000
Loss on sale of machinery	200
Bad debts written off to profit and loss account	8,050
VAT on invoiced sales less returns	36,000
Manufacturing wages	97,000
National insurance, company's contributions	7,400

Bank payments were made during the year as follows:

	£
Creditors, including VAT	203,000
Purchase of plant, excluding VAT	30,000
Purchase of plant VAT	3,000
Creditor for VAT	14,000
Wages control	73,000
Creditor for PAYE	19,700
Creditor for national insurance	12,600

The receipts into the bank account during the year included the following:

	£
Sale of machinery	3,000
VAT on sale of machinery	300

You are also informed that:
1 All amounts shown above are correct.
2 No accounts were settled by contra.
3 The rate of VAT during the year was 10% and applied to all relevant transactions without exception.
4 The machine sold during 1976 originally cost £11,000.
5 Bad debts amounting to £7,900 were written off sundry debtors to the provision for bad debts.
6 VAT charged on materials purchased, less returns, for stock amounted to £19,000.
7 The analysis of the payroll included the following deductions from employees:

PAYE	19,200
National insurance	5,300
	£24,500

(50 marks)
(ICMA Foundation 1977)

2 Using the information given below, you are required to show:
a) the journal entries for the transactions below, including those relating to cash: narratives are required;
b) the trial balance of DHQ Limited at 31 December, 1977 after the transactions below have been included.
Manufacturing, trading, profit and loss accounts, or a balance sheet are not required.
All workings should be clearly shown.
The trial balance of DHQ Limited at 31 December, 1976 was as follows:

Ordinary share capital		80,000
Retained profit		20,000
Fixed assets at cost, and aggregate depreciation	100,000	35,000
Stock of materials	9,000	
Work-in-progress	950	
Stock of finished goods	21,000	
Debtors and creditors	25,000	7,000
Provision for bad debts		1,500
Cash at bank	7,000	
Petty cash	50	

Wages control account		1,000
Creditor for PAYE		150
Creditor for national insurance, etc		50
Prepaid and accrued expenses:		
Manufacturing expenses	40	90
Administration expenses	200	400
Marketing expenses	30	80
Creditor for corporation tax		10,000
Proposed dividend		8,000
	£163,270	£163,270

The following summarised transactions occurred during the year ended 31 December, 1977:

1. Sales on credit amounted to £206,000, and sales returns to £6,000.
2. Purchases of materials on credit amounted to £41,000, and purchase returns to £1,000.
3. Gross wages earned were £60,000, from which £8,000 was deducted for PAYE income tax and £3,000 for employees' contributions to national insurance, etc. Of the gross wages £50,000 referred to direct manufacturing, £1,000 to administration, £3,000 to marketing, and £6,000 to manufacturing expenses.
4. £2,000 was set off by contra by companies who had both debtor and creditor accounts.
5. Discount received amounted to £1,000. It is to be regarded as a reduction in the cost of materials purchased.
6. Discounts allowed amounted to £4,300. It is to be regarded as a marketing expense.
7. Bad debts of £700 were written off against the provision.
8. Payments from petty cash were £2,000, of which £100 related to manufacturing, £1,100 to administration and £800 to marketing.
9. Cash received and banked consisted of:
    (i) £194,000 from debtors;
    (ii) £600 for the sale of fixed assets which had originally cost £5,000 and on which the aggregate depreciation was £4,000. Any profit or loss on sale is to be shown in a separate account.
10. Cheque payments were:
    (i) £1,990 for petty cash replenishment;
    (ii) £36,000 to creditors;
    (iii) £48,500 for net wages;
    (iv) £7,900 for PAYE income tax;
    (v) £6,950 for employees' and company's national insurance contributions;
    (vi) £11,000 for additions to fixed assets;
    (vii) £10,000 for corporation tax;
    (viii) £8,000 for the proposed dividend;
    (ix) £41,150 manufacturing expenses;
    (x) £12,800 administration expenses;
    (xi) £16,050 marketing expenses.
11. The company's contribution to national insurance was £4,000, of which £2,800 was regarded as a manufacturing expense, £300 as administration

and £900 as marketing.

(45 marks)
(ICMA Foundation 1978)

3 You are required for VGH Limited to:
a) write up the transactions stated below for the year ended 31 October, 1978 in the appropriate ledger accounts;
b) show the trial balance of VGH Limited after this has been done.

Do not attempt to prepare manufacturing, trading, profit and loss, and appropriation accounts or a balance sheet.

The trial balances of VGH Limited at 1 November, 1977 was as follows:

	£000	£000
Ordinary shares of £1 each, fully paid		4,000
Share premium account		100
Retained profits		2,000
Fixed assets at cost, and aggregate depreciation	5,620	3,080
Stock of materials	2,000	
Work in progress	300	
Stock of finished products	3,000	
Debtors and creditors	1,800	650
Provision for bad debts		90
Prepayments: Administration expenses	29	
Marketing expenses	1	
Bank balance		2,456
Accruals: Manufacturing expenses		36
Administration expenses		21
Marketing expenses		11
Wages control		250
Creditor for PAYE income tax		41
Creditor for national insurance, etc.		15
	12,750	12,750

The following summarised transactions occurred during the year ended 31 October, 1978:
1. 1,000,000 ordinary shares of £1 each were issued for cash at a price of £1.40 each.
2. Fixed assets were purchased for cash for £1,400,000.
3. Fixed assets which originally cost £20,000 and with a written down book value of £10,000, were sold for £3,000.
4. Sales on credit amounted to £15,500,000, and sales returns to £500,000.
5. Purchases on credit amounted to £6,200,000, and purchase returns to £200,000.
6. Suppliers and customers accounts amounting to £1,200,000 were set off by contra.
7. Discount allowed amounted to £330,000 and discount received to £120,000. Both of these items were regarded as administration expenses.
8. £13,330,000 was received from debtors.
9. Bad debts of £40,000 were written off against the provision.
10. Direct wages earned amounted to £2,700,000 gross, and were allocated as to £1,500,000 manufacturing wages, £800,000 manufacturing expenses,

£100,000 administration expenses and £300,000 marketing expenses.
11 Deductions from employees' wages were £490,000 for PAYE income tax and £170,000 national insurance contributions, etc.
12 The company's proportion of national insurance contributions was £220,000, divided as to £180,000 manufacturing expenses, £10,000 administration expenses and £30,000 marketing expenses.
13 Payments from the bank were:

	£
To creditors	4,630,000
For manufacturing expenses	1,306,000
For administration expenses	422,000
For marketing expenses	1,555,000
For net wages	1,990,000
For PAYE income tax	485,000
For national insurance, company's and employees' contributions	389,000

(35 marks)
(ICMA Foundation 1978)

4 From the information given below you are required to show the rent, rates and insurance account in the ledger of CPF Limited for the year ended 30 June, 1976, showing clearly the prepayments and accruals at that date and the transfer to profit and loss account for the year.

The balances on the account at 1 July, 1975 were:

	£
Rent accrued	200
Rates prepaid	150
Insurance prepaid	180

Payments made during the year ended 30 June, 1976 were as follows:

1975		£
10 August	Rent, three months to 31 July, 1975	300
26 October	Insurance, one year to 31 October, 1976	600
2 November	Rates, six months to 31 March, 1976	350
12 December	Rent, four months to 30 November, 1975	400
1976		
17 April	Rent, four months to 31 March, 1976	400
9 May	Rates, six months to 30 September, 1976	350

(10 marks)
(ICMA Foundation 1977)

5 You are required, using the information given below, to compile a company's stationery and telephone account for the year ended 31 January, 1980 showing clearly the charge to profit and loss account.

The value of the company's stock of stationery on 31 January, 1979 was £241. At that date the prepaid telephone rental amounted to £20, there was an accrued liability of £137 for telephone calls during December 1978 and January 1979, and accrued liability of £25 for stationery.

During the year ended 31 January, 1980 the following transactions occurred:

	1979		£	£
	February 20	Purchase of stationery for		103
	March 19	Payment of telephone account of consisting of:		
		rent for quarter ended 31 May, 1979	60	
		calls for December 1978	79	
		January 1979	58	
		February 1979	65	
	June 28	Payment of telephone account of consisting of:		281
		rent for quarter ended 31 August, 1979	60	
		calls for March, April and May 1979	221	
	August 12	Purchase of stationery for		156
	September 15	Payment of telephone account of consisting of:		305
		rent for quarter ended 30 November, 1979	75	
		calls for June, July and August 1979	230	
	November 13	Purchase of stationery for		74
	December 20	Payment of telephone account of consisting of:		282
		rent for quarter ended 29 February, 1980	75	
		calls for September, October and November, 1979	207	

At 31 January, 1980 the stock of stationery was valued at £199 and there was an accrued liability for stationery of £13. On March 23, 1980 a telephone account of £298 was paid, consisting of:

	£
rent for the quarter ended 31 May, 1980	75
calls for December 1979	86
January 1980	63
February 1980	74

Value added tax (VAT) should be ignored and is not included in the above figures.

(15 marks)
(ICMA Foundation 1980)

6 A company's plant and machinery account at 31 December, 1978 and the corresponding depreciation provision account, broken down into years of purchase, are as follows:

Year of Purchase	Plant and machinery at cost £	Depreciation provision £
1962	20,000	20,000
1968	30,000	30,000
1969	100,000	95,000
1970	70,000	59,500
1977	50,000	7,500
1978	30,000	1,500
	£300,000	£213,500

Depreciation is at the rate of 10% per annum on cost. It is the company's policy to assume that all purchases, sales or disposals of plant occurred on 30 June in the relevant year for the purposes of calculating depreciation, irrespective of the precise date on which these events occurred.

During 1979 the following transactions took place:
1 Purchase of plant and machinery amounted to £150,000.
2 Plant that had been bought in 1968 for £17,000 was scrapped.
3 Plant that had been bought in 1969 for £9,000 was sold for £500.
4 Plant that had been bought in 1970 for £24,000 was sold for £1,500.

You are required to
a) Calculate the provision for depreciation of plant and machinery for the year ended 31 December, 1979. In calculating this provision you should bear in mind that it is the company's policy to show any profit or loss on the sale or disposal of plant as a completely separate item in the profit and loss account.
b) Show the following ledger accounts during 1979:
   (i) plant and machinery, at cost;
   (ii) depreciation provision;
   (iii) sales or disposals of plant and machinery.
c) Show at 31 December, 1979 the breakdown under years of purchase of the balances on the:
   (i) plant and machinery at cost account;
   (ii) depreciation provision account.

(25 marks)
(ICMA Foundation 1980)

7 You are required for APF Limited, a company which manufactures and sells two products X and Y, to prepare in vertical and columnar form:
a) manufacturing, trading and profit and loss accounts for products X and Y for the year ended 30 June, 1977;
b) an appropriation account for the year;
c) a balance sheet as at 30 June, 1977.

The trial balance of APF Limited at 30 June, 1977 was as follows:

	£	£
Ordinary shares of £1, issued and fully paid (authorised £800,000)		800,000
6% Preference shares of £1, issued and fully paid (authorised £200,000)		100,000
Share premium		150,000
Retained profits, at 1 July, 1976		441,000
Fixed assets, at cost £1,200,000	914,000	
Stocks at 1 July, 1976:		
materials	80,000	
work-in-progress:		
product X	34,000	
product Y	29,000	
finished products:		
product X	280,000	
product Y	150,000	
Debtors and creditors	306,000	90,000
Bad debts provision, at 1 July, 1976		12,500
Sales: product X (120,000 units)		1,200,000
product Y (180,000 units)		1,200,000
Purchases of materials	720,000	

Manufacturing wages: product X	100,000	
product Y	200,000	
Manufacturing expenses	208,000	
Creditor for royalties, at 1 July, 1976		62,000
Payments for royalties	391,000	
Administration expenses	139,500	
Selling and distribution expenses	214,000	
Cash at bank and in hand	290,000	
	£4,055,500	£4,055,500

The following information is given:
1. Depreciation is to be provided on fixed assets at the rate of 10% per annum on cost. Additions to fixed assets during the year amounted to £100,000, purchased on 31 December, 1976. The annual depreciation charge is to be apportioned among manufacturing, administration, and selling and distribution in the proportions of 8:1:1.
2. During the year the cost of materials consumed was £300,000 for product X and £400,000 for product Y.
3. Work in progress for both products was constant in quantity and value at the beginning and end of the year.
4. Stocks of finished products were:

	1 July, 1976	30 June, 1977
	in units	in units
Product X	40,000	20,000
Product Y	30,000	50,000

These stocks are to be valued at manufacturing cost (ie materials consumed, manufacturing wages, royalties, manufacturing expenses and the depreciation apportioned to manufacturing).
5. Royalties of £2 per unit for product X and £1 per unit for product Y are payable on the quantities of products completely manufactured.
6. Manufacturing expenses, including the apportionment of depreciation, are to be divided between the products in proportion to the number of completed articles transferred from the factory to the finished product stock. All products are transferred immediately on completion.
7. Bad debts of £6,000 are to be written off and the bad debts provision is to be made equal to £15,000. These items are a selling and distribution expense.
8. Administration expenses, including the proportion of depreciation, are to be divided between the products in proportion to the number of products sold.
9. Selling and distribution expenses, including the proportion of depreciation, bad debts written off and any increase or decrease in the bad debts provision, are to be divided between the products in proportion to sales values.
10. Prepaid and accrued expenses at 30 June, 1977 were:

	Prepaid	Accrued
	£	£
Administration expenses	2,000	1,000
Selling and distribution expenses	1,000	7,000

11 Provision is to be made for:

	£
Corporation tax on the year's profit	135,000
Preference dividend	6,000
Ordinary dividend	120,000

12 Advance corporation tax on dividends is to be ignored.

(50 marks)
(ICMA Foundation 1977)

8 From the information given below you are required to prepare the manufacturing, trading and profit and loss, and appropriation accounts of VBA Limited for the year ended 31 December, 1977 and a balance sheet as at that date.

Trial balance of VBA Limited at 31 December, 1977.

	£000	£000
Ordinary share capital		1,000
Reserves		580
10% Debentures		100
Fixed assets, at cost	2,090	
Provision for depreciation of fixed assets		680
Proceeds of sale of fixed assets		15
Stock of materials	220	
Work-in-progress	40	
Stock of finished goods	230	
Debtors	420	
Provision for doubtful debts		20
Cash at bank and in hand	20	
Creditors		88
Taxation on 1976 profits		118
Sales		3,400
Purchases of materials	1,060	
Manufacturing wages	353	
Manufacturing expenses	555	
Administration expenses	292	
Selling and distribution expenses	666	
Debenture interest	5	
Interim dividend	50	
	6,001	6,001

The following information is also given:

1 The variations in the values of stocks at 31 December, 1977 as compared with the values at 31 December, 1976 were:

		£000
Stock of materials	increase of	30
Work-in-progress	reduction of	10
Stock of finished goods	increase of	70

2 Prepaid and accrued expenses at 31 December, 1977 were:

	Prepaid £000	Accrued £000
Manufacturing wages		7
Manufacturing expenses	1	6
Administration expenses	2	5
Selling and distribution expenses	1	1

3 Debenture interest has been paid to 30 June, 1977 only.
4 Bad debts of £3,000 are to be written off, and the provision for doubtful debts is to be increased by £1,000. These items are to be regarded as selling and distribution expenses.
5 Depreciation is to be provided at the rate of 10% per annum on cost on a strict time basis, and is to be allocated to manufacturing, administration, and selling and distribution expenses in the proportion of 8:1:1.
6 The item appearing in the trial balance 'Proceeds of sale of fixed assets' refers to items which originally cost £100,000 and which were sold on 30 June, 1977, on which date they had a net book value of £10,000.
7 Additional fixed assets were purchased for £160,000 on 31 March, 1977. These were included in the figure of £2,090,000 appearing in the trial balance.
8 A provision of £170,000 is to be made in respect of taxation on the current year's profits.
9 Provision is to be made for a recommended final dividend of 10% on the ordinary shares.

(25 marks)
(ICMA Foundation 1978)

9 Using the information given below you are required to prepare for TLM Limited:
a) manufacturing, trading, profit and loss and appropriation accounts for the year ended 30 June, 1980;
b) a balance sheet as at 30 June, 1980.

Balance Sheet of TLM Limited as at 30 June, 1979

	£	£	£
Fixed assets, at cost		835,000	
less: Depreciation to date		549,000	286,000
Current assets:			
Stock of materials		191,000	
Work-in-progress		30,000	
Stock of finished products		200,000	
Debtors		408,000	
Cash at bank		10,000	
		839,000	
less: Current liabilities:			
Creditors	190,000		
Taxation	50,000		
Proposed dividends	40,000	280,000	559,000
			£845,000

407

Share capital, ordinary shares
  of £1 each fully paid 400,000
Retained profit 445,000
                                                           ─────────
                                                           £845,000
                                                           ═════════

The following information is also given:
1 During the year ended 30 June, 1980 movements in the accounts were:

	£	£
Net operating profit, before tax, for the year		180,000
Depreciation, for the year: manufacturing		80,000
administration and marketing		20,000
Issue for cash of 100,000 ordinary shares of £1 each at a price of £1.20 each		120,000
Sale of fixed assets		2,000
Increase in creditors		10,000
Reduction in work in progress		5,000
Reduction in cash at bank		40,000
Purchase of fixed assets	215,000	
Increase in stock of materials	34,000	
Increase in stock of finished products	50,000	
Increase in debtors	42,000	
Tax paid	51,000	
Dividends paid	65,000	
	£457,000	£457,000

2 There was a profit of £1,000 on the sale of the fixed assets, which originally cost £50,000. This profit is not included in the net operating profit before tax for the year, and is independent of the depreciation charge.
3 Purchases of materials during the year amounted to £784,000.
4 Wages amounted to 30% of materials consumed.
5 Gross profit (sales less the manufacturing cost of goods sold) was 20% of annual sales.
6 The liability for taxation at 30 June, 1980 was £70,000.
7 The amount charged against the appropriation account for dividends during the year to 30 June, 1980 was £75,000.
8 Manufacturing expenses during the year were £430,000. Administration and marketing expenses during the year were £160,000. These amounts do not include depreciation.

(30 marks)
(ICMA Foundation 1980)

10 From the information given below you are required:
a) to prepare balance sheets of HFW Limited as at 1 January, 1976 and 31 December, 1976;
b) to calculate the net profit or loss, before taxation, for the year.

	1 Jan. £	31 Dec. £
Land and buildings: at cost	50,000	50,000
provision for depreciation	7,000	8,000
Plant and machinery: at cost	60,000	70,000
provision for depreciation	24,000	30,000
Stock of materials	18,600	19,400
Work-in-progress	2,200	3,100
Stock of finished products	20,900	21,300
Sundry debtors	23,000	25,000
Provision for bad debts	1,200	1,800
Prepaid expenses	900	1,300
Cash at bank and in hand	9,100	10,700
Sundry creditors	12,000	13,000
Accrued expenses	2,500	3,000
Liability for taxation	9,000	11,000
Recommended dividends	8,000	7,000
10% Debentures	20,000	Nil
Ordinary share capital issued	80,000	
Share premium	3,000	

During 1976 the company issued a further 20,000 ordinary shares of £1 each at a price of £1.25 each. During the year cash payments of £11,000 for dividends and £9,000 for taxation were made.

(15 marks)
(ICMA Foundation 1977)

11 You are required to prepare for CDM Limited:
a) trading, profit and loss and appropriation accounts for the year ended 31 March, 1977; and
b) balance sheets as at 31 March, 1976 and 1977.

CDM Limited is a retail shop which arrives at its selling prices by adding $33\frac{1}{3}$% to the cost of goods purchased for resale. Its position on the two dates was:

	31 March 1976 £	1977 £
Issued ordinary share capital	70,000	70,000
Retained profit	9,000	
Sundry creditors	17,000	18,000
Creditor for taxation	5,000	
Proposed dividend	7,000	3,000
Fixed assets at cost	80,000	
Provision for depreciation of fixed assets	30,800	
Stock	28,000	29,000
Sundry debtors	24,000	20,000
Cash at bank	8,000	7,100
Provision for bad debts	1,200	1,000

The following information is given:
1. Cash payments made during the year were:
   (i) £117,100 to creditors for goods for re-sale;
   (ii) £10,000 for purchase of additional fixed assets;
   (iii) £4,900 for taxation;
   (iv) £14,500 in respect of dividends;
   (v) after allowing for cash received from debtors, the balance on the cash account represents the payment of business expenses.
2. Discount allowed amounted to £3,800, and the discount received to £2,900.
3. Bad debts written off during the year amounted to £1,700.
4. No accounts were settled by contra.
5. Depreciation of fixed assets during the year amounted to £8,700.
6. No fixed assets were sold during the year.
7. Taxation of £8,000 (inclusive of any adjustment of the previous years' liability) should be charged against the profit for the year. Advance corporation tax on dividends is to be ignored.

(25 marks)
(ICMA Foundation 1977)

12 You are required to calculate for each product and for the company as a whole:
a) the values of stock at 31 December, 1977, at cost;
b) the amounts of gross profit, as they would appear in the company's trading account.

The company sells three products, A, B and C on which it earns gross profit percentages, calculated on normal selling prices, of 20, 25 and 33 $\frac{1}{3}$ respectively. The value of its stock at 1 January, 1977, valued at cost, was:

Product	£
A	24,000
B	36,000
C	12,000

During the year ended 31 December, 1977 the actual purchases and sales were:

Product	Purchases £	Sales £
A	146,000	172,500
B	124,000	159,400
C	48,000	74,600

However, certain items were sold during the year at a discount on the normal selling prices, and these discounts were reflected in the values of sales shown above. The items sold at a discount were:

Product	Sales At normal prices £	At actual prices £
A	10,000	7,500
B	3,000	2,400
C	1,000	600

These discounts were not provided for in the cost values of stock at 1 January, 1977 given above.

(15 marks)
(ICMA Foundation 1978)

13 Smith is considering buying a business the final accounts of which for the last three years were as follows:

Profit and loss accounts for the years ended 31 December:

	1977 £000	1978 £000	1979 £000
Sales	200	190	224
Materials consumed	100	95	112
Business expenses	80	80	82
Depreciation	12	13	14
Net profit added to reserves	8	2	16

Balance Sheets as at 31 December:

	1976 £000	1977 £000	1978 £000	1979 £000
Fixed assets, at cost	100	120	140	180
less: depreciation	70	82	95	109
	30	38	45	71
Stock-in-trade	16	17	18.5	21
Debtors	21	24	26	28
Prepaid business expenses	1	0.5	2	1
Cash	32	11	28	13.2
	100	90.5	119.5	134.2
Ordinary share capital	50	50	70	70
Share premium	–	–	5	5
Reserves	16	24	26	42
Debentures	20	–	–	–
Creditors	11	13	14	14
Accrued business expenses	3	3.5	4.5	3.2
	100	90.5	119.5	134.2

Smith wishes his offer for the business to be based upon trading cash flows rather than book profits. By trading cash flows he means cash received from debtors less cash paid to creditors and for business expenses (excluding depreciation) together with an allowance for average annual expenditure on fixed assets of £15,000 per year.

The actual expenditure on fixed assets is to be ignored, as is any cash received or paid out on the issue or redemption of share or loan capital.

Smith wishes the trading cash flows to be calculated for each of the years 1977, 1978 and 1979, and for these to be combined using weightings of 20% for 1977, 30% for 1978 and 50% for 1979 to give an average annual trading cash flow.

He considers that the average annual trading cash flow should show a return of 20% on his investment.

You are required to calculate:
a) the trading cash flows for each of the years 1977, 1978 and 1979;

b) the weighted average annual trading cash flow;
c) the price which Smith should offer for the business.

(15 marks)
(ICMA Foundation 1980)

14 Cash budgets for months 1, 2 and 3 are given. You are required to prepare, using the information supplied, cash budgets for months 4, 5 and 6 in the format shown.

Cash budget

	Month					
	1	2	3	4	5	6
	£	£	£	£	£	£
Balance b/f	(12,705)	(10,215)	100			
Receipts:						
Debtors	15,700	16,000	6,000			
Issue of ordinary shares						
Sale of plant						
	2,995	5,785	6,100			
Payments						
Creditors for materials	12,000	4,500	4,350			
Wages	600	575	595			
Overhead	610	610	615			
Debenture interest						
Taxation						
Dividends						
Purchase of plant						
Repayment of debentures						
	13,210	5,685	5,560			
Balance c/f	(10,215)	100	540			
	2,995	5,785	6,100			

Note: Balances in brackets represent bank overdrafts.

You are given the following information:
1 Material cost is expected to be 75% of invoiced sales.
2 Debtors are given two months' credit.
3 Creditors for materials allow the company one month's credit.
4 No discounts received or allowed, bad debts or items settled by contra are expected.
5 Three quarters of wages earned each month are paid in that month and the remaining quarter in the following month.

6 Overhead expenses are paid, half in the month in which they are incurred and half in the following month.
7 Items other than above are dealt with completely in the month shown in the table of data below.
8 Other relevant information is:

Table of data

	Months					
	1	2	3	4	5	6
	£	£	£	£	£	£
Invoiced sales	6,000	6,200	6,800	7,200	8,400	12,000
Material stocks:						
Increase					700	
Decrease		300	100			
Wages earned	560	580	600	640	700	960
Overhead incurred	600	620	610	630	630	640
Debenture interest paid						1,000
Taxation paid				10,000		
Dividends paid						500
Plant purchased						1,945
Debentures repaid						20,000
Ordinary shares issued at par						35,000
Plant sold					200	

(30 marks)
(ICMA Foundation 1980)

ICMA summary answers

Note: Matters relating to taxation (other than VAT) that have not been dealt with in the text will have a brief explanation within each answer to which it relates.
Final accounts use the vertical format for presentation unless the contrary is stated.

1   *Cash at bank*   Dr Balance 5,000, Debtors 376,000, Sales of machinery 3,000, VAT on machinery 300. Cr Creditors 203,000, Purchase of plant 30,000, VAT on plant 3,000, VAT paid 14,000, Wages 73,000, PAYE 19,700. National insurance 12,600, Balance 29,000.
Sundry debtors   Dr Balance 40,000, Sales 360,000, VAT on sales 36,000. Cr Discount allowed 9,100, Bad debts written off 7,900, Cash 376,000, Balance 43,000.
Materials stock   Dr Balance 54,000, Creditors 190,000. Cr Issues to factory 180,000, Deficit 6,000, Balance 58,000.
Sundry creditors   Dr Cash 203,000, Discounts received 5,000, Balance 23,000. Cr Balance 22,000, Purchases 190,000, VAT on purchases 19,000.
Plant and Machinery (at cost)   Dr Balance 200,000, Purchase 30,000. Cr Profit or loss on sale 11,000, Balance 219,000.
Provision for depreciation   Dr profit or loss on sale 7,800, Balance 94,000. Cr Balance 81,800, Depreciation for year 20,000.
Profit or loss on sale   Dr Plant and machinery (cost) 11,000. Cr

413

Provision 7,800, Cash 3,000, Loss 200.
Creditor for VAT Dr Cash – on purchase of plant 3,000, Cash – paid during year 14,000, Sundry creditors 19,000, Balance 4,400. Cr Balance 4,100, Sundry debtors 36,000, Cash – sale of machinery 300.
Wages control Dr Cash 73,000, PAYE deductions 19,200, NI deductions 5,300, Balance Cr Balance 1,900, Manufacturing wages 97,000.
Provision for bad debts Dr Sundry debtors 7,900, Balance 2,150. Cr Balance 2,000, Profit and Loss 8,050.
Creditor for PAYE Dr Cash 19,700, Balance 1,100. Cr Balance 1,600, Wages control 19,200.
Creditor for NI Dr Cash 12,600, Balance 700. Cr Balance 600, Wages control 5,300, Company's contribution 7,400.

2 a *Journal* Dr 1 Debtors 206,000, Sales returns 6,000; 2 Purchases of materials 41,000, Creditors 1,000; 3 Wages control account 59,500, Direct manufacturing wages 50,000, Administration expenses 1,000, Marketing expenses 3,000, Manufacturing expenses 6,000; 4 Creditors 2,000; 5 Creditors 1,000; 6 Marketing expenses 4,300; 7 Provision for bad debts 700; 8 Manufacturing expenses 100, Administration expenses 1,100, Marketing expenses 800; 9 Cash at bank 194,600; Sale of fixed assets – net book value 1,000, Depreciation provision 4,000; 10 Petty cash 1,990, Creditors 36,000, PAYE 7,900, National insurance 6,950, Fixed assets 11,000, Creditor for corporation tax 10,000, Creditor for proposed dividend 8,000, Manufacturing expenses 41,150, Administration expenses 12,800, Marketing expenses 16,050; 11 Manufacturing expenses 2,800, Administration expenses 300, Marketing expenses 900. Cr 1 Sales 206,000, Debtors 6,000; 2 Creditors 41,000, Purchase returns 1,000; 3 PAYE 8,000, National insurance 3,000, Cash 48,500, Wages control 60,000; 4 Debtors 2,000; 5 Purchases of materials 1,000; 6 Debtors 4,300; 7 Debtors 700; 8 Petty cash 2,000; 9 Debtors 194,000, Sale of fixed asset 600, Fixed asset at cost 5,000; 10 Cash at bank 151,840; 11 National insurance 4,000.

b *Trial balance* Dr Fixed assets at cost 106,000, Stock of material 9,000, Work in progress 950, Stock of finished goods 21,000, Debtors 24,000, Cash at bank 1,260, Petty cash 40, Manufacturing expenses 50,000, Administration expenses 15,000, Marketing expenses 25,000, Direct manufacturing wages 50,000, Purchases of materials 39,000, Loss on sale of fixed assets 400, Total 341,650. Cr Ordinary share capital 80,000, Retained profit 20,000, Depreciation of fixed assets 31,000, Creditors 8,000, Provision for bad debts 800, Wages control 1,500, PAYE 250, National insurance 100, Sales 200,000, Total 341,650.

3 a *Note*: Share accounts are not dealt with in this text. Accounts in £000's.
Ordinary share capital
Dr Balance 5,000; Cr Balance 4,000, Cash 1,000.
Share premium
Dr Balance 500; Cr Balance 100, Cash 400.
Fixed assets
Dr Balance 5,620, Cash 1,400; Cr Sale 20, Balance 7,000.
Depreciation
Dr Sale 10, Balance 3,070; Cr Balance 3,080.
Sale of fixed assets
Dr Fixed assets 20; Cr Depreciation 10, Cash 3, Loss on sale 7.

Wages control
Dr PAYE 490, National Insurance 170, Cash 1,990, Balance 300;
Cr Balance 250, Manufacturing wages 1,500, Manufacturing expenses 800, Administration expenses 100, Marketing expenses 300.
PAYE
Dr Cash 485, Balance 46; Cr Balance 41, Wages control 490.
National Insurance (creditor)
Dr Cash 389, Balance 16; Cr Balance 15, Wages 170, NI expenses Manufacturing 180, Administration 10, Marketing 30.
Manufacturing expenses
Dr Wages 800, National Insurance 180, Cash 1,306;
Cr Balance 36, Balance 2,250.
Manufacturing wages
Dr Wages control 1,500; Cr Balance 1,500.
Sales
Dr Debtors − returns 500, Balance 15,000; Cr Debtors − sales 15,500.
Purchases
Dr Creditors 6,200; Cr Creditors − returns 200, Balance 6,000.
Debtors control
Dr Balance 1,800, Sales 15,500.
Cr Sales − returns 500, Creditors − contra 1,200, Discount allowed 330, Cash 13,330, Bad debts provision 40, Balance 1,900.
Creditors control
Dr Purchases − returns 200, Debtors − contra 1,200, Discounts 120, Cash 4,630, Balance 700.
Cr Balance 650, Purchases 6,200.
Discounts allowed and received
Dr Debtors control 330; Cr Creditors control 120, Administration expenses 210.
Administration expenses
Dr Prepayments 29, Wages 100, National Insurance 10, Cash 422, Discounts − net 210.
Cr Accruals 21, Balance 750.
Marketing expenses
Dr Prepayments 1, Wages 300, National Insurance 30, Cash 1,555.
Cr Accruals 11, Balance 1,875.
Provision for bad debts
Dr Debtors control 40, Balance 50.
Cr Balance 90.
Cash at bank
Dr Share capital 1,000, Share premium 400, Sale of fixed assets 3, Debtors 13,330.
Cr Balance 2,456, Fixed assets 1,400, Creditors 4,630, Manufacturing expenses 1,306, Administration expenses 422, Marketing expenses 1,555, Wages control 1,990, PAYE 485, National Insurance 389, Balance 100.

b *Trial balance*
Dr Fixed assets at cost 7,000, Loss on sale 7, Stock of materials 2,000, Work-in-progress 300, Stock of finished products 3,000, Debtors 1,900, Bank 100, Manufacturing wages 1,500, Expenses 2,250, Administration expenses 750, Marketing expenses 1,875, Purchases, less returns 6,000.
Cr Ordinary shares 5,000, Share premium 500, Retained profits 2,000,

Depreciation 3,070, Creditors 700, Provision for bad debts 50, Wages control 300, PAYE − creditor 46, National insurance − creditor 16, Sales less returns 15,000.
Totals 26,682.

4 *Ledger* Dr 1975 Balances prepaid − Rates 150, Insurance 180, Cash 300, Cash 600, Cash 350, Cash 400. 1976, Cash 400, Cash 350, Balance accrued − Rent 300, Total 3,030. Cr 1975 Balance accrued − Rent 200. 1975 Profit and Loss − Rent 1,200, Rates 675, Insurance 580, Balance prepaid − Rates 175, Insurance 200, Total 3,030.

5 *Ledger* Dr 1979 Balances − Stock 241, Telephone 20; Bank 103, Cash 262, Cash 281, Bank 156, Cash 305, Bank 74, Cash 282. 1980 Balances accrued − Stationery 13, Telephone 149, Total 1,886. Cr 1979 Balances accrued − Stationery 25, Telephone 137. 1980 Profit & Loss − Stationery 363, Telephone 1,137, Balances − Stocks 199, Telephone prepaid 25, Total 1,886.

Note: Payments have been assumed to be by: Cash − telephone and Bank − stationery.

6 *Ledgers* Plant and machinery: Dr Balance 300,000, Purchases 150,000. Cr Disposals − Scrapped 17,000, Sold 33,000, Balance 400,000.

Depreciation in provision Dr Scrapped 17,000, Sold − 1969 assets 9,000, 1970 assets 21,600, Balance 192,200. Cr Balance 213,500, Profit and Loss 26,300.

Disposal. Dr Scrapped 17,000, Sold 33,000. Cr Provision 47,600, Cash proceeds 2,000, Loss on sale 400. Schedule 1962−1979. Cost: 20,000, 13,000, 91,000, 46,000, 50,000, 30,000, 150,000. Depreciation: 20,000, 13,000, 91,000, 43,700, 12,500, 4,500, 7,500.

7 *Manufacturing* (columns X, Y + Total respectively − where given) Units produced 100,000, 200,000, 300,000; Stock 1 July 80,000 (total), Purchases 720,000 (total), Stock 30 June 100,000 (total) − net figure apportioned 300,000, 400,000, 700,000; Manufacturing wages 100,000, 200,000, 300,000; Manufacturing expenses 100,000, 200,000, 300,000; Royalties 200,000, 200,000, 400,000; Work in progress 1 July 34,000 (X), 29,000 (Y), 30 June 34,000 (X), 29,000 (Y); Cost of manufactured goods transferred 700,000, 1,000,000, 1,700,000; cost per unit £7 (X), £5 (Y).

Trading and profit and loss (columns X, Y and Total respectively) Sales 1,200,000, 1,200,000, 2,400,000; Cost of finished goods sold: Stocks 1 July 280,000, 150,000, 430,000; Transferred from production 700,000, 1,000,000, 1,700,000; Stock 30 June 140,000, 250,000, 390,000; Gross profit 360,000, 300,000, 660,000, Administration expenses 60,000, 90,000, 150,000; Selling and distribution expenses 120,000, 120,000, 240,000; Net profit before tax 180,000, 90,000, 270,000.

Appropriations (combined figures) Retained profit 1 July 441,000, Profit before tax 270,000, Preference dividend 6,000, Ordinary dividend 120,000, Corporation tax 135,000, Retained profit 30 June 450,000.

Balance sheet Fixed assets (cost) 1,200,000 less depreciation 401,000, Stock of materials 100,000, Work in progress 63,000, Stock of finished products 390,000, Debtors, less provision 285,000, Prepaid expenses 3,000, Cash at bank and in hand 290,000, Creditors including royalties 161,000. Accrued expenses 8,000, Taxation 135,000, Dividends 126,000, Total 1,500,000.

Issued capital – Ordinary shares 800,000, Preference shares 100,000, Share premium 150,000, Retained profit 450,000, Total 1,500,000.

Taxation – can be treated as a straight forward provision, dealt with as an appropriation, with a corresponding current liability balance.

8   *Manufacturing* (£'s 000)   Materials used: Purchases 1,060, Increase in stocks 30, Manufacturing wages 360, Manufacturing expenses 720, Decrease in work-in-progress 10, Cost of finished goods produced 2,120.

Trading and profit and loss (£'s 000)   Sales 3,400, Cost of finished goods sold: 2,120, Increase in stocks 70, Gross profit 1,350, Administration expenses 315, Selling and distribution expenses 690, Debenture interest 10, Operating profit 335, Profit on sale of fixed assets 5, Profit before taxation 340, Taxation 170, Dividends: Interim 50, Final 100, Transfer to reserves 20.

Balance Sheet (£'000)   Fixed assets (cost) 1,990, less depreciation 790, Stock of materials 250, Work in progress 30, Stock of finished goods 300, Debtors less provision 396, Prepaid expenses 4, Cash at bank and in hand 20, Creditors 93, Accrued expenses 19, Taxation: on 1976 profits 118, on 1977 profits 170, Proposed dividends 500, Total 1,700.

Issued capital – ordinary shares 1,000, Reserves 600, Debentures 100, Total 1,700.

Taxation for both years 1976 and 1977 has been provided for but not paid. It is usually the case that tax on profits is paid (often well) in arrear of when they arise.

9   *Manufacturing* (£'s 000)   Materials consumed: Purchases 784, Increase in stocks 34, Wages 225, Manufacturing expenses 430, Depreciation 80, Cost of production 1,485, Reduction in work in progress 5, Cost of finished goods produced 1,490.

Trading, profit and loss (£'s 000)   Sales 1,800, Cost of goods sold: Finished goods produced 1,490, Increase in stocks 50, Gross profit 360, Administration and marketing expenses 160, Depreciation 20, Operating profit 180, Profit on sale of fixed assets 1, Profit before taxation 181, Taxation: On year's profit 70, Under provision in previous year 1, Dividends: Interim 25, Final 50, Retained profit for the year 35.

Balance sheet (£'s 000)   Fixed assets (cost) 1,000 less depreciation 600, Stocks and work-in-progress 500, Debtors 450, Trade creditors 200, Bank overdraft 30, Taxations 70, Proposed dividends 50, Total 1,000.

Share capital and reserves: Ordinary shares 500, Share premium 20, Retained profit 480, Total 1,000.

Taxation – the provision from the previous year, which is only an estimate has been adjusted upwards after agreement with the Inland Revenue. A further provision has been made out of the current years profits.

10 a *Balance sheet*   Figures for 1 January and 31 December respectively. Fixed assets: Land and buildings (cost) 50,000 less depreciation 7,000, 8,000; Plant and machinery (cost) 60,000, 70,000, less depreciation 24,000, 30,000, Current assets: Stock of materials 18,600, 19,400; Work in progress 2,200, 3,100; Stock of finished products 20,900, 21,300; Sundry debtors less provision 21,800, 23,200; Prepaid expenses 900, 1,300; Cash at bank and in hand 9,100, 10,700; Current liabilities: Creditors and accrued expenses 14,500, 16,000; Taxation 9,000, 11,000; Proposed dividends 8,000, 7,000, Totals 121,000, 127,000. Financed by: Ordinary share

capital 80,000, 100,000; Share premium 3,000, 8,000; General reserves 18,000, 19,000, Debentures 20,000, nil, Totals 121,000, 127,000.

b *Calculation of net profit* Increase in reserves 1,000, Dividends – after recommendation 1 Jan 1976: Paid (11,000 – 8,000), Proposed 7,000, Taxation 11,000, Profit 22,000. Taxation will have been charged in Profit and loss 11,000.

11 *Trading, profit and loss and appropriation* Sales 160,000, Cost of goods sold 120,000, Gross profit 40,000, Business expenses 12,900, Discounts allowed 3,800, Discounts received (2,900), Bad debts 1,700, Decreased provision for bad debts (200), Provision for depreciation 8,700, Profit before taxation 16,000.

Taxation – on profit for year 8,100, overprovided in 1976 100, Profit after taxation 8,000, Balance brought forward 9,000, Dividends – paid 7,500, proposed 3,000, Balance carried forward 6,500.

Balance sheets (columns for 1976 and 1977 respectively) Fixed assets (cost) 80,000, 90,000 less depreciation 30,800, 39,500, Stocks 28,000, 29,000, Debtors less provision 22,800, 19,000, Cash 8,000, 7,100, Totals 108,000, 105,600. Issued ordinary share capital 70,000, Retained profit 9,000, 6,500, Creditors 17,000, 18,000, Proposed dividends 7,000, 3,000, Taxation 5,000, 6,000, Totals 108,000, 105,600.

Taxation – provided in one period may not exactly match settlement. In this case too much was provided in 1976 which releases (in this case) a further 100 to the business.

12 *Calculation of cost of sales* (Products A, B, and C respectively) Sales at actual prices 172,500, 159,400, 74,600; Discounts 2,500, 600, 400, Cost of sales percentage: 80, 75, 66⅔; Cost of sales 140,000, 120,000, 50,000.

Calculation of closing stock (Products A, B, and C respectively) Stock 1 Jan 24,000, 36,000, 12,000; Purchases 146,000, 124,000, 48,000. Cost of sales 140,000, 120,000, 50,000; Stock 31 Dec 30,000, 40,000, 10,000.

Calculation of gross profit (Products A, B, and C respectively) Actual sales 172,000, 159,400, 74,600; Cost of sales 140,000, 120,000, 50,000; Gross profit 32,500, 39,400, 24,600.

13 The weighted average cash flow and its capitalization was not covered in the text but see parts b) and c) below.

a Statement – figures for Years 1977, 1978 and 1979 respectively in £'s 000. Retained profit 8, 12, 16; Depreciation 12, 13, 14; Increase in creditors 2, 1, nil; Increase in accruals 0.5, 1, nil; Decrease in prepayments 0.5, nil, 1; Total 23, 17, 31. Less: Increase in stocks 1, 1.5, 2.5; Increase in debtors 3, 2, 2; Increase in prepayments nil, 1.5, nil; Decrease in accruals nil, nil, 1.3; Totals 4, 5, 5.8. Gross trading cash flow (difference) 19, 12, 25.2. Less average investment in fixed assets 15, 15, 15. Trading cash flow 4, (3), 10.2.

b Weighted average 1977 (20% of 4,000) 800; 1978 (30% of 3,000) (900), 1979 (50% of 10,200) 5,100 = 5,000.

c Price to pay 5,000/20% = 25,000.

14 Statement – figures for months 4, 5 and 6 respectively.

Balances: 540, (9,310), (9,225). Receipts: Debtors 6,200, 6,800, 7,200; Issue of shares nil, nil, 35,000; Sale of plant 200, nil, nil. Payments: Creditors for materials 5,000, 5,400, 7,000; Wages 630, 685, 895; Overhead 620, 630, 635; Debenture interest nil, nil, 1,000; Taxation 10,000, nil, nil; Dividends nil, nil, 500; Purchase of plant nil, nil, 1,945; Repayment of debentures 20,000. Balances: (9,310), (9,225), 1,000.

Glossary

Acid test ratio: a measure of liquidity, taking account of current assets with the exception of stock (that is considered illiquid) and comparing them to current liabilities — forming a ratio, equivalent to the liquid or quick ratio.
Account: a financial statement dealing with monetary transactions, usually presented in a form that relates to specific persons or time periods.
Accounting: the process of preparing accounts.
Accounting period: to assist in the measurement and evaluation of transactions, the accounting process requires accounts to be drawn up for a specific time period eg monthly or yearly.
Accounting policies: concern the choice of specific accounting methods chosen by the management of a particular business, as being the method most suitable to prepare accounts for that business.
Accounting principles: long established accounting concepts and conventions that have over the years formed the bedrock of accounting practice eg the going-concern.
Accounting ratio: a means for making comparison between financial statements of different businesses in one year or different years for the same business, the acid test ratio (above) is an example.
Accounting record: presentation of written evidence of accounting information.
Accounting standards: rules for the preparation of accounts in their present form recently drawn up by the accounting professions to regulate the preparation of accounting statements. This is achieved by narrowing the choice of accounting methods that are permitted in given situations eg SSAP 16 Current Cost Accounting.
Accounting statement: a document containing business figures represented in a way acceptable to accountants. A statement can be issued for an amount due or owed, but in a wider context more usually refers to other presentations, for instance end of period statements ie the Trading, Profit and loss Account. This statement is sometimes referrcd to as the Income Statement and the Balance Sheet is sometimes referred to as the Position Statement.
Accrual: (expense owing or accrued expense) the effect of recording a transaction expense that will require settlement through cash or bank, but in the meantime increases a liability or decreases an asset.
Accumulated fund: the total long term funds employed in a club, society or other non-profit making association, after meeting the current liabilities, that have been built up to support its activities. It is similar to the capital of a trading business, that in the case of the accumulated fund belongs to the club membership after meeting all other liabilities.
Adjustment: in accounting is primarily concerned with the year end, making amendments to cash that affect both income and expenditure and the closing balances (as shown in the balance sheet) according to accepted accounting principles, to as closely as possible make a realistic statement of profit.
Amount outstanding: an amount of money either owed to or owing by the business at the year end, that in the closing balances will be recorded as either an asset or a liability. Often it requires an adjustment in the accounts.
Annual general meeting: in the case of a company, statute lays down a requirement that the owners (ordinary shareholders or members) should meet formally at least once a year to discuss the affairs of the business. The same terminology

applies to clubs and societies where members are similarly expected to meet at least once annually, a right usually stated in the Constitution. One of the main aspects of business, in both cases, is that the final end of year accounts of the business or club will be made available to members, and could be one of the subjects to be discussed at the meeting.

Application of funds: one part of a Funds Flow Statement (the other long term part being the sources) that is designed to show the increased amount of funds committed by a business to its activities, during an accounting period.

Appropriation account: a latter appended part of the profit and loss account, used in the case of companies and partnerships to allocate the net profit to the various claims of owners and other parties that accountants deem to require satisfaction after the calculation of profit.

Asset: an amount recognized by the business as value given, the result of which is expected to provide a further benefit, represented by a current or past transaction:

eg   purchase of machinery
      purchase of goods for re-sale.

An asset is shown as a debit in a ledger account, and is the opposite to a liability in such accounts. Different types of asset are shown in the Balance Sheet where the distinction is generally related to the time span of a transaction:

ie   long term = Fixed Asset
      short term = Current Asset (less than a year).

Auditing: the process for checking final year end accounts, once they have been prepared together with supporting records, for accuracy to determine whether they show a 'true & fair view' of the state of affairs of the business. While auditing is not specifically for the purpose of detecting errors and fraud, the examination of accounting records will assist in this process.

Auditor: the person together with assistants who carries out an auditing role. They may be professionally qualified or not, depending largely on whether they charge for their services, are employed within the business or externally. Statute requires that companies engage the services of suitable professionally qualified accountants to act as auditors. Large organizations, particularly large companies may employ their own auditors, these are known as internal auditors and are not always professionally qualified.

Authorized share capital: that part of company share capital that is regarded as the maximum, that can be issued, until as is usually the case with successful companies, it is revised upwards to make room for further issues. So far as accounting is concerned it is the *issued* share capital that forms part of the balance sheet total.

Average creditors: average amounts owed by a business to its suppliers for purchases and other transactions. The figure for creditors often fluctuate throughout a trading period because of the type of business engaged in and the levels of activity at various times. The figure average creditors is used in the calculation of a ratio to assess the efficiency of management at turning over credit balances.

Average debtors: average amounts owed to a business for sales on credit by its customers. The figure for debtors often fluctuates like that for creditors (see above). The average debtors figure is used in the calculation of a ratio to assess the efficiency of credit control policies, where management chooses and limits its acceptance of debtors according to policy considerations.

Average stock held: Again forms part of a ratio (Rate of Stock Turnover) and is an average, that is one of the most important ratio measures. The average is that for recorded stock figures (often opening and closing) from a given accounting period. Where accurate monthly figures are available, an average of the twelve can be taken, where the accounting period is of one year's duration.

Bad debts: Are those debts where sales have been recorded, but no payment has been forthcoming. This is worse than a provision for bad or doubtful debts, since cash has already been lost.

Balance sheet: the name traditionally given to a formal list of closing balances, prepared for the end of an accounting period, that shows the accepted position of a business in terms of its assets and liabilities, classified as long and short term. Increasingly, in a modern context it is referred to as a position statement.

Balancing-off: the procedure for closing off a ledger account at the end of a specific period of time and carrying any outstanding balance down to the following period, being sure to include it as part of a statement that is devised to assess the business or the outstanding amount.

Bank account: the ledger account (as the usual presentation) recording the amount of business money held at a bank, outside the business and the adjustments made thereto. Amounts could be held in a current or deposit account, but usually such an account is allied to the current account that facilitates many of the non-cash transactions conducted by the business eg paying and receiving cheques.

Bank balance: the latest known figure of money held by the bank. This can be determined from either the bank's or the business' books, subject to adjustment for any transactions that have not been completely recorded.

Bank charges: charges made by banks for maintaining their customer's funds and making available banking facilities, often such figures include commissions.

Bank clearing: the process for adjusting account balances when a cheque is drawn on a current account to be paid into the account of another party.

Bank overdraft: where a current account instead of holding a balance of the customer's money, has been overused leading to a deficiency of customer's money to meet customer's commitments. Therefore, in the case of a business, the bank is (at least) partially funding the activities of the business.

Bank reconciliation: a method of establishing the accuracy of a business bank account balance as recorded in the business books, with the balance recorded by the bank. These figures, after recognized adjustment, should 'balance' exactly.

Bank statement: a record issued by a bank of transactions belonging to a particular account over a given period.

Book adjustment: an adjustment to specific accounts in the books of a business, usually made by accountants for the purpose of producing final accounts.

Book-keeping: the process of recording the day-to-day transactions as they affect the accounting records of a business. Many accounting records today are not kept in the traditional book form – as the name implies, but the principles behind the recording process are still like those of double entry book-keeping.

Books of account: contain the accounting records of the day-to-day transactions, that include ledgers, journals, daybooks and other records that are used to control a business and prepare final accounts.

Brought down: a balance 'brought down' is the end period balance in a ledger account that closes-off one period (Balance c/d) and opens a new period (Balance b/d). The actual amount is said to be 'brought-down' as opposed to 'carried down' (c/d). It is this amount that is brought down that is recognized for the purpose of transfer eg to the Trial Balance.

Budget: a detailed estimate of future activities, expressed in monetary or unitary terms that is prepared to assist in the process of planning and/or control of business decisions.

Capital: comprises the long term funds of owners or proprietors that are committed to the business, including retained surplus in the case of sole traders and partnerships.

Capital accounts: the ledger accounts for those owner's funds, that may include numerous different accounts in the case of companies, and accounts belonging to different people in the case of partnerships.

Capital employed: a technical term used to emphasize the total funds at the command of a business. The term has a variety of definitions eg total assets, and total assets less current liabilities. This can be used as a basis to measure net profit relative to the amount of capital in a business, and expressed as a percentage forms an important ratio.

Carriage inwards: cost of transportation eg delivery or packaging that is paid by the purchaser and added to the cost of purchases, recorded in the trading account.

Carriage outwards: similar costs of transportation that are, in this case, paid by the supplier and amount to normal delivery costs, shown in the expense part of a profit and loss account.

Carried down: (abbreviated c/d) is the end period balance in a ledger account that is used to close-off an account by adding to the deficient side, and making both sides equal one another.

Cash: the most liquid of funds (assets) of a business, money that is retained on business premises, usually under the control of a cashier.

Cash book: the name given to a book of account central to the accounting process, that can be maintained in various forms, but is usually based on a ledger format. It can be restricted to contain just the Cash and Bank accounts (two-column), can contain discount received and allowed rulings, (three column) and maybe the largest part of an accounting system classifying all receipts and payments – including VAT, as they affect cash and bank (multi-column). So far as receipts and payments are concerned it can be referred to as the book of prime entry.

Cash budget: the last statement in a budgeting exercise, where the results of various plans are reflected in liquid funds, leading to a positive or negative projected figure.

Certificate of incorporation: the formal document establishing the legality of a company.

Cheque: a written order addressed to a bank requesting it to pay a certain sum of money to a specified party or bearer. Depending on the conditions of the order, cheques may be negotiable, payable to bearer or permitted only to be transferred into another banking account.

Cheque stubs: the counterfoils of cheques that are retained in a cheque book to serve as a record of cheques drawn, indicating numbers and references that permit a cheque to be traced through the banking system and eventually on to the bank statement.

Concepts: accounting concepts are the main principles of accounting and are often distinguished from conventions that serve to underwrite the concepts.

Consistency: an accounting principle, infers that accounting bases should remain unchanged, from one period to another, and between different parts of a business, unless there is very good reason to change, and then the effect of any changes should be stated in the accounts, and the effect on profits should be quantified. Consistency is often referred to as one of the three main conventions, alongside materiality, and conservatism or prudence.

Contribution from trading: the figure transferred from a revenue account to a funds flow statement, that comprises the net profit, adjusted for relevant provisions that are added back.

Contra: an entry that offsets a corresponding entry eg a debit offsetting a credit, and vice versa. In the case of the Cash Book, a transfer will be entered to credit cash and debit bank where funds are transferred from Cash to Bank. Such entries are often identified as follows: ℂ

Control account: a ledger account in the general ledger, the balance of which represents the total of all the individual account balances in the ledger to which it refers eg creditors' control account. Furthermore each general ledger item reflected in an individual's personal account will be part of a respective aggregate in the control account eg returns outward as they offset a personal account figure will form part of the total returns outward figure appearing in the creditors' control account. Control accounts in the case of debtors and creditors, are clearly only for cases where credit is given in the first place.

Convention: a part of accounting principles (the other being concepts) that underwrites the concepts. Conventions are generally given as: consistency, materiality and conservatism or prudence.

Cost: the amount paid and invoiced for an asset or service, that is utilized in accounts in current or future periods eg as the basis for calculating depreciation. In the case of long-term assets the amount is referred to as historic cost.

Cost of goods sold (cost of sales): presentation of purchases of goods that have been sold as recognized in the Trading Account. Introduced as purchases, adjusted primarily by opening stock and closing stock, but also by returns outwards and carriage inwards where these are applicable.

Credit: in book-keeping, refers to an entry recorded on the credit side of a ledger account, indicating its effect upon an asset or a liability. Applied to a purchase or sale transaction, refers to cases where there is a transfer of goods or service creating compensatory rights, for which no funds are immediately exchanged.

Creditor: the person to whom credit rights are given for the sale of goods or conduct of services.

Credit balance: opening balance on the credit side of a ledger account.

Credit control: the internal process of keeping track of credit sales according to the policy laid down by management, namely a check on: status of customers; the amounts for goods outstanding; and the period of time debts are outstanding.

Cumulative preference shares: preference shares with cumulative rights to dividend. Such rights apply to virtually all preference shares, such that if a dividend is missed, due to lean times in company affairs, it can only be postponed to a future period and remains outstanding alongside any current amounts payable for a future period, and must be paid before any amount is payable to ordinary shareholders.

Current accounts of partners: in a partnership where partners are entitled to a share of profits according to their respective, agreed, proportions; current accounts (as distinct from partners' capital accounts) can be used to adjust for these and other short term amounts leaving the Capital Accounts as a statement of long term amounts.

Current assets: the short term assets of a business as represented in the Balance Sheet, they include: stock, debtors, prepayments, bank and cash.

Current liabilities: the opposite of current assets as shown in the Balance Sheet, they consist of short term liabilities and include: creditors, accruals, dividend proposed, and bank overdraft.

Current ratio: as the name implies, is a ratio comparing current assets to current liabilities, unlike the liquid ratio, stock is included as a current asset.

Daybook: a book of prime (first) entry that collects together in separate listings credit purchases and sales, and likewise credit purchase returns and sales returns. Each entry is taken to the relevant personal ledger account and the period total transferred to the relevant general ledger accounts.

Debenture: a formal acknowledgement of a debt in favour of the debt holder. Debentures are usually negotiable and earn a fixed rate of interest. They may be redeemable or convertible into shares depending on the conditions of issue. Interest payable constitutes the first charge on the profit available for distribution.

Debit: in book-keeping a debit refers to an entry recorded on the debit side of a ledger account, indicating its effect upon an asset or a liability.

Debtor: the person from whom credit rights are taken for the sale of goods or conduct of services.

Debit balance: an opening balance on the debit side of a ledger account.

Deed: an instrument stating the terms of a contract, and the evidence of its due execution eg a debenture deed.

Delivery note: a document sent with goods, the suppliers copy being signed on receipt (usually by the store person) as evidence that goods have been received and meet order requirements.

Department of Trade: the Government department responsible for, among other things, the affairs of companies.

Depreciation: the periodic apportionment of the cost (valuation) of an asset to the business over its expected useful life, according to one of several methods acceptable to accountants. This means that in practice that a part is written-off to the profit and loss account each year, and the remainder is shown as a reduced balance in the balance sheet.

Directors: the officers of a company appointed by the members (ordinary shareholders) to run the company on their behalf, and to report to the members on their activities. The appointment and removal of directors is governed by company law and the internal rules of companies, and is part of the business of an annual general meeting when members appoint or reappoint these officials.

Directors' report: a report made by the directors that is published and filed with the annual accounts.

Direct costs: those costs associated with the production or manufacture of goods that are directly related to the product. Each product has an identifiable input; eg direct labour or direct materials that is used directly contrary to other costs, eg overheads that do not have such a direct relationship. This sometimes subtle distinction is an important feature of costing or management accounting.

Direct debits: payments made directly by a bank on instruction by and on behalf of its customer, out of the customer's funds, usually on a regular basis eg monthly. This means, for the purpose of bank reconciliation, that such transactions will usually be recorded by the bank before being entered in the business books.

Discount allowed: a reduction in the original selling price of goods, following customary terms of trade in a particular business, or to encourage prompt payment. Usually given as a percentage of the selling price, but is recorded in the profit and loss account in its final presentation not the trading account (so far as there has not been a reduction in the invoiced selling price), ie it is shown as a debit or expense, reducing the gross profit.

Discount received: a reduction in the original purchase price of goods, usually shown as a percentage of the purchase price. Like discount allowed, it is recorded in the profit and loss part of final accounts, but in this case reduces the cost of goods to the business, (again so far as the invoiced amount has not incorporated a reduction) ie it is shown as a credit, increasing the gross profit.

Dishonoured cheque: a cheque drawn on an account, that when passed through the banking system is found to be presented against insufficient funds in the drawer's account, and so the obligation cannot be met. Where entries have already been made (in this case somewhat prematurely) they will have to be reversed to restore the original position.

Disposal account: an account drawn up to deal with the sale of an asset, some money may have been received that will have to be compared to the book value, and adjustments made on that basis. Each separate sale asset sold will normally require a disposal adjustment.

Distribution of profit: in the case of a company, contrary to other types of business ownership, a distribution occurs as the method to pay a return to shareholders, that is either fixed or decided (subject to a recommendation by directors) by members, depending on the type of shares.

Dividend: the payment of a return to shareholders by conventional or regular means. Payments can be interim − part way through the year, or final − after the annual general meeting, at which the final dividend is approved by the ordinary shareholders.

Dividend warrant: is fundamentally the cheque payment for the dividend.

Dividend yield: see yield.

Double entry: the method of recording accounting transactions where each entry is supported by an equal and opposite entry for the purpose of maintaining a comprehensive check on financial records and procedures.

Doubtful debts: arise as a year end adjustment to final accounts made by accountants when recovery of amounts due from debtors is uncertain. In practice it is wise to recognize that a proportion of debts will be uncollectable, because a business usually cannot avoid this, and a provision for this reduces the amount of profit available for distribution. The provision is also referred to as a Provision for Bad Debts.

Drawings: the different methods of drawing cash are through cash, goods or use of assets, nominally under business control. The connecting factor is they are removed from the business for the private use of the owners (sole traders and partners) who will usually have the profit (or their part of it) adjusted for the privilege.

Equity: that part of a company belonging to the ordinary shareholders, not only the capital subscribed by them, but also related amounts including, profit and loss cumulative balances, reserves and share premium accounts.

Expenditure: this is a cost operation that has usually required the payment of cash and is partly or wholly attributable to the current accounting period.

Expense: this is a term given to all recorded expenses whether cash has been paid or not, that are recognized by accountants as appropriate to the period in which they arise, and are admitted to the profit and loss account to reduce the net profit figure.

Exposure draft: (abbreviated ED) a preliminary statement issued by the Accounting Standards Committee for discussion prior to the introduction of a Standard on a relevant accounting matter. The exposure draft usually forms the basis of a subsequent standard unless it is amended in the course of following discussions eg ED 24 became S.S.A.P. 16.

Expenses owing (accruals): those expenses that are matched to an appropriate accounting period, ie recognized as relating to that period, that remain unpaid at the close and are therefore payable in the following period.

External audit: in auditing a distinction is made between internal and external audits. An internal audit is often undertaken in larger companies (and other businesses) that are able to sustain the expense of maintaining an internal audit department, whereas the external audit is that where checks are made to test whether the final accounts show a 'true and fair' view, that in the case of companies is performed by independent professional accountants.

Final accounts: consist of the Trading and Profit and Loss account (Income Statement) and Balance Sheet (Position Statement) that form the most important financial accounting statement in any one period.

Final dividend: the period or year end dividend that is recommended by the directors prior to the annual general meeting, the recommendation forms part of the business of the meeting and once passed is usually sent out to shareholders after the conclusion of the meeting.

Financed By (section of a balance sheet): shows the long term funding of a business namely the aggregate of owner's capital, retained income, loans and other funds that are represented as that part of the 'vertical' balance sheet that balances with fixed assets plus *net* current assets.

Financial accounting: that part of accounting procedure and theory that is concerned with the current or immediate past, contrary to alternative, but complimentary procedures and theories that are more concerned with producing cost and management information that is relevant to a present or future time horizon.

Financial reporting: the method of presenting financial information in a manner suitable for users.

Financial statement: shows the state of particular aspects of the business, presented in a recognized standard format, that is capable of recognition and interpretation by practitioners and other interested parties.

Finished goods stock: the stock of goods available for sale at the end of a production process that is distinguished from work in progress ie partly finished goods, and raw materials, as shown in the accounts of manufacturing businesses.

Fixed assets: assets that are intended to be owned for a long period of time are not actively traded in but are used to earn a profit eg buildings, plant and machinery.

Fixed interest: interest payable to service that part of Capital which is loan based, where the payment amounts to a contractual obligation.

Fourth Directive: the collective name given to the rules agreed by member states of the EEC for the preparation of accounts for corporate entities that are

required to publish information for shareholders and others. This information is to be drawn up, so as to be comparable between entities operating within different national boundaries. The Companies Acts of 1980 and 1981 jointly incorporate these provisions into UK law. Small entities mainly those companies that are classified as private are excluded from the more onerous reporting requirements by virtue of their:
a) turnover,
b) assets, or
c) number of employees.

Fully paid shares: shares can be fully or partly paid. Where shares are fully paid this represents the owner's full liability to the business in the case of failure. Otherwise, they may be required to contribute up to the full amount of the shares.

Gearing: the ratio of long-term fixed interest capital to equity. A company with a large amount of fixed interest capital would be high geared, but would otherwise be regarded as low geared.

General ledger: the book or other format containing the non-personal ledger accounts ie those not applicable to debtors and creditors.

General reserve: consists of those retained funds of a company, that while not related to a specific policy eg replacement reserve, are nonetheless regarded by the directors creating it, as more permanent than the profit and loss account balance, and therefore not part of those surplus funds that can be used to supplement a distribution in years where profits are insufficient.

Going concern: an accounting principle (concept) under which a business is evaluated as to whether its continuance or scale of operations is in jeopardy as a result of its (poor) financial state. In a financial assessment most businesses would meet this requirement. Where they do not, it means that the assets cannot be valued at historic cost and may have to be revalued at a realizable value which may be as great as or less than that which would ordinarily be the case.

Goods received note: a document raised internally, copies of which are circulated to departments known to be interested in the arrival of goods in an acceptable condition.

Goodwill: represented in the balance sheet as an intangible asset, so far as it is not written off. Raised on the acquisition of a business, it is the difference between the recorded value of tangible assets (less liabilities) and the agreed aggregate sale price. The difference is usually said to be attributable to the previous owner's trading success.

Gross profit (loss): the difference between the cost of sales (purchases adjusted by opening and closing stock) and sales as recorded in the Trading Account.

Historic cost: the cost at which an asset is introduced into the business verifiable from the invoice, and accepted as a basis by accountants on which financial statements can be prepared.

Imprest system: a method applied to control petty cash payments, whereby a float is established from which payments are made, that is periodically replenished to the initial (maximum) amount.

Income: revenue earned during an accounting period that is opposite to expenses.

Income statements: the modern name for a trading and profit and loss account, usually showing the net profit (or appropriated figure) as the final amount.

Indirect cost: a cost that does not meet the criteria laid down by accountants as being 'direct' that can include an overhead or other cost that is not consumed proportionally to the output, and is therefore regarded as indirect.

Interim dividend: the part year dividend that is customarily paid by many listed companies to maintain the interest of investors in shares quoted on the Stock Exchange and thereby the share price which is regarded as an important consideration by directors in order to facilitate the raising of capital.

Internal audit: the routine or on-going audit that is often conducted in a medium to large organization to secure the accuracy and reliability of a wide range of accounting reports and procedures.

Investment: a business may hold shares in companies or government securities that may be regarded as a long or short term investment, depending on the purpose and time for which they are held. Such holdings in the case of companies may not (and neither be intended to) represent a controlling interest, but should nevertheless be recorded in the balance sheet. Since they are a closing balance, as much as any other.

Investment ratios: in this case, ratios that are particularly relevant to share and fixed interest holdings in listed companies, where holdings have to be evaluated according to their performance. Such ratios are of importance to companies holding shares in other companies just as much as they are to individuals.

Invoice: a document issued by a supplier to the purchaser that specifies the quantity, items, prices, terms of payment and other details of goods sold or services rendered.

Issued share capital: that part of share capital that is in existence and has been paid for i.e. the company has received cash or some other consideration. It is this capital figure that is added into the list of balances contained in the balance sheet, unlike the 'authorized' amounts.

Joint & several: is the legal term referring to the liability of partners, where the claims of creditors will extend to the personal assets of all partners, it covers not only the partner's own share, but the share of other partners where individual partners assets are insufficient to meet their share of the claims on the business.

Journal: a diary of transactions. It is the accounting record where difficult adjustments that cannot be fully explained in the ledgers are listed, and the amending entries recorded as debits and credits, to provide a permanant record of a changed position. This record is of prime importance to auditors when checking through the accounting records that support the final accounts. Entries are posted to ledgers from the journal, it is the ledger that holds the proper double entry transaction.

Ledger accounts: the series of accounts traditionally kept in bound books to record the double entry transactions of a business. The principles of double entry still apply for whatever processing and collation method is used eg computer or mechanized accounting, if satisfactory control is required. In theoretical examples the ledger account is usually portrayed as a 'T' account, but mechanized systems have long shown debit and credit entries in a manner similar to a bank statement.

Liability: an obligation recognized by the business as value received, the result of which is represented by a current or past transaction, requiring settlement. eg capital (funds) provided by the owner(s) for use in the business

sale of goods without immediate payment.
A liability is shown as a credit in a ledger account, and is the opposite to an asset in a balance sheet. There are different types of liability, again (like assets) generally related to the effective time span of the transaction.

ie long term   = Capital
   medium term = Loans
   short term   = Current Liabilities (less than a year).

Limited Company: a company formed where the liability of its owners – ordinary shareholders – is limited to the original (full) amount paid usually for shares. For this privilege, a company has to meet many reporting and other restrictions that are not applicable to other types of enterprise, but these requirements are regarded as part of the price payable for the very significant advantage of limited liability.

Limited liability: where there is a maximum liability that cannot be exceeded in normal circumstances that is applicable to shareholders in limited companies and limited partners in limited partnerships.

Liquid assets: those assets that are represented by cash or near cash ie cash balances, bank balances and debtors balances, but not stock.

Liquid ratios: see Acid Test Ratio

Listed company: a public company that holds a quotation for its shares on a recognized stock exchange, that provides, an up-to-date market price per share for the information and trading requirements of investors and an access point for new capital by the company.

Loans: consists of money lent by outsiders (banks and others) that are not part of ownership capital, that are usually short or medium term and will more than likely be secured by agreement, on the assets of the business or proprietors. Even major shareholders and directors of small, private limited companies find that in order to borrow money from banks and other financiers they have to provide their private property as security, this clearly goes against the spirit of limited liability.

Margin: the gross profit from sales expressed as a proportion of the selling price – usually as a percentage.

Mark-up: the gross profit from sales expressed as a proportion of the cost of sales – usually as a percentage.

Mechanized accounting: there are various methods of maintaining accounting records that have adapted the basic double entry process to suit mechanical and electronic machines that are able to process information much quicker and often provide more comprehensive records.

Members: a collective reference made to groups of people who have by their actions an involvement with or commitment to an organization. In the case of companies they are acknowledged to have a long term financial interest in the capital (equity), in the case of clubs and societies, the right to participate in activities and attend meetings.

Merger: an amalgamation of enterprises, usually corporate (because this type facilitates almost unrestricted capital re-organization) where there is an equal status between the parties, contrary to a take-over where one party takes control of the other and exercises dominant rights.

Monetary value: the use of current sterling amounts (in the United Kingdom) to record financial transactions. To assist in financial measurement, it is helpful if the monetary unit is stable, but this has not been the case in recent years where inflation has become so important as to cause an imbalance in traditionally prepared financial reports.

Net book value: an assessment of the monetary amounts of assets, usually fixed, that are shown in the accounts. So far as fixed assets are concerned net book value is historic cost less an assessment of depreciation to year-end date, that has been deducted from the cost.

Net current assets: is a particular presentation of current assets less current liabilities, in a 'vertical' balance sheet. Net current assets is a different expression for the term *working capital*.

Net profit: the revenue surplus of income over expenses for a given accounting period, where expenses are matched against income according to accepted accounting practice.

Nominal ledger: see general ledger

Nominal value: a value applicable to shares. It is the original price for a share that is distinguished from its current 'market' price that can be more or less than the nominal price.

Notes: are presentations of accounting information, usually examination and other questions that ask for the preparation of final accounts, present notes at the foot of the trial balance for the purpose of making adjustments to those figures recorded in the trial balance. In published accounts, explanatory notes can amount to many pages in order that the accounts are presented in a straightforward manner.

Order: a prepared document issued to a supplier by a purchaser requesting delivery of goods or hiring of services according to the terms stated. The order may be a formal confirmation of an earlier telephone conversation.

Ordinary shares: held by the owners of a company who are entitled to all surplus assets on winding-up, once all preferential claims have been met. The owners of ordinary shares are the owners of equity who stand behind preferential claims not only in the case of a liquidation, but also for the payment of dividend in the normal course of trading.

Overheads: manufacturing costs that are not related to a specific production process, but serve to assist in the process of generating a saleable product eg administrative salaries.

Owner's capital: the term given to all funds belonging to the owner of a business however constituted and represented, eg a sole trader would have claim to his initial capital plus any retained capital, i.e. profits not taken out through drawings, having met all prior claims.

Paid in advance (prepaid or a prepayment): are the terms used to classify the effect of an early cash transaction (settlement) that increases the closing asset concerned but depletes cash or bank balances.

Participative preference shares: some preference shares have rights to participate in extra dividends after ordinary shareholders have received a given amount. These rights are entirely dependent on the terms of issue, and if participative rights are not stated, then preference shares are non-participative.

Partly-paid shares: some shares, preference and ordinary, can be paid on a type of instalment basis, some money is paid on application and allotment (initial purchase), and the remainder can be on call (later notification), by the directors, according to the terms of issue, and rules of the company.

Partners: the persons agreeing to share business profits (and losses) by forming a partnership.

Partnership: a form of business combination, without limited liability, that is governed by either:

a) a partnership agreement drawn up by the partners to formally state the duties, responsibilities and rights of the partners in each specific case, or

b) the minimum statutory requirements according to the Partnership Act 1890.

Partnerships are able to introduce partners with limited liability provided there is at least one general (unlimited) partner, according to the terms of the Limited Partnership Act 1907. The partner with limited liability should not take part in the management of the partnership.

Periodicity: the accounting concept that requires revenue (income net of expenses), to be measured after discrete time intervals, that should be supported by consistent decisions about the recognition and timing of both incomes and expenses.

Personal account: where an account is headed with the name of a person or business, that relates to amounts either owed by or owed to other traders, as a result of acknowledged business transactions. Amounts recorded, rise from the smallest to the largest and are usually presented in a ledger format.

Personal ledger: there are two ledgers where personal accounts are retained, these are for debtors and creditors. An account will be opened and maintained for each individual debtor and creditor in the personal ledgers.

Petty Cash: a small amount of cash retained for small disbursements that occur from time to time. A petty cash book will be kept to record the expenditures, applying the imprest system to replenish the cash float.

Preference shares: a class of shares that have prior rights to specified dividends and to repayment of capital on liquidation of a company. The particular rights attached to any preference shares depend upon the terms of the issue, and the rules of the company.

Prepaid: see prepayment.

Prepayment (prepaid or paid in advance): shows the effect of recording a cash payment, that satisfies a debt, but taken on a time basis belongs to a later period, and is thus an adjustment that decreases current expenses, but increases a current asset.

Price/earnings ratio: provides a relationship between the earnings per share and the market price of that share, expressed as numeric value.

Prime cost: the total of direct material, direct labour and direct expenses used in a productive process.

Prime entry: the initial entry in the accounting system that will not, except where entries in the cash book are considered to be of prime entry, be part of the double entry system. However, such a division of the books assists in the control of a business.

Private limited company: a usually small limited company with, a low maximum membership, restricted share transfer, and restricted access to new capital, that nevertheless has the valuable advantage of limited liability. This type of company will more than likely have reduced reporting requirements after the passing of the Companies Act 1981.

Private ledger: that part of the general or nominal ledger that contains the accounts of ownership requiring restricted access. Such accounts are usually kept by a senior employee, director, partner or the owner.

Production cost: total of manufacturing figures used in the manufacturing account, that is transferred to the final trading account that is then adjusted by opening and closing stocks of finished goods, before the gross profit is determined.

Profit and Loss account: the ledger or other format used to determine the net profit (or net loss) for an accounting period, once the gross profit has been established. It can be called an Income Statement, that will include the presentation of gross profit and earlier figures used in its calculation.

Profit and Loss balance: the balance that is found in the profit & loss account or appended appropriation account that will be taken to the balance sheet or other closing statement.

Promoters: those persons responsible for founding a company who may become its principal shareholders or first directors.

Proposed dividend: the final end of year dividend that has to be recommended by the directors of a company before being finally discussed and voted on by the members in general meeting. During the course of the meeting a resolution is put to members (ordinary shareholders) proposing the dividend.

Proprietor: owner of a one-person trading business.

Provision for bad debts: see doubtful debts and provision for doubtful debts.

Provision for depreciation: arises as a year end adjustment to final accounts, by accountants, to reduce the recorded book value of certain types of fixed asset recorded in a balance sheet, by an amount determined through a pre-set policy, according to the requirements of a business. The assets adjusted are those held at the close of a trading period, although a provision may be raised for assets owned for part of a year. The current period year end adjustment is also shown as an item of expense in a profit and loss account.

Provision for doubtful debts: arises like depreciation (stated above) as a year end adjustment to final accounts. Shown as an adjustment of the current debtors figure – a reduction in the balance sheet. The relevant transfer for the current year is shown in the profit and loss account. See doubtful debts.

Published accounts: those accounts for companies that are required to be published under provisions stated in the Companies Acts. The Act of 1967 states the basic requirements, except where these have been changed for private companies by the Act of 1981.

Public limited company (new abbreviated title plc): a business organization granted the full rights of incorporation, that is also because of the privileges, expected to comply with the full requirements of company legislation, and for listed companies, stock exchange rules. The new title arises in the Companies Act 1980, following the need to distinguish more clearly between public and private limited companies.

Purchases: goods bought by the business either for resale or alternative use. Only purchases for resale are recorded in the trading account. Net purchases will be shown (not so described) but these are purchases after deducting returns.

Purchases ledger: the book or other collection of personal accounts, recording purchases of goods or service on credit for use by the business (not necessarily resale). Often referred to as the Creditors' Ledger.

Quoted shares: those shares of listed companies, holding a market quotation on a recognized stock exchange, distinguishing them from unquoted shares.

Rate of stock turnover: see stock turnover.

Raw materials stock: stock of goods held for the purpose of manufacture that in financial accounting is mainly recorded as opening and closing stock in a manufacturing account, and closing stock in a balance sheet.

Registrar of Companies: the government official who receives and maintains information required by the Companies Acts to be held on public file for the information of interested parties, the Registrar also takes action against defaulting companies.

Registration of Companies: the process of forming a company that requires, among other things that it be registered with the Registrar of Companies.

Retained profit: the surplus from revenue that is kept by the business or organization after meeting recognised reductions. In the case of sole traders and partners it supplements owner's capital, but in the case of companies, can be retained as part of the profit and loss balance or as some type of reserve, or be available for distribution.

Returns inward: sales of goods, that having been invoiced to a customer are returned (hence the alternative description sales returns) for some reason accepted by the seller — eg goods that are faulty or of incorrect specification.

Returns outward: purchases of goods that, in this case, have been invoiced to the business but need to be returned (hence the alternative description purchase returns) for reasons similar to those given under returns inward.

Revenue: income (after deducting expenses) for a period.

Revenue account: another name for the profit & loss account or income statement.

Sales: goods sold by the business recorded in the trading account. Net sales will be shown but not so described as sales after deducting returns.

Sales ledger: the book or other collection of personal accounts recording sales of goods or services on credit. Often referred to as the Debtors Ledger.

Set-off: a case where a previously recorded sum can be diminished by a different accounting flow (usually applicable to goods and services) through an agreement to reduce mutual indebtedness.

Shareholders: individuals or corporate bodies holding either preference or ordinary shares in a company.

Shareholders' funds: long-term funds recognized as belonging to shareholders (mainly ordinary shareholders), excluding various loans.

Share premium: surplus funds raised on the sale of shares, where the directors expect applicants to pay a price in excess of the nominal value to close the gap between this and the (higher) market price. It is a device usually only available to companies raising additional share capital, that already have a trading record which is attractive to potential investors. Once obtained a share premium can only be used in paying off specific, rather unusual obligations, compatible with its introduction in the first place, but more importantly as stated in the Companies Act, 1948.

Share premium account: contains any amounts raised as a premium. These have to be recorded separately in a ledger account opened for the purpose and shown in the 'financed by' section of the balance sheet, usually as part of shareholders' funds.

Sole-trader: the classification for a business person operating his or her own usually small business who neither benefits from limited liability nor shares ownership rights and obligations.

Source of funds: one part of a Funds Flow Statement (the other long term part being applications) that is designed to show the periodic inflow of funds to a business, either through its own internal operations or manipulations, or through external suppliers.

Standards of accounting: the rules narrowing the choices of accounting bases available to business. These rules are drawn up by leading professional members and published, first as exposure drafts and then as statements of practice.

Standing order: a written instruction to a bank to make a fixed periodic payment that remains in force until it is revoked.

Statement: a layout of accounting information, both descriptive and numeric in a form recognized by and compatible with the rules of accounting.

Statement of affairs: a list of known closing balances supplemented by those unknown or estimated to form a complete statement resembling a balance sheet.

Stewardship: that aspect of financial accounting dealing with accurate records of ownership and the preservation of business assets.

Stock: a reference to the closing and opening stocks of consecutive accounting periods these are the same figures carried forward from one accounting period to the next. The stocktake provides the basis for this important figure that serves to increase the profit of an earlier period and reduces that of a later period, as shown in respective trading accounts.

Stock Exchange: a market where shares, debentures, government stocks and other securities are bought and sold. Such exchanges usually have a governing council that makes rules to control the buying and selling of shares; membership by brokers and jobbers; and quotation rules for listed companies.

Stock taking: the periodic process of accounting for the worth of business closing stock by making a physical count and assigning a value to goods.

Stock turnover: the movement of stock in and out of a business accounted for as purchases (inflow) and sales (outflow). This forms an important ratio used to measure overall trading efficiency.

Sundry: a prefix often applied in accounting to minor or miscellaneous items of credit or expense.

Surplus: the excess, usually income over expenses (the opposite would be deficit) — a description sometimes used in accounting.

Take-over: where one business (usually a company) buys or obtains a controlling interest in another business.

Trading activities: where the generation of income comes from buying and selling goods, the prime activities of many businesses.

Trial balance: a list of closing balances extracted from the ledger accounts expressed as debits or credits, that should balance. The balancing exercise forms a preliminary step to preparing final accounts.

True and Fair View: the normal expected circumstance underlying the presentation of information in final accounts, ie that accounts should show a true and fair view of the state of affairs of the business. An undertaking first used in the Companies Act of 1948 but not defined by statute.

Unappropriated profit (undistributed): unused profit that remains in the business to supplement either the profit and loss balance in the case of companies or the cumulative capital of other owners — in the latter case not so described.

Unlimited Company: a limited company by virtue of the Companies Act 1967, can become unlimited. It gains privacy of its affairs, but at the cost of its loss of limited liability status. Such a loss means that creditors, in order to satisfy their

Index

Accountancy, 2, 119
Accounting, classification of, 140–6; concepts, conventions and standards, 315–18; concepts, 316; convention, 316; documentation, 119–21; procedures (diagram), 118; ratios, 363–77; standards, 317
Accruals, 17, 18, 75–9, 199
Accruals concept, 316
Accumulated fund, 197, 198
Acid test (liquid) ratio, 271
Adjustment, 80, 105–6
Adjustments – end of year, 75–9, 79–81, 199; for depreciation in final accounts, 81–9; nature of, 69–74; provisions, 81–9, 89–93, 94–103
Advance receipt, 80–1
Annual general meeting, 178, 181
Application of funds, 281–4
Appropriated profit, 176, 189
Appropriation account, 176, 179, 189
Assets, 15, 29
Assets – disposal, 95, 99; depreciation of, 81–9; intangible, 160–1
Auditing and auditors, 318–20
Auditors, 3
Authorized share capital, 180, 187

Bad debts, 89–93, 104, 230; personal ledger, 90–1; profit and loss, 91, 92; provision for in final accounts, 89–93, 230; provisions, 101–4; provisions in trial balance, 92; trial balance, 90, 92
Balance sheet, 7, 15–20, 56, 197; depreciation provision, 83, 89; doubtful (bad debts) provision, 92
Balancing off, 28; ledger accounts, 45–6, 230; rules, 46
Balancing – trial balance, 47–54
Bank account, 37; balance, 18; overdraft, 17; reconciliation, 237–46; statement, 237, 243
Budgeting – cash, 289–93

Capital, 16, 19, 247; of owners, 17
Carriage inward and outward, 107
Cash, 18, 279, 282
Cash account, 37; book, 125–32, 146, 238, 240; book (extension), 131; budgeting, 289–93; flow statement, 280; projections, 289–93

Classification of accounts, 140–6
Closing balances (ledgers), 47, 228
Closing stock, 10, 49, 135, 136
Club accounts, 195–203
Club subscriptions, 197; trading activities, 199
Collection of creditors ratio, 271
Collection of debtors ratio, 270
Collection of information, 122–5, 147–59
Companies Acts, 175, 313
Company accounts, 174–87
Concepts (accounting), 316
Conservatism (convention), 317
Consistency (convention), 316
Contribution from trading, 283
Control accounts, 227–36
Conventions (accounting), 316
Copyright, 161
Correction of errors – journal, 150, 153–9; trial balance, 49
Cost (concept), 316
Cost and management accounts, 3
Cost of sales (cost of goods sold), 11
Credit, 29, 31
Credit control – bad debts, 90
Credit purchases and sales, 35–9, 228
Creditors, 17, 18, 46, 106, 229; control account, 229, 231, 248, 250; ratio, 271
Current assets, 16, 18; liabilities, 16, 18; ratio, 271, 273, 275

Daybooks, 122–5, 147, 229
Debenture capital, 180, 187
Debenture interest, 179, 186
Debit, 29, 31
Debtors, 16, 18, 46, 106, 229; control account, 229; ratio, 270
Delayed receipt, 80
Depreciation, 82
Depreciation provision – calculation of, 84; trial balance, 88; reducing balance, 86; straight line, 86
Depreciation, provision for, 81–9, 94–100, 283
Direct labour, 204
Directors, 178, 181
Discount, 126, 229
Discount allowed, 106, 127, 130, 231; received, 106, 127, 130, 231
Dishonoured cheque, 229
Disposal of assets, 95, 98, 100

437

Dividend, 178, 283
Dividend yield ratio, 272
Double entry – general principles, 29–34; expenses, 39–40; purchases and sales, 35–9; returns, 40–3; provisions, 94–104
Doubtful (bad) debts provision, 101–3; final accounts, 88–93, 284; trial balance, 92
Drawings, 17, 18, 137–40, 283
Drawings account, 138
Dual aspect (concept), 317

Entity (concept), 316
Expenditure, 195
Expenses, 14
Expenses and expenditure, 6
Expenses – double entry, 39–40; prepayments and accruals, 75–9
Exposure drafts, 318

Factory indirect expenses, 204–7
Final accounts, 5, 70–4, 182; I, 5–8; II, 55–7; examination questions, 106–7; provisions for depreciation, 83, 88, 89
Final dividend, 177, 178
Financed by, 19
Financial accounting, 3
Finished goods, 204, 210
Fixed assets, 16, 18
Fixtures and fittings, 17, 18
Fourth Directive, 175
Funds flow statements, 278–88; layout, 280, 281, 287

General ledger, 141, 145, 163, 164
General reserve, 178, 179, 186–7
Going concern (concept), 10, 316
Goods for proprietor's use, 139
Goodwill, 161
Gross profit, 10, 176, 184, 186, 192, 205; to cash price ratio, 266; to selling price ratio, 266, 275

Historic cost, 82

Imprest system, 133
Income, 195
Income accrued, 79–81
Income and expenditure accounts, 195–203; layout, 196
Income statement, 177
Incomplete records, 246–51
Inflation – depreciation, 83
Intangible asset, 160–1
Interest on capital, 189

Interim dividend, 178, 179, 181
Introduction, 1–3
Investment in shares, 181–3, 185–7
Investment ratios, 272–3
Issued share capital, 180, 187

Journal, 147–59; adjustment method, 105–6; correction of errors, 150–2, 153–9

Land and buildings, 17, 18
Layout of accounts, 8–9; trading account, 9–12; profit and loss account, 13–15; balance sheet, 15–20
Lease, 160
Ledger, 9, 29, 70, 141
Ledger accounts, 28, 45; provisions, 94–104
Liabilities, 15
Liability, 29
Limited companies, 174–87; appropriation account, 176–8; debentures, 180, 187; dividend, 178, 181, 186; general reserve, 178, 186–7; investments, 182, 186–7; share capital, 179, 185, 187; share holders funds, 181, 187; share premium account, 180, 185; undistributed profit, 176, 179, 186–7
Limited partnership, 194
Liquid (acid test) ratio, 271
Loan, 16, 17
Location of errors, 227
Long-term loans, 16, 17

Management accountants, 3
Manufacturing accounts, 203–10; finished goods, 204; prime cost, 205; raw materials, 204; work in progress, 204
Margin, 264, 266–8
Mark-up, 264, 266–8
Matching or accruals (concept), 316
Materiality (convention), 317
Membership fees and subscriptions (clubs), 197
Methods of depreciation, 85
Modern presentation, trading account – 11, profit and loss, 14, balance sheet, 19
Motor vehicles, 16, 17

Net current assets, 19, 187
Net profit, 7, 17, 55, 176, 179, 184, 186, 192, 205; capital employed ratio, 268; owners capital ratio, 269; sales ratio, 268, 275
Nominal ledger, 141

Non-profit organization accounts, 195–202

Objectivity (concept), 317
Opening stock, 10, 99, 140
Ordinary dividend, 178, 186–7
Ordinary share capital, 179, 180, 187
Owners capital, 16, 19

Participative rights, 180
Partners appropriation account, 189, 192; balance of profits, 189, 192; capital, 190; capital account, 190, 192; current account, 190, 193; drawings, 189, 190; interest on capital, 189, 190; interest on drawings, 189, 190; liability, 194; salaries, 189; written agreement, 194
Partnerships, 188–94
Partnership Acts, 189, 194, 315
Partnership deed (agreement), 189, 194
Patent, 161
Periodicity (concept), 316
Personal account, 32–4, 38, 46
Petty cash book, 132–3
Plant and machinery, 17, 18, 85
Preference dividend, 178, 186; shares, 179, 187; share capital, 179, 187
Prepayments, 18, 75–81, 198
Presentation, 5–8
Price/earnings ratio, 273
Prime cost, 204, 205
Prime entry, 28, 70, 122–5, 125–7, 147–59
Private companies, 175, 182
Private ledger, 146
Processing information, 122–5, 147–59
Production cost, 204
Profit, 7, 247
Profit & loss account, 6, 13–15; balance, 181, 186–7; depreciation provision, 83, 89; doubtful (bad) debts provision, 92
Profitability ratios, 268–9
Projections, 290
Proposed dividend, 178, 186–7
Provisions, 82, 84, 89, 92, 93, 98–100, 102–3; for doubtful (bad debts), 89–93, 94–104; for depreciation, 81–9, 94–104
Public companies, 175–82
Purchases, 6, 10, 107, 120; day book, 124; discount, 126, 130; double entry, 35–9; ledger, 141, 152; ledger control account, 229; returns day book, 124

Quoted shares, 182

Rate of stock turnover, 269, 273, 275
Ratios – investment, 272–3; profitability, 268–9; sales, 266–8; turnover, 269–71; working capital, 271–2
Raw material, 204, 210
Realization (concept), 317
Receipts and payments, 289; account, 196
Receipts and revenue, 7
Reducing balance depreciation (method of), 86
Retained net profit, 7, 176
Returns – purchases and sales double entry, 40–3, 229
Returns inward, 40, 124, 229
Returns outward, 40, 124, 229
Revenue, 6–7, 9–15, 176–8, 189, 195–7, 204–5
Royalties, 204

Sales, 6, 10 107, 122; daybook, 123; discount, 125, 135; double entry, 35–9; ledger, 141, 152; ledger control account, 229; ratio, 266–8; returns daybook, 124
Set off, 229
Shares, 179, 182
Shareholders, 178; funds, 181, 187
Share capital, 179
Share premium account, 180
Single-entry, 248
Sole traders, 4
Sources of funds, 281
Stable monetary unit (concept), 316
Standards of accounting, 317
Statement of affairs, 197, 247, 248
Statute, 175, 194, 313–5
Stewardship, 2
Stock, 6, 10, 16, 18, 196, 199, 204, 272; sheet, 140; trading account, 6, 9–12; valuation, 139
Stock Exchange, 181
Stocktake, 139
Straight-line depreciation (methods of), 86
Surplus of income over expenditure (and vice versa), 196, 201–2
Suspense account, 50, 153

Three-column cash book (including two column), 126, 127, 130
Trademark, 161
Trading account, 6, 9–12, 43, 141, 205
Transfer to general reserve, 178, 186–7
Trial balance, 28, 46, 47–54, 70, 92, 183
Turnover ratios, 269–71
Two-column cash book, 126
Types of share capital, 179

439

Unappropriated (undistributed) profit, 176, 179
Unquoted shares, 182

Vertical format (final accounts presentation), 11, 14, 19, 189, 202, 209

Whole page (final accounts presentation), 11, 14, 19, 186, 202, 209
Working capital, 271, 279, 281–2; ratios, 271–2; statement (funds flow), 279, 281, 286
Work in progress, 205, 210